CODEWORD

DICTIONARY

A Compilation of Military and Law Enforcement Codewords from 1904 to Present

Paul Adki

Motorbooks International
Publishers & Wholesalers ®

To
David & Rosemary Mahoney
Caroline Qualey
&
Robert Asbury

First published in 1997 by Motorbooks International Publishers &Wholesalers, 729 Prospect Avenue, PO Box 1, Osceola, WI 54020-0001 USA

© Paul Adkins, 1997

Library of Congress Cataloging-in-Publication Data
Adkins, Paul.
    Codeword dictionary: a compilation of military and law enforcement codewords from 1904 to present/Paul Adkins.
        p. cm.
    Includes index.
    ISBN 0-7603-0368-1 (pbk.: alk. paper)
    1. Raids (Military science)—Acronyms. 2. Special operations (Military science)—Acronyms. 3. Police—Special weapons and tactic units—Acronyms. I. Title.
U167.5.R34A35   1997
355'.01'48—dc21   97-12140

Printed in the United States of America

Contents

Preface

IN SIMPLER TIMES, COMMANDERS, STAFFS, AND HISTORIANS were faced with comparatively few campaigns. They named these informally ("Lee's First Invasion of Maryland") if at all.

Early in the 20th century this system began to break down. In addition to more and more military operations, events generated great numbers of plans and contingencies. Informal names could be confused with one another and often revealed the nature of the plan.

The use of an arbitrary name for a plan seems to have begun in 1904 when the U.S. Army developed plans for war with its traditional enemies. The plan dealing with Mexico was called GREEN, war with Britain was covered by RED, and with Japan in ORANGE.

These names were capitalized to avoid confusion with the actual color and provided some level of security. A page from one of these plans might read "attacks by ORANGE aircraft on the Panama Canal are unlikely given the shortage of ORANGE tankers to resupply the fleet." An agent coming across such a document would not immediately know which country ORANGE was.

Just as importantly, the use of arbitrary code names provided an easy way to refer to these plans. The use of code names was quite common by World War I, and was universal in World War II.

Military, and by extension, law enforcement agencies generate thousands of code names each year. So many are generated that policies to control and regulate their use generally fail.

Broad national characteristics can be seen. The British tend to use one-word code names for their operations (CORPORATE). The French also use one-word names, and in recent times favor names taken from nature (CHEVESNE). The U.S., Canada, and NATO tend to use two-word code names (ABLE MANNER).

Still, so many examples deviate from these norms that no hard and fast rule can be stated.

This work deals with code names of military, law enforcement, and espionage operations and plans. With a few selected exceptions, it excludes acronyms (NATO, U-boat), the names given to equipment (Phantom jet, Typhoon submarine), and geographic designations (Checkpoint Charlie, Porkchop Hill).

The entries are arranged alphabetically in their original language. The name itself is translated into English where required. The country or organization that developed the plan or operations is noted along with the year in the parenthesis notes. The text of the entry explains the nature of the operation and links it to other similar operations.

The index provides a means of seeing operations in major campaigns in chronological order.

No work of this kind can ever be complete. The author welcomes additions and comments directed through the publisher.

POLAR BEAR

1. (GER 43) See EISBAER.

2. (Allied 44) A joint American/Canadian program to test and develop Arctic warfare equipment and techniques. A combined force spent the winter of 1944/45 in the mountains of British Columbia moving between various climatic zones.

POLCO (CN 50) The determination of the exact location of the Earth's magnetic north pole in July 1950 by Royal Canadian Air Force aircraft. POLCO seems to be a contraction of "polar coordinates."

About the Author

Paul Adkins is a retired infantry officer who has served throughout the United States and Central America in a variety of assignments. He is a graduate of the Command and General Staff College at Fort Leavenworth and holds a master's degree from Webster University in Saint Louis.

He maintains a home in western Maryland and teaches at the Technical Institute of Naval Studies in Dhahran, Saudi Arabia.

A

A, OPERATION

1. (Allied 44) Early name for TOENAILS.
2. (JPN 44) See A GO.

A, PLAN (JPN 44) See A GO.

ABC (Allied 41) A series of plans drawn up by the British and Americans in March 1941 that established a "Germany first" policy in the event of American entry into the war. Replaced the RAINBOW series.

ABC 101 (U.S.) See CHARIOTEER.

ABERCROMBIE (Allied 42) Raid launched on 22 April 1942 on the French coastal town of Hardelot by 50 British and 50 Canadian commandos. The landing craft carrying the Canadians stalled offshore in heavy enemy fire. This raid taught important lessons for the larger Dieppe raid (JUBILEE).

ABERLOUR (Allied 44) Planned British and Canadian attack on a German salient north of Caen. To follow EPSOM, but never executed.

ABILENE (U.S. 66) Operation conducted in Phouc Tuy Province, Vietnam, to destroy food and weapons caches. Executed May 1966.

ABLE MANNER (U.S. 92) American-led international operation to discourage Haitians from attempting to flee their country aboard small boats. This operation arrayed over 20 Navy and Coast Guard vessels in international waters surrounding Haiti to interdict boats and return the refugees to their country. This plan was activated when comments by Bill Clinton, then a presidential candidate, seemed to indicate that he would welcome refugees from Haiti. His comments resulted in boats being built in Haiti for a mass exodus by up to 200,000 people. In order to prevent a huge number of deaths on the high seas, Clinton as President ordered this "reverse blockade." See SUPPORT DEMOCRACY.

ABLE SENTRY (U.S. 95) The rotation of U.S. Army units into the former Yugoslavian Republic of Macedonia as part of the U.N. Protection Force. This operation was intended to prevent the Yugoslav civil wars from spreading south into Macedonia and Greece.

ABLE VIGIL (U.S. 94) The use of American Naval and Coast Guard vessels to pick up Cuban refugees at sea. These people were transported not to Miami but to the U.S. Naval Base at Guantanamo Bay. This marked a drastic change of the previous policy of granting immediate political refugee status to Cubans arriving in the U.S.

ABUSIVE (U.S. 47) Early U.S. Navy tests of captured German V-2 missiles, culminating with the PUSHOVER experiment.

ACCOLADE (Allied 43) Planned British amphibious assault on Rhodes and the Dodecanese Islands in the Aegean Sea. Advocated by Winston Churchill as a follow-up to the capture of Sicily in 1943. Never executed. See HERCULES and MANDIBLES.

ACCOUNTABILITY (IS 93) A week-long series of air and artillery attacks launched by Israel on 25 July 1993 against Hezbollah targets in southern Lebanon. These raids were in retaliation for Arab rocket attacks on communities in northern Israel.

ACCURATE TEST (U.S. 81) The first U.S. Central Command deployment to the Persian Gulf region. Conducted in Oman and Egypt in February 1981, this exercise set the stage for an ever-greater defense relationship between the U.S. and the Arab world, which culminated in DESERT SHIELD/DESERT STORM.

ACES NORTH (AUS/U.S.) An Australian air defense exercise that used visiting U.S. Air Force and Navy units to simulate an attacking force.

ACHILLES (GER 18) Alternative plan to HEILIGER MICHAEL. Plan for an attack on Allied forces near the Aisne River, scheduled for the spring of 1918. Renamed BLÜCHER. Never executed.

ACHSE "AXIS" (GER 43) Plan for the emergency occupation of Italy in the event of that country abandoning the Germans in World War II. Covert preparation began by 1 August 1944; additional German troops moved into Italy under the guise of reinforcing the defense of Sicily. On 3 September 1943 the Italians defected and the plan was executed on the order of Field Marshal Kesselring. ACHSE was an elaboration on the smaller ALARICH plan. See KOPENHAGEN and SIEGFRIED.

ACID GAMBIT (U.S. 89) A plan to rescue Central Intelligence Agency (CIA) operative Kurt Muse from a Panamanian prison in which he was held in 1989. Muse had been arrested while attempting to set up a covert anti-Noriega radio station in Panama City. Political considerations delayed the raid by the elite "Delta Force" until the U.S. invaded Panama to topple the local dictator (JUST CAUSE). The rescue went smoothly, and was carried out more quickly than any of the elaborate rehearsals. The helicopter flying Muse out crashed shortly after leaving the *Comandancia*. Another aircraft had to rescue him from the crash.

ACONIT "ACONITE" (FR 90) The operations of French aircraft to protect the Kurds in northern Iraq as part of PROVIDE COMFORT. An aconite is a type of flower.

ACROBAT (Allied 42) Planned British advance from Cyrenaica (the eastern part of Libya) into Tripolotana in the west by the British 8th Army. Scheduled for January 1942, this attack never took place; a German spoiling attack drove the British forces back to Gazala before it could be launched.

ADDITION (Allied 41) Evacuation of British and Commonwealth troops from Bardia, Libya, on the night of 19-20 April 1941.

ADELAIDE I (U.S. 66) Operation involving the destruction of enemy positions in and near the Ong Dong jungle near Tan Uyen (Bihn Duong Province, Vietnam). Executed June 1966.

ADLER "EAGLE"

1. (GER 40) Series of air attacks beginning on 13 August 1940 that began the Battle of Britain. A German victory was a prerequisite for the invasion of England (SEELOWE). During this period, the Royal Air Force lost 415 of its 1,500 pilots. The German Air Force redeployed its bombers to support the

invasion of the Soviet Union (BAR-BAROSSA) in June 1941 ending the threat to England. See CW.

2. (GER 42) Anti-partisan operation centered on the Chechivichi region of Belarus begun on 20 July 1942.

ADVENT (U.S. 62) Program to launch the first U.S. Army communication satellite. Canceled in 1962 due to budget and weight considerations.

AFRICAN EAGLE (US/Mor 96) A combined American/Moroccan air exercise in which USAFE units based in Britain deployed to Morocco as if for a contingency operation. Units were housed in tents at austere bases where they deployed their F-15 aircraft against host-nation F-5s and Mirage jets. Conducted in mid-December 1996.

AGENT (Allied 45) See NEST EGG.

AGREEMENT (Allied 42) British ground and amphibious attack on German-held Tobruk launched on 13 September 1942. The assault failed; the British lost three ships and several hundred soldiers.

A GO "OPERATION A" (JPN 44) 1944 Japanese plan for a climactic naval and air battle with U.S. forces in the Pacific. Forces for this attack were assembled in April 1944 but were dissipated in a series of counterattacks on U.S. forces throughout the Southwest Pacific region. The key portion of these battles became known as the Battle of the Philippine Sea (See FORAGER). A GO included KON, the movement of reinforcements to Biak, in the Schouten Islands northwest of New Guinea, as bait for the American Fleet.

AIDA (GER 42) Ground attack launched by Rommel in June 1942 that pushed British forces east as far as El Alamein, 60 miles west of Alexandria. The Germans captured over 6,000 British prisoners. This advance was the furthest advance of German forces

in North Africa, although it failed to reach its objectives of Cairo and the Suez Canal.

AJAX (U.S./U.K. 51) Plan for the covert 1951 overthrow of the Iranian Prime Minister Mossadegh in response to his nationalization of the Anglo-Iranian Oil Company. The collapse of the Mossadegh regime led to the reestablishment of a monarchy headed by Reza Shah Pahlavi.

AL (JPN 42) The invasion of the Aleutian Islands in Alaska as a diversion for the attack on Midway Island, Operation MI. Subordinate operations were Operation AQ (invasion of Attu and Adak) and Operation AOB (insertion of occupation troops on islands secured by invasion). Executed 7 June 1942.

ALADDIN (Allied) Plan for an emergency invasion of northern Norway in the event of an unexpected local or general German collapse. Never executed. See APOSTLE I and II.

ALAMO (U.S./R.V.N. 75) Plan for a last-ditch defense of the Tan Son Nhut airbase by South Vietnamese troops in the face of the final Communist offensive. This would provide a secure base for an orderly evacuation. Never executed. See EAGLE PULL, FREQUENT WIND, and NEW LIFE.

ALARICH (GER 43) Plan to protect German interests in Italy and to occupy the northern part of that country in the event of a major political change. The Italians surrendered on 3 September 1943. The plan was executed as ACHSE, with the Germans occupying northern Italy and quickly disarming their former allies. "Alarich" is the proper name of a king of the West Goths. See ACHSE, KOPENHAGEN, and SIEGFRIED.

ALBACORE (Allied 43) Overall plan for the Chinese army in India to retake northern Burma. ALBACORE had three sequential sub-plans. Never executed.

ALBACORE ONE Plan for the defense of the British supply base at Ledo, India.

ALBACORE TWO The occupation of Shingbwiyang on 15 November 1943, and for sending out patrols to the lines of the Tarung and Tanai streams.

ALBACORE THREE This part of the overall ALBACORE plan had four phases. Phase 3A: the seizure of Jambu Bay and the air movement of one regiment of the Chinese 22nd Division from Ledo to Fort Hertz, China (LEDO STRIPTEASE). Phase 3B: the capture of the Lonkin-Kamaing line. Phase 3C: the capture of the towns of Mogaung and Myitkyina. Phase 3D: the seizure of Katha and Bhamo.

ALBATROS "ALBATROSS" (FR 54) Plan for the escape of the French Union forces surrounded at Dien Bien Phu. All able-bodied troops would take only their personal weapons, abandoning their artillery and wounded comrades. The escaping troops would link up with the French forces at Muong Nha. Scheduled for May 1954 but never executed.

ALBERTA (Allied 44) The actual fabrication of the early American atomic weapons. One of these was used for the TRINITY test, and the other two ("Fat Man" and "Little Boy") were dropped on Japanese cities (CENTER-BOARD). See MANHATTAN ENGINEER DISTRICT and SILVERPLATE.

ALLEGHENY (U.S./R.V.N. 64) A large-scale search-and-destroy operation conducted by American and South Korean marines and units of the Army of the Republic of South Vietnam in Quang Tri and Thua Thien provinces in late 1964. Launched by the American First Corps on 28 August, this sweep included the A Shau Valley and the Ding Lam Mountains in the North Vietnamese Military Region J.

ALLEGIANT SENTRY 95 (U.S. 95) A month-long port security training exercise

conducted along the east coast of the U.S. in May 1955. This included a large number of reserve units, who are responsible for the protection of American ports in wartime.

ALPENVEILCHEN "ALPINE VIOLET" (GER 41) Proposed German operation designed to help the Italians break out of their Albanian colony into Greece. Never executed; the Italians invaded Greece without German help and were quickly driven to retreat.

ALPHA (Allied 44) Plan drawn up in November 1944 to defend the Chinese cities of Kunming and Chungking from the Japanese ICHI-GO attack.

ALPHABET (Allied 40) The evacuation of British troops from the Norwegian town of Narvik; authorized on 24 May 1940 (shortly before the ground forces had actually entered the port) and completed by 8 June. This evacuation was made necessary by the launch of the German attack on France in the spring of 1940, which reduced operations in Scandinavia to a sideshow. See WILFRED, WESERUEBÜNG. Several nights after final evacuation, the civilians of the town were rescued by British Sub-Lieutenant Patrick Dalzael-Job. Against orders, he organized local fishing boats to remove the population just before a German reprisal bombing. The town was largely destroyed, but only four people were killed. The Royal Navy wanted to discipline Dalzael-Job but was unable to after King Haakon VII awarded him the Knights Cross of the Order of Saint Olav (First Class). Later in the war, he served with Ian Fleming. Many sources cite Dalzael-Job as the inspiration for the James Bond character.

ALSOS (U.S. 44) Overall name for American operations to seize German nuclear resources, materials, and personnel in the final stage of World War II to prevent their capture by the Soviets.

"Alsos" is Greek for "groves," and so this designation is a play on the name of Major General Leslie M. Groves, the head of the MANHATTAN ENGINEER DISTRICT, the American nuclear weapon program. Included BIG, HARBORAGE, OVERCAST, and PAPERCLIP.

ALYSSE (FR 92) The French contribution to the SOUTHERN WATCH, the international effort beginning on 27 August 1992 to prohibit Iraqi aircraft south of the 32nd parallel. This was to protect religious minorities in the southern portion of that country. An alyssum is a flower. See JURAL.

AMBASSADOR (Allied 40) A small British commando raid launched on 14 July 1940 against the 469-man German garrison of the Channel Island of Guernsey. The British captured two Germans and lost one soldier who drowned.

AMHERST (Allied 45) British ground attack in the last weeks of World War II designed to capture intact Dutch canals, bridges, and airfields. Executed in April 1945.

AMIGOS "FRIENDS" (U.S. 60) Emergency humanitarian airlift of supplies to Chile after a series of earthquakes and tidal waves.

AMPLE EXPRESS (NATO 83) A 4-week training exercise begun in September 1983 that involved over 11,000 soldiers from 17 countries who deployed to Denmark to improve their quick-reaction capabilities.

AMSTERDAM (Allied 44) Two flights by 2 heavily-escorted B-17 Flying Fortress bombers from Italy to a primitive airstrip at Tri Duby, Slovenia; the first mission was conducted on 19 September 1944. The bombers carried 4.4 tons of supplies to Tito's partisans and returned with 12 American, a British, and a Czech airmen who had been sheltered by Yugoslavs. A second flight was conducted on 6 October 1944.

ANAKIM (Allied 42) A proposed three-pronged attack to liberate Burma and reopen the Burma road in the dry season of 1942/43. This plan included an amphibious landing to recapture the port of Rangoon as well as ground assaults launched by Chinese and British forces. Never executed due to the low priority given to the China-Burma-India Theater by the Allies and the difficulty of coordinating their actions across such a large area. Variants of this plan included BUCCANEER, BULLDOZER, GRIPFAST, TARZAN, and PIGSTICK. See SAUCY.

ANGEL MOVE (Allied 40) Proposal to reinforce the British Expeditionary Force trapped at Dunkirk with fresh Canadian troops in May 1940. Never executed. See DYNAMO.

ANGUS (Allied 44) Canadian ground attack west of Korteven, Netherlands, launched on 13 October 1944.

ANKLET (Allied 41) British commando raid on the Lofoten Islands, Norway, on 26 December 1941. See CLAYMORE.

ANLACE (U.S. Law Enforcement 86) See LACE.

ANNIE (Allied 44) Psychological operations conducted by the U.S. 12th Army Group during the last five months of World War II in Europe from a high-powered radio transmitter in Luxembourg. This was "black propaganda" as the station claimed to be a Nazi transmitter and gave out false information and orders to its listeners.

ANNIVERSARY VICTORY No. 2 (U.S./Laos 64) See SALEUMSAY.

ANTHROPOID (Allied 41) The assassination of Reinhard Heydrich, the Nazi "Protector of Czechoslovakia." Two resistance fighters, Josef Gabcik and Jan Kubis, flew into Czechoslovakia on the night of 28 December 1941 landing near Pilsen. The attackers wounded Heydrich in May 1942;

he died in early June. Over 15,000 Czechs were killed in reprisal (HEYDRICH).

ANTLER (UK 57) A series of three open-air nuclear tests conducted in September and October 1957 at Maralinga, Australia. The first two bombs were placed in towers, while the third was dropped from an aircraft and exploded high over the test site. Followed BUFFALO, preceded GRAPPLE.

ANTLER 1	14 September 57	1 kiloton
ANTLER 2		6 kilotons
ANTLER 3	October	25 kilotons

ANTON (GER 42) The invasion of the unoccupied zone of France ("Vichy France") by the German Army. Executed 11 November 1942. "Anton" is a proper name. See ATTILA.

ANVIL

1. (Allied 44) Planning name for the Allied amphibious invasion of southern France in the Toulon-Marseilles area on 15 August 1944. The actual invasion was a modified version of ANVIL; renamed DRAGOON by Winston Churchill, who claimed to have been "dragooned" into accepting it. This drew German forces away from the OVERLORD beach heads. See BODYGUARD.

2. (U.S. 75) A series of 19 underground nuclear tests conducted in 1975 and 1976 at the Nevada Test Site. These tests followed the BEDROCK series and preceded the FULCRUM series. The individual shots were:

MARSH	9 June 75	about 15 kilotons
HUSKY PUP	24 October	about 15 kilotons
KASSERI	28 October	1.2 megatons
(Unknown)	18 November	(unknown)
INLET	20 November	500 kilotons
LEYDEN	26 November	5 kilotons
CHIBERTA	20 December	160 kilotons
MUENSTER	3 January 76	600 kilotons
KEELSON	4 February	200 kilotons
ESROM	4 February	150 kilotons
FONTINA	12 February	900 kilotons
CHESHIRE	14 February	350 kilotons
ESTUARY	9 March	350 kilotons
COLBY·	14 March	900 kilotons
POOL	17 March	500 kilotons
STRAIT	17 March	200 kilotons
MIGHTY EPIC	12 May	<20 kilotons
BILLET	27 July	20-150 kilotons
BANON	26 August	20-150 kilotons

AOB (JPN 42) See AL.

APEX (U.S. 76) A proposed reorganization of the American system of assigning codewords designed to reduce overlap and facilitate the sharing of classified information. This system, advanced by the Carter Administration, was resisted by the military services and intelligence agencies and was never implemented.

APHRODITE (Allied 44) Program that attempted to attack difficult-to-destroy German targets by use of explosive-laden remote-controlled bombers guided from a second manned aircraft. A pilot and engineer flew the bomb to altitude, armed it, and bailed out, allowing the robot bomb to be controlled by radio. On 12 August 1944 Joseph P. Kennedy Jr., the older brother of the future president, was killed when the B-24 he was flying exploded, apparently when he set the arming switch. The target was a submarine pen in France. The destroyer *Joseph P. Kennedy Jr.* was christened in his honor a year later. Robert F. Kennedy, later the U.S. Attorney General and Senator, served aboard the ship. Also called BATTY, CASTOR, ORPHAN, and WEARY WILLIE. See EISENHAMMER.

APOSTLE (Allied 45) Plans and operations relating to the liberation of Norway. APOSTLE II called for a quick reoccupation in the event of a localized German collapse in Scandinavia and was never executed. APOSTLE I was the name given to the actual operation conducted after the fall of Germany in May 1945. See ALADDIN and JUPITER.

APPLE (Chinese 45) Commando raid against Japanese supply lines near Kaiping launched on 12 July 1945.

AQUATONE (U.S.) An early name for the secret design and construction of the U-2 reconnaissance aircraft.

ARBOR (U.S. 73) A series of 7 nuclear tests conducted in 1973 and 1974 at the Nevada Test Site. This series of tests followed the TOGGLE test and preceded BEDROCK. The individual shots were:

HUSKY ACE	12 November 73	about 4 kilotons
BERNAL	28 November	<20 kilotons
(Unknown)	27 February 74	about 150 kilotons
(Unknown)	22 May	(unknown)
FALLON	23 May	20-200 kilotons
(Unknown)	6 June	(unknown)
MING BLADE	19 June	about 20 kilotons

ARCADIA (Allied 42) Conference held between Churchill and Roosevelt in Washington from 22 December 1941 to 14 January 1942. This meeting confirmed the basic "Germany First" policy of the Allies and resulted in the Joint Declaration and the creation of the Combined Chiefs of Staffs to co-ordinate overall military activity.

ARCHANGEL (GER 18) See ERZENGEL.

ARCHERY (Allied 41) British commando raid launched against the naval base at Maloy in western Norway on 27 December 1941. Five merchant ships totaling 16,000 tons were sunk in the harbor.

ARC LIGHT (U.S. 65) The deployment of heavy bombers to bases in Guam. By extension, the Air Force term for B-52 Stratofortress bomber missions flown during the Vietnam War in support of ground troops. The first use of these heavy bombers in Southeast Asia occurred on 18 June 1965. Flying out of Guam, 27 aircraft used 750- and 1,000-pound bombs to attack a Viet Cong stronghold. Two of the bombers collided in midair. See NEU-TRALIZE, NIAGARA, and WOWSER.

ARDECHE (FR 54) The last convoy to the French Union garrison at Dien Bien Phu. The troops from the fortress met up with a column from Laos at the tiny village of Sop Nao, 50 miles from Dien Bien Phu. The difficulty of the terrain and harassment of the column by local forces showed ground reinforcement of the garrison to be impractical. The name Ardeche is a region of metropolitan France.

ARGONAUT (Allied 45) A series of 2 conferences between Allied leaders in early 1945. CRICKET was a meeting between Roosevelt and Churchill on Malta as the 2 leaders were en route to the Black Sea. MAGENTO was held between Stalin, Churchill, and Roosevelt in Yalta 4 through 11 February 1945.

ARGUMENT (Allied 44) A coordinated series of intensified air attacks conducted by the Royal and U.S. Army Forces on the German aircraft industry. The operation ran from 11 January 1944 to 1 March, but reached its peak during 20-26 February ("Big Week") when over 3,500 bomber sorties were flown. The Allies lost over 2,600 airmen killed wounded or captured, but failed to make a long-term impact on Nazi aircraft production. Although aircraft production quickly recovered, the Germans were unable to replace the experienced pilots killed defending against this onslaught. Part of POINTBLANK.

ARGUS (U.S. 58) A series of 3 very-high altitude nuclear tests conducted in 1958 above the South Atlantic 1,100 miles southwest of Capetown. All yielded less than 2 kilotons and tested the effect of electromagnetic pulse on communications. These experiments led to a clearer understanding of the Van Allen Radiation Belt. These tests were unannounced and were secret at the time. Followed HARDTACK I and preceded HARDTACK II. The individual tests were:

ARGUS I   27 August 58
ARGUS II   30 August
ARGUS III   6 September

ARID THUNDER (U.S./U.K. 95) A combined American-British training exercise conducted at the Yuma Marine Corps Air Base in 1995 and 1996. Eight British Tornado fighter-bombers were based at the facility. British and American units rotated through the base to improve air-ground cooperation between units from the two nations.

ARIEGE (FR 54) A name used for ALBATROSS beginning in early May 1954 for fear the original name had been compromised to the Vietminh forces.

ARIEL (Allied 40) Escape of French and British forces from northern France after the collapse of that country. This evacuation was conducted from several ports (Cherbourg, St. Malo, Brest, Ste. Nazaire, La Pallice, and Nantes) during the period 16 to 24 June 1940. Over 163,000 British, French, Polish, and Canadian soldiers were brought to safety. See DYNAMO.

ARMADA JAYA (Indonesia 73) Annual unilateral naval and air exercise. Designated by number.

ARME (U.S. 55) A U.S. experiment that tested the ability to detect radioactive fallout from aircraft. The detection of radioactive elements was critical in this period as a means of monitoring Soviet nuclear tests. The name may be an acronym for Atomic Radiological Meteorological Experiment. See RAIN BARREL.

ASHTRAY (U.S. 51) The emergency wartime conversion of F-86A Sabre fighters to reconnaissance aircraft. American forces quickly discovered that elderly World War II propeller-driven aircraft were incapable of surviving against communist jet fighters, prompting this hurried modification.

ASKARI (R.S.A. 83) A series of air strikes conducted in December 1983 against Angolan air defense units.

ASPIDISTRA (Allied 39) Extremely powerful radio transmitter installed near Camden, England, during World War II. By extension, the propaganda operations were conducted by the British Ministry of Political Warfare from this installation.

ASSURED RESPONSE (U.S. 96) The evacuation of Western civilians from Monrovia, Liberia, conducted in early April 1996. American helicopters, gunships, and electronic warfare aircraft operated out of the airport at Freetown, Sierra Leone, flying into the seaside U.S. Embassy compound. Over 2,000 civilians were rescued from an outbreak of Liberia's long-running civil war. The operation ended on 14 April 1996 without any injury or loss of life. See SHARP EDGE.

AT (Allied) Convoys of large, fast ships (such as the *Queen Mary*) sailing from North America to Great Britain in World War II. Designated by number (i.e., AT 123).

ATLANTE "ATALANTE" (FR 54) An offensive by French Union forces through south-central Vietnam launched on 20 January. At the same time as the French were searching for the shadowy guerrillas, Vietminh forces sidestepped the French and encircled the fortress at Dien Bien Phu. An Atlante is a statue or column used in architecture.

ATLANTIC (Allied 44) The Canadian portion of GOODWOOD. Second Canadian Corps crossed the Orne River south of Caen in an attack beginning on 19 July 1944.

ATOLL OUVERTE "OPEN ATOLL" (FR) A public relations effort launched by the French government in response to anti-nuclear testing groups. Sixty journalists were invited to visit the French nuclear test site on Fangataufa Atoll in French Polynesia. The tour was designed to show the reporters that the atoll was not being destroyed by the explosions.

ATTICA (GER 42) Abortive ground attack launched on 23 September 1942 along the north coast of the Black Sea to capture Tuapse, Sochi, Suchmi, and Batum. Strong Soviet defenses halted the advance short of even its first objective.

ATTILA (GER 40) The Nazi occupation of Vichy France. This plan was drawn up in 1940 to capture the French Navy, and was executed on 11 November 1941 in response to the TORCH landings in North Africa. Most of the French fleet at Toulon was scuttled by order of Admiral de Laborde to prevent its capture. As a result of this action, the Germans lost the use of 3 battleships, 7 cruisers, 28 destroyers, and 20 submarines. See ANTON and CATAPULT.

ATTLEBORO (U.S. 66) Operation that sparked the Battle of Dau Tieng (or Dong Minh Chau) involving U.S. 3rd Corps units conducting search and destroy operations throughout a broad area in November 1966.

AUDACIOUS (U.N. 51) Fighting withdrawal conducted by U.N. forces from KANSAS and WYOMING lines to the vicinity of the 38th parallel in response to the long-expected Chinese 1951 spring offensive. The plan called for a quick, orderly pullback before becoming decisively engaged. The U.N. forces would halt on prepared positions while 2 American divisions would strike at the right flank of the advancing Chinese. The 5th Chinese Offensive began on 24 April 1951 with 2 U.N. units (the

South Korean Sixth Division and the Commonwealth Brigade) unable to quickly disengage. As a result, the plan was executed in a piece-meal fashion, opening gaps in the U.N. line.

AUTUMN FOG (GER 40) See HERBST-NEBEL.

AUTUMN FORGE (NATO 75) Annual fall exercise begun in 1975 and denominated by year (i.e., "AUTUMN FORGE 80").

AVALANCHE (Allied 43) The invasion of Italy near the port of Salerno, executed on 9 September 1943. Allied units participating included U.S. 7th Corps and British 10th Corps. Salerno was an obvious choice for an invasion and the defenders were not surprised. Heavy naval bombardment, reinforcement by the American 82nd Airborne Division, and a secondary flanking landing at Reggio de Calabria and Taranto were needed to overcome the strong defenses. Planned under the name TOPHAT. Supported by the deception plan BOARDMAN.

AVENGER

AVENGER II (Allied 44) A pair of deception plans prepared in late 1944 designed to convince the Germans that a major Allied thrust toward southern Germany was being prepared. These deception plans were never executed as the actual planned Allied attack into northern Germany was canceled.

AXIOM (Allied) Plan proposed by Lord Mountbatten to retake northern Burma and so render the torturous Burma Road obsolete. This plan emphasized sea power and the recapture of Malaya, Sumatra, and Hong Kong. Never executed.

AXIS (GER 44) See ACHSE.

AZTEC PACKAGE (U.S.) U.S. Air Force term for "force packages" of units, equipment, and personnel in support of certain special operations.

B

B1 (R.V.N. 63) See BRAVO ONE.

B2 (R.V.N. 63) See BRAVO TWO.

BABYLIFT (U.S. Unofficial 75) The evacuation of Vietnamese war orphans from Saigon in the face of the final North Vietnamese offensive. Tragically, one of the aircraft crashed on takeoff, killing all on board.

BACKBONE
BACKBONE II (Allied 42) Plan for an American invasion of Spanish Morocco as part of the larger invasion of North Africa (TORCH) if the Franco government entered World War II on the side of the Axis. Revised in January 1943 and rechristened BACKBONE II. Never executed.

BACK BREAKER (U.S. 51) See FANDANGO.

BACKFIRE (U.K. 45) A post-war operation by British scientists who fired a captured German V-2 rocket from the Altenwalde on 2 October 1945. The German V-2 served as the basis of the American and Soviet space efforts. See ABUSIVE.

BACKHANDLER (Allied 43) American amphibious assault on the western tip of New Britain on 15 December 1943. DEXTERITY invaded the opposite end of the island at the same time. Part of CARTWHEEL.

BACKLASH III (CN 50) Cargo and other flights by the Royal Canadian Air Force in support of the construction of air-defense radar stations in remote areas of that country.

BAEDEKER (GER 42) A series of air attacks on the British cities of Bath, Norwich, Exeter, York, and Canterbury in April 1942 launched in retaliation for British fire-bomb attacks on Rostock and Lubeck. Supposedly, the targets were selected from a tourist guide book. The most popular publisher of guidebooks in Germany was Baedeker. Often, the word is mistranslated as "tour guide" or "guide book."

BAGRATION (S.U. 44) General attack by Soviet forces to clear the Nazis from Belorussia that resulted in the destruction of the German Army Group Center and ended with Soviet forces near Warsaw. This attack began on the morning of 22 June 1944, 3 years to the day after the Nazi attack on the Soviet Union. The Germans had transferred units to meet the invasion of Normandy (OVERLORD) 2 weeks before. Four Soviet "Fronts" (i.e., Armies) totaling over 120 divisions smashed into the thinly-held German line. The Soviets achieved a ratio of 10 to 1 in tanks and 7 to 1 in aircraft. At the points of attack, the numerical and quality advantages of the Soviets were overwhelming. The Germans crumbled. Minsk fell on 3 July, trapping

50,000 Germans. Ten days later the Red Army reached the prewar Polish border. Overall the annihilation of Army Group Center cost the Germans 2,000 tanks, 57,000 other vehicles, and over 150,000 soldiers. Named after General Bagration, who died at Borodino.

BAKER 60 (Allied 45) Plan for the air transport of the U.S. 11th Airborne Division to air bases on the Tokyo Plain in the event of an unexpected Japanese collapse. Part of BLACKLIST.

BALBUZARD (FR 94) French naval patrols as part of DENY FLIGHT and MARITIME GUARD.

BALIKATAN "WORKING TOGETHER" (U.S./PH 94) A series of periodic joint U.S./Filipino training exercises. These exercises have included amphibious operations as well as medical training and engineer operations aimed at improving the life of Filipinos in remote regions of the country. Designated by year (as in BALIKATAN 94).

BALTOPS (NATO 73) The annual NATO air and naval exercise held in the Baltic Sea. During the Cold War, NATO training in the Baltic was a means of monitoring Soviet naval developments and was conducted without the cooperation of nearby countries. The 1995 exercise included ships from 13 nations including all the nations surrounding the Baltic. Denominated by year (as in BALTOPS 85). BALTOPS may be a contraction of "Baltic Operations."

BAMBERG (GER 43) Anti-partisan sweep centered near Bobruisk, Russia, in March 1943. In the barbarism typical of these operations, numerous villages were burned and over 3,000 civilians were killed.

BAMBOO (Allied 44) The overall plan for an Allied ground attack in the fall of 1944 on the Kra Isthmus in Burma. Never executed. Included CLINCH.

BAMBOO TREE (U.S. 61) A program that upgraded Berlin's airfields and navigational aids to improve the ability to conduct a second Berlin Airlift (VITTLES). Emergency supplies of food and fuel were also stockpiled in the city, further reducing the vulnerability of the city to a blockade. Completed by the end of 1961.

BAN (JPN 45) Plan for the Japanese 15th Army of the Burma Area Army to defend Mandalay, Burma's second largest city. The city fell to British and Chinese forces in March 1945.

BANANA BELT (U.S./CN 55) Acceptance tests for CF-100 fighters conducted at Cold Lake, Alberta, and Eglin Air Force Base, Florida, from November to May 1955. Also known informally as FROZEN BANANA BELT.

BANISH BEACH (U.S.) A proposal to attack the Ho Chi Minh Trail with C-130 cargo aircraft loaded with fire bombs. Never executed. See COMMANDO LAVA and CAROLINA MOON.

BANQUET (U.K. 40) Contingency plan to employ training aircraft in the ground-attack role in the event of a German amphibious landing (SEELOWE). Part of JULIUS CAESAR.

BÄR "BEAR" (GER 44) The Nazi evacuation from Rumania conducted under heavy Soviet pressure beginning on 21 August 1944.

BARBAROSSA (GER 40) The German invasion of the Soviet Union. Hitler ordered planning for the opening of Germany's Eastern Front as early as September 1940. The attack was originally scheduled for 15 May 1941 but was delayed by the unexpected requirement for Germany to move into Yugoslavia and Greece to save the Italian effort in those countries (MARITA). The BARBAROSSA invasion was launched at 0300, 22 June 1941 by 3,000,000 German and Axis troops along a 2,000 mile front. By noon, over 1,000 Soviet aircraft were destroyed on the ground. The original objective of this attack was to establish German control west of the general line of the Volga River to Archangelsk. After victory, the Soviet Union was to be turned into a vast resource base for a greater Germany. Economic exploitation of the conquered area was covered by the OLDENBURG Plan. The high water mark of German operations was reached on 12 December 1941 on the outskirts of Moscow. Named after the medieval Kaiser "Red Beard," who died during the Crusades. See OTTO and WARTBURG.

BARCLAY (Allied) Deception plan in support of the invasion of Sicily (HUSKY). This operation kept the Axis guessing as to the location of the Allied jump across the Mediterranean by use of bogus troop movements and radio traffic. See MINCEMEAT, TROJAN HORSE, WAREHOUSE, WATERFALL, and WITHSTAND.

BARITONE (Allied 42) The delivery of Spitfire fighters to Malta on 17 August 1942.

BARKER (Allied 44) The insertion of several French resistance fighters by air near Salornay on the night of 13 August 1944. These agents worked to disrupt the retreat of German forces from the Normandy area. See COBRA.

BARNEY (Allied 45) A wolf-pack of 9 U.S. submarines in the Sea of Japan during June 1945. The force destroyed 28 Japanese ships. The operation was named after the man who planned it: Admiral Barney Sieglaff.

BARRACUDA (Allied 44) Planned invasion aimed directly at the port city of Naples, Italy. Never executed, although elements of this plan were integrated into AVALANCHE. See GANGWAY and TOPHAT.

BARREL ROLL (U.S. 64) The use of American aircraft to attack communist supply routes in Laos, authorized in December 1964 by President Johnson. On 14 December, the American 428th Tactical Fighter Wing began flying F-100 Super Sabre jets from Takhli Royal Thai Air Force Base. Part of OPLAN 34-A. See STEEL TIGER.

BARRISTER (Allied) Plan for the seizure of Dakar. In planning, this operation was first called BLACK, then BARRISTER, followed by PICADOR, and was finally executed as MENACE.

BARROOM (U.S. 53) The modification of B-36 Peacemaker bombers to carry the early, very large thermonuclear bombs. Conducted in 1953 and 54. Followed by CAUTERIZE.

BASALT (Allied 42) Commando raid on the German-held channel island of Sark on 4 October 1942. Eight Germans were killed outright; 5 others were killed while trying to escape with their hands bound. When the news of the killing of the prisoners reached Berlin, Hitler ordered that no British commandos were to be captured. This directive is popularly called the "Commando Order."

BASEPLATE (GER 45) See BODENPLATTE and HERMANN.

BASTION (Allied 42) A deception operation that inflated the number and capability of British units in North Africa using fake radio transmissions and phony vehicles. Began in early 1942. These fake units were later used in BOARDMAN and FAIRLANDS deceptions.

BAT (Allied Law Enforcement 83) A joint counter-narcotics program conducted by the governments of the U.S. and its regional partners in the area of the Bahamas, Antilles, and the Turks Islands. Military and law enforcement agencies cooperated sharing radar and other surveillance information.

BATTLEAXE

BATTLE AXE (Allied 41) Ground attack launched by British forces in Egypt to push the Axis back across the Egyptian frontier. An earlier attack (BREVITY) had failed, but with the addition of over 200 tanks General Wavell felt his Western Desert Army could recapture Tobruk. Launched on 15 June 1941 the attackers squandered their 4 to 1 advantage in armor by dividing it into a number of smaller thrusts. These attacks were chopped to bits by German armor and batteries of anti-aircraft guns. After 2 days the British found themselves in retreat, having lost 91 tanks to the Germans' 12. As a result of this disaster, General Wavell was relieved of his command. The next British attack from Egypt was CRUSADER.

BATTERING RAM (Allied 43) The insertion of 8 resistance fighters into an area between Saumur and Chinon, France, by air on the night of 12 September 1943. Eight other men were returned to Britain.

BATTY (Allied 44) See APHRODITE.

BAUMIER "BALM TREE" (FR 91) The French evacuation of over 2,000 European refugees from the civil unrest in Zaire in 1991. The transport aircraft operated from bases in Chad and the Central African Republic.

BAYTOWN (Allied 43) Invasion of the Italian mainland at Reggio di Calabria, across the Straits of Messina from Sicily, by British forces under the command of Field Marshal Bernard Montgomery. Executed 3 landings at Salerno (AVALANCHE) and Taranto (SLAPSTICK). The initial landings were unopposed, but Axis demolitions along the narrow defiles of the rugged landscape delayed the advance of the British forces. See BOOTHBY, BUTTRESS, and HOOKER.

BAZAAR (Allied 44) Plan for U.S. air support of Soviet forces in Siberia in the event of a Japanese attack. By extension, the survey of air bases and other facilities in Siberia to support this plan. Allowing U.S. heavy bombers to use Soviet bases would have increased the tempo of the American air attacks on the Japanese. Never executed.

"BAZOOKA" (GER 44) See MICKEY MOUSE.

BEARSKIN (Yugoslavia 44) Offensive by partisan forces led by Tito against German road and rail networks in Slovenia launched in May 1944. The strategic intent of these attacks was to prevent the Nazis from shifting forces to France in response to the invasion of France scheduled for the next month.

BEAR TRAP (U.S.) A U.S. Navy program that used P-3 Orion long-range aircraft to monitor electronic emissions of Soviet "Bear" bombers.

BEAVER

1. (Allied 42) A series of 4 training exercises conducted by Canadian I Corps in England in spring 1942.

2. (Allied 44) A training exercise conducted by elements of the U.S. 7th Corps at Slapton Sands, England, to simulate the OVERLORD landings.

BEDROCK (U.S. 74) A series of 18 nuclear tests conducted in 1974 and 1975 at the Nevada Test Site. These tests followed ARBOR and preceded ANVIL. The individual shots were:

ESCABOSA	10 July 74	about 170 kilotons
(Unknown)	18 July	(unknown)
PUYE	14 August	about 40 kilotons
PORT-MANTEAU	30 August	200 kilotons

(Unknown)	25 September	(unknown)
STANYAN	26 September	100 kilotons
HYBLA FAIR	28 October	<20 kilotons
(Unknown)	16 December 75	about 4 kilotons
TOPGALLANT	28 February	about 185 kilotons
CABRILLO	7 March	about 120 kilotons
DINING CAR	5 April	about 20 kilotons
EDAM	24 April	about 9 kilotons
OBAR	30 April	about 41 kilotons
TYBO	14 May	about 380 kilotons
STILTON	3 June	about 275 kilotons
MIZZEN	3 June	about 160 kilotons
MAST	19 June	about 520 kilotons
CAMEMBERT	26 June	about 750 kilotons

BEEF BROTH (U.S. 65) The buildup of Tactical Air Command units in the U.S. to replace units deployed to Vietnam.

BEGGAR (Allied 44) Plan for the aerial supply of weapons and ammunition to resistance forces in Paris conducting the uprising of August 1944. The liberation of the city by Allied ground forces proceeded very rapidly and political considerations led to modifications. Rather than providing weapons to the Communist-led uprising, the aircraft dropped food and fuel in Paris in advance of the arrival of ground troops controlled by General DeGaulle.

BELL BOY (U.S. 51) Program to equip American F-89 interceptors with air-to-air nuclear weapons.

BELLICOSE (Allied 43) The first shuttle bombing mission of World War II. American bombers left Britain on 20 June 1943 attacking the steel works at Friedrichshafen and flying on to Algeria. On their return flight, these aircraft hit the Italian naval base at La Spezia. An unexpected benefit of the raid on Friedrichshafen was the accidental destruction of an undetected V1 "Buzz Bomb" factory. The factory was relocated

underground, forcing a delay in the use of these weapons. See FRANTIC.

BELLOWS (Allied 42) The reinforcement of Malta with Spitfire fighters on 11 August 1942.

BENEFICIARY (Allied 44) Plan for breaking out of the Normandy lodgment by means of airborne and amphibious attacks near Saint Malo. Never executed. See COBRA, GOODWOOD.

BENITO (Allied 41) Exercise by Canadian troops involved in the defense of Britain against a German invasion (SEELOWE). Conducted in mid-April 1941.

BENT SPEAR (U.S.) The flag-word used to designate an accident or incident involving a nuclear weapon less severe than BROKEN ARROW, but more dangerous than a DULL SWORD incident. Such an event would include damage to a weapon requiring major repair, the release of classified information, the possibility of a nuclear weapon being armed, or of adverse public reaction. See CRESTED ICE.

BERM BUSTER (Coalition 91) A deception operation designed to falsely portray preparations for a Coalition attack into occupied Kuwait via the Wadi Al Batin. Conducted by the U.S. 1st Cavalry Division with supporting psychological warfare units on 15 February 1991. Followed by RED STORM.

BERNHARD (GER 43) Operation to undermine the British economy by counterfeiting 5-pound bank notes. By early 1943, large amounts of these bogus bills appeared in neutral cities around Europe. Eventually, up to £140,000,000 sterling were produced, forcing the Bank of England to redesign the notes.

BERTRAM (Allied 42) Deception operation designed to disguise British preparations for the LIGHTFOOT attack. The success of this early deception inspired elaborate deceptions in support of other allied operations. See TREATMENT.

BERYL (FR 62) French nuclear test conducted on 1 May 1962 at the Hoggar Massif in the Algerian Sahara. A single AN-11 bomb was released from a Mirage bomber. The resulting mushroom cloud contaminated at least a dozen soldiers with radiation.

BESTRAUFUNG "PUNISHMENT" (GER 41) German terror-bombing attacks against the city of Belgrade, Serbia (then the capital of Yugoslavia) conducted from 6 to 8 April 1941. These attacks launched the German invasion of that country. Seventeen thousand civilians were killed. The name "Punishment" refers to the political intent to punish Yugoslavia for refusing to allow German troops to move freely into Albania and Greece. See MARITA.

BETTELSTAB "BEGGAR'S STAFF" (GER 42) Planned German assault to destroy the Oranienbaum Bridgehead, west of Stalingrad (now Volgograd) scheduled for the summer of 1942. Never executed.

BIG (Allied 45) Operations to move nuclear intelligence teams from - Freudenstadt through Horb to Haigerloch in southwest Germany. Troops taking part in this operation (dubbed "Task Force A") captured a German atomic pile at Haigerloch that only needed additional heavy water to become operational. Nearby at Hechtingen they uncovered the heavy water plant shipped from Norway after the FRESHMAN and GUNNERSIDE attacks. Conducted in April 1945.

BIG BLOW (GER 45) See HERMANN.

BIG BOY (U.N. 51) See SPITFIRE.

BIG DROP (NATO 96) The U.S. Air Force portion of PURPLE STAR.

BIGEARD (FR 54) A local counterattack launched by the besieged French Union

forces at Dien Bien Phu to destroy Vietnamese antiaircraft positions that were interfering with air resupply flights. Launched on 26 March 1954, the attackers came under artillery bombardment and suffered heavy casualties. Named after the attack's commander, Bruno Bigeard.

BIG LIFT (U.S. 63) Exercise involving the first airlift of an entire U.S. Army division from the U.S. to Europe. Conducted in 1963, presaging REFORGER.

BIGOT (Allied 43) A security marking on OVERLORD documents created after September 1943 that revealed the actual names and locations of objectives. As such, it was not a code word, but rather designated the document as belonging in a "security compartment"; today we would call this "Sensitive Compartmentalized Information." Bigot information was limited to selected personnel, who naturally were called "Bigots."

BIG SAM (U.S. 60) An evaluation of the application of U.S. airlift operations in small counterinsurgency operations conducted in March 1960. The Army portion of this exercise was called PEERTO PINE.

BIG SANDY LAKE (U.S./CN 55) A joint American/Canadian search and rescue effort conducted in mid-February 1955. An American B-47 bomber had exploded above northern Saskatchewan while en route to Greenland. Three of the airmen were rescued.

BIG STICK

1. (U.N. 51) Plan to destroy a communist supply at Sibyon-ni, Korea, by ground assault thereby capturing Kaesong and advancing the left flank on the U.S. 8th Army. Planned for 15 April 1951, never executed. See HOME COMING.

2. (U.S. 53) A major month-long deployment of B-36 Peacemaker bombers from the

U.S. to Japan. This training took place in August and September 1953, shortly after the armistice was signed in Korea. The deployment served to display American determination to protect South Korea.

3. (U.S. 80) Computer-assisted "war game" used by the Air Command and Staff College at Maxwell Air Base, Alabama. Conducted in the 1980s as a student exercise, the game simulated a nuclear war between the U.S. and the Soviet Union.

BIG SWITCH (U.N. 53) The final exchange of prisoners at the end of the Korean War. Beginning soon after the signing of the armistice on 27 July, a total of 12,733 U.N. prisoners were exchanged for 75,823 communists (70,183 North Koreans and 5,640 Chinese.) The U.N. insisted on a voluntary repatriation of the communist prisoners. This was a central sticking point in the negotiations to the end of the war. The large number of communist prisoners who refused repatriation (SCATTER) caused a major embarrassment to the communist governments. A total of 22 U.N. personnel (1 Briton, the remainder American) refused repatriation. See LITTLE SWITCH and HOME COMING.

"BIG WEEK" (Allied 44) See ARGUMENT.

BINGHAM (Allied 45) The establishment of a secret Allied air base at Zara in the former Yugoslavia in April 1945.

BINGO (Allied 44) Attacks by the U.S. 12th Air Force against rail targets in the Brenner Pass region of Italy beginning in November 1944. The bombers quickly knocked out electrical power on the rail line from Brennero to Vicenza. The attacks peaked in March 1945 with 6,500 sorties in a single week. The surrender of German forces in Italy on 29 April ended the operation.

BIRDCAGE (Allied 45) Operations to inform outlying areas in Malaya, Burma, and Siam that the Japanese had surrendered, ending

World War II. Over 33,000,000 leaflets were dropped on 90 POW camps and 150 other Japanese military installations. Executed in August 1945. See MASTIFF.

BIRD SONG (GER 42) See VOGEL-GEZWITSCHER.

BIRMINGHAM (U.S. 66) Search and destroy operation conducted in Tay Ninh Province in South Vietnam along the border with Cambodia. Conducted in April 1966. Over 160 B-50 ARC LIGHT sorties were in flown in support of this operation.

BISHOP (Allied 45) Supporting attack for DRACULA.

BITING (Allied 42) British commando raid to capture components of the German radar set at Brunefal, France, executed on 27 February 1942. Two Germans were captured, one of whom was a radar operator who provided a great deal of classified information.

BLACK

1. (U.S. 04) American contingency plan for war with Germany first drawn up in 1904 and periodically updated. One of the "Color Series" of plans that were replaced in 1938 with the RAINBOW series. Never executed. See COLOR SERIES.

2. (Allied 40) First plan for the seizure of the French naval base at Dakar. Later called PICADOR, then BARRISTER, and finally MENACE.

3. (U.S. 41) American diplomatic code thought by the Americans to be unbreakable. The Italian intelligence service began reading this traffic late 1941 after photographing the code books. As a result of this code break, the German forces under Rommel received sensitive information on British forces in Egypt that was sent from the U.S. embassy in Cairo to Washington.

4. (GER 43) See SCHWARZ.

BLACK ARROW (IS 55) Commando raid by an Israeli paratroop company commanded by Captain (later Defense Minister) Ariel Sharon on 28 February 1955 against Egyptian forces in the Gaza Strip. Thirty-six Egyptians and 8 Israelis were killed in the attack against the local railroad and the city's water plant. See MUSKETEER.

BLACKBOY (Allied 42) An anti-invasion training exercise conducted by the Canadian 1st Division in November 1942 in Britain. See SEELOWE.

BLACK BUCK 1-6 (U.K. 82) A series of 6 extremely long-range bombing attacks by British Vulcan bombers on Argentine positions in the Falkland Islands. The missions flew from the British air base on Ascension Island starting on the night of 30 April 1982. Victor tankers provided multiple refuelings. Each aircraft carried more than 21 1,000-pound bombs or a number of anti-radar missiles. At the time, these 6 raids were the longest combat flights in history (see SECRET SQUIR-REL). The results were more psychological than physical, as the Argentines were quickly able to repair damage to the radars and the Port Stanley runway. The raids prompted the Argentines to keep their best aircraft on the mainland to protect against possible raids on Argentine cities. See CORPORATE.

BLACK DRAGON (BG 64) See DRAGON NOIR.

BLACK JACK (U.S./R.V.N.) The designation (with a number such as BLACK JACK 123) used for operations by Mobile Guerrilla Forces in Vietnam. These operations involved long patrols by American Special Forces and South Vietnamese guerrillas and were frequently resupplied by air.

BLACK JACK 22 (U.S./R.V.N. 66) Staged from Ban Me Thout and ran for 34 days, ending in January 1967.

BLACK JACK 33 (U.S./R.V.N. 67) Was conducted by Special Forces Detachment B-56 in the 3rd Corps area in April-May, 1967.

BLACK JACK 41 (U.S./R.V.N. 67) Conducted in the spring of 1967 in the Seven Mountains region.

BLACKLIST (Allied 45) The Allied contingency plan dated 15 August 1945 for the sudden, unexpected collapse of Japan in World War II. BLACKLIST called for General Stillwell's 10th Army to occupy the Japanese colony of Korea to prevent the Soviets from extending their influence in the region. See BAKER 60.

BLADE JEWEL (U.S. 89) The reduction of the number of military families in Panama during the period of tension before the American invasion of that country (JUST CAUSE). The U.S. government feared the large number of Americans in Panama might be held hostage in the event of hostilities. After a set date, additional families were prohibited from arriving and those families already in the country were sent back to the U.S. Ran concurrently with NIMROD DANCER.

BLAST (U.N. 52) A program of dropping propaganda leaflets on North Korean settlements near military targets warning of upcoming air attacks. After the air strikes, more leaflets were dropped (under a program called STRIKE) reminding the civilians of the earlier warning.

BLAU "BLUE" (GER 43) The German strategy for the southern portion of their Eastern Front in 1943. Planned under the name "SIEGFRIED," this operation was based on an attack by Army Group South past Rostov into the Caucus oil fields. It had 3 phases. BLAU I (also called FRED-ERICUS II), called for a northward thrust toward Kursk. This phase began on 28 June 1943, and resulted in the Battle of Kursk. The Soviets, having captured a copy of this plan when a German staff officer's plane crashed, were prepared for the attack. The action around Kursk unhinged BLAU II (an eastward attack toward Kursk) and BLAU III (also called CLAUSEWITZ), the ill-fated attack into Stalingrad. The focus on Stalingrad (now Volgograd) was a political objective, which distracted the Germans from reaching the critical oil facilities at Grozny and Maikop. The German Army was forced into a battle of attrition from which it would never recover. Axis losses at Stalingrad included 2 Rumanian, an Italian, and a Hungarian army as well as 240,000 German troops killed and another 94,000 captured. See KREMLIN.

BLAZING TRAILS (U.S. 85) See FUERTES CAMINOS.

BLIND BAT (U.S.) The general term for illumination missions flown by C-130 Hercules aircraft over Vietnam. The large cargo aircraft could loiter over areas for a long period of time dropping hundreds of flares.

BLIND LOGIC (U.S. 90) Operation to conduct civil-military stability operations in Panama in the aftermath of the American invasion (JUST CAUSE). Replaced KRYSTAL BALL. Executed in a modified form as PROMOTE LIBERTY in January 1990. See PRAYER BOOK.

BLITZ "FLASH" (U.S. Unofficial 45) The first 5 fire-bomb raids against Japanese cities conducted by B-29 Superfortress bombers based in the Marianas. These bases had improved logistical support over those in China (MATTERHORN). A new commander, Major General Curtis LeMay, abandoned the use of high-explosive bombs delivered from high altitude in favor of a large number of incendiaries spread across a wide area of cities at low levels. The available supply of these bombs limited the number of initial attacks (dubbed BLITZ) to 5. BLITZ 1 was flown by 325 aircraft against Tokyo on 9 March. This was the single most destructive air attack of the war. Almost 16 square miles of the city burned, killing 83,000 people and wounding another 41,000. A million people were left homeless. The Americans lost only 14 aircraft. BLITZ 2 and 5 hit Nagoya on 11 and 18 March burning over 5 square miles, more than half the city. BLITZ 3 and 4 burned 11 square miles of Osaka and Kobe on 13 and 16 March.

BLOCKADE (U.S. Law Enforcement 93) An intensified program of border security along a 20-mile sector centered on El Paso, Texas, that began as a local initiative in September 1993. The Border Patrol commander in the area positioned his officers closely together (as little as 50 meters apart) to prevent illegal border crossings from Mexico. To man this effort, he removed officers from positions further in depth. This technique dramatically reduced the number of illegal border crossings in the area. Both the local business community and the Mexican government protested this action. In October, the name BLOCKADE was discontinued and the new tactic was dubbed HOLD THE LINE and extended to other regions of the U.S./Mexican border. See GATEKEEPER and SAFEGUARD.

BLOCKBUSTER (Allied 45) Ground attack by Canadian 2nd Corps east of the Rhine toward Calcar in February 1945.

BLOODLETTING (FR 54) A planned escape of the besieged French Union forces from Bien Dien Phu, a variant of ALBATROS. Never executed.

BLÜCHER Marshal Blücher was the Prussian commander at Waterloo. His name is commonly anglicized as "Bluecher."

1. (GER 18) An alternate plan to HEILGER MICHAEL. This plan called for an

attack on Allied forces near the Aisne River, scheduled for spring 1918. Never executed.

2. (GER 42) A planned 5-division attack from the Crimean Peninsula across the Kerch Straits into the Caucasus, as part of BLAU. Executed in a much smaller form 2 September 1942.

BLUE (GER 42) See BLAU.

BLUEBAT (U.S. 58) Intervention by U.S. forces in Lebanon (in conjunction with British forces based in Jordan) to counter unrest caused by agitators controlled by the United Arab Republic (Egypt and Syria). The American Marines landed unopposed on 15 July 1958. Army units arrived 4 days later. The American units quickly sealed off Beirut, freeing the Lebanese Army for other duties. American strategic forces went on increased alert during the period of tension surrounding the American intervention.

BLUEBIRD (U.S. 45) A planned U.S. invasion of Japanese-occupied Formosa. Taiwan was a natural stepping-stone between the Philippines and Japan and so its invasion was favored by General Douglas MacArthur. The invasion was canceled, but elements of the plan were used to falsely portray an invasion threat as a deception to protect assault on Okinawa (ICEBERG).

BLUE BOOK (U.S. 50) Study conducted by the U.S. Air Force's Office of Scientific Research, which began in the 1950s to examine the potential threat to American security posed by Unidentified Flying Objects (UFOs). The report issued in 1969 discounted any such threat. This result inspired some segments in society to attack the report as a cover-up. See MAJESTIC.

BLUECOAT (Allied 44) Attack by British 2nd Army south of Caumont, France. Executed 29 July 1944. This assault followed in the steps of GOODWOOD, which also failed to break through the German defenses.

BLUE FALCON (U.K. 90) A series of company-level training exercises conducted by the Royal Marines in Kuwait after that nation's liberation in Operation DESERT STORM. Four rotations of about 100 men each had taken place by mid-1994.

BLUE FLAG (U.S.) Training exercises periodically conducted by U.S. Air Force units at Eglin Air Force Base, Florida, where a large area is fitted out to simulate a dense antiaircraft array. This event is hosted by the U.S. Central Command and includes units from all the military services. See CHECKERED FLAG, GREEN FLAG, and RED FLAG.

BLUE HARRIER (NATO) Annual naval mine-hunting exercise. Denominated by year (i.e., BLUE HARRIER 94).

BLUEHEARTS (U.N. 50) The first American amphibious landing in Korea, conducted at Pohang on 18 July 1950 by the 1st Cavalry Division. The town was still in friendly hands, but was in the path of the rapid North Korean advance. The American units quickly joined the defenders. This landing, planned on extremely short notice, attracted little attention at the time, but pointed the way towards critical landing at Inchon (CHROMITE).

BLUE NOSE (U.S. 60) The test launch of a GAM-77/AGM-28 Hound Dog missile from a Strategic Air Command B-52G Stratofortress bomber on 12 April 1960. Although the Hound Dog was carried on a pylon under the aircraft's wing on a 20-hour flight in the Arctic, it functioned perfectly. These weapons were accepted into the Air Force arsenal in 1961 and were retired in 1976.

BLUES (Allied 44) British naval air attacks on southern Norway in June 1944 as part of LOMBARD.

BLUE SPOON (U.S. 88) The first name given to U.S. Southern Command Operations Plan 1-90 for offensive actions against the Panama Defense Forces. Drawn up in April 1988, approved on 30 October. Executed in modified form in December 1989 as JUST CAUSE.

BLUE SPRINGS (U.S. 64) A "sensitive intelligence operation" mentioned in the "Pentagon Papers." From context, it seems likely this was a covert American operation directed against communist forces operating in Laos in 1964 and was part of OPLAN 34-A.

BLUE STRAW (U.S. 61) Nuclear weapons test proposed for 1961. This plan called for a W-49 warhead to be fired on an Atlas missile and set to explode high over Taongi Atoll. Never executed. See GIANT PATRIOT.

BLUE SWORD (NATO 94) Close air support for NATO ground units in Bosnia.

BOARDMAN (Allied 43) The deception operation that supported the AVALANCHE invasion at Salerno, Italy. This deception continued the false threat of an Allied invasion of the Balkans. See CHETTYFORD and FAIRWINDS.

BODENPLATTE "BASEPLATE" (GER 45) See HERMANN.

BODYGUARD (Allied 43) The overall Allied deception plan in Europe for 1944. The major objective of this plan was to conceal the intentions of the Allies to invade northern and southern France (OVERLORD and DRAGOON). BODYGUARD included FORTITUDE (deception plans in support of OVERLORD), which in turn had two major parts: SKYE (conducted by the British) and QUICKSILVER (conducted mostly by the Americans). Followed JAEL. Other deception plans in support of the invasion of

Normandy included FERDINAND, FORTITUDE, IRONSIDE, MINCEMEAT, OVERTHROW, ROYAL FLUSH, and ZEPPELIN.

BODYLINE (Allied) Scientific investigation of the possibility of the German development of rocket- and jet-powered flying bombs.

BOLD FIRE 3-74 (U.S. 74) Combined Army/Air Force exercise conducted in May 1974 at Yakima Firing Center in Washington state.

BOLERO (Allied 42) The buildup of American troops in Britain for use in Europe (OVERLORD and ANVIL). This major movement was concealed by the LARKHILL deception. See MAGNET and SHADOW 82.

BOLO (U.S. 67) A large air sweep by American F-4 Phantoms conducted on 2 January 1967 that resulted in the destruction of seven North Vietnamese MiG-21s.

BOOMERANG (Allied 44) American air attack on refineries on Palmebang on Sumatra by aircraft based on Ceylon. The fifth MATTERHORN mission.

BONG SONG I (U.S./R.V.N. 65) Operations north of Bong Song (Binh Dinh Province, Vietnam) and west of Highway I to seize a series of enemy-held villages. Executed January 1965.

BONUS (Allied 42) Planning name for IRONCLAD.

BOOTHBY (Allied 43) Deception plan that portrayed a false threat of an Allied invasion at Crotone, Italy. This drew attention away from the site of the actual AVALANCHE invasion, Naples.

BOOTLEG (NATO 61) Local training exercise conducted by the U.S. 37th Engineer Group in Germany in September 1961.

BOOTY (Allied 45) See NEST EGG.

BORDERTOWN (U.S. 59) American over-flights of Eastern Europe conducted from 1959 to 1964. American RB-57 Canberra bombers could violate airspace in the region safely until the introduction of the MiG-21.

BOWERY (Allied 42) The ferrying of fighter aircraft to the besieged island of Malta by the aircraft carriers HMS *Eagle* and USS *Wasp* in early May 1942. Eagle was sunk on a similar operation, PEDESTAL.

BOWLINE (U.S. 68) A series of 30 nuclear test explosions conducted in 1968 and 1969 at the Nevada Test Site. These blasts followed CROSSTIE and preceded MANDREL. The individual tests of this series were:

TANYA	30 July 68	about 20 kilotons
DIANA MOON	27 August	<20 kilotons
SLED	29 August	about 260 kilotons
NOGGIN	6 September	about 110 kilotons
KNIFE A	12 September	<20 kilotons
STODDARD	17 September	about 13 kilotons, see PLOWSHARE
HUDSON SEAL	24 September	about 10 kilotons
KNIFE C	3 October	about 3 kilotons
(Unknown)	10 October	(unknown)
(Unknown)	31 October	(unknown)
CREW	4 November	about 22 kilotons
KNIFE B	15 November	about 8 kilotons
(Unknown)	15 November	(unknown)
MING VASE	20 November	about 12 kilotons
TINDERBOX	22 November	about 3 kilotons
SCHOONER	8 December	30 kilotons, see PLOWSHARE
TYG	12 December	about 20 kilotons
(Unknown)	12 December	(unknown)
BENHAM	19 December	1.15 megatons
PACKARD	15 January 69	10 kilotons
WINESKIN	15 January	about 40 kilotons
VISE	30 January	about 40 kilotons
CYPRESS	12 February	about 15 kilotons
BARSAC	20 March	about 10 kilotons
COFFER	21 March	about 35 kilotons
THISTLE	30 April	20-200 kilotons
BLENTON	20 April	20-200 kilotons
PURSE	7 May	about 180 kilotons
TORRIDO	27 May	about 22 kilotons
TAPPER	12 June	about 12 kilotons

BOXER I (U.N. 53)

BOXER II (U.N. 53) The naval insertion of two South Korean 12-man sabotage teams near Hungnam on Korea's east coast on the night of 7 February 1953. Neither team was ever heard of again.

BOXER III (U.N. 53) The air insertion of a 12-man South Korean special operations team on 9 February 1953. They were never heard from again.

BOXER IV (U.N. 53) The air insertion of a 12-man South Korean special operations team on 11 February 1953. They were never heard from again.

BOX TOP (U.S. 64) A "sensitive intelligence operation" mentioned in the "Pentagon Papers." This operation was a series of secret reconnaissance flights flown by RB-47 aircraft in Southeast Asia.

BRADDOCK II (Allied 44) Dropping of incendiary charges to foreign workers in Germany in 1944 to encourage sabotage against German war production.

BRADMAN (Allied 44) The air attack on German positions near Casino, Italy, that preceded the DICKENS attack.

BRASSARD (Allied 44) The capture of the Italian island of Elba by the Free French on 17 June 1944. Attacking units staged on nearby Corsica.

BRASS RING (U.S. 50) An Air Force program to develop a drone aircraft (a modified B-47 bomber) to deliver thermonuclear weapons. The first American hydrogen bombs were designed to provide an "Emergency Capability" and lacked parachutes or other means to allow a manned aircraft the means of clearing the area before the explosion. By July 1952, parachutes were available and this effort was canceled. See APHRODITE.

BRAVE SHIELD (U.S. 80) A training exercise conducted by elements of the U.S. 18th Airborne Corps at Forts Bragg and Polk in the southeastern U.S. in August 1980.

BRAVE SHIELD 17 (U.S. 78) A deployment of elements of the U.S. 18th Airborne Corps to Fort Irwin, California, in April 1978. This exercise was highlighted by the first use of an E-3 Sentry aircraft in support of an Army exercise.

BRAVO ONE (R.V.N. 63) A plan for South Vietnamese troops to falsely portray a pro-Communist coup d'état in Saigon in October 1963. This would provide sufficient confusion to allow forces loyal to President Diem to kill political rivals and force the Americans to more closely align themselves with the Diem regime. See BRAVO TWO.

BRAVO TWO (R.V.N. 63) An actual coup d'état conducted against the government of President Diem under the cover of the false BRAVO ONE coup. The troops were moved into the capital to crush the BRAVO ONE coup. On 1 November 1963 rebel forces under General Dinh attacked the presidential palace and the barracks of loyal troops. Diem was unable to reach safety; both he and his brother were captured and murdered by the plotters. Major General Nguyen Khanh was established as President, and the anniversary of Diem's murder was made a holiday.

BRAWN (Allied 44) A series of follow-up air attacks on the damaged German battleship *Tirpitz* in its harbor at Kaafjord, Norway. Due to the heavy German defenses and steep sides of the fjord, these attacks did not damage their target. See TUNGSTEN.

BREACH (Allied 41) British air attacks and aerial mining that closed the port at Mogadishu, Italian Somaliland (now Somalia) in February 1941.

BREVITY (Allied 41) Ground attack on the Germans near the Halfaya Pass by British forces in Egypt to break through to the besieged garrison at Tobruk. Begun early on 15 May 1941 the pass quickly fell, but was recaptured by a German counterattack on 27 May. Tobruk was resupplied by sea and continued to hold out until relieved by the more deliberate CRUSADER offensive. Followed by BATTLEAXE.

BREWER (Allied 44) Invasion of the Admiralty Islands, northeast of Papua New Guinea launched on 19 February 1944.

BRIARPATCH (US 68) The name for a North Vietnamese prisoner of war compound near Ap Lo. By extension, the name was used for a raid proposed in 1968 to rescue Americans held at that facility. The plan called for an agent on the ground to observe enemy activity and to call for a helicopter raid when the prisoners were moved outside the compound for a work party. Never executed. See IVORY COAST.

BRIDE (U.S./U.K. 45) A worldwide effort to completely decipher Soviet transmissions. Soon after the end of World War II, a U.S. code breaker using a partially destroyed Soviet code book found a weakness in Soviet communications. Rather than using one-use pads properly, a method that seems to be unbreakable, the Soviets used the same series of pads at stations around the world. This allowed a partial solution that required massive amounts of Soviet wartime coded transmissions in order to further the break. BRIDE was designation for both the collection of these coded messages and the intelligence produced by that effort. BRIDE intercepts provided important counterintelligence to the Americans, allowing them to uncover the Rosenbergs and Klaus Fuchs, Soviet spies in the U.S. nuclear programs. Other spies were uncovered, in some cases years later, in various military and civilian government agencies. Later designated VERONA.

BRIGHT STAR

1. (U.S. 60) A large U.S. Air Force training exercise conducted in August 1960. The co-incident Army training was called PINE CONE II.

2. (U.S./Egypt 81) Combined training exercises by U.S. forces in Egypt. These exercises began in 1981 and are conducted every other year. They are denominated by year number (e.g., BRIGHT STAR 85). Designed to strengthen ties between the Egyptian and American militaries and demonstrate and enhance the ability of the Americans to reinforce their allies in the Mideast in the event of war, these deployments usually are centered at the large Cairo West air base.

BRILLIANT FOIL (NATO 95) A 3-day exercise conducted in late 1995 at the Royal Air Force Base at Church Fenton, England. British, Belgian, and Norwegian fighters as well as British and Belgian paratroops took part in the training.

BRIM FROST (U.S.) Biennial exercises designed to test plans for the defense of Alaska and to provide cold-weather training.

BRIMSTONE (Allied 43) Plan for invasion of Italy at Cagliari, Sardinia, by the U.S. 5th Army. Never executed. Abandoned on 20 July 1943 in favor of AVALANCHE. After the plan was abandoned, its outline was used in the MINCEMEAT deception. Copies of the plan were allowed to fall into German hands in order to mislead them as to Allied intention.

BRISSEX (Allied 44) See SUSSEX.

BRIZ 95 (NATO 95) A multinational peace-keeping and convoy-defense exercise hosted by Bulgaria in the Black Sea in late August 1995. Ships from Bulgaria, Greece, Italy, Turkey, Ukraine, and the U.S. took part under the Partnership for Peace program.

BROADAXE (Allied 45) An overall deception plan to protect the invasion of Japan (DOWNFALL). This plan would have falsely portrayed Allied invasion threats to French Indochina, the Chinese coast, and Formosa. See BLUEBIRD.

BROILER (U.S.) An early plan for nuclear war with the Soviet Union. This plan was one of a series of plans developed by Strategic Air Command. Other plans of this series were HALF MOON, FROLIC, DOUBLESTAR, TOTALITY, TROJAN, OFF TACKLE, SHAKEDOWN, and CROSS PIECE. Eventually, these plans were superseded by a series of numbered Single Integrate Operations Plans (SIOPs). The first SIOP was CHARIOTEER which was prepared in 1948.

BROKEN ARROW (U.S.) The flag-word used to designate the most severe class of nuclear weapon accident. Such an accident would involve any hazard to the public, the loss or theft of a weapon, a nuclear or a non-nuclear detonation, or an accidental or unauthorized use of any nuclear-capable weapon (such as nuclear-capable missile without its warhead).

BROKEN FAITH (U.S. Law Enforcement 92) A FBI probe of corruption in the District of Columbia police department. The federal investigators posed as drug dealers seeking to expand their operation in the District in mid-1992. Several members of the police offered to serve as spies, guards, or enforcers for the supposed drug gang. Eighteen months later, 12 policemen were arrested.

BRONX SHIPMENT (Allied 45) Shipment of nuclear weapon components to Tinian in July 1945. The first bomb used was shipped to the island base aboard the cruiser Indianapolis. Shortly after making its delivery, the ship was sunk by a Japanese submarine. The loss of electrical power made it impossible to send a final message, and the ship was not missed for several days. By the time a search found the survivors, many had died in the shark-infested waters. See ALBERTA and SILVERPLATE.

BROOM (IS 60) The Israeli designation for the sudden Egyptian movement of three divisions into the demilitarized Sinai Peninsula in February 1960. This deployment was undetected by the much-vaunted Israeli intelligence, and the entire episode was considered an intelligence disaster.

BROTHERHOOD (U.S./R.V.N. 54) An American-sponsored program that encouraged "free Asian" nations (mostly Philippines) to send medical teams to rural areas in South Vietnam to build goodwill toward the Saigon government. The plan was conceived in the summer of 1954 and was quickly adopted by the CIA who co-opted elements in the International Junior Chamber of Commerce (the "Jaycees") as a cover for American involvement.

BRUMBY (U.K. 67) The clean-up of radioactive material scattered about the British nuclear test facility at Maralinga, Australia. Conducted from April to July 1967, at least 20 kilograms of highly-poisonous plutonium was plowed just below the surface. See VIXENS.

BRUNNENKRESSE "WATERCRESS" (Allied 42) The insertion of a Special Operations Executive (SOE) agent (Arnoldus Baatsen) and a large amount of matériel into the Netherlands on the night of 27 March 1942. Unfortunately, the Dutch SOE agent who was ordered to meet Baatsen had been "turned" by the Nazi security apparatus as part of NORDPOL. Baatsen was captured upon landing.

BRUTUS (Allied 44) Parachute insertion of the Belgian Independent Parachute Company near the village of Yvoir on the Meuse River on 5 September 1944 to assist local resistance fighters.

BT (Allied) The designation of Allied convoys from Australia to the U.S. in World War II.

BUBBLE (U.S.) A reserved first word for programs and projects of the former U.S. Strategic Air Command. For example, BUBBLE DANCER was a program of high-altitude weather research flights conducted by U-2 aircraft.

BUCCANEER (Allied 42) Plan for the invasion of the Andaman Islands, in the Bay of Bengal. Due to the worldwide shortage of landing craft, the operation was scaled back in size and finally canceled in December 1943. Planned under the name UTOPIA. See ANAKIM and BUNKUM.

BUCKSKIN (U.S./AUS 66) Infantry operation in Vietnam in January 1966 in Ho Bo Woods. The 173d (U.S.) Airborne Brigade and the Royal Australian Regiment destroyed a massive series of tunnels. Planned under the name of CRIMP.

BUFFALO

1. (Allied 44) The breakout from the Anzio beachhead conducted by U.S. 6th Corps on 23 May 1994. See CRAWDAD.

2. (U.K. 56) Four open-air nuclear test explosions conducted in late 1956 at the Maralinga test site in South Australia. Over 200 Commonwealth troops observed the explosions from 4½ miles away. Critics charged the planning for these blasts did not take the safety of local aborigines into

account. See BRUMBY. Followed MOSA-IC, preceded ANTLER.

BUFFALO I	September 56	15 kilotons
BUFFALO 2		15 kilotons
BUFFALO 3		10 kilotons
BUFFALO 4	October	1.5 kilotons

BUFFALO HORN (U.S.) A flag-word used in electronic messages reporting a disaster at airbases operated by the former U.S. Strategic Air Command.

BÜFFEL BEWEGUNG "BUFFALO MOVEMENT" (GER 43) Local retreats conducted by the German Army on the Russian Front during the period 1-22 March 1943. This movement eliminated the Rzhev Salient and shortened the front by 230 kilometers, saving 21 divisions for use elsewhere.

BUGLE (Allied 45) Air attacks in support of ground troops crossing the Rhine in May 1945.

BULBASKET (Allied 44) Sabotage and intelligence operation conducted by a 50-man Special Air Service team in support of the invasion of Normandy (OVERLORD). Inserted by parachute on 6 June 1944 these fighters attacked German convoys and rail traffic near Poitiers and Tours. Cornered by the SS on 3 July, more than a third of the force was captured and murdered.

BULLDOZER (Allied 42) Plan for a reduced-scale amphibious landing in the Arakan region of Burma of Bengal, proposed by Lord Mountbatten as a follow-on to the canceled PIGSTICK. Never executed. See ANAKIM.

BULLET SHOT (US 72) The deployment of the B-52 bombers of the Second Bomb Wing in May 1972 to support combat in Southeast Asia (LINEBACKER II).

BULLFROG (Allied) Plan for an amphibious operation against the Burmese coast during World War II. Never executed.

BULLSEYE (U.S. 60s) American airborne electronic eavesdropping missions conducted in the Far East in the 1960s. One EC-121 aircraft was shot down by the Soviets during a BULLSEYE flight in 1969.

BUMBER (Allied 41) A large anti-invasion training exercise held northwest of London in September 1941.

BUMPY ROAD (U.S. 61) See PLUTO.

BUNBURY (GER 44) A plan to sabotage the English power plant at Bury Saint Edmunds in East Anglia by 2 German agents. On 18 August 1944 British and Nazi media reported the destruction of the plant. In fact, both agents had been "turned" by the British security services. The attack never happened. The reports were part of a deception program designed to convince the Germans that their agents were effective.

BUNKUM (Allied 43) Intelligence patrol carried out by a 6-man team landed by submarine on 19 January 1943 on Japanese-held Middle Andaman Island, 1,000 miles southeast of Calcutta, south of Rangoon. The operation lasted 32 days. Part of BUCCANEER. Preceded CANNIBAL.

BURDOCK (GER 43) See GROSSE KLETTE.

BURNING ARROW (U.S./R.V.N. 63) A raid conducted by South Vietnamese troops on the Central Office for South Vietnam, the main communist headquarters for the war. The attackers were ferried into the Duong Minh Chau area aboard H-21 helicopters but were unable to locate their target. Launched on 2 January 1963.

BUSHEL (U.K. 85) Royal Air Force famine-relief operations in Ethiopia in 1985.

BUSHMASTER

1. (U.S. 87) The use of infantry units to supplement Military Police patrols of areas

surrounding the Panama Canal and other American installations in Panama. These patrols were in response to criminal activity that increased during the period before the American invasion of that country. Began in December 1987. See JUST CAUSE and BLADE JEWEL.

2. (U.S.) A series of minor exercises throughout Latin America conducted by U.S. troops based in Panama.

BUSTER-JANGLE (U.S. 51) A series of 7 nuclear test explosions conducted at the Nevada Test Site west of Las Vegas. BUSTER consisted of the first 5 shots. JANGLE was the final 2. U.S. Army troops participated in tests and tactical exercise DESERT ROCK I, II, and III in conjunction with BUSTER BAKER, CHARLIE, and DOG. JANGLE UNCLE was the first American underground test. Followed GREENHOUSE and preceded TUMBLER-SNAPPER. The individual shots of this series were:

BUSTER

ABLE	22 October 51	misfired
BAKER	28 October	3.5 kilotons
CHARLIE	30 October	14 kilotons
DOG	1 November	21 kilotons
EASY	5 November	31 kilotons

JANGLE

SUGAR	19 November	1.2 kilotons
UNCLE	29 November	1.2 kilotons

BUSY (U.S.) A first word used for missions flown by U.S. Air Force B-52 bombers in support of training by other units.

BUTTRESS (Allied 43) Plan for an invasion of Italy at Gioia in the toe of Italy, by the U.S. 8th Army scheduled for 1 September 1943. Never executed. Abandoned in favor of AVALANCHE and BAYTOWN.

C

C (JPN 42) Raid conducted by 5 aircraft carriers on Colombo (now the capital of Sri Lanka) and British maritime activity in the Indian Ocean. The operation began on 1 April 1942 and sank a British aircraft carrier, 2 cruisers, 2 destroyers, and an armed merchant cruiser, as well as 23 merchant ships totaling over 100,000 tons. The Japanese lost 36 aircraft.

C3

1. (IT 42) Plan for a combined German/ Italian invasion of Malta. Called HERKULES by the Germans.

2. (U.S.) In current U.S. military vernacular, "C3" refers to "Command, Control, and Communications," and is often pronounced "See Cubed."

C 38M (IT) The Italian World War II naval code. This cipher was broken in June 1941 by the British. Intelligence produced by this effort was later combined with PURPLE and ENIGMA intercepts under the general designation ULTRA.

CACTUS (IN 88) The November 1988 airlift 1,240 Indian troops to the island nation of the Maldives to foil an attempted coup d' état by foreign mercenaries. This action, undertaken at the request of the legitimate government, marked India's debut as a regional power. The troops were flown in on Indian Air Force transports and were supported by Indian Mirage 2000 jets. The foreign plot quickly collapsed under this unexpected intervention.

CALENDAR (Allied 42) The reinforcement of the air garrison on Malta with 47 fighters flown from the U.S. aircraft carrier *Wasp* on 20 April 1942. Upon landing, most of the aircraft were destroyed by a German air raid.

CALLBOY

1. (Allied 41) October 1941 British convoy to the besieged island of Malta. Followed HALBERD, preceded SPOTTER.

2. (Allied 45) Allied deception operation designed to falsely portray the British crossing of the Rhine in February 1945 as a feint for a (non-existent) attack aimed at Kassel.

CAMEL HUMP (U.S.) Operations by U-2 aircraft from Taif, Saudi Arabia, monitoring Iraq after the Gulf War.

CAMID (U.S. 50) Exercise by the U.S. 2nd Marine Division and its associated air wing at Little Creek, Virginia, shortly before the outbreak of the Korean War.

CAMILLA (Allied 40) Deception operation in support of the British attack into Italian Somaliland. This plan portrayed the false threat of an amphibious landing to draw attention away from preparations for an overland assault.

CAMPUS (Allied 44) U.S. Navy plan for the occupation and governance of Japan. See BLACKLIST.

CANNIBAL (Allied 43) A British attack launched on 1 January 1943 from Chittagong war Donbaik, with a final objective of Akyab, a port in western Burma. The attack lost momentum in the face of stiff Japanese resistance and ended on 4 March with a Japanese counterattack. The British were pushed back to their start-point in India.

CAPITAL (Allied 43) A broad British offensive launched from Assam, India, across the Chinwin River into northeast Burma near Mandalay on 19 November 1943. The British 14th Army struck the Japanese 15th Army near Imphal and Kohima. The Japanese were forced to pull back to a line from Indaw to Mandalay, vacating most of Burma. Some sources call this operation EXTENDED CAPITAL.

CARBON GRAPE (NATO 94) A small NATO exercise held in late October 1994 in Denmark. A Polish contingent of 37 soldiers also took part under the Partnership for Peace program. Followed COOPERATIVE SPIRIT.

CARGO (Allied 44) Training exercise conducted by Allied logistical units in preparation for the invasion of northern France (OVERLORD).

CARIBEX (U.S. 50) A general term for American training in Panama during the 1950s and '60s. The term seems to be a contraction of "Caribbean Exercise." During this period, the American headquarters in the region was Caribbean Command (now U.S. Southern Command).

CAROLINA MOON (U.S.) Attempt to use C-130 Hercules cargo aircraft to bomb bridges in Vietnam. Never executed. See BANISH BEACH and COMMANDO LAVA.

CARPET (Allied 44) A planning name for the concept of laying a "carpet" of paratroops along the planned advance of an armored thrust. This general idea grew into the MARKET-GARDEN attack.

CARPETBAGGER (Allied 44) Aerial resupply of weapons and other supplies to resistance fighters in France, Italy, and the Low Countries by the U.S. Army Air Forces that began on 4 January 1944.

CARRYALL (U.S./CN 51) Combined American/Canadian winter training exercise held at Fort Churchill, Manitoba, over the winter of 1951/52 to develop equipment and techniques for Arctic warfare.

CARTE BLANCHE (NATO 55) Large NATO air defense exercise conducted by 3,000 aircraft in late June 1955.

CARTWHEEL (Allied 43) Planned as ELK-TON III, CARTWHEEL called for a series of 13 separate amphibious operations converging on the twin harbors at Rabaul on New Britain. The operation began on 31 June 1943 and ran for 9 months. The first move was the seizure of Woodlark and Kiriwina Islands (CORONET and CHRONICLE) off the east coast of New Guinea. This was followed by TOENAILS, the seizure of the Japanese airfield at Munda Point, then POSTERN, the amphibious landing at Nassau Bay. DEXTERITY and BACKHANDLER, the landings on New Britain, came in December. By 1 March 1944 CARTWHEEL was completed, although the Japanese strongpoint of Rabaul itself (with its 98,000 man garrison) was bypassed and isolated by massive air and sea attacks.

CASANOVA (Allied 44) Attack launched by the U.S. 377th Infantry Regiment, 95th Infantry Division, as a demonstration to distract German attention from the main U.S. 11th Corps crossing of the Moselle River at Metz by the U.S. 19th

Infantry Division. Executed on 8 November 1944.

CASCADE (Allied 42) An early Allied deception operation in the Mideast beginning in March 1942. At this time, Allied forces were rather weak, and so to preclude further Axis attacks a number of phony Allied units were created. Fake radio traffic, double agents, and other means were used to ensure the enemy noted the presence of these phantom units.

CASEY JONES (U.S. 45) Operation planned by the Office of Strategic Services and conducted by the Army Air Forces to photograph Soviet-occupied portions of Europe immediately following World War II. At least 3 American aircraft were shot down by Soviet air defenses. See DICK TRACY and TOTALITY.

CASTLE (U.S. 54) Seven planned nuclear tests conducted at the Pacific Proving Ground in early 1954. This series was plagued by problems. The first blast (of an experimental lithium deuteride device) was almost three times as large as planned, making it the largest known U.S. nuclear test. The blast damaged the test range, forcing drastic changes in the schedule. Radiation from this explosion drifted over a Japanese fishing boat, the Fukuryu Maru, 80 miles away, causing over 20 cases of radiation sickness. The fourth test (ECHO) was canceled. Followed UPSHOT-KNOTHOLE and preceded TEAPOT. The shots used experimental warheads, which were designated by nicknames.

BRAVO	28 February 54	"Shrimp"	15 megatons
ROMEO	27 March	"Runt"	11 megatons
KOON	7 April	"Morgenstern"	110 kilotons
ECHO	(canceled)	"Ramrod" (canceled)	
UNION	26 April	"Alarm Clock"	6.9 megatons
YANKEE	5 May	"Runt II"	13.5 megatons
NECTAR	14 May	"Zombie"	1.7 megatons

CASTOR Castor is one of the twins in the constellation of Gemini. The other is Pollux.

1. (GER 18) Alternate plan of the HEILGER MICHAEL series. This called for a pincer attack on French forces north of Verdun in the spring of 1918. Never executed. See KAISERSCHLACHT.

2. (Allied 44) See APHRODITE.

3. (FR 53) The airdrop of 2 regiments of French paratroops into the fortress of Dien Bien Phu on 20 November 1953.

CATAPULT (Allied 40) A complex, worldwide operation executed by British forces on 3 July 1940 to seize, disable, or destroy the French fleet to prevent it being captured by the Nazis. The largest and most dangerous French naval flotilla was in port at Mers-El-Kebir near Oran. After the French commander rejected a British ultimatum, the Royal Navy attacked with a massive barrage that killed over 1,200 French sailors. The commander of the French flotilla at Alexandria agreed to have his ships disarmed; his men lived in the harbor for the entire war, their salaries paid by the British.

CATCHPOLE (Allied 44) The American invasion of Eniwetok Atoll, the northernmost of the Marshall Islands, on 16 February 1944. The island was fully secured by 23 February. Eniwetok Atoll provided a forward base for the U.S. Navy for its later operations.

CATHERINE (Allied 39) Plan to extend British sea power into the Baltic Sea in the winter of 1939/40. Proposed by Churchill; the general idea was to modify one or more old "Class R" battleships with additional flotation to reduce their draft. A task force, perhaps including an aircraft carrier, would be built around these ships to prevent

German trade with Scandinavia and disrupt U-Boat operations. Never executed.

CAUCASIAN (U.S. 50) The development of parachute-retarded nuclear weapons by the U.S. Air Force.

CAUSEWAY (Allied 44) Proposed American invasion of Formosa scheduled for 1945. This assault was designed to cap the thrust toward Japan from the south by forces commanded by General MacArthur. Never executed. Part of CRASHER, see BLUE-BIRD and INDUCTION.

CAUTERIZE (U.S.) A modification program carried out by the U.S. Air Force to update its B-36 Peacemaker bombers to carry thermonuclear weapons. Followed BAR-ROOM.

CAVE (Allied 45) Capture of Piscopione in the Dodecanse Islands in early March 1945. In 1947, these islands were transferred from Italy to Greece.

CAVENDISH (Allied 42) Part of the OVER-THROW deception in Europe. CAVENDISH called for a phony raid to cross the English Channel in order to lure the German Air Force into a major air battle. Scheduled for October 1942 but never executed due to bad weather.

CEDAR FALLS (U.S./R.V.N. 67) The first large American "Search and Destroy" mission of the Vietnam War. Launched on 8 January 1967, the attack ran for 19 days and was centered on the "Iron Triangle" in Binh Duong province bounded by National Route 13 and the Saigon River, 13 miles northwest of the capitol. Sixty square miles were saturated with American and South Vietnamese troops who destroyed tunnels, cleared undergrowth, and captured a large amount of documents and supplies. More than 7,000 Vietnamese civilians were displaced by this operation. The Allied forces were unable to maintain a presence in the area; within weeks the Viet Cong and North Vietnamese had reestablished themselves. Cedar Falls is a city in Iowa. Followed by JUNCTION CITY.

CELLOPHANE (Allied 44) Training exercise conducted by logistics troops earmarked for the invasion of northern France (OVER-LORD) in April 1944. This operation focused on moving large amounts of supplies over the beach. See CARGO and TONNAGE.

CENTERBOARD (Allied 45) The nuclear attack on the Japanese city of Hiroshima on 6 August 1945. This bombing, carried out by the B-29 "Enola Gay" from Tinian Island, killed 80,000 people outright, wounding another 35,000. The memorial erected at "Ground Zero" lists 138,890 victims, but includes those who died years later due to radiation and other causes. Despite the appalling destruction, the Japanese government failed to surrender, necessitating the attack on Nagasaki on 9 August. The 2 nuclear attacks on Japanese cities rendered an amphibious invasion of Japan unnecessary (DOWN-FALL). See MANHATTAN ENGINEER DISTRICT.

CENTER LANE (U.S.) One of a series of names given to a team of psychics that the CIA established in the early 1980s at Fort Meade, Maryland. This team attempted to "remotely image" Soviet activities in order to direct more conventional intelligence assets where they could be best utilized. The term CENTER LANE replace GRILL FLAME and was in turn replaced by SUN-STREAK.

CENTRAL ENTERPRISE (NATO) A major NATO fall exercise, designated by year (e.g., CENTRAL ENTERPRISE 93) and held each autumn. These exercises focus on the ability of the U.S. Air Force to quickly reinforce Europe with air power.

CERBERUS (GER 43) See ZERBERUS.

CERTAIN CARAVAN (NATO) A mobile command post exercise conducted in Europe in conjunction with the annual REFORGER exercise. Designed by year (e.g., CERTAIN CARAVAN 92).

CERTAIN SHIELD (NATO 91) A joint exercise conducted in Germany in 1991.

CHAMFROM (U.K. 63) The deployment of British units to Malaya from 1963 to 1966. See MATTERHORN.

CHAMPION

1. (Allied 43) Plan for a general Allied offensive in Burma in late 1943. Changed to CAPITAL due to compromise. See ANAKIM.

2. (Allied 45) British commando raid behind Japanese lines in Burma that began on 18 April 1945. Due to the poor communications in the region, the operation went on until 8 September, after the war ended.

CHANNEL STOP (Allied 41) Attempt to close the English Channel to German surface ships by air power beginning in April 1941. See ZERBERUS.

CHAOS (U.S. 67) Joint CIA/FBI project to investigate and infiltrate groups in the U.S. opposed to the Vietnam War. A major goal of this work was to determine if these groups were supported or controlled by groups outside the U.S. The project was officially designated MHChaos. CHAOS began in 1967 and ran until 1972 when the Director of Central Intelligence changed its focus toward international terrorism. The charter of the CIA does not allow it to operate in the U.S. One part of this program was called RESISTANCE.

CHARACTER (Allied 45) Fighting by British forces against Japanese defenders near Moulmein on Burma's southern coast that ended on 8 September 1945, after the formal end of the war.

CHARIOT (Allied 42) Naval and commando raid to destroy the large *Normandie* dry dock at the French port of Ste. Nazaire on the night of 27 March 1942. An old U.S. destroyer, HMS *Cambeltown*, one of the 50 sent to Britain in exchange for naval bases, was modified to resemble a German ship and to carry a 5-ton high explosive charge. Using German flags and recognition signals, the flotilla breached the port defenses and the destroyer rammed the gates of the dry-dock, disgorging commandos to attack submarine pens and other nearby installations. Small boats sent to retrieve the raiders were mostly driven off by the now-alert harbor defenses, leading to a large number of commandos being killed or captured. The *Cambeltown* exploded the next day with an inspection party of high-ranking officers aboard, killing at least 130. The dock, the only one in northern France capable of repairing the battleship *Tirpitz*, was out of action for the rest of the war.

CHARIOTEER

1. (U.S. 48) The first U.S. plan for nuclear war with the Soviet Union that integrated the actions of all the U.S. armed forces. It was, therefore, the first "Single Integrated Operations Plan" (SIOP). Prepared in 1948, it assumed the Soviet Union had already occupied Europe by a conventional invasion. The goal was to force the Soviet Union back to its 1939 borders. The plan called for a U.S. arsenal of 133 atomic bombs to be delivered to 70 Soviet cities in the first 30 days. After the initial supply of weapons was used, conventional and atomic strikes would continue until the Soviets surrendered. Moscow was to receive 8 bombs, Leningrad (now St. Petersburg) was scheduled for 7. This plan was repeatedly modified and was the basis for a number of studies. These variations included ABC 101, COGWHEEL,

DUALISM, and GUNPOWDER. It was superseded in 1949 by the DROPSHOT plan (which in turn became SIOP-63). Never executed. See TOTALITY.

2. (U.S. 85) A series of 15 underground nuclear tests conducted in 1985 at the Nevada Test Site. These tests followed the GRENADIER series. Identified shots were:

MILL YARD	9 October 85	<20 kilotons
DIAMOND BEECH	9 October	<20 kilotons
ROQUEFORT	16 October	20-150 kilotons
KINIBITO	5 December	20-150 kilotons
GOLDSTONE	28 December	20-150 kilotons

CHARNWOOD (Allied 44) British ground attack on Caen, France, launched on 7 July 1944. The attack was preceded by a Royal Air Force "carpet bombing" attack on the city itself. British forces succeeded in capturing the outskirts of the city and isolated it from German positions elsewhere in Normandy. Followed EPSOM. See COBRA and GOODWOOD.

CHASTISE (Allied 43) An air attack carried out by specially-equipped British bombers against 3 Ruhr River dams on 16 May 1943 as part of the "Battle of the Ruhr." The raiders used unique bombs designed to skip across the lake surface before diving deeply against the dam face to explode. Two of the 3 targeted dams were ruptured. Flooding killed over 1,200 people, including 700 Soviet slave laborers. The British lost 8 of the 18 bombers and 56 of the 133 airmen committed to the attack. As a result of this raid, the German moved anti-aircraft units to defend dams across Germany. The precision-bombing unit, 617 Squadron, sank the German battleship Tirpitz in the harbor of Tromso, Norway in November 1944.

CHASTITY (Allied 44) Plan for the construction of an artificial harbor (called a "Mulberry") in Quiberon Bay, France, to support Allied operations in northern France. Never executed.

CHATTANOOGA-CHOO-CHOO (Allied 44) A massive air campaign launched against locomotives and other rolling stock throughout France in support of the Normandy invasion (OVERLORD). These attacks used a large number of free-roaming fighter-bombers and began on 21 May 1944 and continued until the invasion on 6 June.

CHECKERED FLAG (U.S.) A series of individually-named exercises designed to improve the ability of U.S. Air Force units to deploy overseas. Exercises in this program that deploy units to Italy generally use the word "Salty" in their designation (i.e., "SALTY BEE"), in the same way deployments to Germany use the words "Coronet" or "Creek" (i.e., "CORONET CASTLE"). These large deployments are conducted several times each year and feature massive Allied cooperation including basing rights, air tanker support, and maintenance facilities. See CENTRAL ENTERPRISE.

CHECKMATE

1. (IN 88) Indian peacekeeping operations in Sri Lanka.

2. (U.S. 91) An American Air Force planning cell, based in Washington, which produced the INSTANT THUNDER plan. See EAGER ANVIL.

CHECKMATE II (NATO 61) Large Greek/Turkish training exercise conducted in mid-September 1961.

CHEERFUL (Allied 45) Attack by Free French forces that reduced the Colmar pocket in a 20-day battle ending on 8 February 1945. Over 22,000 Germans were captured, at a cost of 1,600 French and 540 American dead.

CHEROKEE (U.N. 52) Term used by American naval aviators for close support missions flown in Korea from October 1952 to the end of that war.

CHERRY BLOSSOMS AT NIGHT (JPN 45) Planned Japanese chemical or biological attack on the U.S. mainland in mid-1945. Three large aircraft-carrying submarines survived late into the war. Seaplanes launched from these boats would scatter plague-infected fleas over California. Never executed.

CHERRY TREE (Allied 44) American naval air raid on Japanese targets on Saipan and Tinian in the Marianas Islands. Executed on 22 February 1944, George Washington's Birthday.

CHESHIRE (U.K. 93) The British contribution to PROVIDE PROMISE. Four Royal Air Force C-130 Hercules planes were assigned to the effort.

CHESTERFIELD (Allied 44) Attack by the Canadian 1st Corps on the German "Adolph Hitler Line" in Italy. Launched on 23 May 1944 in rough coordination with the breakout from the Anzio beach head (BUFFALO).

CHESTNUT (Allied 43) A series of 4 small commando raids inserted by air to harass enemy lines of communications in support of the 10 July 1943 invasion of Sicily (HUSKY).

CHESTNUT 1	12 July	(2 aircraft)
CHESTNUT 2	13 July	(2 aircraft)
CHESTNUT 3	14 July	(2 aircraft)
CHESTNUT 4	19 July	(1 aircraft)

CHETTYFORD (Allied 44) Tactical deception in support of the Allied invasion at Anzio (SHINGLE). George Patton made a well-publicized visit to units based around Cairo. A number of double-agents were used to misinform the Germans that a major invasion of the Balkans was planned. See BOARDMAN and FAIRLANDS.

CHEVESNE "CHUB" (FR 83) French support to U.N. peacekeeping efforts in Lebanon in 1983 and 1984. This operation came to an end when a series of car-bombs destroyed the headquarters of the French and American contingents nearly simultaneously. Chevesne is French for the fish, which is called a chub in English.

CHEVROLET (Allied 44) Marshaling exercise conducted in February 1944 in England in preparation for the invasion of northern France (OVERLORD).

CHICAGO (Allied 44) The airborne insertion of the U.S. 101st Airborne Division into Normandy as part of the invasion of northern France (OVERLORD). See DETROIT.

CHICKEN 53 (IS 69) Israeli special forces raid conducted in December 1969. A commando team by helicopter on an Egyptian base captured a then-secret Soviet radar.

CHICKENPOX (U.S. 45) A program of modifications made to C-97 cargo aircraft to allow them to transport the early large nuclear weapons.

CHICKEN STEALER (U.N. 52) A shore bombardment by the USS *Halsey Powell* on communist positions using spotting parties in the destroyer's whale boats.

CHILDHOOD (Allied 43) Attack by British motor torpedo boats based on Malta against German and Italian craft attempting to close the harbor at Valetta. Conducted on 20 January 1943.

"CHRISTMAS TREE" (GER 40) See TANNENBAUM.

CHRISTROSE (GER 44) Draft plan for a winter offensive to be launched against the Western Allies in the winter of 1944. Prepared by Colonel General Alfred Jodl and presented to Hitler on 21 October. The dictator was very impressed, and the plan was modified to become WACHT AM RHEIN.

CHOKER I (Allied 45) Planned airborne attack on the German "Siegfried Line" defenses near Saarbrüken. Never executed.

CHOKER II (Allied 45) Planned airborne attack behind the Rhine River near the city of Frankfurt. Never executed.

CHOPSTICK 6
CHOPSTICK 16 (U.N. 52) Limited attacks planned to seize the high ground south of Pyongyang, North Korea, by a single South Korean division or 2 South Korean divisions respectively. General Ridgeway approved CHOPSTICK 6 to begin in April 1952, but it was later canceled.

CHOWHOUND (Allied, Informal 44) The nickname given by Allied airmen in Europe to food-supply missions at the end of World War II. See MANNA, VITTLES.

CHROME DOME (US) Strategic alert missions flown by American B-52 bombers during the Cold War. During these operational missions, the long-range bombers armed with nuclear weapons flew to advanced bases in Iceland, Korea, and other locations to stage for potential strikes on the Soviet Union. Flying missions with nuclear weapons were by their nature dangerous. CHROME DOME missions ended in 1967.

CHROMITE (U.N. 50) U.N. amphibious invasion at Inchon, Korea. This assault flanked the entire North Korean thrust into the Republic of Korea and took the strategic initiative from the invaders. Executed at 0630 hours, 15 September 1950 the lead elements of U.S. 10th Corps hit 3 beaches near the center of the city. The sudden appearance of the U.N. forces so far behind North Korean lines unhinged their entire attack. U.N. forces quickly took the offensive, driving north. Their assault continued

until the Chinese sent troops into the war. See COMMON KNOWLEDGE.

CHRONICLE (Allied 44) Invasion of Woodlark and Kiriwina Islands in the South Pacific as part of CARTWHEEL. An early planning name for this operation was CORONET. Executed without opposition on 30 June 1944.

CHRONOMETER (Allied 41) The British capture of the port of Ascab, Eritrea, on 11 June 1941.

CHRYSLER (Allied 44) Parachute insertion of a 3-man team into Italy to provide advisers and supplies to partisan units then fighting the Germans. Conducted 26 September 1944.

CHUB (FR 83) See CHEVESNE.

CHUCKLE (Allied 44) Canadian attack toward Bologna, Italy, in November 1944.

CIMARRON DRIVE (U.S. 60) A major exercise by the U.S. 4th Army at Fort Hood, Texas, in 1960.

CISCO (Allied 44) Air strikes launched by bombers in support of an assault by the U.S. 30th Infantry Division against the German "West Wall" defenses. Executed on 20 October 1944.

CITADEL (GER 43) See ZITADELLE.

CLAM UP (U.N. 52) Deception conducted from 10 to 15 February 1952 by U.N. forces in Korea. No patrolling, artillery fire, air support, or radio communications was permitted. The intent was to encourage enemy patrols into U.N. positions where they could be captured. The Chinese did not seem to notice the inactivity and no patrols were captured.

CLARENCE (BG 39) Intelligence and resistance network established in 1939 by Walthere Dewe to organize Belgian resistance to the impending German occupation.

Dewe was a hero for his resistance work during the German occupation of his country in World War I.

CLARION (Allied 45) Air operations beginning on 22 February 1945 by over 10,000 aircraft from bases in England, France, Holland, Belgium, and Italy directed against the German rail system. The object of these attacks was to overwhelm the ability of the system to repair itself. As a result, the Germans lost 90 percent of their rail capability, ending their ability to shift forces. On the first night of the offensive, the Swiss towns of Stein Am Rhein and Rafz were bombed by mistake, killing 17 Swiss nationals.

CLASSICA (NATO 95) See COOPERATIVE MERMAID/CLASSICA.

CLAUSEWITZ (GER)

1. (GER 43) Phase III of BLAU.

2. (GER 44) The defense of central Berlin from the encircling Red Army. The Soviets claimed that over 6,000,000 troops in 3 "fronts" (i.e., Armies) took part in the battle that began on 12 January 1944 several hundred miles east of the city. The Reichstag building was stormed on 30 April, the same day Hitler killed himself. On 2 May, the remnants of the Berlin garrison surrendered.

CLAWHAMMER (Allied 42) Planned British commando raid on a German radar and communication site near Cherbourg, France. Canceled in October 1942.

CLAYMORE (Allied 41) Naval raid on 4 March 1941 against German forces on and around the Lofoten Islands (off the coast of Norway, north of the Arctic Circle), centered on the armed trawler *Krebs*. The British captured documents and equipment critical to breaking German naval codes. A Claymore is a traditional Scottish broadsword.

CLEAN HANDS (IT Law Enforcement 93) The anti-corruption and anti-Mafia investigations conducted by the Italian judiciary that centered on the Christian Democratic Party in the early 1990s. More than 2,000 officials, including over 20 percent of the entire Parliament, were implicated in the wide-ranging bribery scandal, which had roots in the establishment of the party in the period after World War II.

CLEANSLATE (Allied 43) Occupation of Russell Island about 60 miles northwest of Guadalcanal by the U.S. in August 1942. The Japanese had captured the island in January 1942.

CLEAR LAKE (U.S. 62) Exercise conducted by U.S. Army and Air Force units at Eglin Air Force Base, Florida, in May and June 1962.

CLINCH (Allied 44) British plan to capture the Mergui-Tavoy area of the Kra Isthmus in Burma. Never executed. Part of BAMBOO.

CLIPPER (Allied 45) Offensive by 30th British Corps (including the American 84th Infantry Division) to reduce the Geilenkirchen Salient. Executed on 18 November 1945.

CLOCKWORK (NATO 79) Deployment of Royal Marines to northern Norway in late 1979 to rehearse their wartime role of protecting NATO's northern flank.

COAT (Allied 40) An uneventful British convoy of 5 warships (including the battleship *Barham*) from Gibraltar to Alexandria. The ships departed on their Mediterranean transit on 8 November 1940.

COBRA

1. (Allied 44) The breakout from the Normandy lodgment by 1st U.S. Army launched on 25 July 1944 from the city of Saint Lo. As with GOODWOOD, the

41

nearly-simultaneous British attempt at a breakout, a massive carpet-bombing attack by over 2,500 sorties, preceded this attack by one day. Over 600 Americans, including Lieutenant General Leslie McNair, were killed while forming up for the attack by bombers that were unable to locate the markers laid out on the ground. The drive broke the German defenses and reached the city of Avranches on 31 July. See BARKER, GOODWOOD, and SPRING.

2. (U.S.) A reserved first word for nicknames of projects and programs by the U.S. Air Force. See COBRA BALL, COBRA DANE, COBRA JUDY.

COBRA BALL
COBRA DANE
COBRA JUDY (U.S.) Air-, ground-, and sea-based radars used to monitor Soviet missile tests in the Pacific.

COBRA GOLD (U.S./Thai 81) Annual joint U.S./Thai training exercises, designated by year (e.g., COBRA GOLD 89) beginning in 1981. Early exercises include the deployment of combat troops, but later the series became more humanitarian in nature. American military units deployed to build schools, provide basic medical services, and improve rural infrastructure. Military and naval units also participated in these exercises. This joint training took on greater significance with the withdrawal of the U.S. presence from the Philippines in 1992.

COCKADE (Allied 42) The overall 1943 Allied deception plan for Europe. The goal was to convince the Germans that the Western Allies would invade Europe in 1943. By forcing the Germans to redeploy troops from the Eastern Front, COCKADE was aimed at reducing pressure on the Soviet Union. Included 3 sequential elements: STARKEY, WADHAM, and TINDALL. STARKEY falsely depicted the threat of a large British inva-

sion near Bourlogne in mid-September. An American attack (WADHAM) would supposedly follow 3 weeks later. After these 2 phony invasions were "canceled," 5 divisions would be diverted for a false invasion of Norway (TINDALL). See HARLEQUIN, DUNDAS, and LARKHILL.

COCKPIT (Allied 45) Raid by a British naval force of 22 warships, including 2 aircraft carriers, on Japanese port and oil facilities on Sabang Island (off the northern tip of Sumatra) executed on 25 July 1945. Followed MERIDIAN.

COGWHEEL (U.S.) See CHARIOTEER.

COLD (U.S.) A reserved first word for nicknames of programs and projects of the Military Airlift Command of the U.S. Air Force. See COLD FIRE.

COLD FIRE (U.S. 74) A periodic airlift operation conducted by the various NATO air forces in Europe, denominated by year (e.g., COLD FIRE 84).

COLD SHAFT (NORAD 82) A major NORAD exercise conducted in July 1982 in Canada.

COLD WATER
COLDWATER (Allied 40) A series of British revenge attacks on German cities following their air raids on Coventry and Birmingham.

COLLAR (Allied 40) A small, 3-ship convoy that left Gibraltar on 24 November 1940 escorted by 2 cruisers for Malta and Alexandria. The flotilla encountered no difficulties.

COLLECT (U.S.) A reserved first word for the programs and projects of the U.S. Air Force.

COLLEGE (U.S.) A reserved first word for the programs and projects of the former U.S. Air Defense Command.

COLONY (U.S.) A reserved first word for the programs and projects of the U.S. Air Force.

COLOR SERIES (U.S. 04) Plans originated by the American Chief of Staff of the Army Lieutenant General Chaffee in April 1904 to deal with a series of contingencies. The plans were updated periodically in response to developments. The RED plans dealt with war with the British Empire, ORANGE with Japan, RED-ORANGE with both, GREEN with Mexico, and BLACK with Germany. These plans were designated by color as both a convenient name and as a security measure. This appears to be the first use of "codewords" in the modern sense. The "Color Series" was superseded in 1938 by a series of plans envisioning war against a coalition of enemies, the RAINBOW plans.

COLOSSUS (Allied 41) Commando raid by 38 paratroopers against the railroad viaduct at Trigano (near Potenza, in southern Italy) on 10 February 1941. This British airborne raid ended in disaster when all of the raiders were captured after causing only slight damage to their target.

COLT (U.S.) A reserved first word for the programs and projects of the U.S. Air Force Europe.

COLUMBIA CLIFF (U.S. 60) A major U.S. 6th Army exercise at Fort Lewis, Washington, in 1960.

COMBAT (U.S.) A reserved first word for the programs and projects of the U.S. Air Force.

COMBAT LANCER (U.S. 67) The deployment of the first 6 F-111A aircraft to Southeast Asia for combat testing. Three of the aircraft were lost in only 55 missions, two to unknown causes and one to faulty welds. This deployment of the immature system into combat was designed to take the wind out of the sails of the detractors of the "Aardvark" but in fact

the entire program was called into question by this poor first showing. The aircraft were recalled to the U.S. on 22 November. See CONSTANT GUARD V and HARVEST REAPER.

COMBAT TRIDENT (U.S. 67) The initial training of the first F-111A pilots conducted at Nellis Air Force Base in 1967. These airmen then deployed to Southeast Asia as part of COMBAT LANCER and HARVEST REAPER.

COMBINED DEVELOPMENT TRUST (U.S. 42) Part of the MANHATTAN ENGINEER DISTRICT that attempted to corner the world's supply of uranium. The Americans focused on buying the rights to Belgian ores mined in Africa. Later, the effort was keyed to ensuring that the Soviet Union was unable to buy ore on the world market. Unknown to the American military, the Soviet Union had vast ore reserves. An unintended result of this worldwide buying effort was that as the price of uranium went higher, prospectors brought additional supplies on-line, defeating the American effort. Replaced the term MURRAY HILL AREA.

COMET (U.S.) A reserved first word for the programs and projects of the U.S. Air Force.

COMFORT (U.S.) A reserved first word for the program and projects of the U.S. Air Force Reserve.

COMFY (U.S.) A reserved first word for the programs and projects of the U.S. Air Force Security Service.

COMMANDO

1. (U.N. 52) The last major U.N. attack in the Korean War. The U.S. 1st Corps (including 4 U.S. Divisions, the Commonwealth Division, and the 1st South Korean Division) seized the Jamestown Line destroying elements of the 42nd, 47th, 64th, and 65th Chinese

Armies. This prevented the Communist forces from interdicting the U.N. supply lines near Seoul. The attack began on 3 October 1952 and ended on 15 October, with a few hills south of the line still in communist hands, requiring a follow-up operation, POLECHARGE. As a result of this 6-mile advance, the badly mauled U.S. 1st Cavalry Division was withdrawn to Japan for refitting.

2. (U.S.) A reserved first word for the programs and projects of the U.S. Pacific Air Forces.

COMMANDO HUNT III (U.S. 69) A series of B-52 Stratofortress raids conducted against communist supply lines in southern Laos from November 1969 to April 1970. The aircraft were based at U Tapao Royal Thai Air Base.

COMMANDO LAVA (U.S.) A proposal to use C-130 Hercules cargo aircraft for attacks on the Ho Chi Minh Trail. Never executed. See BANISH BEACH and CAROLINA MOON.

COMMANDO VAULT (U.S.) The general term for missions flown by C-130 Hercules aircraft to deliver large 10,000- and 15,000-pound bombs in Vietnam. These "daisy cutter" bombs were used to clear jungle areas, producing instant helicopter landing zones.

COMMON CAUSE (U.S. 62) American electronic surveillance air patrols of Cuban military activity conducted by RB-47 aircraft during the Cuban Missile Crisis.

COMMON ENERGY (NATO 94) A long-range air training exercise that featured Belgian F-16s using American KC-10 tankers to attack targets in Spain.

COMMON KNOWLEDGE (Unofficial 50) A term used by media people in Tokyo to describe the not-quite secret plan to invade Korea (CHROMITE).

COMPASS

1. (Allied 40) The first major British ground attack against Italian forces in North Africa. This action, launched on 7 December 1940, has often been described as a large raid, which forced the Italian units in Egypt from Sidi Barrani to retreat to Bardia. The Italian defeat prompted the Germans to reinforce their ally in North Africa (SONNENBLUME). Troops that could have been used to make the British victory complete were diverted to Greece and Cypress (SCORCHER). As a result the war in the desert continued for years.

2. (U.S.) A reserved first word for the programs and projects of the U.S. Air Force. These programs generally deal with electronic warfare, battlefield surveillance, and control.

COMPATRIOT (U.S. 67) See POPEYE.

COMPLY (U.S.) A reserved first word for the programs and projects of the U.S. Air Force Headquarters.

CONCRETE (U.S.) A reserved first word for the programs and projects of the U.S. Air Force Headquarters. Examples include CONCRETE BEET and CONCRETE TRACTION. The names generally apply to civil engineering projects.

CONDOR

1. (FR 54) An attempt to break through to the besieged French Union forces at Dien Bien Phu. Launched in much-reduced form on 13 April, the relief columns were delayed by the rugged terrain and were cut up by the surrounding Viet Minh.

2. (Latin America 74) A counter-terrorism campaign of assassination and intelligence-gathering conducted jointly by the security services of Argentina, Bolivia, Brazil, Chile, and Uruguay in the mid-1970s. The right-wing governments of these countries agreed to cooperate in sending teams into

third countries, including France, Portugal, and the U.S. to locate, observe, and assassinate terrorists. One target in September 1974 was the Venezuelan-born Illich Ramirez Sanchez (a.k.a., "The Jackal"). After his involvement in murder of the Bolivian ambassador and a Chilean attaché in Paris as well as a Chilean diplomat in the Middle East, Ramirez was located by the Latin Americans in Europe. The American CIA detected the CONDOR operation and alerted France and Portugal. They warned Ramirez, allowing him to escape.

CONJOUR (Allied 43) The insertion of 6 French resistance fighters on the night of 15 November 1943 into a primitive landing field near Angers, France. One of the partisans was Francois Mitterand, who was later elected President of France.

CONSTANT (U.S.) A reserved first word for the programs and projects of the U.S. Air Force.

CONSTANT GUARD V (U.S. 72) The deployment of 2 F-111A squadrons from the U.S. to Takhli, Thailand, conducted in September 1972 as part of LINEBACKER I. Compared to the high loss rate experienced during COMBAT LANCER, Aardvark gained a reputation as a highly survivable aircraft experiencing a loss rate of .015 percent throughout the rest of the war.

CONSTANTINE (GER) See KONSTANTIN.

CONTINUE HOPE (U.S. 93) U.S. Central Command operations in Somalia in support of the U.N. Somalia II mission from May through December 1993.

CONTRARY (U.K.) The installation of electronic monitoring devices in the Polish trade mission building in Brussels, Belgium, by British intelligence.

COOL (U.S.) A reserved first word for the programs and projects of the U.S. Air Force's Alaska Air Command.

COOPERATION FROM THE SEA 1995 (U.S./RU 95) A Joint American/Russian amphibious exercise conducted at the U.S. Marine Corps Base at Kanehohe Bay, Hawaii, in late August 1995. After landing 250 Russian naval infantrymen, the 3 Russian ships also took part in ceremonies at Pearl Harbor commemorating the 50th anniversary of the end of the World War II.

COOPERATIVE BRIDGE 94 (NATO 94) The first military exercise conducted by the Western Alliance and its former Warsaw Pact enemies. The 5-day exercise began on 12 September 1994 at Biedrusko, Poland. The training focused on interoperability issues. Five 150-man companies were organized with 4 platoons from the various countries. Poland, Bulgaria, the Czech Republic, Lithuania, Rumania, Slovakia, and Ukraine joined with units from the U.S., U.K., Germany, Denmark, Italy, and the Netherlands in this training.

COOPERATIVE CHALLENGE (NATO 95) A Partnership for Peace exercise conducted by elements from 14 nations in the Czech Republic in September 1995.

COOPERATIVE JAGUAR (NATO 95) NATO naval exercise in the Baltic Sea that included major participation by Partnership for Peace countries conducted from 2 to 12 October 1995. This operation focused on communication and interoperability between 18 ships from 15 countries.

COOPERATIVE MERMAID/CLASSICA 95 (NATO 95) A naval exercise conducted in late November 1995 in the Ligurian Sea by naval units from NATO and Eastern European nations under the Partnership for Peace program.

COOPERATIVE NUGGET 95 (NATO 95) The third NATO exercise with Eastern

European nations under the Partnership for Peace. COOPERATIVE NUGGET 95 was conducted of Fort Polk, Louisiana, and featured training on peacekeeping and mine-clearing procedures.

COOPERATIVE SPIDER (NATO 94) NATO exercise conducted in the Netherlands with units from the Partnership for Peace.

COOPERATIVE SPIRIT 94 (NATO 94) The second exercise between NATO and Eastern European armies under the Partnership for Peace program. Conducted in the Netherlands' Harzkamp Training Area, it included American, Swedish, German, Polish, and Dutch troops.

COOPERATIVE TIDE 96 (NATO 96) A small exercise conducted in late February 1996 in Houston, Texas, that focused on the naval control of shipping. Four NATO and 8 Eastern European nations took part including Russia, Poland, and Finland.

COOPERATIVE VENTURE (NATO 94) NATO naval exercise held in the North Sea for NATO and Partnership for Peace nations.

COPE (U.S.) A reserved first word for the programs and projects of the U.S. Air Force's Pacific Air Force. See COPE THUNDER and COPE WEST.

COPE THUNDER (U.S. 76) U.S. Pacific Command annual air-to-ground training held beginning in 1976 at the highly-instrumented Crow Valley Range complex at Clark Air Force Base in Alaska after Clark was closed in 1992. Units fly to Eielson as if it were a wartime overseas deployment and conduct air, support, and other operations. See FIERY VIGIL.

COPE TIGER (U.S./Thai/Sing) Annual fighter exercise conducted by American and Thai or Singapore Air Forces. Designated by year (e.g., COPE TIGER 95).

COPE WEST (U.S./Singapore 91) Bilateral air exercise that took place in Singapore in March 1991.

COPENHAGEN (GER 43) See KOPEN-HAGEN.

COPPER (U.S.) A reserved first word for the programs and projects of the U.S. Air Force generally dealing with supply and logistics functions. See COZY.

COPPERHEAD (Allied 44) See HAMBONE.

CORKSCREW (Allied 43) Invasion of the Italian island of Pantelleria (between Sicily and Tunisia) on 10 June 1943. Following a 10-day bombardment, the Italian garrison surrendered when the British forces landed on the island. The Italian garrisons on other nearby islands (Linosa and Lampedusa) quickly fell. This cleared the way for the invasion of Sicily (HUSKY) a month later.

CORNCOB

1. (Allied 45) A series of air attacks on bridges crossing the Adige and Brenta rivers designed to disrupt the retreat of German forces from Italy. Conducted over a 3-day period beginning 20 April 1945.

2. (GER) See MAISKOLBEN.

CORNERSTONE (U.S. Law Enforcement 93) A federal investigation of the money-laundering and legal-defense activities of the Cali drug cartel. This investigation was made public on 5 June 1995 when 59 indictments were announced. Key among those accused were a number of lawyers who allegedly acted as "house counsels" to drug kingpins, advising them on ways to minimize their legal exposure. Three former federal prosecutors with ties to the Justice Department and the Drug Enforcement Administration were among those indicted.

CORONA (U.S.) A reserved first word for the programs and projects of the U.S. Air Force Headquarters.

CORONET

1. (Allied 44) Planning name for the capture of Woodlark and Kiriwina Islands, off the eastern tip of New Guinea, by U.S. forces on 30 June 1944. Executed under the name CHRONICLE. The landings were unopposed. Part of CARTWHEEL.

2. (Allied 45) Planned invasion of the Japanese home island of Honshu at the Tokyo Plain south of the capital. First scheduled for 1 December 1945 and later postponed to March 1946. This would have been the largest amphibious operation of all time, with 15 divisions (including the floating reserve) earmarked for the operation. This invasion would have followed OLYMPIC; both attacks were components of the DOWNFALL plan. Never executed.

3. (U.S.) A reserved first word for the programs and projects of the U.S. Air Force's former Tactical Air Command.

CORPORATE (U.K. 82) Liberation of the Falkland Islands from Argentine occupation. The 2 April 1982 Argentine invasion took the British by surprise. Their counter-invasion was launched on 21 May, the capital city of Port Stanley fell on 14 June. Included KEYHOLE and BLACK BUCK. See PURPLE WARRIOR.

CORREO (U.S. 83) See FUSILEER.

COSECHA AMISTAD "HARVEST FRIEND-SHIP" (U.S./PN 94) An engineer training exercise conducted in the remote Panamanian province of Darien, near the Colombian border. U.S. National Guard units rotated into a series of work sites where they built schools and other civic improvements during their 2-week annual training period.

COSMIC (Allied 44) Contingency plan for the deployment of British naval units in the event the German battle cruiser Tirpitz broke out of Altendiord in Norway. Never executed.

COTTAGE (Allied 43) U.S. liberation of Kiska, Alaska, in August 1943 from the Japanese. These islands were captured by the Japanese in support of the Battle of Midway.

COTTBUS (GER 43) Anti-partisan operation conducted in the Polotsk-Label-Borisov region of Belorussia. Launched on 3 June 1943, it was the largest such operation of the war. Five thousand Russians were killed as partisans or sympathizers. It seems unlikely the sweep was targeted at combatants. Official reports indicate that fewer than 500 rifles were captured and that many of those killed were children. Cottbus is a German city; the name is sometimes anglicized as "Kottbus."

COUGAR (U.S.) A reserved first word for the programs and projects of the U.S. Air Force's Accounting and Finance Center.

COUNCIL (U.S.) A reserved first word for the programs and projects of the U.S. Air Force's Base Support Agency.

COUNTENANCE (Allied 41) The partition of Iran between the British (based in the south) and the Soviets (operating from the north) executed on 25 August 1941 to secure an ice-free supply route for lend-lease supplies sent to bolster the Soviets. Soviet efforts to preserve this division of Iran in the post-war period led to an early showdown in the U.N. See AJAX.

COUNTER (U.S.) A reserved first word for the programs and projects of the U.S. Air Force's Accounting and Finance Center. See COUGAR.

COURAGEOUS (U.N. 51) See RIPPER.

COURIER (GER 43) See EILBOTE.

COURLIS "CURLEW" (FR 93) French deployment of cargo aircraft to the Frankfurt am Main airbase to fly relief missions to war-torn Yugoslavia as part of PROVIDE PROMISE.

COVER (U.S.) A reserved first word for the programs and projects of the U.S. Air Force's Strategic Air Command.

COWPUNCHER (Allied 43) Amphibious training exercises conducted before the invasion of Italy (AVALANCHE).

COZY (U.S.) A reserved first word for the programs and projects of the U.S. Air Force's former Air Logistics Command.

CRACKERJACK (NORAD 55) North American Air Defense Command exercise conducted in 1955.

CRASHER (Allied 44) Proposed Allied amphibious landing in the general area of south China to include Formosa or Luzon. This would bring forces under the command of General Douglas MacArthur closer to Japan for the final invasion. Never executed. Included CAUSEWAY.

CRAWDAD (Allied 44) Alternate plan to break out from the beach head at Anzio. Never executed. See BUFFALO.

CRAZY HORSE

1. (U.S. 66) Operations by elements of the 1st Cavalry Division in the Vinh Thanh Valley, Vietnam. Executed May 1966.

2. (NATO 78) A mine-clearing exercise conducted off La Spezia, Italy, in 1978. See OLIVE NOIRES.

CRECERELLE "KESTREL" (FR 95) The deployment of French aircraft to air bases in Italy in support of Operation DENY FLIGHT.

CREDIBLE (U.S.) A reserved first word for the programs and projects of the U.S. Air Force Europe.

CREEK (U.S.) A reserved first word for the programs and projects of the U.S. Air Force Europe. See CREEK MISTY, CREEK SWING, CHECKERED FLAG.

CREEK MISTY (U.S.) The use of specially equipped cargo aircraft to gather intelligence while flying in the aerial corridors between West Germany and Berlin. A C-130 Hercules on a CREEK MISTY mission was shot down on 2 September 1958 when it strayed from its assigned flight path.

CREEK SWING (U.S. 77) The worldwide reshuffling of American F-111 units conducted in 1977 before the provisions of the Strategic Arms Limitation Talks (SALT I) came into effect. Also called READY SWITCH.

CRESCENT (U.S. 77) A series of 19 underground nuclear tests conducted at the Nevada Test Site. This series of explosions followed FULCRUM and preceded QUICKSILVER. The individual shots of this series were:

BOBSTAY	26 October 77	<20 kilotons
HYBLA GOLD	1 November	<20 kilotons
SANDREEF	9 November	20-150 kilotons
SEAMOUNT	17 November	20 kilotons
FARALLONES	14 December	20-150 kilotons
CAMPOS	13 February 78	<20 kilotons
REBLOCHON	23 February	20-150 kilotons
(Unknown)	16 March	(unknown)
ICEBERG	23 March	20-150 kilotons
BACKBEACH	11 April	20-150 kilotons
FONDUTTA	11 April	201-50 kilotons
TRANSOM	10 May	failed to detonate
(Unknown)	1 June	(unknown)
(Unknown)	7 July	(unknown)
LOWBALL	12 July	20-150 kilotons
PANIR	31 August	20-150 kilotons
DIABLO HAWK	13 September	<20 kilotons
DRAUGHTS	27 September	20-150 kilotons
RUMMY	27 September	20-150 kilotons

CRESTED (U.S.) A reserved first word for the programs and projects of the U.S. Air Force headquarters. See CRESTED CAP and CRESTED ICE.

CRESTED CAP (NATO) Annual practice reinforcement of Europe by U.S. Air Force units. See CENTRAL ENTERPRISE and CHECKERED FLAG.

CRESTED ICE (U.S. 68) The cleanup after a major accident involving nuclear weapons in Greenland. On 21 January 1968 a B-52 bomber crashed 7 miles short of the runway of the U.S. air base at Thule. One crewman was killed by the extreme cold. Both the aircraft and its weapons broke apart on impact with the ice, with some parts crashing to the sea floor. In a massive effort, over 230,000 cubic feet of ice were removed by the Americans under the supervision of the Danish government. See BROKEN ARROW.

CREW (U.S.) A reserved first word for the programs and projects of the U.S. Air Force's Technical Application Center.

CRICKET

1. (Allied 45) See ARGONAUT.

2. (U.S. 66) Operation mentioned in the leaked "Pentagon Papers." This operation monitored or interdicted communist infiltration through the Demilitarized Zone that formed the northern border of the former Republic of South Vietnam.

CRIMP (U.S./AUS 66) Planning name for BUCKSKIN.

CRISEX (U.S./SP 83) Exercise run in late October 1983, which included B-52 bombers operating with Spanish forces. King Juan Carlos watched 1 bombing attack. CRISEX seems to be contraction of "Crisis Exercise."

CRISPY (U.S.) A reserved first word for the program and projects of the U.S. Air Force's Military Airlift Command.

CROMWELL (Allied 40) Second British plan to defend their home islands from a German invasion (SEELOWE). Replaced the JULIUS CAESAR plan on 5 June 1940. The operational concept was for stiff initial resistance on the landing beaches followed by a heavy counterattack.

CROSSBOLT I

CROSSBOLT II (U.S. 93) A series of exercises designed to perfect methods to detect and quickly attack tactical ballistic missile launchers. During the Gulf War, the U.S. was befuddled by its inability to attack Iraqi Scud missile launchers before their highly trained crews could escape. In January 1993 during CROSSBOLT I, air units managed to detect and simulate an attack on a Lance missile launcher in 32 minutes. In December 1993 a Cobra Ball airborne radar was used to detect missile launchers during Phase I of CROSSBOLT II. Phase II was conducted in March 1994 when the tactical aircraft attempted to hit the launcher within 10 minutes.

CROSSBOW (Allied 44) Allied designation for the V-1 "Buzz Bomb" attacks on England. The first few bombs fell on London on the night of 12 June 1944. Over 200 were launched three nights later. See NOBALL.

CROSSKEYS (Allied 45) Plan for an American amphibious invasion of Denmark to cut off German forces in Scandinavia. Never executed.

CROSS PIECE (U.S.) An early plan for nuclear operations against the Soviet Union. This was one of a series of plans developed by the Strategic Air Command. Others were HALF MOON, BROILER, FROLIC, DOUBLESTAR, TROJAN, OFF TACKLE, and SHAKEDOWN. Eventually, these plans were superseded by a series of Single Integrated Operations Plans (SIOPs). The first SIOP was DROPSHOT.

CROSSROADS (U.S. 46) The test detonation of 2 first-generation ("Fat Man") atomic bombs on Bikini Atoll in the summer of

1946. ABLE, an air burst yielding 23 kilotons was conducted on 1 July; BAKER, an underwater explosion of the same yield was conducted on 25 July. A second underwater burst, CHARLIE, was canceled. These early tests were to determine the effects of nuclear detonation using weapons drawn from the operational nuclear stockpile. The health impact of exposure to radiation was not yet clearly understood, and so a large number of servicemen were exposed to hazardous levels. This resulted in lawsuits decades later. A fleet of 73 target ships, including the American aircraft carrier *Saratoga* and a number of captured ships, were sunk by these blasts. Preceded by TRINITY, followed by SANDSTONE.

CROSSTIE (U.S. 67) A series of 33 nuclear tests conducted in Nevada during 1967 and 1968. These tests followed the LATCHKEY series and preceded BOWLINE. The blast designated GASBUGGY involved the simultaneous detonation of 5 nuclear devices to produce a ditch of 855 feet long, 254 feet across, and 65 feet deep. The individual tests of this series were:

STANLEY	27 August 67	prob. 8 kilotons
(Unknown)	4 August	(unknown)
WASHER	10 August	<20 kilotons
BORDEAUX	18 August	<20 kilotons
DOOR MIST	31 August	prob. 9 kilotons
YARD	7 September	20-200 kilotons
MARVEL	21 September	2.2 kilotons, see PLOWSHARE
ZAZA	27 September	prob. 170 kilotons
LANPHER	18 October	prob. 140 kilotons
SAZERAC	25 October	<20 kilotons
COBBLER	8 November	prob. 7 kilotons
GASBUGGY	10 December	29 kilotons, near Farmington, New Mexico. See PLOWSHARE.
STILT	15 December	prob. 2 kilotons
HUPMOBILE	18 January 68	7.4 kilotons
STACCATO	19 January	20-200 kilotons

FAULTLESS	19 January	prob. 200 kilotons
CABRIOLET	26 January	2.3 kilotons, see PLOWSHARE
(Unknown)	31 January	(unknown)
KNOX	21 February	prob. 200 kilotons
DORSAL FIN	29 February	prob. 20 kilotons
BUGGY	12 March	5.4 kilotons, see PLOWSHARE
POMMARD	14 March	1.5 kilotons
STINGER	22 March	prob. 160 kilotons
MILK SHAKE	25 March	prob. 10 kilotons
NOOR	10 April	prob. 20 kilotons
SHUFFLE	18 April	prob. 25 kilotons
SCROLL	23 April	prob. 6 kilotons
BOXCAR	26 April	1.3 megatons
(Unknown)	3 May	(unknown)
CLARKSMOBILE	17 May	prob. 15 kilotons
TUB	6 June	<20 kilotons
RICKEY	15 June	prob. 300 kilotons
CHATEAUGAY	28 June	prob. 50 kilotons

CROSSWORD (Allied 45) Secret negotiations conducted in Switzerland through Italian intermediaries to arrange a local surrender of German forces in northern Italy. These negotiations upset the Soviets greatly; they accused the western powers of trying to reach a separate peace. The actual surrender in Italy occurred in April 1945. Some American sources refer to these talks as SUNRISE.

CRUMPET I (Allied 44) Plan for Allied air attacks on Italian supply bases near Pesaro. Never executed.

CRUMPET II (Allied 44) Allied air attacks on Axis defenses near Rimini, Italy, in September 1944.

CRUSADER (Allied 41) British attack launched on 18 November 1941, which relieved the garrison at Tobruk on the 27th. This operation, commanded by Field Marshal Claude Auchinleck, forced

Rommel to withdrawal to El Agheila, where he had begun his advance 8 months before, thus ending the Axis threat to Egypt. The British enjoyed a large advantage in the number of tanks and aircraft available for this operation but deployed their tanks in small units to push the enemy back uniformly across the front. This resulted in the Germans being able to inflict enormous losses on the British in selected portions of the battle such as Gabr Saleh and Sidi Razegh. These counterattacks began on 24 November. The British could replace material losses more readily than could Axis. Followed by BATTLEAXE.

CUCUMBER (Allied 43) British air attacks on shipping off the Dutch coast from August 1943 to April 1944.

CUDGEL (U.N. 51) Plan to seize communist artillery positions that threatened the rail center at Ch'orwon-Kumhwa, Korea, which was required for WRANGLER, scheduled for October 1951. Never executed.

CULVERIN (Allied 43) Plan for an Allied amphibious assault on northern Sumatra and the Netherlands East Indies during the 1943/44 dry season. Never executed. Replaced by DRACULA.

"CURLEW" (FR 93) See COURLIS.

CURRENCY (GER 45) See WAHRUNG.

CUTTER (U.N. 52) The first phase of the STRANGLE air attacks on North Korea.

CUT THROAT (Allied 44) American air attacks on Japanese positions in northeast New Guinea in late January 1944.

CW (Allied 40) The designator for westbound English Channel convoys. The individual convoys were assigned a sequential number (e.g., CW6). The most famous of these convoys was CW9, which came under heavy German air attacks in the early stage of the Battle of Britain in late July 1940. Eventually, Channel convoys were suspended and their cargo shifted to rail transport.

CYCLE (Allied 40) The evacuation of Allied troops from La Havre, France, in June 1940. See DYNAMO.

D

D (U.S.) See Federal Emergency Plan D.

D Plan (U.S. 40) See Dog Plan.

DAGUET "FAWN" (FR 91) French participation in the coalition effort to liberate Kuwait. See DESERT SHIELD, DESERT STORM, and HORUS.

DAISY (R.S.A. 81) Raids by South African forces against guerrilla camps at Cheraqurera and Bambi, Angola.

DAME BLANCHE "WHITE LADY" (BG 14) Intelligence and resistance network established by Walthere Dewe in occupied Belgium in World War I. See CLARENCE, ZERO, and LUC.

DAMOCLES (IS 62) Assassination campaign conducted by the Israeli intelligence services against German rocket scientists during the 1960s. The Israelis feared these scientists, led by Eugen Saenger, would assist the Arabs to build a V-2 type rocket to be used against the Jewish state. The major weapon of this campaign was the letter bomb. Several Egyptian officers were killed, and some German scientists were injured. The intimidation worked; although two types of missiles were tested in July 1962, the program failed.

DAN (JPN 42) Japanese plan to prevent the Allies from opening a land route from Ledo (Assam Province, India) to Bhamo, Burma, the "Ledo Road." This would bypass areas captured by the Japanese and reestablish a land supply route to China. Construction of the new route began in June 1942 and was completed in August 1944. The Japanese attack was never launched.

DANI (IS 48) Israeli attack that began on 9 July 1948 that resulted in the capture of Tel Aviv and the towns of Lydda and Ramle as well as the nearby Lydda Airport. About 50,000 Arab residents left their homes as a result of this 10-day battle.

DARRINGTON II (Allied 44) One of a series of rescues launched along the Italian coast during that country's collapse in World War II. In this mission, 2 small boats left Termoli for the mouth of the Tenna River on the night of 24 May 1944 to recover 153 Allied escapees.

DAUNTLESS

1. (Allied 44) A preliminary ground attack by the British 30th Corps west of Caen, France, to capture jumping-off points for the EPSOM attack. Launched on 25 June 1944.

2. (U.N. 52) An attack launched by the U.S. 1st and 9th Corps on 11 April 1952 toward Chorwon in the "Iron Triangle" region. Chinese forces withdrew ahead from the American advance. Conducted in conjunction with RUGGED.

DAWN PATROL (NATO 73) A 5-nation naval and air exercise conducted throughout the Mediterranean in 1973.

"D DAY" The term used in planning for an as yet unspecified date on which military operations will begin. The time operations will begin is called "H Hour." The first use of this term seems to have been in an operations order issued on 7 September 1918 by the American Expeditionary Force in France. The "D Day" designation is so convenient in military planning that its use has become universal. The most famous "D Day" is 6 June 1944 when the Allies invaded Normandy (OVERLORD). In the postwar era, to avoid confusion with the OVERLORD invasion, some military operations have avoided the "D Day" designation. The Allied invasion of Iraq and Kuwait began on "G Day."

DEAD EYE (NATO 95) A NATO contingency plan to destroy rebel Bosnian air defense radar and missile sites in order to allow safe NATO overflights of Bosnian territory. Rejected in favor of DELIBERATE FORCE.

DEADLIGHT (Allied 46) The postwar sinking of captured German submarines begun on 25 November 1946. At Loch Ryan in western Scotland, 86 boats were sunk. Another two dozen were sunk off Lisahally in Ulster.

DECISION (JPN 45) See KETSU-GO.

DECOY (Allied 52) A deception operation that falsely portrayed an amphibious fleet approaching Kojo on Korea's east coast on 15 October 1952. This feint drew defenders out of their shelters where they were exposed to American air and naval bombardment.

DEEP FREEZE I
DEEP FREEZE II (U.S. 56) Antarctic expeditions conducted by U.S. Navy units during the (Antarctic) summers of 1955-56 and

1956-57 respectively. During DEEP FREEZE I, research bases were established at Little America on Kianan Bay and at McMurdo Sound near Hot Point as part of the International Geophysical Year. On 31 October 1956, a U.S. Navy Skytrain landed with a crew of 7 at the South Pole. This was the first team to reach this destination since Captain Robert Scott in January 1912. DEEP FREEZE II was more far-ranging, using a fleet of 12 ships including an aircraft carrier to explore the continent.

DEEP PROUD ALPHA (U.S. 71) A short series of American air strikes against targets in North Vietnam from 26 to 30 December 1971.

DEEP STRIKE (Coalition 91) Raids conducted by the Second Brigade of the U.S. 1st Cavalry Division against Iraqi border positions in the Wadi al Batin on 24 February 1991. These attacks captured prisoners, collected intelligence, and prevented Iraqi forces from identifying the main axis of attack of the U.S. 5th and 18th Airborne Corps to the west. Followed the BERM BUSTER/RED STORM/KNIGHT STRIKE series.

DELIBERATE FORCE (NATO 95) An air campaign aimed at forcing rebel Bosnians to withdraw heavy weapons used to besiege the capital city of Sarajevo for more than 3 years. Prompted by a series of artillery attacks on civilians, the U.N. Security Council extracted a promise from the rebels to move their artillery from a "safe zone" surrounding the city. The shelling continued, however, including an attack that killed over 30 shoppers in the city center. NATO, acting as military agent for the U.N., responded on 30 August, with the destruction of the rebel air defense air network and infrastructure. The Bosnian Serbs, pressured by their Serbian allies, agreed to live up to their obligations and lifted the siege after 2 weeks of bombardment by aircraft and cruise missiles. The international airport reopened on 15 September 1995, allowing PROVIDE PROMISE flights to resume. This cease-fire by heavy weapons later led to the "Dayton Agreement" in 1996. See DEAD EYE and DELIBERATE FURY.

DELIBERATE FURY (NATO 95) The naval component of DELIBERATE FORCE. NATO ships launched missiles and air-craft, provided command and control and coordinated the activities of both land and sea-based aircraft.

DEMON (Allied 41)

1. Evacuation of Allied forces from Greece. Thanks to a defense at the historic pass at Thermopylae, over 50,000 British, Australian, Polish, and New Zealand sol-diers were moved to Crete. Executed 24-30 April 1941.

2. The British occupation of Abaden, Iran, on 25 August 1941. See COUNTENANCE.

DEMON III (U.S. 50) Exercise by the 1st Marine Division and its associated air wing at Fort Leavenworth, Kansas, in May 1950.

DENY FLIGHT (NATO 93) The use of fighter aircraft from several NATO nations flying from bases in Italy and from an American aircraft carrier to prevent Serbian aircraft from entering Bosnian air-space. This operation began on 12 April 1993, long after the Serbians had captured large portions of Bosnia using ground forces. On 15 March 1993, the Serbians attacked the besieged Muslim city of Srebrenica with 3 An-2 aircraft. The U.N. ordered a no-fly zone over Bosnia and Herzegovina. NATO provided aircraft to monitor compliance (SKY MONITOR). The Bosnians so blatantly violated the ban that the U.N. ordered enforcement of the ban. NATO again provided aircraft, this time under operation DENY FLIGHT. The effort eventually became discredited as the

Serbs began helicopter operations in the no-fly area. On 28 February 1994, American aircraft shot down 4 Bosnian Serb jet fighters as part of this operation, marking the first time NATO had used force in its history. The operation ended on 21 December 1995 when authority for operations in the region passed to the new NATO Implementing Force headquarters. Followed PROVIDE PROMISE. See CRE-CERELLE and GRAPPLE.

DERFFLINGER (GER 42) Plan to cut off the Toropets Salient from the south by a thrust northwest from Rzhev by the German 9th Army. Scheduled for late July or early August 1942. Never executed. Named for Georg Derfflinger, a military hero of the 1600s.

DERVISH (Allied 44) Aborted Allied decep-tion plan tailored to lure infantry units away from the Western Front. This plan would have falsely portrayed the threat of an Allied airborne attack deep behind German lines. Never executed.

DESERT DRAGON (U.S. 90) Series of plans drawn up for the defense of Saudi Arabia by U.S. forces against an attack launched from Iraqi-occupied Kuwait. These plans evolved into DESERT SHIELD. As the forces actually on the ground changed, the DESERT DRAGON plan was modified, expanding the area to be defended. DESERT DRAGON was based on the pre-war Central Command plan 90-1002 and included lessons learned from the INTER-NAL LOOK 90 exercise. Major versions of the rapidly-changing plan were:

DESERT DRAGON I (U.S. 90) Plan for the defense of Saudi Arabia using available units, in effect from 9 to 12 August 1990. At this time the only U.S. unit available was 4th Battalion, 325th Parachute Infantry. This unit was to defend the air and seaports in the Dhahran/Ad Dammam area in order to allow other U.S. units to arrive.

DESERT DRAGON II (U.S. 90) Plan for the defense of Saudi Arabia using available units, in effect from 13 August to 3 September 1990. This plan used the 2nd Brigade, 82nd Airborne Division to expand the defended area north to include the port of Al Jubayl.

DESERT DRAGON III (Coalition 90) Plan for the defense of Saudi Arabia using available units, in effect from 4 to 30 September 1990. This plan made use of the newly arrived Marines, the entire 18th Airborne Corps and other units, to include the British 7th Armoured Brigade (the "Desert Rats") and French units. The defended area expanded to include King Khalid Military City.

DESERT DRAGON IV (U.S. 90) The final plan for the defense of Saudi Arabia against an Iraqi attack. This plan was an extensive modification of the original CENTCOM plan 1002 and was renamed DESERT SHIELD.

DESERT FAREWELL (U.S. 91) Name given to the return of American units and equipment to the U.S. after the liberation of Kuwait. Some U.S. Marine Corps units were diverted in route to conduct humanitarian assistance in flooded Bangladesh (SEA ANGEL).

DESERT FLAG (U.S. 90) A realistic training program conducted in the deserts of the American Southwest for U.S. Air Force units scheduled to deploy to Saudi Arabia as part of DESERT SHIELD. Based on the RED FLAG program, DESERT FLAG included opportunities to fire live ammunition against realistic ground and air targets.

DESERT ROCK I-VIII (U.S. 51) A series of training exercises conducted by U.S. Army troops from 1951 to 1957 in conjunction with nuclear test detonations conducted at the Nevada Test Site. Typically, soldiers would place a "test array" of vehicles and equipment to be destroyed by the blast. They would huddle in the trenches and bunkers during the detonations and finally conduct a simulated breakthrough of the "ruptured enemy lines" in vehicles and on foot. The earlier exercises in this series served the additional purpose of "sending a message" to communist forces during the Korean War. A series of lawsuits have resulted from injuries to soldiers who took part in these operations. See IVY FLATS.

BUSTER-JANGLE	1951	DESERT ROCK I, II, and III
TUMBLER-SNAPPER	1952	DESERT ROCK IV
UPSHOT-KNOTHOLE	1953	DESERT ROCK V
TEAPOT	1955	DESERT ROCK VI
PLUMBOB	1957	DESERT ROCK VII and VIII

DESERT SHIELD (Coalition 90) Operation by Coalition forces to defend Saudi Arabia from Iraqi forces in Kuwait. Based on DESERT DRAGON. The Iraqi invasion of Kuwait on 2 August 1990 was accomplished with such overwhelming force that an invasion of Saudi Arabia looked likely. U.S. Central Command began deploying units to the Gulf region on 7 August. It was estimated that the Saudi capital could fall in as little as 3 days without American troops. See DAGUET, DESERT DRAGON, FRICTION, and GRANBY.

DESERT STORM (Coalition 91) Operation by Coalition forces to liberate Kuwait. After a short crisis initiated by the Iraqi dictator, Iraq invaded its much smaller neighbor at 0200, 2 August 1990. With few forces in the region, an American-led Coalition began moving units into the area to deter further Iraq aggression (DESERT SHIELD) and then to eject the invader (DESERT STORM). The air portion of the attack began on 15 January 1991. Massive Coalition air strikes quickly destroyed Iraqi infrastructure, leaving their ground forces exposed to an exceptionally harsh environment without supplies, transportation, or communications. The ground assault began on "G-Day," 24 February when Central Command headquarters issued the one-word order "Wolfpack." President Bush ordered a halt to the advance effective 100 hours later, at 0800 hours, 28 February. It was perhaps the most one-sided victory in military history. Coalition losses from all causes were fewer than 500 dead, the Iraqis lost more than 100,000 killed, a 200:1 exchange ratio. No Coalition aircraft were lost in air-to-air combat, compared to 35 downed Iraqi airplanes. The Iraqi Air Force, its air-defense network, and its small navy were essentially destroyed, while its army and parallel Republican Guard organization were ravaged and much reduced in combat capability. See PROVEN FORCE.

DESERT STRIKE (U.S. 96) The American missile strike on Iraq in early September 1996. Concerned over Iraqi ground actions in the Kurd-dominated north, the Americans launched over 40 cruise missiles at targets in southern Iraq. The main target was the Iraqi air-defense system. Simultaneously, the Americans extended the southern no-fly zone (SOUTHERN WATCH) north to just below Baghdad.

DE SOTO

DESOTO (U.S. 64) Aggressive patrolling of the Gulf of Tonkin off North Vietnam by U.S. Navy destroyers that began in February 1964. On the night of 2 August 1964 the USS *Maddox* was conducting a DESOTO mission off the coast of North Vietnam in international waters when it was attacked unsuccessfully by several North Vietnamese patrol boats. This attack and the confused action fought the next night in the same general area became known as the Gulf of Tonkin incident. A resolution framed by President Johnson was passed by the American Congress authorizing him to use force in the region. This served as a legal basis for American entry in the war in Vietnam. Part of OPLAN 34-A.

DESTINED GLORY 95 (NATO 95) An amphibious training exercise conducted by ships from 6 nations in the Mediterranean in May 1995.

DESTINED GLORY 96 (NATO 96) Two week exercise featuring 7 navies operating in the Mediterranean in June 1996.

DESTROYER (Allied 45) Attack by Canadian 1st Corps to capture the area between the Waal and Neder Rijn Rivers on 2 April 1945. The Germans destroyed dams and levees upstream leaving the objective a soggy island. The Canadians were forced to evacuate the area. Planned as SIESTA.

DETACHMENT (Allied 45) American invasion of the Japanese island of Iwo Jima on 19 February 1945. The Japanese garrison of about 20,000 had dug an extensive fortification complex centered on Mount Suribachi. They thereby avoided the massive preinvasion bombardment. Three airfields for American B-29 bombers were operating by March despite strong resistance. Just 216 defenders were captured. Many of the civilian inhabitants committed mass suicide rather than be captured, often jumping off cliffs.

DETAINED I (Allied 44) A Yugoslav commando raid on the island of Slota off the former Yugoslavia on the night of 18 March.

DETAINED II (Allied 44) The landing of a large force of Yugoslav partisans on Slota on the night of 8 May 1944. The force was withdrawn on 9 April.

DETROIT (U.S. 44) The insertion of the 82nd Airborne division into Normandy as part of OVERLORD. See CHICAGO.

DEWEY CANNON (U.S. 69) An American sweep of the A Shau and Da Krong Valleys, Vietnam, conducted in April 1969.

DEXTERITY (Allied 43) Seizure of Cape Gloucester, New Britain, by amphibious and airborne attacks that cut off the Japanese troops on the eastern tip off the island. Executed on 15 December 1943 simultaneously with BACKHANDLER. Part of CARTWHEEL.

DIADEM (Allied 44) The 1944 Allied spring ground offensive in Italy launched on 12 May 1944 to turn the German defenses at Cassino and open up the Liri Valley. The breakthrough was achieved by Free French and Moroccan troops on the 14th. This caused the German "Gustav Line" to collapse, reducing pressure on the Anzio beachhead (SHINGLE) and allowing a breakout from that encirclement (BUFFALO). The Germans retreated northward to the new "Gothic Line." DIADEM was roughly coordinated with the invasion of northern France (OVERLORD) and was supported by the air attacks of Operation STRANGLE. A diadem is a primitive royal crown. Followed DICKENS. Included HASTY.

DIAMOND (U.S.) A reserved first word for the programs and projects of the U.S. Defense Nuclear Agency dealing with underground nuclear tests.

DIAPER (U.S., Unofficial 46) The transport of European war brides and their dependents to the U.S. beginning in January 1946.

DICKENS (Allied 44) Ground attack on German fortifications near Cassino, Italy, and its ruined abbey on 15 March 1944. Preceded by a major carpet bombing attack (BRADMAN).

DICK TRACY (Allied/GER 45) The hurried transfer of Nazi intelligence information on the Soviet armed forces from Luftwaffe to American and British intelligence agencies.

Conducted in May 1945 as the German forces collapsed; truckloads of aerial photographs and order of battle information were moved westward. This action is often cited as the beginning of the Cold War and marks the first steps of Germany into the Western Alliance.

DIPLOMAT (Allied 44) Allied naval operations to protect shipping lanes between India and Australia in March and April 1994.

DIPLOMATIC (Allied 43) A series of secret talks between the British and the neutral Portuguese to secure air bases in the Azores for use as anti-submarine bases.

DIPPER

1. (Allied 42) Invasion of Bougainville by the U.S. 3rd Marine Division, executed 1 November 1942. The small Japanese garrison was brushed aside by the end of the year. Four airfields built on the captured portion of the island were used to attack the Japanese defenses on Rabaul. Part of the large CARTWHEEL operation.

2. (Allied 43) Amphibious training exercise held in England by Canadian troops earmarked for the invasion of northern France (OVERLORD) in August 1943.

DISCLAIM (Allied 42) The insertion of partisans by parachute near Sarajevo, Herzegovina (then part of Yugoslavia), on the night of 5 February 1942.

DISTANT FRONTIER (U.S./U.K. 92) Large exercise by U.S. and Royal Air Force units in Alaska in April 1992.

DIVIDER (U.S. 92) The last U.S. nuclear test. Conducted on 23 September 1992.

DIXIE

1. (U.S. 45) A delegation of military observers sent by the Americans to investigate the activities and future usefulness of the Chinese Communist People's Liberation Army. The report of this mission predicted

the defeat of the Nationalist Kuomintang forces. The name DIXIE may have referred to the "rebel" Chinese, or come from a song popular at the time "Is It True What They Say About Dixie?"

2. (U.S. 56) Planned U.S. open-air nuclear test scheduled for 1956; the DIXIE tests were combined into the REDWING series.

DOG PLAN "PLAN D" (U.S. 40) Plan drawn up by Admiral Stark in late 1940 for joint US/British operations in World War II. This plan was heavily influenced by and similar to RAINBOW-5, which also clearly stated a "Germany first" policy.

DOMINIC (U.S. 58) A series of 105 nuclear test explosions conducted in 1962 and 1963. This test series was scheduled quickly, in order to take advantage of the Soviet abandonment on the 1958-61 test moratorium. Most of these shots were conducted with free-fall bombs dropped from B-52 aircraft. Those conducted in the Pacific are sometimes called DOMINIC I. The blasts in Nevada are DOMINIC II. Twenty of these shots were to test new weapons designs, 6 to test weapons effects, and several shots to confirm the reliability of existing weapons. The Thor Missile was used to loft the warhead into near-space to conduct tests; these shots were collectively called FISHBOWL. The individual detonations were:

"DOMINIC I"

ADOBE	25 April 62	Christmas Island
AZTEC	27 April	Christmas Island
BLACK	27 April	Nevada Test Site
ARKANSAS	2 May	Christmas Island
QUESTA	4 May	Christmas Island
FRIGATE BIRD	6 May	Polaris A2 Missile 600 kilotons
PACA	7 May	Nevada Test Site
YUKON	8 May	Christmas Island
MESILLA	9 May	Christmas Island
ARIKAREE	10 May	Nevada Test Site
MUSKEGON	11 May	Christmas Island
SWORDFISH	11 MAY	off San Diego, California
ENCINO	12 May	Christmas Island
AARDVARK	12 May	Nevada Test Site 40 kilotons
SWANEE	14 May	Christmas Island
EEL	19 May	Nevada Test Site
CHETCO	19 May	Christmas Island
WHITE	25 May	Nevada Test Site
TANANA	25 May	Christmas Island "fizzled"
NAMBE	27 May	Christmas Island
RACCOON	1 June	Nevada Test Site
BLUEGILL	3 June	Johnston Island failed
PACKRAT	6 June	Nevada Test Site
ALMA	8 June	Christmas Island
TRUCKEE	9 June	Christmas Island
YESO	10 June	Christmas Island
HARLEM	12 June	Christmas Island
DES MOINES	13 June	Nevada Test Site
RINCONADA	15 June	Christmas Island
DULCE	17 June	Christmas Island
PETIT	19 June	Christmas Island "fizzled"
STARFISH	20 June	Johnston Atoll failed
DAMAN I	21 June	Nevada Test Site
OTOWI	21 June	Nevada Test Site
BIGHORN	27 June	Christmas Island
HAYMAKER	27 June	Nevada Test Site 67 kilotons
MASH- MALLOW	28 June	Nevada Test Site
BLUESTONE	30 June	Christmas Island
SACRAMENTO	30 June	Nevada Test Site
SEDAN	6 July	Nevada Test Site See PLOWSHARE
BLUEGILL PRIME	25 July	Johnston Island failed

"DOMINIC II" (See IVY FLATS)

LITTLE FELLER II	7 July	Nevada Test Site

STARFISH PRIME	9 July	Johnston Island 1.4 megatons
SUNSET	10 July	Christmas Island
PAMLICO	11 July	Christmas Island
JOHNIE BOY	11 July	Nevada Test Site 500 tons
MERRIMAC	13 July	Nevada Test Site
SMALL BOY	14 July	Nevada Test Site
LITTLE FELLER I	17 July	Nevada Test Site
WICHITA	27 July	Nevada Test Site
YORK	24 August	Nevada Test Site
BOBAC	24 August	Nevada Test Site
RARITAN	6 September	Nevada Test Site
HYRAX	4 September	Nevada Test Site
PEBA	20 September	Nevada Test Site
TOCITO	Canceled	Christmas Island
ALLEGHENY	29 September	Nevada Test Site
ANDRO-SCOGGIN	2 October	Johnston Island
MISSISSIPPI	5 October	Nevada Test Site 115 kilotons
BUMPING	6 October	Johnston Island
ROANOKE	12 October	Nevada Test Site
WOLVERINE	12 October	Nevada Test Site
BLUEGILL DOUBLE PRIME	15 October	Johnston Island
CHAMA	18 October	Johnston Island
TIOGA	18 October	Nevada Test Site
BANDICOOT	19 October	Nevada Test Site
CHECKMATE	20 October	Johnston Island
BLUEGILL TRIPLE PRIME	26 October	Johnston Island
SANTEE	27 October	Nevada Test Site
CALAMITY	27 October	Johnston Island
HOUSATONIC	30 October	Johnston Island
KINGFISH	1 November	Johnston Island
TIGHTROPE	4 November	Johnston Island
ST LAWRENCE	9 November	Nevada Test Site
GUNDI	15 November	Nevada Test Site
ANACOSTIA	27 November	Nevada Test Site See PLOWSHARE
TAUNTON	4 December	Nevada Test Site
TENDRAC	7 December	Nevada Test Site

MADISON	12 December	Nevada Test Site
NUMBAT	12 December	Nevada Test Site
MANATEE	12 December	Nevada Test Site
CASSELMAN	8 February 63	Nevada Test Site
ACUSHI	8 February	Nevada Test Site
FERRET	8 February	Nevada Test Site
HATCHIE	8 February	Nevada Test Site
CHIPMUNK	15 February	Nevada Test Site
KAWEAH	21 February	Nevada Test Site See PLOWSHARE
CARMEL	21 February	Nevada Test Site
JERBOA	1 March	Nevada Test Site
TOYAH	15 March	Nevada Test Site
GERBIL	29 March	Nevada Test Site
FERRET PRIME	5 April	Nevada Test Site
COYPU	10 April	Nevada Test Site
CUMBERLAND	11 April	Nevada Test Site
KOOTANAI	24 April	Nevada Test Site
PAISANO	24 April	Nevada Test Site
GUNDI PRIME	9 May	Nevada Test Site
DOUBLE TRACKS	15 May	Nevada Bombing Range
HARKEE	17 May	Nevada Test Site
TEJON	17 May	Nevada Test Site
STONES	22 May	Nevada Test Site
CLEAN SLATE I	25 May	Nevada Bombing Range
PLEASANT	29 May	Nevada Test Site
CLEAN SLATE II	31 May	Nevada Bombing Range
YUBA	5 June	Nevada Test Site
HUTIA	6 June	Nevada Test Site
APSHAPA	6 June	Nevada Test Site
CLEAN SLATE III	9 June	Nevada Bombing Range
MATACO	14 June	Nevada Test Site
KENNEBEC	25 June	Nevada Test Site

DONNERSCHLAG "THUNDERCLAP"

1. (GER 43) Plan for a breakout from the besieged city of Stalingrad (now Volgograd) by the ill-fated German 6th Army. This operation was canceled by Hitler who insisted that the German Air Force resupply

the garrison. This effort failed totally, leaving the 6th Army to starve under the Soviet attacks.

2. (GER 42) The breakout from Brest, France, of German ships led by the *Scharnhorst, Gneisenau,* and *Prinz Eugen* on 12 February 1942.

DOORSTOP (U.N. 53) Contingency plan to disperse jet fighters to remote locations in the event of a surprise communist air or commando attacks on South Korean air bases. Never executed. Replaced by FAST SHUFFLE plan.

DOUBLESTAR (U.S. after 49, before 63) See CHARIOTEER.

DOVE (Allied 44) The glider-borne assault conducted as part of the invasion of southern France (DRAGOON) on 15 August 1944. Over 300 gliders carried 3,000 soldiers and critical equipment to reinforce paratroopers who had already landed.

DOVECOT (GER 42) Plan for the destruction of the Toropet Salient from the north. Scheduled for late 1942. Canceled due to the demands of the Battle of Stalingrad.

DOVETAIL (Allied 42) Rehearsal for the invasion of Guadalcanal (WATCHTOWER) conducted on Fiji.

DOWNFALL (Allied 43) Overall Allied plan for the invasion of Japan to end World War II. This plan had its genesis in 1943 and the "Strategic Plan for the Defeat of Japan." It envisioned two subordinate attacks: OLYMPIC, the invasion of the southern island of Kyushu, and CORONET, the attack of the main island of Honshu. These invasions would have dwarfed the invasion of Normandy (OVERLORD) in terms of the number of troops involved, the difficulty of logistics, and projected casualties. Canceled as a result of the surrender of Japan.

DRACULA (Allied 45) Land, airborne, and amphibious attack on Rangoon by British forces. Launched 3 May 1945, the DRACULA landings included the parachute insertion of a Ghurka battalion at Elephant Point. British units converged on the city on all sides. When a Burmese unit raised by the Japanese occupation government defected, the defense came unglued. Rangoon fell without a fight, capping a 26-day campaign that had covered over 300 miles and ended the major fighting in Burma. Japanese units tried to escape on rafts down the swollen Sittang River. British air attacks and ambushes by local resistance fighters killed over 11,000 retreating Japanese. Replaced proposed invasion of Sumatra (CULVERIN). Initially called PLAN Z and then VANGUARD.

DRAGON BLANC "WHITE DRAGON"
DRAGON NOIR "BLACK DRAGON"
DRAGON ROUGE "RED DRAGON"
DRAGON VERT "GREEN DRAGON"
(U.S./BG 64) Plans for Belgian operations (supported by U.S. military and paramilitary forces) to rescue Western hostages held in the Republic of the Congo (now Zaire) by rebel forces. BLACK DRAGON (executed 26 November 1964) and RED DRAGON (executed 23 November 1964) centered on operations at Paulis and Stanleyville respectively. Plans for WHITE DRAGON (centered on Bunia) and GREEN DRAGON (centered on Watsa) were never executed. See FLAG POLE and GOLDEN HAWK.

DRAGON HAMMER (NATO 90) A NATO air-to-air training exercise conducted in May 1990 at bases in Italy. In addition to Italian units, American F-16s and A-10s deployed from as far away as Mississippi and Utah.

DRAGON HEAD (U.S. 59) American training exercise held at Fort Bragg,

North Carolina, in 1959 by the 18th Airborne Corps. The corps insignia is a blue dragon.

DRAGONSTRIKE
DRAGON STRIKE (U.S. 95) An air defense exercise conducted by the 5th Battalion, 5th U.S. Air Defense Artillery in Korea in mid-1995.

DRAGOON (Allied 44) Invasion of southern France between Toulon and Cannes executed on 15 August 1944. Originally called ANVIL, the name was changed by Churchill, who claimed to having been "dragooned" into accepting it. Over 94,000 troops and 11,000 vehicles were landed on the first day. The quick success of this invasion, with a 20-mile penetration in 24 hours, sparked a major uprising by resistance fighters in Paris (ZEPPELIN). The rapid retreat of the German 19th Army gave the resulting battle the flavor of a race up the Rhone Valley. Allied forces from DRAGOON moving northward met up with southern thrusts from Normandy (OVERLORD) near Dijon in mid-September. Included a glider landing (DOVE) and a deception (SPAN).

DRAKE (Allied 43) An early plan to conduct a strategic bombing campaign against Japan from bases in China. The aircraft were to be based in India and would fly to intermediate staging fields in China. After some maintenance and crew rest, the aircraft would continue on to targets in Japan. Abandoned in favor of MATTERHORN in the fall of 1943. Also called TWILIGHT and SETTING SUN.

DREIECK "TRIANGLE" (GER 42) An anti-partisan operation conducted (concurrently with VIERECK) in the Bryansk region of southern Russia in September 1942.

DROPSHOT (U.S. 49) A 1949 American plan for war against the Soviet Union using nuclear weapons. This plan assumed such a war would begin with the forces available on 1 January 1957; in many respects it was more an academic study than a contingency plan. The goal was to limit the spread of Soviet power beyond the Rhine. This plan was released in 1977 under the Freedom of Information Act. See TOTALITY.

DRUM ROLL (GER 42) See PAUKEN-SCHLAG.

DRYGOODS
DRY GOODS (Allied 43) Assembly of supplies in the Guadalcanal-Tulagi area to support the offensive against Japanese forces in New Georgia in February 1943.

DRYSHOD (Allied 42) Large British amphibious training exercise held in August 1942 in Scotland by troops earmarked for the invasion of North Africa (TORCH). This exercise was integrated into the SOLO deception operation.

DUALISM (U.S.) A variant of CHARIOTEER.

DUCK
1. (Allied 40) The Anglo-French naval bombardment of Stavanger, Norway, on 17 April 1940.
2. (Allied 44) Series of training exercises (DUCK I, II, and III) conducted at Slapton Sands, England, to perfect amphibious assault, support, and other techniques. Conducted in January and February 1944.

DUEL BLADE (U.S./R.V.N.) A plan to protect South Vietnam with an electronic fence (later renamed an "automated battlefield") along the Demilitarized Zone between North and South Vietnam. This plan was partially implemented with sensors being installed to detect and target ground movement through the region. See IGLOO WHITE.

DULL SWORD (U.S.) Flag-word used to designate the least severe category of incidents involving a nuclear weapon. Such an incident would include the unscheduled landing of an aircraft with a nuclear weapon, minor damage to such a weapon, or to any of its safety devices. See BENT SPEAR and BROKEN ARROW.

DUNDAS (Allied 42) Allied deception operation that used "turned" enemy agents, phony radio traffic and other means to exaggerate the size and capability of British forces in the British Isles. Part of COCKADE. See LARKHILL.

DUNLOP (Allied 41) British convoy to the island of Malta in April 1941. Followed PERPETUAL, preceded ROCKET.

DUNN (Allied 45) The evacuation of refugees by air from Griblje, Yugoslavia, in late March 1945.

DYNAMO (Allied 40) The evacuation from Dunkirk conducted from 27 May to 4 June 1940. In 9 days, 338,226 French and British soldiers were taken off the beach by a ragtag fleet of over 900 vessels. Despite the success of this operation, over 50,000 vehicles and 40,000 French troops were abandoned after a valiant rearguard action. The British also lost 235 ships of various types. The British commander, Sir Harold Alexander, was the last British soldier taken off the beach. After the French surrender, a majority of the rescued French troops returned to their homeland. See ARIEL and CYCLE.

E

E, PROJECT (U.S./U.K. 58) A secret program under which the Americans provided the British with nuclear weapons from 1958 until British-designed weapons became available. By sharing their nuclear arsenal with the U.K., the Americans gained a bomber force base close to the Soviet Union and complicated the Soviet air defense situation.

EAGER (U.S.) A reserved first word for the programs and projects of the U.S. Central Command. Examples include EAGER ANVIL, EAGER GLACIER, EAGER MACE, and EAGER SENTRY. See GALLANT.

EAGER ANVIL (U.S. 91) A planning cell built around the cadre of the U.S. Army's School for Advanced Military Studies at Fort Leavenworth. This shadow staff studied many potential ground campaigns to liberate Kuwait before developing the extremely wide northeastern swing through Iraq. This concept was refined into the actual DESERT STORM plan. Similar to CHECKMATE.

EAGER GLACIER (U.S. 87) A series of reconnaissance flights conducted covertly by the U.S. CIA over Iran beginning in July 1987. Followed by CAMEL HUMP.

EAGER MACE (U.S. 92) A "war game" conducted by U.S. Central Command in conjunction with INTRINSIC ACTION and NATIVE FURY in August 1992.

EAGER MACE 96-1 (U.S./Kuwait 95) An amphibious training exercise that included the landing of elements of the 11th Marine Expeditionary Unit from the landing ships *Juneau* and *New Orleans*.

EAGER SENTRY (U.S./Kuwait 92) Combined naval training exercises conducted in the northern Persian Gulf under a bilateral defense cooperation agreement signed in the aftermath of the Gulf War. Designated by number, the first of the series EAGER SENTRY 93-1 began on 1 November 1992.

EAGLE (GER 40) See ADLER.

EAGLE CLAW (U.S. 79) The attempted rescue of the staff of the U.S. embassy taken hostage in Tehran, Iran, by the revolutionary government of that country on 4 November 1979. The mission failed when aircraft collided on 24 April 1980 at an intermediate staging area designated "Desert One." The hostages were released after 444 days of captivity on 20 January 1981, the day President Jimmy Carter left office.

EAGLE PULL (U.S. 75) The evacuation of the remaining U.S. personnel from Phnom Penh, Cambodia, on 11 April 1975. This operation was conducted largely by naval forces based on the carrier USS *Hancock* and brought an end to American involvement in the conflict in Southeast Asia. See FREQUENT WIND and NEW LIFE.

EARDRUM (U.S. 47) The aerial mapping of Greenland by the U.S. Air Force. The most direct routes for nuclear attacks between the U.S. and the former Soviet Union lay over Greenland, Canada, and Alaska, making accurate maps critical.

EARNEST WILL (U.S. 87) The protection of Kuwaiti oil tankers by the U.S. Navy from Iranian attacks in 1987 and '88 during the Iran/Iraq War. To provide a legal justification for this operation, the Kuwaiti vessels reflagged as American ships. See PRIME CHANCE, PRAYING MANTIS.

EASEFUL (U.S. 46) The secret positioning of about 80 underground caches of arms in the American-occupied sector of Austria in the period before that country regained full independence after World War II. These stockpiles were to be used by resistance fighters in the event of a Soviet invasion of Austria. The Americans publicly revealed the program in 1996, although it was apparently known by members of the Austrian government throughout the period. See FREEBORN.

EASTERN EXIT (U.S. 91) The evacuation of the American embassy and other Westerners from Mogadishu, Somalia, conducted from 2 to 11 January 1991 by the 13th Marine Expeditionary Unit. Somalia continued its descent into anarchy, despite an international relief effort (PROVIDE RELIEF) mounted in 1992.

EASTERN EXPRESS (NATO) Routine patrols of West German and other NATO maritime aircraft to monitor Eastern European activity in the North and Baltic Seas.

EASTWIND (Allied 45) The forced repatriation of Soviet citizens interned by the Allies in Italy at the conclusion of World War II. Part of KEELHAUL.

ECLIPSE (Allied 44)

1. Plan for the initial military occupation and government of Germany in World War II.

2. Plan for an airborne assault by the Western Allies on Berlin in the event of a sudden Nazi collapse. The paratroopers would seize the city's main airports, ensuring that the Western powers would be a full player in discussions of the city's future. Never executed. See JUBILANT.

EDELWEISS (GER 42) A German attack launched near Stalingrad in August 1942. The Edelweiss is a mountain flower and traditional symbol of the Alpine regions of Germany and Austria.

EGRET (R.S.A. 85) A September 1985 ground attack by South African forces against the SWAPO faction in Angola's civil war.

EICHE "OAK" (GER 43) The rescue of the Italian dictator Mussolini by German commandos on 12 September 1943 from a hotel at Gran Sasso d'Italia. The team was commanded by Otto Skorzeny who then flew the deposed leader from captivity in an overloaded light airplane.

EIGHT BELLS 79 (U.S./R.O.K. 79) One of an annual series of combined U.S./R.O.K. exercises to test the command and control relationship between the local commander (Commander, 8th U.S. Army, Korea) and the American Joint Chiefs of Staff. Canceled. The name may be a play on "8th Army."

EILBOTE "COURIER" (Axis 41) Attack by German and Italian troops in January 1941 in the Bou Arada-Pont-du-Fahs area to capture the Kebir River Dam in central Tunisia.

EISBAER "POLAR BEAR" (GER 43)

1. German evacuation of the French island of Corsica on 3 October 1943.

2. An anti-partisan operation conducted in January 1943 in the area between Bryansk and Dmitriev, Russia.

EISENHAMMER "IRON HAMMER" (GER 44) A German program to develop remote-controlled drone bombers to hit targets in the Soviet Union. The Germans mated a manned fighter atop an unmanned bomber on the ground, the aircraft would take off together and separate before the drone would crash into its target. See APHRODITE.

ELABORATE MAZE (U.S. 89) American plan for the defense of the Panama Canal prepared in 1989. Unlike previous plans, this one assumed Panamanian forces to be neutral or hostile. Part of PRAYER BOOK. See POST TIME.

ELDER FOREST (NATO 90) A major air defense exercise conducted in late April 1990 that focused on the protection of Iceland and the British Isles.

ELDER STATESMAN (U.S. 88) Plan for the defense of the Panama Canal drawn up in April 1988. Successor to ELABORATE MAZE, succeeded by POST TIME. Never executed. Part of PRAYER BOOK.

EL DORADO CANYON (U.S. 86) The American air strike on Tripoli, Benghazi, and other targets in Libya conducted on the night of 14-15 April 1986 by 48th Tactical Fighter Wing in retaliation for a terrorist bomb planted in a Berlin nightclub by Libyan diplomatic personnel. Twelve Air Force F-111 bombers flew from bases in Great Britain using air-to-air refueling during the 7-hour flight to avoid French airspace. Fighter and electronic warfare aircraft from the aircraft carriers *America* and *Coral Sea* covered the Air Force's approach to Tripoli and hit secondary targets in Benghazi. One American aircraft was downed by ground fire, and its 2-man crew killed. Although the Americans claimed that the Libyan dictator Moammar Gahafi was not targeted, many of his usual haunts were attacked.

ELEFANT (GER 41) The January 1941 confiscation by the German Army of all trucks not essential to the civilian economy. These vehicles were used to support the attack on the Soviet Union (BARBAROSSA).

ELEPHANT

1. (GER 42) See ELEFANT.

2. (Allied 45) Attack by the Canadian 4th Armoured Division to the Maas River harbor in the Netherlands. Launched on 26 January 1945.

ELKTON (Allied 43) Series of plans designed to capture Rabaul during World War II. These plans evolved from the earlier TULSA scheme, which called for a 5-stage campaign. Eventually, ELKTON III was executed as CARTWHEEL.

ELKTON I (Allied 43) The initial revision of TULSA, dated 12 February 1943. This plan called for a massive assault by 23 Allied divisions. Never executed.

ELKTON II (Allied 43) Revision of ELKTON I based upon initial estimates of troops available.

ELKTON III (Allied 43) A revision of ELKTON II and the planning name for CARTWHEEL, the seizure of the New Britain, New Guinea, and New Ireland area. See DRYGOODS and TOENAILS.

ELOQUENT BANQUET (U.S. 87) The deployment of elements of the 18th Airborne Corps to Panama in support of BLUE SPOON/JUST CAUSE. Approved in November 1987, the reinforcement included Sheridan light tanks and Apache attack helicopters. This movement was part of a general increase in American activity in Panama that overwhelmed the ability of the Panamanians to keep track of the complex movements.

EMERY (U.S. 70) A series of 12 nuclear test conducted at the Nevada Test Site. These explosions occurred after the MANDREL series and before GROMMET. The BANEBERRY blast was notable for the 3,000,000 curies of radiation that escaped through cracks in the ground. This was the "dirtiest" acknowledged American nuclear test. The individual tests of this series were:

TIJERAS	14 October 70	prob. 94 kilotons
(Unknown)	28 October	(unknown)
ABEYTAS	5 November	prob. 11 kilotons
(Unknown)	19 November	(unknown)
ARTESIA	16 December	20-200 kilotons
CREAM	16 December	<20 kilotons
CARPETBAG	17 December	220 kilotons
BANEBERRY	19 December	10 kilotons
EMBUDO	16 June 71	18 kilotons
LAGUNA	23 June	10 kilotons
HAREBELL	24 June	prob. 10 kilotons
CAMPHOR	29 June	<20 kilotons

ENCLOSE (Allied 43) Air attacks beginning 20 March 1943 against German submarines passing through the Bay of Biscay. Although a great many submarines were spotted and attacked, only one was sunk during the 8-day operation.

END RUN (Allied 44) Attack by "Merrill's Marauders," a specially trained U.S. Army unit against Japanese rear areas in Burma. The all-volunteer unit left India on 24 February 1944 bypassing local defenders to set up roadblock in the rear. Indian troops then hit the Japanese, driving them to panic. This scenario was repeated several times, deeper and deeper into the harsh Burmese jungle. In mid-July the remnants of the unit captured the Japanese airfield at Myitkyina. The rear-echelon Japanese tried to escape down the Irrawaddy River, but were repeatedly ambushed by local fighters who killed several hundred. Removing this fighter base allowed planes flying to China over "the Hump" to use a shorter, less-dangerous route.

END SWEEP (U.S. 75) The American effort to remove naval mines planted in Vietnamese waters during the war. This operation was conducted by the U.S. as part of the Paris peace agreement.

ENHANCE
ENHANCE PLUS (U.S./R.V.N. 72) The emergency transfer of American military supplies and bases to the South Vietnamese government in advance of the cease-fire that ended American involvement in the war. Conducted in an intense month-and-a-half flurry of activity in late 1972.

ENIGMA (Allied/German) The machine used by the Germans to encrypt messages before and during World War II. By extension, the code itself and information obtained from breaking it. See ULTRA.

ENORMOUS (Allied 42) British naval bombardment of the harbor at Mersa Matruh, Egypt, on 6 August 1942. This port is located 150 miles east of the Libyan frontier.

ENTERPRISE (Allied 44) Plan to establish a string of American air bases in China to support bombing attacks on Japan. Several facilities were built, but the logistical difficulties in moving fuel, bombs, and other supplies to China from India limited the number of attacks. Capture of Pacific island bases made the bombardment of Japan much more effective. See DRAKE and MATTERHORN.

ENTERTAINMENT (Allied 43) A deception operation in support of the liberation of Sicily (HUSKY) that falsely presented a threat of an Allied landing at Keers Bay, Greece.

EPERVIER "SPARROWHAWK" (FR 86) French support to the government of Chad in their battle with Libyan-supported rebels in the northern portion of that country. On 16 February 1986, 8 Jaguar fighter bombers destroyed the rebel air base at Wadi Doum. A second attack was launched on the base on 7 January 1987. The French Foreign Legion provided ground support.

EPSOM (Allied 44) British attack to seize Caen, France. Three assaults by Canadian and Scottish units from 26 June to 1 July 1944 achieved local objective but failed to take the city despite heavy casualties. See ABERLOUR, DAUNTLESS, and WINDSOR. Followed by CHARNWOOD.

ERZENGEL "ARCHANGEL" (GER 18) Alternative plan to the HEILGER MICHAEL series. This plan called for an attack near the juncture of the British and French armies at Barisis, France, to be executed in the spring of 1918. See KAISERSCHLACHT.

ESKIMO (Allied 44) A joint American/Canadian exercise in Saskatchewan during the winter of 1944-45. The soldiers conducted a 150-mile foot march to test new cold weather equipment.

EUREKA (Allied 43) Conference between Roosevelt, Churchill, and Stalin held in Teheran from 26 November to 2 December 1943. At this meeting, Stalin announced the Soviet Union would declare war on Japan after the defeat of Germany.

EXCESS (Allied 41) A small convoy of 3 merchant ships and 5 escorts that departed Gibraltar for Alexandria on 6 January 1941. They encountered no enemy activity and arrived safely.

EXODUS (U.S./R.V.N. 54) The movement of refugees south from North Vietnam in the period immediately before the division of the country in the summer of 1954. About 1,000,000 people left the north in order to avoid communist rule. They migrated by foot, in U.S. Navy ships, and aboard an airline run by the CIA from Taiwan. Weapons, supplies, and personnel were secretly transported north in order to destabilize the new Hanoi government. Many of the refugees were Roman Catholics who became staunch supporters of the regime of the Catholic President Diem.

EXPLOIT (Allied 44) Deception plan to convince the Germans that the Allies would cross the Rhine River at Uerdingen, 15 miles south of the actual crossing point at Rheinburg.

EXPLOSION (U.S. Unofficial 62) A plan developed by General Paul Harkins, commander of U.S. forces in Vietnam in 1962 to defeat the communists. EXPLOSION was presented to General Maxwell Taylor as being a 4-phased operation, with the first two ("Planning" and "Preparation") already being complete. It envisioned a Phase III, "Execution," involving a massive military assault that would grind down the communist forces. This plan assumed the South Vietnamese would have an uninterrupted flow of resources from the U.S. and so could successfully engage the communists in a war of attrition. This plan was never adopted but it does show the outlook of some members of the U.S. military to the war in Vietnam. Little attention was paid to maneuvers, the collection of intelligence, or to civic action programs to reestablish the authority of the Saigon government over the countryside. SUNRISE, the establishment of "strategic hamlets" throughout the country, was originally part of EXPLOSION.

EXPORTER (Allied 41) Allied operations in Vichy-controlled Syria to liberate Beirut and Damascus. Launched 8 June 1941. The highlight of this operation was an overland expedition by Australian, British, and Free French troops from Palestine who conducted a wide-ranging 5-week campaign. It was during this fighting that Moshe Dayan, then a young Jewish guerrilla, lost his eye when a bullet struck the telescope he was using.

EXTENDED CAPITAL (Allied 43) See CAPITAL.

F

FA3 (U.S. 50) See FOX ABLE 3.

FABIUS (Allied 44) A series of practice exercises (FABIUS I through VI) for the invasion of northern France (OVERLORD) conducted by Allied units in Britain. Executed in early May 1944.

FADED GIANT (U.S.) American civil defense plan to deal with a major nuclear reactor accident.

FAIRLANDS (Allied 43) Deception operation that portrayed the false threat of an Allied invasion of the Balkans with forces based in Egypt. Followed by CHETTYFORD.

FAIRWINDS (US 96) Annual U.S. Atlantic Command sponsored exercise of its Fleet Marine Force units. In April 1996, units trained to conduct an emergency reinforcement of the U.S. embassy in Port au Prince, Haiti.

FALL BLAU "PLAN BLUE" (GER 42) See BLAU.

FALLEX (NATO 62) A series of NATO command post exercises that began in the autumn of 1962. FALLEXs are denominated by year (e.g., FALLEX 66) and generally focus on communications and civil-military cooperation. Often conducted simultaneously with the major CENTRAL ENTERPRISE Air Force exercise. FALLEX seems to be a contraction of "Fall Exercise."

FALL GELB "PLAN YELLOW" (GER 40) See GELB.

FALL ROT "PLAN RED" (GER 40) See ROT.

FALL SCHWARZ "PLAN BLACK" (GER 43) See SCHWARZ.

FALL WEISS "PLAN WHITE" (GER 39 and 42 respectively) See WEISS.

FAMILY JEWELS (U.S. Informal 73) A list of CIA improprieties complied by James Schlesinger when he became director of that agency in 1973.

FANDANGO (U.S. 51) A program of modifications to Tactical Air Command aircraft to allow them to carry nuclear weapons. Followed by RETAINER. Also called BACK BREAKER.

FANTASTIC (U.K.) The installation of electronic eavesdropping devices in the offices of the Soviet trade attaché in Copenhagen, Denmark, by British agents.

FAST FLY (U.S. 65) The accelerated phase-out of B-47 Stratojet bombers and KC-97 tankers from the U.S. Air Force. Scheduled to be closed out in June 1966, the action was completed by the end of 1965.

FAST SHUFFLE (U.N. 53) Plan to quickly disperse American jet fighters in the event of communist attacks on South Korean airbases. Replaced DOORSTOP.

FAUST

1. (U.S. 51) Planning name for RANGER.

2. (Allied 45) Ground transportation of food into German-occupied portions of the Netherlands in 1945. This effort was conducted in conjunction with the CHOWHOUND and MANNA airdrops to reduce the level of civilian starvation. These shipments were conducted with the permission of local German commanders.

FEDERAL EMERGENCY PLAN D (U.S. 69) The basic American civil defense plan to maintain the continuity of government and to begin recovery after a crippling nuclear strike on the U.S. This plan was first issued in 1969, revised the next year and again in 1980. See JEEP.

FEEDBACK (U.S. 52) A study conducted in 1952 by the RAND Corporation on the potential use of satellites for aerial surveillance.

FELIX (GER 41) Plan for a German/Spanish seizure of Gibraltar. Scheduled for 10 January 1941 but never executed. This plan was discussed at a meeting held between Franco and Hitler in late October 1940 in Hitler's railroad car at Hendaye, France. Hitler later said he would rather have 3 teeth extracted than to meet with Franco again. It is subject to historical debate if Franco overplayed his hand demanding too much from Hitler for Spanish entry into the war, or if he deliberately stymied the German dictator.

FERDINAND

1. (Allied 44) A deception plan, which as part of BODYGUARD, supported the invasion of Normandy (OVERLORD). This operation falsely threatened an Allied invasion along the central west coast of Italy. Other portions of BODYGUARD included IRONSIDE, JAEL, MINCEMEAT, ROYAL FLUSH, SKYE, and ZEPPELIN.

2. (Allied 42) The network of coast-watchers operating on Japanese-held islands throughout the Philippines and the South Pacific region. This system of observers consisted of civilians and some military volunteers who radioed reports on Japanese ship movements.

FERDY (Allied 43) Allied amphibious landing at Vilo Valentia, Italy, on 8 September 1943.

FERNBANK (Allied 44) A deception operation that used a number of double agents to convince the Germans the British had a secret weapon, which was most effective against deep-running submarines. It was hoped the German U-boats would run at shallower depths, exposing themselves to conventional weapons.

FEUERLAND "TIERRA DEL FUEGO" (GER 43) The movement of gold, art, and other valuables from Germany to safe havens in Argentina by submarine beginning in late 1943. This activity has led to persistent speculation that high-raking Nazis managed to escape to South America.

FIERY VIGIL (U.S. 91) The evacuation of American airmen and their families from Clark Air Force Base and the Subic Bay and Cubi Point Naval Air Stations in the Philippines following the eruption, in June 1991, of nearby Mount Pinatubo. This eruption effectively ended the American occupation of these bases.

FIREBRAND (Allied 43) Planned invasion of Ajaccio, on the French island of Corsica. Abandoned in favor of VESUVIUS.

FIREDOG (U.K./MY 48) Operations against communist infiltration in Malaya from 1948 to 1960.

FIREFLY

1. (U.N.) Night attacks by U.S. naval aircraft on targets in Korea. One set of aircraft

would illuminate the target using flares; a second set could then attack using rockets and cannon. See INSOMNIA.

2. (U.S.) Alternate name for missions flown as part of UNITED EFFORT.

FIRST LIGHTNING (S.U. 48) The first Soviet nuclear test, called JOE 1 by Western intelligence. Conducted on 29 August 1948 at the secret Semipalatinsk-21 facility, in what is now Kazakhstan. Detected in the West by RAIN BARREL. See RDS-1.

"FIRST SPECIAL AVIATION PROJECT" (Allied 42) The "Doolittle Raid" on Japan conducted by 16 U.S. Army B-25 bombers launched from the USS *Hornet* on 18 April 1942. The crews were specially trained to take off from a flight deck. Landing on the carrier was impossible so the plan called for the raiders to attack the cities of Tokyo, Yokohama, Yokosuka, Kobe, and Nagoya and then fly on to airfields in China. The attack had little physical impact, but provided a large psychological boost to the Americans and a nasty shock to the Japanese. Few of the planes landed safely, mostly due to poor navigation. See HAL PRO.

"FIR TREE" (GER 40) See TANNENBAUM.

FISCHFALLE "FISHTRAP" (GER 44) German counterattack against the Anzio beachhead on 3 February 1944. The attack failed to force the Americans into the sea, but did achieve local successes.

FISHBOWL (U.S. 62) A subset of 5 nuclear tests in the DOMINIC series conducted in near-space above Johnston Island using missiles. The tests were:

BLUEGILL	3 June 62	missile malfunctioned and destroyed in flight.
STARFISH	20 June	missile malfunctioned and destroyed in flight.
STARFISH PRIME	8 July	1.4 megatons
BLUEGILL PRIME	25 July	missile malfunctioned and destroyed on the launch pad.
BLUEGILL DOUBLE PRIME	15 October	missile malfunctioned and destroyed in flight
CHECKMATE	19 October	successful
BLUEGILL TRIPLE PRIME	26 October	successful
KINGFISH	1 November	successful
TIGHTROPE	4 November	successful

FISHTRAP (GER 44) See FISCHFALLE.

FLAG POLE (U.S. 64) Plan written in July 1964 by the U.S. Embassy in Leopoldville (Republic of the Congo, now Zaire) to rescue U.S. Counsel Michael Hoyt from insurgents. Never executed.

FLAMING DART
FLAMING DART I (U.S. 65) The first U.S. air strikes on North Vietnam. Conducted on 7 February 1965 by fighter-bombers from the aircraft carriers *Coral Sea*, *Hancock*, and *Ranger*. The original plan called for ground-based aircraft from the South Vietnamese Air Force to join in the attack on the guerrilla base at Dong Hai, 40 miles north of the Demilitarized Zone, but bad weather prevented them from taking off. President Johnson ordered the attack in retaliation for the raid on U.S. forces at Pleiku the night before. See MAYFLOWER.

FLAP (Allied 44) The parachute insertion of Captain Neville Temple of the British Army into Italy in mid-July 1944 to serve as a partisan leader. He was killed 3 months later in a traffic accident escaping German troops.

FLASH (GER 44) See BLITZ.

FLASH BURN
FLASHBURN (U.S. 54) See TREE TOP.

FLAX (Allied 43) Air operation designed to cut the air supply lines between Italy and the Axis troops in Tunis. Conducted in

April 1943 this interdiction operation led to the 18 April "Palm Sunday Massacre" in which the U.S. 9th Air Force attacked over 100 Ju-52 tri-motored transports over Cape Bon loaded with soldiers escaping the VULCAN attack. Over half the transports were destroyed. See RETRIBUTION.

FLEETWOOD (U.S. 48) A plan for an American nuclear attack on the Soviet Union prepared in response to the Berlin blockade which began in June 1948. A variation of CHARIOTEER, this plan assumed a war would begin about 31 December 1948. The Soviet rail system was a prime target. While CHARIOTEER had many aspects of an academic study, FLEETWOOD was an actual contingency plan. Never executed.

FLIGHT (Zionist 45) The movement of Jews from post-war Europe to Palestine in violation of British policy. In some cases official-looking uniforms and documents capitalized on the confused post-war situation to allow refugees to commandeer Allied transportation.

FLINTLOCK

1. (Allied 44) The invasion of Kwajalein Atoll in the Marshall Islands. This attack sank a large number of Japanese ships and stripped the air base at Truk of its offensive potential. With Truk neutralized, it could be bypassed, forgoing a costly invasion. Executed on 31 January 1944, Kwajalein fell on 7 February after stiff Japanese resistance. See ELKTON.

2. (U.S. 65) A series of 40 nuclear tests conducted with one exception at the Nevada Test Site. These tests followed WHETSTONE and were in turn followed by LATCHKEY. The RED HOT test was notable for the release of 1,000,000 curies of radioactivity, which drifted as far as eastern Iowa. The individual test shots were:

BRONZE	23 July 65	prob. 60 kilotons
MAUVE	6 August	prob. 18 kilotons
CENTAUR	27 August	<20 kilotons
SCREAMER	1 September	prob. 12 kilotons
CHARCOAL	10 September	20-200 kilotons
ELKHART	17 September	<20 kilotons
LONG SHOT	29 October	80 kilotons, near Amchitka, Alaska
SEPIA	12 November	<20 kilotons
CORDUROY	3 December	prob. 100 kilotons
EMERSON	16 December	<20 kilotons
BUFF	16 December	prob. 36 kilotons
MAXWELL	13 January 66	<20 kilotons
LAMPBLACK	18 January	prob. 36 kilotons
DOVEKIE	21 January	<20 kilotons
PLAID II	3 February	prob. 32 kilotons
REX	24 February	19 kilotons
RED HOT	5 March	<20 kilotons
FINFOOT	7 March	<20 kilotons
CLYMER	12 March	<20 kilotons
PURPLE	18 March	<20 kilotons
TEMPLAR	24 March	<20 kilotons, see PLOWSHARE
LIME	1 April	<20 kilotons
STUTZ	6 April	<20 kilotons
TOMATO	7 April	<20 kilotons
DURYEA	14 April	70 kilotons
PIN STRIPE	25 April	prob. 4 kilotons
TRAVELER	4 May	<20 kilotons
CYCLAMEN	5 May	12 kilotons
CHARTREUSE	6 May	73 kilotons
TAPESTRY	12 May	<20 kilotons
PIRANHA	13 May	prob. 100 kilotons
DUMONT	19 May	prob. 190 kilotons
DISCUS THROWER	27 May	22 kilotons
PILE DRIVER	2 June	62 kilotons
TAN	3 June	prob. 140 kilotons
PUCE	10 June	<20 kilotons
DOUBLE PLAY	15 June	<20 kilotons
KANKAKEE	15 June	20-200 kilotons
VULCAN	25 June	25 kilotons, see PLOWSHARE
HALFBREAK	30 June	365 kilotons

FLIT (Allied 44) A training exercise conducted in England by the Canadian 1st Army and the Royal Air Force's 84th Group in May 1944.

FLOATING CHRYSANTHEMUMS (JPN 45) The Japanese kamikaze defense of Okinawa from the American invasion (ICEBERG). Part of the overall TEN ICHI plan. Okinawa is an integral part of Japan, so the same methods were used to defend it as would have been used had the Americans been forced to invade the home islands (DOWNFALL). Over 350 aircraft and pilots were used in a massive series of attacks that destroyed over 30 American ships; another 300 were damaged.

FLORESCENCE (IS 70) Air attacks on air bases, troops, and other targets deep inside Egypt launched on 7 January 1970. These attacks were designed to force the Nasser regime to halt the War of Attrition. Instead, the Egyptians turned to the Soviet Union for massive amounts of defense aid. This reduced Egyptian flexibility in dealing with the Israelis, other Arab countries, and the U.S. Also called PRICHA.

FOAL EAGLE (U.S./R.O.K. 95) An annual combined American/South Korean port defense exercise.

FOCUS (IS 67) See MOKED.

FOCUSED DISPATCH (U.S. 95) An "Advanced Warfighting Exercise" conducted at Fort Knox, Kentucky, in mid-1995. This exercise equipped soldiers with experimental and prototype equipment in order to see how advances in communications, sensing, and computing would impact future operations.

FOOTLIGHTS (Allied 40) Blockade of the Vichy-controlled French West Indies.

FORAGER (U.S. 44) U.S. invasion in the Marianas Islands (Guam, Saipan, and Tinian) to secure bases for B-29 attacks on the Japanese home islands. The amphibious assault on Saipan was conducted on 15 June 1944. The Japanese launched a carrier-based counterattack, resulting in the massacre of their young pilots in the "Great Marianas Turkey Shoot," more formally called the Battle of the Philippine Sea. The Japanese lost 3 carriers and 400 planes. Only a few of the 24,000 Japanese defenders on the island were captured; large numbers of local civilians threw themselves and their children off high cliffs rather than be captured. The liberation of Guam was achieved on 21 July 1944. Part of GRANITE and GRANITE II.

FORD I
FORD II
FORD III (Allied 42) A series of amphibious training exercise held by Canadian troops earmarked for the JUBILEE raid.

FOREMOST (Allied 44) An Allied submarine wolfpack that was deployed in March 1944 to bottle up the German battlecruiser *Tirpitz* in Norway.

FORTITUDE (Allied 44) Part of BODYGUARD, the overall deception operations in support of the invasion of northern France (OVERLORD). FORTITUDE had 2 subelements: FORTITUDE NORTH and FORTITUDE SOUTH. FORTITUDE NORTH was a mostly-British effort that falsely depicted a threat of an invasion of Scandinavia by forces in Scotland (see TINDALL). The key portion of FORTITUDE SOUTH was QUICKSILVER, which depicted a fictitious "1st U.S. Army Group" commanded by George Patton aimed at invading France at the Pas de Calais (see STARKEY).

FOX (Allied 44) Last major invasion rehearsal before the invasion of Normandy (OVERLORD), conducted by U.S. 5th Corps in March 1944.

FOX ABLE 3 (U.S. 50) The movement of 180 F-84E Thunderjet fighters of the 27th Fighter Escort Wing from Texas to Furstenfeldbruck, Germany, conducted in September and October 1950. "FOX ABLE 3" is a phonetic pronunciation of "FA3." See FOX PETER 1, FOX PETER 2, and LONGSTRIDE.

FOX PETER 1 (U.S. 52) The deployment of 58 F-84G Thunderjet fighters of the 31st Fighter Escort Wing from Turner Air Force Base, Georgia to Misawa and Chitose, Japan in July 1952. This was the first large deployment of fighters using air-to-air refueling to fly from California to Hawaii. The jets then hopped from island to island across the Pacific to complete their journey. See LONGSTRIDE.

FOX PETER 2 (U.S. 52) The deployment of 75 F-86G Thunderjet fighters from Bergstrom Air Force Base, Texas, to Misawa, Japan, in early October 1952. This operation allowed the 31st Fighter Escort Wing (see FOX PETER I) to be relieved by the 27th Fighter Escort Wing. See LONGSTRIDE.

FOYNES (Allied 44) Allied deception that attempted to mislead the Germans as to the location and capabilities of Allied amphibious forces in Europe. In early 1944, over 70 landing craft were moved from the Mediterranean to the British Isles to support the OVERLORD invasion of northern France. This deception attempted to convince the Germans that the vessels were damaged and were being returned for extensive repairs.

FRANCIS MARION (U.S. 66) One of a series of American search-and-destroy operations conducted in Vietnam in 1966. Together these operations killed a great many of the local Viet Cong and so increased the proportion of North Vietnamese regulars arrayed against the Americans and South Vietnamese. Francis Marion was a guerrilla leader in the American War for Independence.

FRANKTON (Allied 42) British commando raid on shipping at the mouth of the Gironde River near Bordeaux, France, in December 1942. The strike force made their approach in canoes that were carried to the area by the British submarine HMS *Tuna*.

FRANTIC (Allied 44) Raids conducted by American bombers based in Britain or the Mediterranean, which then landed in Ukraine. This shuttle bombing technique complicated the defense of German targets. Originally, this program was to lead to establishing 3 heavy bomber groups in Soviet territory permanently. Only 7 missions were actually flown and only a small contingent of U.S. troops were based on the Eastern Front. The first mission was designated FRANTIC JOE. See BELLICOSE.

FRANTIC JOE (Allied 44) The first bombing raid of the FRANTIC series, conducted on 2 June 1944. American bombers flew from bases in southern Italy attacking Debrecen en route to Soviet airfields at Focsani. This attack supported Red Army operations, which in turn neatly coincided with the OVERLORD invasion. A German spotter plane located the American aircraft, which were quickly attacked on the ground by the German Air Force. Concerns raised by this effective German air raid derailed plans to maintain a large force of American bombers in the Soviet Union permanently. The name FRANTIC JOE was changed to FRANTIC to avoid any possible reference to Joseph Stalin, the Soviet dictator.

FREDERICUS

FREDERICUS I (GER 42) The German attack into Ukraine launched on 18 May 1942. This assault tore a 50-mile gap in Soviet lines and eventually led to the encirclement of 4 Soviet armies.

FREDERICUS II (GER 43) The main stage of BLAU. The Soviets upset BLAU by attacking first, on 12 May 1943, which began the Battle of Kursk. FREDERICUS II was launched on 28 June as a counterattack. The resulting encirclement captured 239,000 Soviet prisoners and 1,240 tanks. See ZITADELLE.

FREEBORN (Allied 44) Plan by the Western Allies to partition and govern Austria after World War II. See EASEFUL.

FREEDOM (Allied 44) The rescue of over 300 Allied prisoners held in Bulgaria in the fall of 1944. The prisoners were moved by air through Turkey and Egypt to Italy.

FREEDOM BANNER 95 (U.S./R.O.K. 95) A joint American/South Korean amphibious exercise conducted along the east coast of Korea in July and August 1995.

FREEDOM TRAIN (U.S. 72) Following the ROLLING THUNDER offensive that ended on 31 October 1968, the U.S. observed a moratorium on air attacks on North Vietnam. This unilateral action continued until the LINEBACKER strikes, which began on 8 May 1972. FREEDOM TRAIN and DEEP PROUD ALPHA were the only two exceptions to this general policy. DEEP PROUD ALPHA attacked targets in North Vietnam from 26 to 30 December 1971 and FREEDOM TRAIN attacks were conducted from 6 April to 7 May 1972.

FREEZE (Allied 45) Local defense along the Senio River in Italy conducted in January 1945 by Indian troops.

FREQUENT WIND (U.S. 75) The evacuation of the remaining U.S. personnel and selected Vietnamese from Saigon on 29 and 30 April 1975. This operation was conducted largely by naval forces based on the carrier USS *Hancock*. A number of U.S. Air Force flights (BABYLIFT) were conducted during this period carrying "Amerasian" children out of the country. One of these crashed on takeoff killing the evacuees and the crew. See EAGLE PULL and NEW LIFE.

FRESH APPROACH (U.S. 57) The third and final exercise conducted by the Strategic Air Command to develop and refine organizations, techniques, and procedures needed to keep one-third of its aircraft on alert at all times. This exercise was conducted by the 9th Air Wing in September 1957; it followed TRY OUT and WATCHTOWER.

FRESHMAN (Allied 42) The first attempt to destroy the Vermork-Rjuked nitrate factory in Rjuked, Norway. The plant was the largest producer of heavy water in Europe. Heavy water was needed to modulate reactors that could produce material needed for an atomic bomb. A small pathfinder team (SWALLOW) jumped into Norway on the night of 18 October. Two gliders full of Norwegian commandos (GROUSE) attempted to find the landing zone, but got lost in bad weather. Both gliders crashed and their teams were killed. The SWALLOW team was not detected and later linked up with GUNNERSIDE team that attacked the factory.

FRICTION (CN 90) Canadian naval participation in DESERT STORM and DESERT SHIELD. The Canadians contributed 2 destroyers and a supply ship. Canadian air and ground units sent to support the international effort were called SCIMITAR.

FRIENDSHIP PROJECT (Allied 42) Program that established a string of weather observation stations throughout remote areas of China.

FRIO TEJAS "COLD TEXAS" (U.S. 96) American anti-smuggling sweep that culminated in 15 arrests in January 1996. This operation was the first major law-enforcement effort aimed at contraband chlorofluorocarbons (CFCs). These chemicals were banned in the U.S. in the mid-1990s but were still available in Mexico. Smugglers brought canisters of the banned refrigerant into the U.S. to be used to recharge automobile air-conditioning systems.

FRITZ (GER) Early name during planning for the invasion of the Soviet Union (BARBAROSSA). Named by Colonel Bernhard von Lossberg, who drafted the plan, after his son.

FROLIC (U.S.) An early American plan for nuclear war with the Soviet Union. This was one of a series of plans developed by Strategic Air Command. Others were: HALF MOON, BROILER, GRABBER, DOUBLESTAR, TROJAN, OFF TACKLE, SHAKEDOWN, and CROSS PIECE. Eventually, these plans were superseded by a series of numbered Single Integrated Operations Plans (SIOPs), the first of which was named DROPSHOT.

FRONT BURNER (U.S.) A flag-word used in electronic communications to highlight messages that report any incident that might result in war. See NUCFLASH.

FROSTBITE (U.S. 46) Operations by the carrier *Midway* and other ships in the Arctic during the winter of 1946. This exercise tested techniques for extreme cold weather operations. Operations in the Arctic became more important in the post-war era as U.S.-Soviet tensions increased.

FROZEN BANANA BELT (U.S./CN 55) See BANANA BELT.

FRÜHLING "SPRING" (GER 44) Large antipartisan operation in the Jura Mountains surrounding Gex and Oyonnax, France, beginning on 7 April 1944. Six regiments of German troops, supplemented by a regiment of turncoat Soviets, conducted the sweep.

FRÜHLINGSERWACHEN "SPRING AWAKENING" (GER 45) An abortive German attack in northern Hungary launched on 5 March 1945 to turn away Soviet spearheads directed at Vienna. The assault was plagued by shortages of manpower and fuel. Exceptionally muddy conditions further limited the mobility of the attackers who accomplished little.

FRÜHLINGSWIND "SPRING WIND" (Axis 43) Last Axis offensive in Tunisia. Executed 14 February 1943 by the battered remnants of 5th Panzer Army against British positions at Sidi Bou Zid.

FU GO (JPN 44) A series of air attacks launched by the Japanese on the continental U.S. beginning in November 1944. Large balloons were released from the Home Islands carrying incendiary bombs. The goal was to start massive fires in the forests of the Pacific Northwest, but little damage was actually done.

FUERTAS CAMINOS "BLAZING TRAILS" (U.S. 85) Exercises involving U.S. Army engineers building roads and conducting incidental humanitarian relief operations in various Latin American countries. These exercises are designated by year and nation as in "FUERTAS CAMINOS 92 (HONDURAS)." The work in this program was generally performed by National Guard engineer battalions who spent their annual 2-week training period overseas. The road between the Aguan and Yoro Valleys in Honduras was begun in 1985 and completed in 1992. Other exercises in this series were conducted in Peru and Panama.

FULCRUM (U.S. 76) A series of 11 underground nuclear tests conducted at the Nevada Test Site. This series followed ANVIL and preceded CRESCENT. The individual shots of this test were:

CHEVRE	23 November 76	<20 kilotons
REDMUD	8 December	<20 kilotons

ASIAGO	21 December	<20 kilotons
RUDDER	28 December	20-150 kilotons
MARSILLY	5 April 77	20-150 kilotons
BULKHEAD	27 April	20-150 kilotons
CREWLINE	25 May	20-150 kilotons
STRAKE	4 August	20-150 kilotons
SCANTLING	19 August	20-150 kilotons
EBBTIDE	15 September	<20 kilotons
COULOM-MIERS	27 September	20-150 kilotons

FULLER (Allied 42) British interdiction of major German warships attempting to transit the English Channel. Convinced of an imminent British invasion of Norway, Hitler ordered the cruisers *Prinz Eugen, Scharnhorst,* and *Gneisenau* to return to Germany from France (ZERBERUS). Despite espionage reports of the planned departure time, the British were caught off guard by the nighttime departure of the flotilla from Brest on 12 February 1942. The British attacks throughout the next day were piecemeal and uncoordinated. The *Scharnhorst* and *Gneisenau* were slightly damaged, at a cost of 71 aircraft lost to the heavy German fighter cover. This episode was called the "Channel Dash" in the British press.

FULL FLOW (NATO 84) The deployment of 35,000 American troops to Germany by air in 1984.

FULL HOUSE (Allied 44) One of a series of fighter-bomber sweeps through Normandy after the invasion of northern France (OVERLORD). These attacks were designed to catch German units in the open as they moved to counterattack the invading force. See STUD and ROYAL FLUSH.

FURTIVE BEAR (U.S. 92) Anti-drug missions flown by U.S. Air Force aircraft throughout Latin America. On 24 April 1992 an American C-130 Hercules equipped with electronic monitoring equipment was fired on by 2 Peruvian Su-22 Fitter interceptors. The Peruvians claimed the American plane had strayed from its agreed-upon flight path. One crewman was killed but the C-130 was able to land safely.

FUSILEER (U.S. 83) A series of 16 underground nuclear tests conducted at the Nevada Test Site. The principal blast of this series was designated CORREO, testing a W-84 20-kilotons cruise missile warhead to confirm its reliability. This series followed PHALANX and preceded GRENADIER. Four explosions detected outside the test site have never been publicly admitted. The individual shots of this series were:

(Unknown)	9 December 83	(unknown)
ROMANO	16 December	20-150 kilotons
GORBEA	31 January 84	20-150 kilotons
MIDAS-MYTH/MILAGRO	15 February	<20 kilotons
TORTUGAS	1 March	20-150 kilotons
AGRINI	31 March	<20 kilotons
MUNDO	1 May	20-150 kilotons
(Unknown)	2 May	(unknown)
(Unknown)	16 May	(unknown)
CAPROCK	31 May	20-150 kilotons
DUORO	20 June	20-150 kilotons
(Unknown)	12 July	(unknown)
KAPPELI	25 July	20-150 kilotons
CORREO	2 August	<20 kilotons
DOLCETTO	30 August	<20 kilotons
BRETON	13 September	20-150 kilotons

FUSILLADE (Allied 44) The occupation of Dieppe, France, by Canadian troops on 1 September 1944. See JUBILEE.

FUSTIAN (Allied 43) Airborne assault by British paratroops to seize and hold Primrose Bridge, south of Mount Etna, Italy, until relieved by the main HUSKY invasion force. Executed on 14 July 1943.

G

GABEL ADDER (U.S.) Plan maintained by the U.S. Special Operations Command to rescue American hostages or capture foreign leaders anywhere in the world using a small force of highly-trained soldiers. Never executed, but served as the basis for NIFTY PACKAGE.

GAIN (Allied 44) Parachute insertion of a Special Air Service unit near Orleans, France, in June 1944 to support the OVER-LORD invasion. The group was captured on 4 July after successfully interdicting German supply lines. After over a month of torture, most of the prisoners were shot. Only one of the team survived. After the war, the commander of the German unit, Josef Kieffer, was tried and executed.

GALAHAD (Allied 44) The radio call sign of "Merrill's Marauders" as they conducted the END RUN attack.

GALLANT (U.S.) A first word used to designate training exercises conducted by the U.S. Central Command and its predecessor the Rapid Deployment Force in the California desert. Individual exercises are designated by name and year number. Examples are GALLANT EAGLE 84 and GALLANT KNIGHT 88. See EAGER.

GALLANT EAGLE 84 (U.S. 84) A U.S. Central Command exercise conducted from 4 to 12 September 1984 in California. The largest military exercise conducted in the U.S. since 1962.

GALLANT KNIGHT 81 (U.S. 80) A command post exercise conducted at Fort Bragg, North Carolina, by U.S. Central Command from 23 to 30 October 1980.

GALVANIC (Allied 43) The invasion of Makin, Tarawa, and Abemana in the Gilbert Islands secure them as bases for future operations. "Dog Day" for the main attack on Tarawa was 20 November 1943. The invasion involved the largest fleet assembled anywhere in the world up to that time, including a dozen aircraft carriers, 13 battleships, 8 heavy and 4 light cruisers, and 70 destroyers and destroyer escorts. The largest town on the atoll, Makin, fell 3 days later. The enormous losses inflicted on the attackers by the outnumbered Japanese caused the U.S. to rework its amphibious doctrine, adopting specialized tracked landing craft to move troops safely through coral shallows.

GAMBIT (Allied 44) A sub-pan of NEP-TUNE, the naval portion of the invasion of northern France (OVERLORD). This involved two midget submarines who marked the extreme left and right limits of the British and Canadian invasion beaches with navigation lights and flags.

GAME WARDEN (U.S.) The general U.S. Navy term for "brown-water" operations in the Mekong River in Vietnam.

GAMMA GILT
GAMMA GOAT
GAMMA GYRO
GAMMA DELTA (U.S. 69) A series of National Security Agency interception operations directed against foreign and domestic targets conducted during the Vietnam-war era. Although illegal, the Agency monitored the telephone, mail, and other communications of identified left-wing radicals within the U.S. Tom Hayden, Jane Fonda, and Cora Weiss were among the Americans who were monitored.

GANGWAY (Allied 44) Plan for an unopposed invasion of the Italian mainland at the beaches just north of Naples in the event of an Italian collapse. See BARRACUDA. Never executed.

GARDEN (Allied 44) Ground portion of MARKET-GARDEN. On 17 September 1944 the 1st Allied Airborne Corps landed an airborne division on each of 3 bridges behind German defenses (MARKET). GARDEN was a ground attack by the British 30th Corps to relieve the paratroops guarding the critical bridges. The 2 American divisions were relieved as planned, but the British unit was stranded when GARDEN stalled against unexpectedly stiff German resistance.

GARDENING (Allied 44) Aerial mining of the Danube River near Belgrade which began on 8 April 1944. These attacks disrupted the movement of oil-bearing barges from the facilities at Ploesti, Rumania.

GARDEN PLOT (U.S.) Contingency plan for the use of U.S. Army units to control civil disturbances within the U.S. See GROWN TALL.

GATEKEEPER (U.S. Law Enforcement 95) Adoption of the border-control tactics developed in BLOCKADE near San Diego, California.

GAUNTLET (Allied 41) Raid by British, Canadian, and Norwegian commandos on the Norwegian island of Spitzbergen, north of the Arctic Circle to destroy German port facilities and naval stores. An additional objective was the rescue of over 2,000 Soviet citizens and some Allied prisoners. Executed on 27 August 1941.

GAZELLE (IS 73) Attack across the Suez Canal by Israeli forces on 16 October 1973. This operation threatened the Egyptian city of Ismailia and outflanked the entire Egyptian 3rd Army. Egyptian counterattacks on the northern flank of this thrust resulted in the Battle of the Chinese Farm. A cease-fire took effect on 24 October, with some Israeli forces west of the canal, and some Egyptian units trapped in the east.

GERBOISE BLEUE "BLUE JERBOA" (FR 60) The first French nuclear test conducted at Reggane, Algeria. A jerboa is a large desert rodent.

GELB "YELLOW" (GER 40) The German invasion of France and the Low Countries in World War II. Executed 10 May 1940. German armored units punched through the Ardennes, outflanking the Maginot Line, and unhinging the Allied defenders. France fell in less than a month. Much of the British army was able to escape in a series of evacuations (ARIEL, DYNAMO). The French Republic collapsed and was replaced by "Etat Français" headed by Marshall Henri Pétain. His government based in Vichy became a loyal partner of the Axis for the rest of the war. Included ROT.

GEM (U.S. 47) Part of SADDLETREE, the modification of B-29 bombers as tanker aircraft (SUPERMAN) and delivery aircraft (RURALIST) to support the early, very large nuclear weapons. See SILVERPLATE.

GEMSTONE (U.S. Political 71) The overarching plan for political intelligence and "dirty tricks" designed to ensure the reelection of President Richard Nixon. This plan contained a number of potential operations that were aimed at the Democratic Party. Initial planning included the possibility of electronic eavesdropping, burglaries, and the sabotage of the air conditioner at the Democratic convention. The overall objective was to discredit the Democratic Party and to damage the campaigns of potential strong Democratic candidates. A similar operation was planned as SANDWEDGE by Jack Caulfield but was not approved. GEMSTONE was planned by Howard Hunt. The most infamous portion of this plan was the break-in of the National Democratic headquarters at the Watergate.

GENERAL DEVELOPMENT TRUST (U.S. 41 or so) An American attempt in the late 1940s to control the world supply of uranium and other nuclear materials. Much of this effort went into securing contracts for high-grade ore from the Belgian Congo. This effort failed when it drove the price of these ores up, which in turn increased production. Replaced the name MURRAY HILL AREA.

GENERALPLAN OST "GENERAL PLAN EAST" (GER 41) Political plan to deport or murder the populations of Eastern Europe in order to open the area for "Germanic" settlers.

GEORG "GEORGE" (GER 18) A planned attack on British positions in Flanders during World War I in support of the HEILGER MICHAEL offensives. Replaced the earlier HEILGER GEORG plan, replaced by GEORGETTE. Never executed. See KAISERSCHLACHT.

GEORGETTE (GER 18) A much-reduced version of the GEORG plan. This attack was launched too late in World War I and with too few troops to effectively support HEILGER MICHAEL. The final objective was the rail center of Hazebrouck, although Ludendorff may have intended to continue the drive to the sea. These attacks (GEORGETTE and HEILGER MICHAEL), forced the British Expeditionary Force into a difficult battle on a wide front. Finally, on 19 April, French reinforcements arrived in time to relieve the over-extended British forces. Executed from 9 to 29 April 1918. See KAISERSCHLACHT.

GIANT

1. GIANT I (Allied 43) Plan for an airborne and air-landing assault along the Volturno River. Never executed.

2. GIANT II (Allied 43) Plan for airborne attack centered on the 3 airfields north of Rome. Aircraft were actually loaded on 8 September 1943 to carry the soldiers to Rome, but the operation was canceled at the last minute. Complex political considerations revolving around the ability of the Italians to provide promised assistance played a major role in the cancellation.

3. (U.S.) A reserved first word for nicknames that designate the programs and projects of the U.S. Air Force's former Strategic Air Command. See GIANT ELK and GIANT PATRIOT.

GIANT ELK (U.S. 62) The program for the maintenance and operation of the fleet of SR-71 Blackbird aircraft. The SR-71 was in operation with the U.S. Air Force from 1962 to 1990.

GIANT PATRIOT (U.S. 65) Plan to fire an instrumented Minuteman II missile from an operational silo in the U.S. to the Pacific Test Range. Quashed by Congress in July 1974. See LONG LIFE.

GIBBON (Allied 43) Alternate name for SLAPSTICK.

GLASS (U.S.) A reserved first word for the programs and projects of the U.S. Air Force's former Strategic Air Command.

GLIMMER (Allied 44) Deception plan in support of the invasion of northern France (OVERLORD). In order to convince the Germans the invasion at Normandy was a feint, electronic devices and strips of aluminum foil were used to portray the illusion of a fleet off the coast of Boulogne.

GLOBAL SHIELD (U.S.) Annual readiness conducted by the former Strategic Air Command. These exercises were designated by number (e.g. GLOBAL SHIELD 79) and simulated a period of tension culminating in a nuclear attack on the U.S.

GLOBETROTTER (Allied 44) The capture of Sansapor on the north coast of New Guinea by Allied forces on 30 June 1944. This operation closed out major combat on the island.

GO (JPN) The general Japanese word for "plan."

GOBLET (Allied 43) Planned invasion of Italy at Cotrone. Never executed; abandoned in favor of BRIMSTONE.

GOLD (U.S./U.K. 54) A joint operation conducted by the U.S. CIA and the British Secret Intelligence Service to tap into landline communication of the Soviet Army headquarters in Berlin using a tunnel into the Soviet-occupied zone. This was a much more complex variation of the earlier SILVER project. The covert construction of a 1,476-foot tunnel 20 feet under the world's most heavily patrolled border to intersect a series of cables less than 18 inches below a busy street was an exceptional engineering challenge. Work began in August 1954 and was completed on 25 February the following year. The tunnel entrance was concealed as a new CIA radio intercept site. Spoil was stored in warehouses built for the purpose. The intercepts were not decoded, but were read in plain text due to an electronic echo produced by the Soviet equipment. Interestingly, the Soviet knew of the tunnel due to George Blake, a "mole" in the British intelligence apparatus. To protect this operative, and thinking their codes were secure, the Soviets allowed the tunnel to operate until 21 April 1956 when the tunnel was dramatically "discovered" by an outraged Soviet commander who showed it to the world's press. Directly under the border was a steel door marked "Entry Forbidden by the Commanding General." The tunnel was hailed throughout the free world as an engineering triumph.

GOLDEN CARGO (U.S. 91) Annual training exercise for American Army Reserve and National Guard logistic units. Soldiers move actual wartime tonnage of ammunition and other supplies and equipment under the control of Army Reserve Theater Army Commands.

GOLDEN EAGLE

1. (U.S. 69) Plan for American special forces, Thai government forces, and various tribal elements to harass North Vietnamese supply routes in Laos during 1969. Never executed.

2. (U.K. 88) An around-the-world flight by 4 Royal Air Force Tornado interceptors conducted from 21 August to 26 October 1988. En route, the aircraft participated in exercises in the U.S., Australia, Malaysia, and Thailand.

GOLDEN EYE (Allied 40) British contingency plan to seal off and defend Gibraltar in the event of Spain entering the war on the side of the Axis powers. FELIX was the German plan to capture the colony. Never executed.

GOLDEN HAWK (U.S. 64) 1964 plan for a unilateral rescue of Westerners from Zaire (then the Congo), which was racked by civil war. Never executed. See DRAGON BLANC, DRAGON NOIR, DRAGON ROUGE, DRAGON VERT, and FLAG POLE.

GOLDEN PHEASANT (U.S. 87) Emergency deployment of American troops to Honduras as a show of force as a result of threatening actions by the forces of the (then Socialist) Nicaraguans.

GOLDEN THRUST 88 (U.S. 87) The largest peacetime test of mobilization procedures conducted by the U.S. during the Cold War. Executed from 6 to 22 November 1987 by over 24,000 reservists in New England and the Mid-Atlantic region.

GOLDFLAKE (Allied 44) The transfer of Canadian 1st Corps from the Mediterranean to England in preparation for the invasion of northern France (OVERLORD). See PENKNIFE.

GOMORRAH (Allied 43) Allied air attacks on Hamburg, Germany, conducted from 24 to 30 July 1943. Over 3,000 aircraft were involved. In the climatic attack on the night of 28 July 1943, the bombers dropped over 2,326 tons of bombs, a high percentage of which were incendiaries. Weather conditions and the depletion of the city's fire services provided the conditions for a "firestorm." The winds were strong enough to uproot trees and suck the air from underground shelters. That night over 42,000 people were killed, more than the number of British casualties during the entire "Blitz." The entire series of raids destroyed 277,330 housing units. Despite the massive destruction, in a few weeks industrial production had reach pre-attack levels.

GOODWOOD

1. (Allied 44) Attempt by British forces to break out from the Normandy beachhead toward Paris. Preceded by an extraordinarily heavy carpet bombing centered on the French city of Caen. The bombardment killed over 3,000 Frenchmen. This followup to the failed CHARNWOOD attack began on 18 July 1944. The British assault inadvertently served as a supporting attack for the successful American breakthrough (COBRA) on 31 July. This heavy fighting depleted German forces in France and so contributed to the rapid Allied advance through that country. See ATLANTIC, BLUECOAT.

2. GOODWOOD I.

GOODWOOD II
GOODWOOD III (Allied 44) A series of carrier-borne air attacks against the German battleship *Tirpitz* in its harbor at Kaafjord during August 1944. GOODWOOD I and II were canceled due to poor weather. GOODWOOD III was conducted on 24 August with 77 aircraft flying off HMS *Formidable*, *Furious*, *Emperor*, *Searcher*, and *Pursuer*. Two bombs hit the target, but one 1,600 pounder crashed through 8 decks and failed to explode. The British lost 4 aircraft; the *Tirpitz* was crippled and never moved again under her own power. She was towed to Tromso to be used as a coast defense battery. She was sunk there by Royal Air Force Lancaster bombers on 12 November 1944. See TUNGSTEN.

GOOSE (U.N. 51) Armored raid conducted on 13 June 1951 by elements of the U.S. 3rd Infantry Division from its defensive line near Chorwon to Pyongyang. The area was believed to be heavily defended, so the raid was designed to collect intelligence and prevent a communist attack. In fact the "Iron triangle" has largely been abandoned, apparently in an attempt to avoid American firepower.

GRABBER (U.S.) An early American plan for nuclear war with the Soviet Union. This was one of a series of plans developed by Strategic Air Command. Others were: HALF MOON, BROILER, FROLIC, DOUBLESTAR, TROJAN, OFF TACKLE, SHAKEDOWN, and CROSS PIECE. Eventually, these plans were superseded by a series of numbered Single Integrated Operations Plans (SIOPs), the first of which was named DROPSHOT.

GRAFFHAM (Allied 44) A deception plan in support of the invasion of northern France (OVERLORD). This operation depicted the threat of an Allied invasion of central Norway in 1944. Part of BODYGUARD.

GRANBY (U.K. 91) British participation in the defense of Saudi Arabia (DESERT SHIELD) and the liberation of Kuwait (DESERT STORM).

GRANITE (Allied 44) Plan for operations in the central Pacific region drawn up in January 1944 to cover that entire year. It included a series of amphibious assaults via the Marshall Islands, the Carolines, including Truk, and the Marianas, eventually leading to a link-up with MacArthur's forces in the Philippines. See RENO III.

GRAPES OF WRATH (IS 96) The Israeli attack into south Lebanon in April 1996. Israel had declared that region to be part of a "Security Zone." The weak central government of Lebanon allowed militant Iranian-inspired Arabs to establish bases that repeatedly shelled Israel. On 11 April, Israeli forces launched a series of air and artillery strikes aimed at destroying the bases of these attackers. Using reconnaissance drone aircraft and elaborate counter-battery radars, the Israelis quickly identified and hit terrorist positions. Many of these targets were in populated areas and the attacks forced many from their homes. A U.N. base packed with refugees was deliberately targeted by repeated attacks that killed many civilians. The Israelis purposely fired into the protected area, killing and wounding a large number of civilians.

GRAPHIC HAND (U.S.) Contingency plan to use military personnel to deliver mail in the event of nationwide postage strike.

GRAPPLE

1. (U.K. 57) A series of 9 open-air nuclear tests conducted from May 1957 to September 1958 at Christmas Island. Both nuclear and thermonuclear weapons were tested but the size and dates of these blasts remain classified. One of these tests has been referred to as GAPPLE1/SHORT GRANITE and another as GRAPPLE Z. Followed ANTLER. See E.

2. (U.K. 93) Royal Air Force participation in operations over Bosnia-Hersegovina as part of the overall DENY FLIGHT plan.

GRAYLING (Allied 44) A disastrous air raid on Nuremberg on the night of 30 March 1944. Of the 800 Royal Air Force bombers taking part, about 95 were lost along with 545 highly-skilled airmen. The attack caused little damage and killed about 200 Germans on the ground.

GRAY PAN (U.S. 78) A joint effort of the Central and Defense Intelligence Agencies in 1978 to acquire a radar-directed anti-aircraft gun sold by the Soviets to the Iranian military. Information on this operation was seized by the new revolutionary government of Iran when it captured the U.S. embassy in Teheran on 4 November 1979.

GRAZING HERD (U.S.) Flag-word used to identify messages dealing with exercises concerning the mobilization of reserve units and personnel. The key word used for an actual mobilization is "Roaring Bull."

GREASED LIGHTNING (U.S. 63) The record-breaking flight of a B-58 Hustler bomber of the former Strategic Air Command conducted on 16 October 1963. The aircraft set a new Tokyo to London record of 8:35:20.4 (averaging 938 miles per hour).

GRECIAN FIREBOLT (U.S. 94) A series of large annual communications training exercises that feature extensive participation by Army Reserve and National Guard units. Designated by year (GRECIAN FIREBOLT 95).

GREEN

1. (U.S. 04) American plan for war against Mexico first drawn up in 1904 and periodically updated. One of the Color Plans. Superseded by the RAINBOW series. Never executed.

2. (GER 38) See GRUEN.

3. (FR 44) See VERTE.

GREEN ARROW (GER 40) See GRUENER PFEIL.

"GREEN BEAN" (BG 90) See HARICOT VERT.

GREEN DRAGON

1. (U.N. 53) A disastrous South Korean special operation. On 22 April 1953, the GREEN DRAGON team, then far behind enemy lines, reported rescuing 5 American pilots. A 57-man team was dropped in to aid in the extraction of the Americans. The rescue plane was ambushed by North Korean anti-aircraft fire and the GREEN DRAGON team was never heard from again. In hindsight, it is clear that the North Koreans had captured and "turned" GREEN DRAGON.

2. (BG 64) See DRAGON VERT.

GREEN FLAG (U.S.) An annual Air Force exercise conducted at the remote Nellis Air Force Base in Nevada. This training features the use of actual air-defense radars, jammers, and other electronic devices as they would be encountered in a conflict. The use of these devices is very restricted due to their interference with civilian transmissions.

GREENHOUSE (U.S. 51) A series of 2 nuclear and 2 thermonuclear tests conducted in 1951 at the newly-established Pacific Proving Ground. This was the fourth post-war nuclear test series (following CROSSROADS, SANDSTONE, and RANGER). All of the devices were mounted in tall towers to simulate airbursts. A number of target buildings, including bunkers, homes, and factories, were built on Mujinkarikku Island as test subjects. GEORGE was the world's first thermonuclear device; ITEM used a tritium booster. The individual shots were:

DOG	8 April 51	70 kilotons
EASY	21 April	47 kilotons
GEORGE	9 May	225 kilotons
ITEM	25 May	45.5 kilotons

GREEN ICE (Allied Law Enforcement 89) Undercover, multinational investigation into the worldwide underground drug economy. As a result of this investigation, begun in 1989, over 200 people were arrested in a simultaneous sweep in 6 countries conducted in early October 1992. The extent of cooperation between Colombian, Italian, French, and American criminal organizations was discovered to be surprisingly extensive.

GREENLINE (Allied 44) The British ground attack launched on 15 July 1944 by 12th Corps south of Evrecy, France, to support GOODWOOD.

GREIF "GRIFFIN" (GER 44)

1. Deception special operation designed to support the Battle of the Bulge (WACHT AM RHEIN) by using German soldiers in captured Allied uniforms and vehicles to cause confusion in the rear of the Allied

defense. A lack of transport aircraft, uniforms, and English-speaking soldiers limited this operation. Many GREIF personnel went into action as a conventional unit using captured equipment. However, the effect of the few personnel who infiltrated Allied lines was out of proportion to their numbers. A rumored assassination mission against Eisenhower kept the Supreme Allied Commander in his headquarters for several days. Personnel captured in Allied uniforms were shot as spies. Executed 16 December 1944. See WAHRUNG.

2. Anti-guerrilla operation begun on 14 August 1944 in the vicinity of Orsha and Vitebsk, Russia.

GRENADE (Allied 45) The February 1945 attack by the American 9th and Canadian 1st Armies across the Rhine into the area between Dusseldorf and Wesel, Germany. The crossing was made more difficult by the German destruction of dams upstream.

GRENADIER (U.S. 84) A series of 16 underground nuclear tests at the Nevada Test Site. These tests followed the FUSILEER series and preceded the CHARIOTEER tests. The individual shots of this series were:

(Unknown)	2 October 84	(unknown)
VILLITA	20 November	<20 kilotons
EGMONT	9 December	20-150 kilotons
TIERRA	15 December	20-150 kilotons
(Unknown)	20 December	(unknown)
VAUGHN	15 March 85	20-150 kilotons
COTTAGE	23 March	20-150 kilotons
HERMOSA	2 April	20-150 kilotons
MISTY RAIN	6 April	<20 kilotons
TOWANDA	2 May	20-150 kilotons
SALUT	12 June	20-150 kilotons
VILLE	12 June	<20 kilotons
MARIBO	26 June	<20 kilotons
SERENA	25 July	20-150 kilotons
CHAMITA	17 August	<20 kilotons
PONIL	27 September	<20 kilotons

"GRIFFIN" (GER 44) See GREIF.

GRILL FLAME (U.S. 84) A team of psychics used by the CIA to "remotely view" areas of interest to the U.S. See SCANATE, CENTER LANE, STARGATE, and SUN-STREAK.

GRIPFAST (Allied 42) Proposed Allied offensive to liberate Burma in the 1942/43 dry season. Never executed. See ANAKIM.

GRISLY HUNTER (U.S. 80 or so) U.S. spyplane flights conducted over Central America (mostly Nicaragua and Guatemala) during the Reagan Administration.

GRIZZLY (Allied 43) A Canadian training exercise held in England in the fall of 1943.

GROMMET (U.S. 71) A series of 20 underground nuclear tests conducted at the Nevada Test Site (with one exception). These tests followed EMERY and preceded TOGGLE. The individual shots were:

DIAMOND MINE	1 July 71	<20 kilotons
MINIATA	8 July	83 kilotons, see PLOWSHARE
ALGODONES	18 August	20-200 kilotons
(Unknown)	22 September	(unknown)
PEDERNAL	29 September	<20 kilotons
CATHAY	8 October	<20 kilotons
(Unknown)	14 October	(unknown)
CANNIKIN	6 November	<5 megatons, Amchitka, Alaska
DIAGONAL LINE	24 November	<20 kilotons
(Unknown)	30 November	(unknown)
CHAENACTIS	14 December	20-100 kilotons
(Unknown)	3 February 72	(unknown)
(Unknown)	30 March	(unknown)
LONGCHAMPS	19 April	<20 kilotons
MISTY NORTH	2 May	<20 kilotons
(Unknown)	11 May	(unknown)

ZINNA	17 May	<20 kilotons
MONERO	19 May	<20 kilotons
(Unknown)	28 June	(unknown)
(Unknown)	29 June	(unknown)

GROSSE KLETTE "BURDOCK" (GER 43) German anti-partisan operation centered on Kletnya, Russia, conducted in January 1943. Burdocks are a family of wild herbs.

GROUSE (Allied 42) The second phase of the FRESHMAN attack on the heavy water plant at Rjuked, Norway. Two gliders with 17 Norwegian commandos on each were sent to land on a rough strip prepared by the SWALLOW team. Due to bad weather both gliders crashed. Everyone aboard 1 glider died, 14 commandos in the second glider survived, only to be captured and killed by the Germans. Followed by GUNNERSIDE.

GROWN TALL (U.S.) Contingency plan for the U.S. Marine Corps to supplement the Army in the suppression of civil unrest in the U.S. See GARDEN PLOT.

GRUBWORM (Allied 44) The air transport of the Chinese 14th and 22nd Divisions from Burma to China beginning in early December 1944. These American-trained units were used to defend key Chinese cities from the Japanese ICHI-GO offensive. See ALPHA.

GRUEN "GREEN" (GER 38) The Nazi invasion of Czechoslovakia that began on 14 March 1938. The areas of Czechoslovakia with a majority of ethnic Germans were ceded to Germany on 1 October 1938 at the infamous Munich Conference. The Czechs were therefore without their formidable border defenses. When the Germans invaded, the Czechs were abandoned by their British and French allies. They surrendered with only local resistance. The Germans annexed the Czech areas and created a puppet Slovak Republic in the east. The destruction of Czechoslovakia outflanked Poland to the north in much the same way as the annexation of Austria outflanked the Czechs themselves. Czechoslovakia was re-created after World War II but has since divided itself into Slovakia and the Czech Republic.

GRUENER PFEIL "GREEN ARROW" (GER 40) German invasion of the Channel Islands of Guernsey and Jersey. The local population were ordered by the British government not to resist the invasion, which occurred on the afternoon of 1 July 1940.

GUARDIAN (U.S. 80) A series of 16 nuclear tests conducted at the Nevada Test Site. This test series followed TINDERBOX and preceded PRAETORIAN. The individual shots of GUARDIAN were:

DUCHESS	24 October 80	<20 kilotons
MINERS IRON	31 October	<20 kilotons
DAUPHIN	14 November	<20 kilotons
SERPA	17 December	20-150 kilotons
BASEBALL	15 January 81	20-150 kilotons
CLAIRETTE	5 February	<20 kilotons
SECO	25 February	<20 kilotons
VIDE	30 April	<20 kilotons
ALIGOTE	29 May	<20 kilotons
HARZER	6 June	20-150 kilotons
NIZA	10 July	<20 kilotons
PINEAU	16 July	<20 kilotons
HAVARTI	5 August	<20 kilotons
ISLAY	27 August	<20 kilotons
TREBIANO	4 September	<20 kilotons
CERNADA	24 September	<20 kilotons

GULF STREAM (BG 90) Belgian logistic flights during DESERT SHIELD and DESERT STORM.

GUNNERSIDE (Allied 43) The second commando raid on the Norwegian heavy water plant at Rjuked. After the FRESHMAN attack failed, the SWALLOW team escaped detection and prepared for a second attempt. On the night of 16 February

1943, 6 Norwegian commandos jumped into a landing zone prepared by the SWAL-LOW pathfinders. The team climbed down steep cliffs to place charges at key points in the factory and escaped before the explosives went off. All members of both teams were able to escape to neutral Sweden. The attack destroyed a great deal of the valuable heavy water, but the plant resumed production quickly. After a series of air attacks on the facility, the Germans moved its critical components to Germany for greater security. The disassembled factory was captured in April 1944 by the BIG operation in southern Germany.

GUNPOWDER (U.S. 48) See CHARIOTEER.

GUNSMOKE (U.S.) "Gunsmoke" was a popular American television program set in the old West.

1. (U.S.) Annual U.S. Air Force training exercise/competition for close air support pilots and crews. Designated by year and held at Nellis Air Force Base, Nevada.

2. GUNSMOKE I (U.S. Law Enforcement 92) Operation conducted by the U.S. Marshal's Service to capture violent offenders wanted by federal law enforcement agencies. Conducted in the spring of 1992, this 10-week sweep netted more than 3,000 criminals in 40 cities. In addition to the 730 weapons seized, $6,000,000 in drugs and other contraband were impounded.

3. GUNSMOKE II (U.S. Law Enforcement 92) Operation conducted by the U.S. Marshal's Service to capture sex offenders in major American cities. Launched on 13 October 1992, the 6-week sweep coordinated the activity of over 100 state and local law enforcement agencies and resulted in the capture of more than 1,000 fugitives.

GUNTHER (GER 43) Anti-partisan sweep conducted in the Smolensk area in early July 1943 area to clear the way for the Kursk offensive. See ZITADELLE.

GUN VAL (U.N. 53) A combat test in Korea of the F-86F Sabre variant in the spring of 1953. The F model was equipped with a new 20-millimeter cannon and so the operation name may be a contraction of "Gun Validation."

GYMNAST (Allied 41) Early plan for the invasion of North Africa. Replaced by SUPER-GYMNAST and finally TORCH.

GYPSY BARON (GER 43) See ZIGEUNER-BARON.

H

HADDOCK (Allied 40) A series of British air attacks on Italian airfields launched from bases in southern France.

HAGEN (GER 18) A planned renewed attack on British forces in Flanders scheduled for mid-June 1918. Never executed. Hagen was a Teutonic mythological figure.

HAGEN BEWEGUNG "HAGEN'S MOVE-MENT" (GER 43) Retreat of German troops along the Eastern Front after the German defeat at the Battle of Kursk (ZITADELLE). Began on 1 August 1943.

HA-GO (JPN 44) The southern thrust of the U-GO attack from Burma into India in March 1944.

HAILSTORM (Allied 44) A massive naval air attack launched on 16 and 17 February 1944 against the Japanese naval facility on Truk in the Caroline Islands. American dive and torpedo bombers sunk 15 warships and 25 merchantmen. Over 250 Japanese aircraft were destroyed, mostly on the ground. The attackers lost only 25 aircraft. This attack was conducted in support of the invasion of Eniwetok Atoll (CATCH-POLE) and has often been compared to the Japanese attack on Pearl Harbor.

HALBERD (Allied 41) Convoy to Malta that arrived in September 1941. Followed SUB-SISTENCE, preceded CALLBOY.

HALF MOON (U.S.) An early plan for nuclear operations against the Soviet Union. This plan was one of a series of plans developed by the former Strategic Air Command. Eventually, these plans were superseded by a series of Single Integrated Operations Plans (SIOPs), the first of which was named DROPSHOT.

HAL PRO (Allied 42) See HALVERSON PROJECT.

HALVERSON PROJECT (Allied 42) An early plan to bomb Japan. A force of 24 B-24 bombers, commanded by Colonel Harry Halverson, was to strike at the Home Islands from a base in China. The aircraft left from the east coast of the U.S. and flew as far as Egypt, where the plan was canceled and the aircraft used for other purposes. See FIRST SPECIAL AVIATION PROJECT.

HAMBONE (Allied 44) One of the many deception operations in support of the invasion of northern France (OVERLORD). A British actor, E. Clifton-James, depicted Field Marshal Montgomery on a well-publicized inspection tour through the Mediterranean. This operation was the subject of the book and movie I Was Montie's Double. Also called COPPERHEAD.

HAMMER

1. (Allied 40) Proposed British attack on Trondheim, Norway, during the "phony

war" in 1940. It was canceled due to inadequate naval support. See WESERÜBUNG.

2. (Allied 43) The naval bombardment of Reggion, Italy, on 31 August 1943.

3. (U.S.) A reserved first word to designate the programs and projects of the U.S. Air Force's Communication Service.

HAMPDEN (U.K. 94) Royal Air Force reconnaissance flights over Bosnia. See GRAPPLE.

HANDCUFF (Allied 43) A 1943 plan for British troops to occupy the island of Rhodes. In the confusion following the Italian collapse, Hitler ordered the small German contingent on the island to seize the Italian garrison, which they did on 11 September 1943, preempting the planned British move. See ACCOLADE and HERCULES.

HANDS UP (Allied 44) Plan for breaking out of Normandy lodgment by means of airborne and amphibious attacks on Quiberon Bay, France, to outflank the German defenses. Never executed. See COBRA, GOODWOOD.

HANDY (U.S.) A reserved first word for the programs and projects of the U.S. Air Force's Aeronautical Chart and Information Center.

HARBORAGE (U.S. 45) Operation to capture German atomic weapons scientists, material, and facilities in the cities of Hechingen, Bisingen, and Haigerloch. These centers of the German nuclear effort were all scheduled to be occupied by the French. By ensuring American technical intelligence units swept the area, the French were locked out of the lively post-war trade in nuclear scientists. See BIG.

HARDGATE (Allied 43) Attack launched by the British 8th Army on Sicily on 29 July 1943.

HARDIHOOD (Allied 43) Secret 1943 Anglo-Turkish program to provide British troops and equipment to Turkey in exchange for that country joining the war. Never executed. See SATURN.

HARDNOSE (U.S. 64) Part of OPLAN 34-A. This was one of several "sensitive intelligence operations" mentioned briefly in the "Pentagon Papers." It appears to have involved U.S. or South Vietnamese units and personnel crossing the Laotian border covertly.

HARDTACK

1. (Allied 43) A series of small, covert landings by British reconnaissance parties on the Channel Islands. Known HARDTACK landings are:

HARDTACK 28	at Gifford Bay, Island of Jersey on 25 December 1943
HARDTACK 4	Near Le Treport on 26 December 1943
HARDTACK 21	Near Point Terrible, Island of Sark on 27 December 1943

2. (U.S. 58) A series of 35 nuclear tests conducted at the Pacific Proving Grounds in 1958. These tests were made to ensure the reliability of weapons in the American stockpile, to improve the "cleanliness" of U.S. thermonuclear weapons, and to develop new weapons. The shots were:

ENIWETOK ATOLL

CACTUS	6 May 58	18 kilotons
BUTTERNUT	12 May	
KOA	13 May	1.37 kilotons
WAHOO	16 May	
HOLLY	21 May	
YELLOWWOOD	26 May	"fizzle"
MAGNOLIA	27 May	
TOBACCO	30 May	"fizzle"
ROSE	3 June	
UMBRELLA	9 June	
WALNUT	15 June	"fizzle"
LINDEN	18 June	

ELDER	28 June		MORA	29 September	2 kilotons
OAK	29 June	8.9 megatons	COLFAX	5 October	5.5 tons
SEQUOIA	2 July		HIDALGO	5 October	77 tons
DOGWOOD	6 July		TAMALPAIS	8 October	72 tons
SCAVEOLA	14 July		QUAY	10 October	79 tons
PISONIA	18 July		LEA	13 October	1.4 kilotons
OLIVE	23 July		NEPTUNE	14 October	115 tons
PINE	27 July		HAMILTON	15 October	1.2 tons
QUINCE	6 August Nuclear components failed to explode, radioactive material was widely scattered.		LOGAN	16 October	5 tons
			DONA ANA	16 October	37 tons
			VESTA	17 October	24 tons
FIG	18 August		RIO ARRIBA	18 October	90 tons
BIKINI ATOLL			SAN JUAN	20 October	zero
YUCCA	28 April		SOCORRO	22 October	6 kilotons
FIR	12 May		WRANGELL	22 October	115 tons
NUTMEG	22 May		RUSHMORE	22 October	188 tons
SYCAMORE	31 May		OBERON	22 October	zero
MAPLE	11 June		CATRON	24 October	21 tons
ASPEN	15 June		JUNO	24 October	1.7 tons
REDWOOD	28 June		CERES	26 October	.7 tons
HICKORY	29 June		SANFORD	26 October	4.6 kilotons
CEDAR	3 July		DEBACA	26 October	2.2 tons
POPLAR	12 July		CHAVEZ	27 October	.6 tons
JUNIPER	22 July		EVANS	29 October	55 tons
JOHNSTON ISLAND			HUMBOLT	29 October	7.8 tons
TEAK	31 July	2.5 megatons	MAZAMA	29 October	zero
ORANGE	11 August	2.5 megatons	SANTA FE	30 October	1.3 kilotons
			BLANCA	30 October	22 kilotons
			GANYMEDE	30 October	zero
			TITANIA	30 October	.2 ton

HARDTACK II (U.S. 58) A series of 37 nuclear test explosions conducted at the Nevada Test Site in 1958. This series was marked by a flurry of activity at the end of October; a test moratorium took effect in November. The U.S. did not conduct any test detonations until the NOUGAT series 34 months later. The individual explosions were:

OTERO	12 September 58	38 tons
BERNALILLO	17 September	15 tons
EDDY	19 September	83 tons
LUNA	21 September	1.5 tons
MERCURY	23 September	"sight"
VALENCIA	26 September	2 tons
MARS	28 September	13 tons

HARE (Allied 41) Canadian anti-invasion exercise conducted in England in April 1941.

"HARE CHASE" (GER 43) See HASENJAGD.

HARICOT ROUGE "RED BEAN" (BG 78) Humanitarian intervention in Zaire.

HARICOT VERT "GREEN BEAN" (BG 90) Belgian evacuation of Westerners from Rwanda in 1990.

HARLEQUIN (Allied 43) A combined amphibious feint/training exercise conducted on 8 September 1943 as part of STARKEY. STARKEY falsely depicted the threat of an Allied invasion of Europe in 1943 with fake radio traffic and other means. It culminated in HARLEQUIN, a large convoy sent across the Channel to provoke a German response. Troops did not embark; the convoy was designed to serve as bait to lure the German Air Force into a large air battle. Strangely, the Germans did not attack the decoy force. See COCKADE.

HARMONY (CN 92) Canadian participation in the U. N. Protection Force (UNPROFOR) in the former Yugoslavia. The Canadian Battle Group was based on the 22nd Regiment with attached military engineers.

HAROLD (Allied 42) Anti-invasion exercise in which the British 12th Corps defended against Canadian "invader" in July 1942.

HARPOON

1. (Allied 42) The overall plan for 2 convoys in the Mediterranean. One convoy (VIGOUROUS) left Alexandria for Gibraltar by way of Malta. The second (HARPOON) went in the opposite direction. The convoys met with fierce Axis opposition and only 2 of 17 merchant ships completed the journey. Executed in mid-June 1942.

2. (GER 41) See HARPUNE.

HARPUNE "HARPOON" (GER 41) The major German deception plan of 1941. This operation falsely portrayed as inevitable the invasion of England (SEELOWE) while concealing preparation for war with the Soviet Union (BARBAROSSA). HARPUNE had 2 parts, HARPUNE SUD (South) operated from the French channel ports, while HARPUNE NORD (North) did the same in Scandinavia.

HARRY (Allied 44) The Allied crossing of the Cosina River in Italy by the British 8th Army in May 1944.

HARTMUT (GER 40) The general term for German submarine operations in support of the invasions of Denmark and Norway in April 1940 (WESERÜBUNG). All 36 available submarines screened the invasion force from the Royal Navy. Hartmut is a proper name.

HARVEST

1. (Unofficial Anglo-Dutch 75) The recovery of aircraft from the bottom of the Zuider Zee, which was being drained in 1975. Parts of over 1,000 aircraft are thought to be on the bottom of the shallow bay. A German Gotha bomber from World War I was the oldest relic discovered.

2. (U.S.) A reserved first word to designate the programs and projects of the U.S. Air Force. See SCHEUNE.

HARVEST HOUSE (GER 43) See HARVEST REAPER.

HARVEST FRIENDSHIP (U.S./PN 94) See COSECHA AMISTAD.

HARVEST REAPER (U.S. 67) The preparation of 6 early F-111A aircraft for combat testing in Southeast Asia. See COMBAT LANCER.

HASENJAGD "HARE CHASE" (GER 43) An anti-partisan sweep begun on 6 February 1943 in the vicinity of Novorossiisk and Gomel, Russia.

HASTY

1. (Allied 44) Small airborne raid on bridges in Italy as part of DIADEM in June 1944.

2. (U.S.) A reserved first word designated the programs and projects of the U.S. Air Force's Air Training Command.

HAT (U.S. 66) A CIA operation to place an unmanned nuclear-powered seismic sensor to observe Chinese nuclear tests from an isolated location high in the Indian Himalayas. The first device was lost in an avalanche in the winter of 1966 and never recovered. A second sensor was put in position in 1967 and was later removed.

HAVE (U.S.) A reserved first word that designates the programs and projects of the U.S. Air Force's System Command. This command is responsible for the development of many items of equipment that inevitably keep the name under which they were developed.

HAVEN (U.S.) A reserved first word for the programs and projects of the U.S. Air Force's Office of Aerospace Research.

HAWK

1. (CN 50) Flights by Royal Canadian Air Force transports to support U.N. operations in Korea. Began in July 1950 when 426 Transport Squadron was transferred to McCord Air Force Base in the U.S. Ended on 9 June 1954.

2. (U.N. 51) Planned airborne assault to be conducted by the U.S. 187th Airborne Combat Team on 22 March 1951 near Chunchon. After extensive preparation, a final reconnaissance showed the communist forces had already withdrawn from the area in response to a U.N. ground offensive. Never executed. See TOMAHAWK.

HAWKEYE (U.S. 89) Military support to civil authorities in the U.S. Virgin Islands following a hurricane.

HAZEL FLUTE (NATO 95) A NATO tactical evaluation of British Harrier "jump jets" in an austere field-operating environment. Conducted 11 to 22 September 1995.

HEAD (U.S.) A reserved first word that designates the programs and projects of the Headquarters of the U.S. Air Force. See HEAD COP.

HEADACHE (Allied 40) Allied spoofing of German night guidance systems for aircraft by transmitting spurious signals.

HEAD COP (U.S.) Air Force plan for continuity and reconstruction in a post-nuclear attack scenario.

HEAT RISE (U.S. 62) The record-setting flight of a B-58 Hustler bomber conducted on 5 March 1962. The aircraft averaged 1,044.46 miles per hours on its trip from New York and Los Angeles and 1,214.65 miles per hour on the return leg. The Hustler was in service with the U.S. Air Force from 1960 to 1969.

HEAVEN BOUND (U.S. 52) A U.S. project that studied the use of nuclear weapons as antiaircraft weapons in the air-to-air or ground-to-air role. Led to development of the "Bomarc" missile for the defense of North America.

HEAVY (U.S.) A reserved word that designates the programs and projects of the U.S. Air Force.

HEAVY DOOR (U.S. 80) A plan, current in the early 1980s, to use elements of the U.S. Air Force to conduct special operations, shows of force, and deception operations in the Pacific region.

HEAVY HURDLE (U.S.) A proposed American bombing campaign in Southeast Asia. Never executed.

HEAVY STONE (U.S. 80) A plan, current in the early 1980s, to use elements of the U.S. Air Force to conduct special operations, shows of force, and deception operations in the Pacific region.

HECTOR (GER 18) See HEKTOR.

HEILIGER GEORG I "SAINT GEORGE I"
HEILIGER GEORG II "SAINT GEORGE II" (GER 18) Alternate plans designed to attack British forces along their left (northern) flank from south of Armentieres north

to the sea. Two simultaneous attacks into the Ypres Salient would converge near Hazebrouck. These were two of a series of confusing, overlapping plans drawn up by German staffs in January 1918. These plans were presented as options to General Erich Ludendorff, along with HEILIGER MICHAEL, HEILIGER QUENTIN, ACHILLES, BLÜCHER, CASTOR, KAISERSCHLACHT, and POLLUX. In much-diminished form, this plan became GEORG and was executed as GEORGETTE in April 1918.

HEILIGER MICHAEL 1 "SAINT MICHAEL 1" HEILIGER MICHAEL 2 "SAINT MICHAEL 2" HEILIGER MICHAEL 3 "SAINT MICHAEL 3" (GER 18) German attacks in World War I against British forces on a 43-mile front from Vimy to La Fere, France, during the period 21 March to 4 April 1918. The goal of the attack was to rupture the British line and drive north to the sea. Seventy-three German divisions faced fewer than 26 British divisions. The German troops used "Storm Troops" for the first time on their western front. Over 350,000 men died; the Germans gained 1,200 square miles of French territory. This attack was supported by operations GEORGETTE and MARS. See ACHILLES, BLÜCHER, and ROLAND.

HEINRICH (GER 44) The movement of German forces from the surrounding countryside into the fortress city of Cherbourg, France. By preserving these forces from destruction in the field, the Germans ensured sufficient units would be available to defend to critical port from Allied attacks well into 1945.

HEKTOR "HECTOR" (GER 18) Alternate plan to the HEILGER MICHAEL series. This plan called for a German attack on French units in the Champagne district in the spring of 1918. Never executed. See KAISERSCHLACHT.

HELLHOUND (Allied 44) Planned assassination attempt against Hitler to be conducted by heavy bombers of U.S. 15th Air Force operating from bases in Italy. From radio intercepts, the Allies knew Hitler would be at his Bavarian retreat of Berchtesgaden in June 1944. The attack was canceled, perhaps to protect the fact that the Allied were decoding German radio traffic.

HENRY (Allied 40) A preliminary landing of a small British force near Namgos, Norway, on 14 April 1940 as part of MAURICE.

HERBSTNEBEL "AUTUMN FOG"

1. (GER 44) Plan created by Field Marshal Walther Model as an alternative to MARTIN and WACHT AM RHINE. Never executed.

2. (GER 44) A plan rejected by Hitler to withdraw German troops in Italy behind the Po River.

HERBSTREISE "AUTUMN JOURNEY" (GER 40) Deception operations to support the planned German invasion of Britain (SEELOWE). This would have involved an empty convoy of large transports threatening the east coast of England while the actual invasion force in small barges would hit the southern coast.

HERCULES

1. (Allied 45) The British capture of Rhodes on 1 May 1945. This attack, only 8 days before the surrender of the Germans, was part of an overall goal of the British to maintain a post-war presence in the eastern Mediterranean. See ACCOLADE, HANDCUFF, and MANDIBLES.

2. (GER) See HERKULES.

HERKULES "HERCULES" (GER 42) German plan for an airborne invasion of Malta. The concept was approved at a meeting between Hitler and Mussolini on 29-30 April 1942. The planning for this

93

attack was extensive. Over a thousand gliders and other aircraft were to cover the assault and drop 1 Italian and 1 German airborne division onto the southern portion of the island. After the initial assault, 70,000 Italian troops would land by sea at 2 points to link up with the paratroops. A number of special operations were to be carried out by Axis commandos to destroy key targets in the hours before the airdrop. The Italian Navy would be committed to a fleet action to protect the seaborne troops. This attack was to be over 5 times as large as the airborne attack on Crete (see MERKUR). Scheduled for September it was repeatedly delayed and finally canceled after the Axis defeat at Tobruk on 13 November. Called C3 by the Italians.

HERMANN (GER 44)

1. Operation by about 1,100 German Air Force planes designed to destroy Allied air power in the West in support of Operation WACHT AM RHEIN. Twenty-seven Allied air bases in Belgium, Holland, and France were attacked, 439 Allied aircraft were destroyed, mostly on the ground. Also called BIG BLOW and BODENPLATTE. Executed 1 January 1945.

2. A month-long anti-partisan operation between Vilnius, Lithuania and Polotek, Belorussia launched on 15 June 1944.

HEYDRICH (GER 42)

A frenzy of revenge against Jews and other minorities in eastern Europe, especially Czechoslovakia, beginning on 10 June 1942. The operation was named after the SS chief Reinhard Heydrich, who was ambushed by resistance fighters in Prague on 27 May (ANTHROPOID). He died in early June.

HG (Allied convoy)

The designation for Allied convoys from Gibraltar to Britain.

HIGHBOY (U.N. 52)

A local operation conducted in January 1952, which used 155-millimeter howitzers to fire directly into enemy bunkers. Conducted by U.S. 1st Corps in front of a high-ranking group of observers; poor coordination between the infantry and artillery produced disappointing results.

HIGHJUMP

1. (Allied 45) The forced repatriation of Croat nationals to Yugoslavia at the end of World War II. Part of KEELHAUL.

2. (U.S. 46) Expedition conducted by the U.S. Navy during the Antarctic summer of 1946-47 using a fleet of 13 ships including a submarine and an aircraft cruiser. This was the first major American exploration of the Antarctic continent since the Second Byrd Expedition in 1933-35 and served to establish the U.S. as an interested party in postwar discussions of the future of the region.

HIGHJUMP II (U.S. 48)

A proposed follow-up to the first HIGHJUMP expedition to Antarctica scheduled for 1948, but canceled.

HIGH NOON (U.S.)

The annual bombing competition held by the Strategic Air Command. Replaced by the PROUD SHIELD series.

HILL FOIL (NATO 92)

A training exercise that centered around a deployment of British Harrier jump-jets to a field location near Sennelager, West Germany, in June 1992.

HIMMLER (GER 39)

Deception operation that was designed to make it appear that the Poles attacked the Germans in 1939; this would then provide an excuse for war. Nazi operatives took prisoners (called "canned goods") from various prison camps, dressed them in Polish uniforms, and killed them on the night of 31 August 1939 near the German radio station at Gleiwitz. International reporters were then brought to see the aftermath of the supposed "Polish raid."

HIRAM (IS 48)

A 60-hour attack by Zionist forces in October 1948 against the Arab Liberation Army in what is now northern

Israel. The name seems to be a reference to Hiram, the biblical king of Tyre.

HI TIDE (U.N. 51) The first combat missions flown using air-to-air refueling. F-84G Thunderjets flown by the 116th Fighter Bomber Wing used tankers operating out of Japan to extend their reach into North Korea.

HOLD THE LINE (U.S. Law Enforcement 93) See BLOCKADE.

HOME COMING

1. (U.N. 52) Plan developed as a more limited alternative to BIG STICK using only Korean troops. Scheduled for 1 April 1952 but never executed.

2. (U.N. 52) The release of about 27,000 Korean civilians who were reclassified from prisoners of war to civilian detainees in the summer of 1952. The South Korean government applied a great deal to release prisoners before they were exposed to communist propaganda teams. This denied North Korea that manpower needed to rebuild after the war.

3. (U.S. 73) Military operations in support of the release of 591 American prisoners by North Vietnam in accordance with the January 1973 Paris Peace Accord.

HONEY BADGER (U.S. 79) A proposed second attempt to the failed attempt to rescue the hostages held at the U.S. embassy in Tehran (EAGLE CLAW). This much larger operation would have involved 2 Ranger battalions capturing an intermediate airfield at Mehrabad. Air Force cargo aircraft would then fly in helicopters and a rescue team who would liberate the hostages and fly them out from a landing zone in a major stadium. Liberal use of airpower would have ensured a large number of civilian dead. Never executed. See YELLOW FRUIT.

HOOKER (Allied 43) The landing of a British brigade north of Pizzo, Italy, on 8 September 1943 as part of BAYTOWN.

HOOLIGAN BUSTER (U.N./DN Unofficial 94) The largest combat operation by Danish forces since World War II. In May 1994, a Danish contingent on peacekeeping duty in Bosnia was ambushed by Serb forces. Despite restrictive rules of engagement imposed by the U.N., Lt. Col. Lars Moller ordered an attack. His German-made Leopard II tanks destroyed several Serb artillery pieces, an ammunition dump, and several bunkers.

HOOPER (R.S.A. 88) The last major South African ground attack in Angola. Conducted in January 1988 following MODULER.

HOPE FOR THE WORLD (U.S./AL 95) American humanitarian relief airlift that began in January 1995. Albania became an important American listening post in the 1990s as nearby Yugoslavia continued to self-destruct.

HOREV (IS 48) A major Israeli attack into the Negev during the 1948 War of Independence.

HORNBLOWER (Allied 42) British preparation to demolish the harbor facilities at Alexandria, Egypt, in the event of a German breakthrough. Never executed.

HORUS (FR 90) The deployment of French troops to the Persian Gulf as part of DAGUET.

HOT BOX (U.K. 53) British air sampling of the radiation from the TOTEM I test in Australia.

HOTFOOT (Allied 44) Proposed raid to be conducted by naval aviation against the Japanese fleet and other targets on the Japanese mainland scheduled for October 1944. This would have been the first carrier-based raid on the Japanese homeland since the famous Dolittle Raid in April 1942. The element of surprise would contribute to what was hoped to be a "reverse

Pearl Harbor." The operation was canceled when the naval aircraft were required in the Battle of Leyte Gulf.

HUNGARIAN VENTURE (U.K./HU 94) A combined exercise by British and Hungarian troops conducted in Hungary in September 1994 under the Partnership for Peace program.

HURRICANE

1. (GER 42) See WIRBELSTRUM.

2. (Allied 44) Invasion of Biak, north of New Guinea, by U.S. forces on 27 May 1944. Japanese attempts to reinforce Biak (KON) failed, but the garrison conducted an effective defense, holding out until 28 June, when the last 150 defenders escaped, protected by the last stand of their wounded comrades.

3. HURRICANE I (Allied 44) A planned massive air attack on industrial targets in that Ruhr region using all available tactical and strategic aircraft. Scheduled for October 1944 but never executed.

4. (U.K. 52) The first British nuclear test. A 25-kiloton nuclear device was exploded in an obsolete frigate anchored in the Monte Bello Islands, northwest of Australia on 3 October 1952. Followed by TOTEM.

HURRY (Allied 40) The first British wartime convoy to Malta in April 1940. Followed by WHITE.

HUSKY (Allied 43) Invasion of Sicily on 10 July 1943. In the first day of the landing over 160,000 troops and 600 tanks arrived and seized Syracuse. The entire island was in Allied hands after 39 days of fighting. See BARCLAY, CORKSCREW, FUSTIAN, and LADBROKE.

HUSTON PLAN (U.S. Political 70) An aborted plan devised by Tom C. Huston to coordinate various intelligence and law enforcement agencies in a vigorous and illegal suppression of anti-war youth groups. At a White House meeting in early July 1970, President Nixon emphasized the need for closer cooperation between the FBI, CIA, the Military Intelligence branches, and other federal organizations to suppress the unrest on American campuses. Huston attended the meeting as a presidential aide. In early July, he prepared an analysis of the meeting and proposed several means of improving cooperation. He then attached a secret addendum to the memorandum outlining a program of eavesdropping, postal interception, and burglaries. This "Huston Plan" was patently illegal and was quickly suppressed by the Justice Department before it could be implemented. See CHAOS and GEMSTONE.

HX (Allied convoy) Fast Allied convoys from Halifax, Nova Scotia, to England. Designated by number (e.g., HX 123).

HYDRA (Allied 43) A 17 August 1943 air raid by the Royal Air Force on the German rocket test and production facility at Peenemunde. A special target was the housing for the scientists, 130 of these key personnel were killed. In addition, 600 slave laborers died when British bombs accidentally struck their compound. As a result of this raid, production of the "V-Weapons" was moved to an underground factory at Nordhausen. The German effort was set back at least 2 months.

I

IBEX (GER 44) See STEINBOCK.

ICARUS (GER 40) See IKARUS.

ICEBERG (Allied 45) The American invasion of Okinawa on Easter Sunday, 1 April 1945. The Japanese consider Okinawa an integral part of Japan, and so they defended the island using the same techniques they planned to employ against an Allied invasion of the home islands. The 100,000 defenders avoided the massive pre-invasion bombardment by establishing their defensive lines inland (TENICHI). The resulting battle was the largest in the Pacific theater. The island was secured after 82 days, at a cost of over 107,000 Japanese soldiers and 150,000 local civilians. This was a rate of over 1,300 Japanese soldiers killed each day. At sea and in the air, the Japanese countered with a massive kamikaze attack (FLOATING CHRYSANTHEMUMS), sinking 34 ships, and damaging an additional 368. Over 7,500 Americans were killed on the ground, and another 5,000 in the surrounding sea. The deception operation for this invasion was BLUEBIRD.

ICE CUBE (N.Z.) Supply flights flown by the Royal New Zealand Air Force to support Antarctic research at McMurdo Station.

ICHI-GO "PLAN ONE" (JPN 44) The overall plan for the 1944 Japanese offensive in eastern China. Launched on 17 April 1944 it called for a massive attack to open a direct north-south route between Peking and Nanking, end Chinese resistance between the Hwang Ho and Yangtze Rivers, and destroy U.S. airbases. It consisted of 2 parts: the KA-GO attack was launched from French Indo-China and northern China near Wuhan to converge southeast of the Nationalist wartime capital of Chunking. At the same time, the TO-GO attack thrust southeasterly from Zhengzhou to meet the other two forces. These attacks were successful, forcing the U.S. to abandon its bases in Szechwan, Kiangsi, and Kwangsi provinces. Massive panic spread throughout the region. American-trained units had to be flown in to prevent complete collapse (ALPHA, GRUBWORM). These losses made the capture of the island Saipan to replace the lost airfields all the more important.

IDEALIST (U.S.) One of several names used for the U.S. for its program of high-altitude reconnaissance flights by U-2 aircraft.

IGLOO WHITE (U.S.) Plan to use naval sonar buoys dropped into the demilitarized zone between North and South Vietnam as primitive ground sensors to detect the movement of communist trucks along the Ho Chi Minh Trail. The barrier these sensors would create was dubbed the

"Automated Battlefield" by American planners. See DUEL BLADE.

I GO "PLAN I" (JPN 43) Attacks made against Allied bases and air power around Guadalcanal, New Guinea, in early April 1943. This operation was divided into 2 phases, Operations X and Y. X called for attacks by 200 aircraft on the Solomons (Guadalcanal and Tulagi) between 5 and 10 April. Operation Y required attacks on New Guinea from 11 to 20 April. Japanese pilots grossly exaggerated their effectiveness, leading their commanders to think this operation was a success. Allied losses were 25 aircraft, 2 merchant ships, a tanker, and 2 small naval vessels. Japanese losses were about 42 aircraft. See WATCHTOWER.

IKARUS "ICARUS" (GER 40) Planned German invasion of Iceland scheduled for mid-June 1940. The invasion force was built around the 163rd Infantry Division and was to be landed from high-speed passenger liners at both ends of the Reyjavik/Akureyri highway. The invaders would then establish an air base that could effectively close the North Atlantic to British shipping. At the time the invasion was planned, the British Army, decimated by its retreat from Europe, guarded the island with a single territorial (i.e., reserve) brigade. This force was heavily reinforced by the British by the projected invasion date. This reinforcement and German naval inferiority led to the invasion being canceled. See INDIGO.

ILL WIND (U.S. Law Enforcement 88) Investigation conducted by the FBI of corruption in procurement contracting in the American Department of Defense. This probe was made public in 1988 and resulted in over 60 convictions of high-ranking officials. In early 1993, the ITV Corporation admitted fraud and paid a large fine.

IMMINENT THUNDER (Coalition 90) Deception operations conducted as "training exercises" by naval and marine units along the Saudi coast to falsely reinforce the threat of an amphibious landing along the Iraqi or Kuwaiti coast during Operation DESERT STORM. The word-press sent images of this training around the world, and presumably to Baghdad. Executed beginning 15 November 1990.

IMMUNE (AUS 89) Royal Australian Air Force operation that mitigated the effects of a 5-month long strike by civilian airline pilots.

IMPERATOR (Allied 42) A plan for a large raid against German-occupied France using land forces available in 1942 or 1943. This raid, to be conducted by at least 1 infantry division and available armored units, was to land in the Cherbourg region and fight for several days before being withdrawn. This was a contingency for use in the event of a sudden German or Soviet collapse. One goal was to force the German Air Force into a final battle over France with the then-dominant Royal Air Force. Never executed. See ECLIPSE.

INDIGO (Allied 41) Relief of British forces occupying Iceland by U.S. troops. Began 7 July 1941 with the landing of a Marine brigade. These troops were later replaced by the Army's 10th Infantry Regiment. See IKARUS.

INDUCTION (Allied 45) Alternate plan to CAUSEWAY. Never executed.

INFATUATE (Allied 44) A ground attack by British and Canadian forces launched on 1 November 1944 to seize the island of Walcheren in the Scheldt river to open the port of Antwerp. Determined German resistance and extensive demolition of the port delayed the reopening of this critical facility. The island fell on 8 November, and the first Allied convoy entered the repaired port on 1 December.

INFINITE (U.S.) A reserved first word used to designated the programs and projects of the U.S. Central Command.

INFINITE MOONLIGHT (U.S./JOR 95) A 2-week joint U.S./Jordanian training exercise conducted beginning 18 August 1995. The Jordanians were passive allies of the Iraqis during the Gulf War. In early August, a number of Iraqi dictator Saddam Hussein's family fled to Jordan. By granting them asylum, the Jordanians dramatically changed their policy, aligning with the West and other Arab states against Iraq. Over 3,000 U.S. troops went to the Wadi Rum area, 175 miles south of Amman to bolster the security of the Jordanians.

INLAND SEA (U.S. 59) The tour of the Great Lakes by a U.S. naval task force of 28 ships based on the heavy cruiser USS *Macon* conducted in June and July 1959. This publicity and recruiting visit marked the first major U.S. Navy presence in the region since 1813.

INMATE (Allied 45) American air attacks on Japanese bases on Truk in the Caroline Islands conducted from 12 to 16 June 1945.

INNOCENT IMAGES (U.S. Law Enforcement 95) A 2-year investigation of pedophile activity on computer on-line services. Begun in late 1993, it was publicly announced in September 1995 with a dozen arrests in Miami, Dallas, and the New York City area.

INSECT (Allied 42) The delivery of Spitfire fighters to Malta on 21 July 1942 by the carrier HMS *Eagle*.

INSOMNIA (U.N. 52) Nighttime ground-attack missions flown by American naval aircraft using the light of the moon, flares, and bright snow on the ground to illuminate North Korean supply convoys and other targets in the spring of 1952. See FIREFLY.

INSTANT THUNDER (Coalition 90) The initial planning name for air operations designed to force the Iraqis to leave Kuwait. Executed in modified form as part of DESERT STORM. INSTANT THUNDER was the product of a U.S. Air Force planning cell ("Checkmate"), which envisioned air power as the key to the liberation of Kuwait. When presented by the Air Force officers to the field commanders (who were mostly Army personnel) the plan was rejected in form, but adopted in practice. The plan called for a classic air campaign that would first destroy the enemy air defenses, followed by the establishment of air supremacy. Air power would then hit key "centers of gravity" throughout the theater. The original plan called for a 6-day attack on 100 targets to disrupt Iraqi command, economic, and military systems. The actual campaign used a 30-day air attack aimed at many more targets than originally planned. These included Iraqi nuclear and chemical facilities as well as military units. The initial strikes on Baghdad were made by the newly-fielded F-117 Nighthawk operating behind a curtain of target drones who forced the defending radars to reveal their positions. INSTANT THUNDER was perceived as an Air Force "dream plan" that was expanded into a joint (that is all-services) plan.

INTERMEDIARY (U.S. 68) See POPEYE.

INTERNAL LOOK (U.S.) Series of annual command post exercises conducted by U.S. Central Command to validate its operational plans. INTERNAL LOOK 90 was directed at the CENTCOM Plan 1002, the defense of Kuwait and Saudi Arabia against an attack by Iraq. Strangely, this exercise took place at the same time as the actual Iraqi invasion. As a result of lessons learned during INTERNAL LOOK 90, the 1002 plan was modified into the DESERT DRAGON series.

INTRINSIC ACTION (U.S. 92) Combined U.S./Kuwaiti exercise originally scheduled for September 1992. The operation was executed in early August due to saber rattling by the Iraqi regime. Over 2,000 troops from the 5th Special Forces Group and 1st Cavalry Division arrived by air to link up with heavy equipment already in storage in Kuwait. See EAGER MACE, NATIVE FURY.

IRONCLAD (Allied 42) British amphibious assault on the French island of Madagascar conducted on 5 May 1942. This attack ensured Japanese naval units would not use the Vichy-controlled island as base to interdict British convoys in the Indian Ocean. The French commander surrendered after 2 days of sharp fighting although sporadic resistance to the British continued until September. Planned as BONUS.

IRON CROSS (Allied 45) A plan to raise a company of German defectors to conduct an airborne raid into the Nazi "National Redoubt" in Bavaria during the closing days of World War II. The soldiers would wear German uniforms and carry false papers in order to conduct sabotage, reconnaissance, and other operations. The head of the American Office of Special Services, Colonel William "Wild Bill" Donovan, hoped the unit would be able to kill or capture Hitler. The unit was to be dropped in the Inn River Valley near Schwarz. Bad weather and the rapid advance of conventional ground units forced the cancellation of this operation.

IRONSIDE (Allied 44) A deception in support of the June 1944 invasion of Normandy (OVERLORD). This operation falsely threatened an Allied invasion of France along the Bay of Biscay, near Bordeaux in the summer of 1944. IRONSIDE was a part of the larger deception FORTITUDE SOUTH, which was in turn part of BODYGUARD.

IRVING (U.S. 66) Operation near Hoa Hoi, Binh Dinh Province, Vietnam, in which the 12th U.S. Cavalry Regiment with elements of the 5th U.S. Cavalry Regiment defeated the 7th and 8th North Vietnamese Regiments in October 1966.

ISABELLA (GER 41) A plan to be put into effect after the collapse of the Soviet Union to secure bases in Spain and Portugal for the continuation of the strangulation of Great Britain. This concept was laid out by Hitler in June 1941 but was never executed. See FELIX.

ISKRA "SPARK" (S.U. 43) The final breakthrough to Leningrad (now St. Petersburg), ending the German siege of that city on 13 January 1943. The narrow route south of Lake Ladoga was under Axis commandment for another year, but food and supplies could be brought into the city. The term "Spark" in Leninist thought indicates the act that sparks revolution.

IVORY COAST (U.S. 70) The 21 November 1970 American raid to rescue prisoners thought to be held at the North Vietnamese complex near Son Tay. To preserve security, the raiders trained in Florida and were flown to their staging base in Thailand only hours before the mission. The U.S. Navy conducted a diversionary attack along the coast of North Vietnam as the raiding force approached from the opposite direction. The 52-man team avoided detection during the long flight. They launched their raid by deliberately crashing a helicopter into the compound with a team that destroyed the guard barracks and rushed the prisoner compound. Other helicopters pulverized guard towers with heavy machine-gun fire after landing their elements outside the facility. Over 200 Vietnamese (and perhaps some Soviet) personnel were killed. The raiding party suffered only 2 slight injuries but found no prisoners in the compound. American intelligence had purposely avoided paying too much attention to the region in the weeks before the raid, and so did not detect the movement of the prisoners a week before the rescue attempt.

IVY (U.S. 52) Two nuclear tests conducted in late 1952 on Eniwetok Atoll at the Pacific Proving Ground. The MIKE explosion was the first experimental "fusion" or thermonuclear device (i.e., a "hydrogen bomb"). The KING blast was of the most powerful American fission weapon ever tested. Followed by TUMBLER-SNAPPER, preceded UPSHOT-KNOTHOLE. See TEXAN.

MIKE	1 November 52	10.2 megatons
KING	16 November	500 kilotons

IVY FLATS (U.S. 62) Ground forces exercises conducted in conjunction with the DOMINIC II nuclear tests in 1962 and 1963. See DESERT ROCK.

IVY LEAGUE (U.S. 83) Periodic U.S. national-level exercises of command and control systems to be used in the event of nuclear war. Open sources indicate one of these exercises was conducted beginning in March 1983 and another in conjunction with WINTEX/CIMEX 85 and REX 82 ALPHA.

J

JACK FROST (U.S. 77) Arctic testing of the newly-fielded A-10 ground-attack aircraft conducted at Eielson Air Force base in Alaska in January 1977.

JACK POT (U.S.) See TREE TOP.

JACOB (GER 43) See JAKOB.

JAEL (Allied 44) Allied deception operation conducted from November 1943 to February 1944 in Europe to convince the Germans that the center of Allied operations would continue to be in the Mediterranean area. The large buildup of Allied forces in Britain in preparation for the invasion of northern France (OVERLORD) was impossible to completely conceal. Followed by BODYGUARD.

JAGUAR (Allied 41) A convoy with supplies to reinforce Malta in 1941.

JAKOB "JACOB" (GER 43) Anti-partisan operation begun on 8 October 1943 north of Uzda, Russia.

JALOPY (Allied 44) American amphibious training exercise conducted in northern Ireland in the spring of 1944 by troops earmarked for the invasion of northern France (OVERLORD).

JANTZEN (Allied 43) A major amphibious training exercise conducted in April and May 1943 near Tenby, Wales, for administrative and logistics troops earmarked to take part in the invasion of northern France (OVERLORD).

JEEP

1. (Allied 43) Marshaling exercise held by the American 2nd Infantry Division in northern Ireland in preparation for the invasion of northern France (OVERLORD).

2. (U.S.) Plan to evacuate key members of the U.S. government from Washington to prepared positions in Maryland, Pennsylvania, Virginia, and West Virginia (the "Federal Relocation Arc") in the event of nuclear war. Although periodically exercised, it has never been executed. The name JEEP is an acronym for "Joint Emergency Evacuation Plan."

JENNIFER (U.S. Espionage 74) A CIA project to recover a sunken Soviet submarine from the Pacific Ocean conducted in the summer of 1974 using the purpose-built Glomar Explorer. In February 1975 the *Los Angeles Times* reported on this operation, which was denied by the U.S. government. The operations of the Explorer were explained as being an undersea mining experiment financed by Howard Hughes. In fact, JENNIFER was one of the most complex and secretive known intelligence operations of the Cold War. On 11 April

1968 the American 'Sea Spider' hydrophone network detected an accidental explosion on a Soviet submarine. After the Soviets were unable to locate their lost boat, Henry Kissinger, then National Security Advisor, approved the plan to raise the wreckage. The Glomar Explorer and the submersible barge HMB-1 used a large mechanical claw to grab the submarine and lift it 17,000 feet. Published reports indicate the boat broke in half when being raised. The front was recovered; it did not have the missiles and code books that were the main prize, but did include a number of nuclear torpedoes and other valuable intelligence documents along with the bodies of 6 crewmen.

JERICHO (Allied 44) An air raid on the prison at Amiens, France, designed to rescue resistance fighters held there. Alerted that the Nazis intended to execute a dozen partisans, the Royal Air Force used 19 Mosquito bombers on 18 February 1944 in an attempt to skip bombs off the ground and into the walls of the prison. Fifty prisoners escaped, but 96 were killed when the walls were breached. In addition, bombs that missed the prison entirely struck a nearby school and other buildings, causing a number of civilian casualties.

JESSE JAMES I (U.N. 52) The insertion of a 10-man South Korean special operations team near Kaesun on the night of 20 December 1952. The entire team was captured on landing.

JESSE JAMES II

JESSE JAMES III (U.N. 52) The insertion of two 10-man South Korean special operations teams north of Kaesun on the night of 28 December 1952. Neither team was ever heard from again.

JESSICA (Allied 45) Minor Allied deception operation that falsely depicted preparations for an Allied ground attack from France into Italy. This was meant to tie down German units in the Alps as the Allies continued their attacks from the south. See KNIFEEDGE.

JET STREAM (U.S. 57) A flight by a single KC-135 *Stratotanker* of the former Strategic Air Command, which began on 17 September and which set several aviation records. These included distance without refueling on a closed circuit (3,125 miles), speed over 2,000 kilometers (589 miles per hours), and speed over 5,000 kilometers (587 miles per hours). See TOP SAIL.

JOE I (U.S. 48) Western term for the first Soviet nuclear test conducted on 29 August 1948 at Semipalatinsk. This detonation was detected in September by Project RAIN BARREL and was informally called JOE 1. Later tests were designated by number (JOE 2, 3, 4, and so on) for a number of years. The Soviet name for this explosion was FIRST LIGHTNING.

JOE 2 (U.S. 51) The second Soviet nuclear test. Conducted at Semipalatinsk on 24 September 1951.

JOE 3 (U.S. 51) The third Soviet nuclear test. Air-dropped on 18 October 1951 at Semipalatinsk.

JOE 4 (U.S. 53) The first test of a Soviet thermonuclear ("hydrogen") bomb. Detonated on 12 August 1953 on a tower at Semipalatinsk, it had a yield of 400 kilotons.

JOINT EMERGENCY EVACUATION PLAN (U.S.) See JEEP.

JOINT ENDEAVOR (NATO 95) The deployment of over 50,000 NATO troops to supervise the peace between Bosnia, Croatia, and Serbia. This movement, which began in early December 1995, was the largest actual deployment of NATO troops in the alliance's history. Due to political considerations, a Russian brigade, along with troops from Hungary, Poland, and Finland were also included in the effort.

JUBILANT (Allied 45) Part of the ECLIPSE plan for the occupation of Nazi Germany in the event of its sudden collapse. This plan called for the Allied 1st Airborne Army to protect prisoner of war compounds until ground forces could arrive. Never executed.

JUBILEE (Allied 42) The raid on Dieppe, France, conducted by British and Canadian forces on 19 August 1942. This raid was a smaller version of the RUTTER plan. The raid was approved for execution on 16 July by Winston Churchill in response to Soviet demands for a second front. The raiders came up against stiffer-than-expected resistance from the alerted defenders and suffered over 3,000 casualties. Seven battalion commanders were captured, reflecting the magnitude of the defeat. JUBILEE served as a rehearsal for the planned invasion of northern France; this raid proved that even minor French ports were too heavily defended for a direct assault. The British learned the importance of close air support, deception, and security as well as the need for specialized invasion equipment, lessons incorporated into planning for OVER-LORD.

JUDAS (PN) Panamanian strongman Manuel Noriega's program to compromise the local Catholic church. His Panamanian Defense Forces collected information that allowed them to blackmail priests and other officials with charges of homosexuality. This plan was revealed by documents captured by Americans during their invasion (JUST CAUSE).

JUDGMENT (Allied 40) The British aerial attack on the Italian fleet anchored at Taranto on 11 November 1940. One Italian battleship was sunk and 2 damaged along with 2 cruisers. In its use of carrier-based torpedo bombers against a fleet in harbor,

this attack had many of the key elements later used by the Japanese in their attack on Pearl Harbor.

JUGGLER (Allied 43) A 2-pronged attack on the German aircraft factories at Regensburg conducted on 14 August 1943. The U.S. 9th Air Force, operating from bases in Britain, and the U.S. 8th Air Force, flying from Italy, conducted the coordinated attack to split the Nazi fighter defenses.

JU JITSU (U.K./U.S. 52) A series of overflights of the former Soviet Union by RB-47C aircraft. The Americans loaned the aircraft to the Royal Air Force who flew the actual missions. Both countries shared the intelligence. One aircraft was lost in 1952, and another in 1954.

JULIUS CAESAR (Allied 39) The general plan for the British defense of their home islands against a German invasion (SEELOWE). Initial resistance on the beach was to be provided by Home Guard and other relatively immobile units, while the Canadian Corps provided a mobile reserve to counterattack. Replaced by the CROMWELL plan in June 1940.

JUNCTION CITY (U.S./R.V.N. 67) The second major American "Search and Destroy" mission of the Vietnam War. Conducted from 22 February to 14 May 1967 by over 45,000 Allied troops centered on the U.S. 25th Infantry Division. The main communist force in the area was the Viet Cong 9th Division. The area of operations was northwest of Saigon near the Cambodian border. This attack was much larger that the earlier CEDAR FALLS operation but had the same transient success. Allied forces claimed 3,000 enemy dead, at a cost of 202 American dead and another 1,570 wounded. A highlight of this operation was the parachute jump by 845 soldiers of the 503d Parachute Infantry Regiment in the first operational airdrop since the Korean War and the only such operation by conventional airborne forces during this conflict. Junction City is a town in Kansas.

JUNGLE JIM

1. (U.S. 62) The training of Latin American air forces in counterinsurgency techniques at the School of the Americas in Panama in 1962.

2. (U.S./R.V.N. 63) The deployment of 2 U.S. Army helicopter companies and an Air Force air commando unit to Vietnam in 1963. Officially, they simply instructed the Vietnamese in air support techniques, but in reality they also conducted operations.

JUNKET (U.N. 52) American naval operation that captured small Korean junks and interrogated their crews for intelligence. Began in January 1952.

JUNO

1. (GER 40) Naval offensive in support of the German invasion of Norway and Denmark (WESWEÜNG). French and British forces landed in the northern part of Norway to aid in its defense. The Germans sank several British transports as well as the carrier HMS *Glorius* and 2 destroyers. These losses made the Allied situation ashore more difficult. The Allies torpedoed the cruisers *Scharnhorst* and *Gneisenau*, damaging both. See HARTMUT.

2. (Allied 44) The Canadian beach at Normandy, France, invaded on 6 June 1944 as part of OVERLORD.

JUPITER (Allied 44) Plan for a British invasion of German-occupied northern Norway. Although advocated by Churchill, it was never executed due to opposition by the Admiralty. See FORTITUDE NORTH.

JURAL (U.K. 92) The British contribution to SOUTHERN WATCH, the international effort beginning on 27 August 1992 to enforce a prohibition on Iraqi aircraft flying south of the 32nd parallel. See WARDEN.

JURIST (Allied 45) The Allied occupation of Malaya on 18 August 1945 shortly after the Japanese surrender.

JUST CAUSE (U.S. 89) Invasion of Panama that deposed Manuel Noriega in December 1989. H-Hour was 0045 hours, 20 December 1989. The Americans used overwhelming force. Over 300 aircraft moved troops, attacked targets, or provided other support. Twenty-four thousand U.S. troops were deployed against the 16,000 members of the Panama Defense Force. The Panamanian force was quickly decapitated. Senior officers were killed, captured, or more commonly abandoned their men. The attack touched off fires and looting by impoverished Panamanians. The operation quickly lost focus as decentralized resistance, criminal activity, and the hunt for Noriega replaced clear-cut objectives. By January, combat forces had begun to withdraw and reconstruction of the Panamanian government began under the name PROMOTE LIBERTY. The Americans lost 23 killed and 324 wounded. Panamanian deaths are more difficult to calculate. The Defense Forces lost 314 dead, and another 200 civilians are known to have died, although this number may not include people in destroyed buildings whose bodies were never recovered. Planned under the name BLUE SPOON the actual invasion incorporated elements of the NIFTY PACKAGE and ACID GAMBIT plans. See BLADE JEWEL, NIMROD DANCER, PURPLE STORM, PRAYER BOOK, and SAND FLEA.

JW (Allied convoy) Allied convoys from England to the northern Soviet ports. Designated by number (e.g., JW 123). Replaced the PQ designation in December 1942.

K

KA
KA GO

1. (JPN 42) Attack to clear U.S. forces out of the southern Solomons by launching an amphibious counter-invasion of Guadalcanal on 18 August 1942. The invasion troops were transported from Truk in a flotilla of old destroyers. American intelligence detected the massing of Japanese naval forces, resulting in the Battle of the Eastern Solomons the next day. The Americans interdicted the Japanese fleet, which was forced back to Truk after losing a carrier and 60 aircraft. See WATCHTOWER and KE.

2. (JPN 44) One prong of the 1944 ICHI-GO offensive in China launched on 19 April 1944 that cleared the rail lines north of Hankow.

KADESH (IS 56) Israeli preemptive attack launched on 29 October 1956 against Arab (Egyptian and Palestinian) forces in the Sinai. "Operation Kadesh" is a common name in Israel for the entire 1956 war. Conducted in conjunction with the Anglo-French invasion of the area surrounding the Suez Canal (MUSKETEER), this war resulted in the capture of the canal and its facilities by the Western forces shortly after the Arabs sank hundreds of obstacles in the canal. In addition, the entire Gaza and Sinai were occupied by the Israelis. Political considerations forced a mutual withdrawal from the occupied area; a U.N. force was stationed in the Gaza to separate the 2 sides. The canal remained closed until 1974 (NIMBUS MOON, NIMBUS STREAM, NIMBUS STAR). "Kadesh" is a biblical name (Numbers 14:26) for the modern settlement of Ain Kadis in the Sinai.

KAISERSCHLACHT "EMPEROR'S BATTLE" (GER 18) The overall plan for the German spring 1918 offensive. This battle aimed to destroy the Allies in France before the arrival of significant American units. The plan had a number of confusing, overlapping alternatives to be used as events dictated.

KAN (JPN 44) Plan for the Japanese Burma Area Army to defend the Burmese coast from British amphibious landings in the fall of 1944.

KANGAROO (Allied 82) Periodic joint defense exercise hosted by Australia. Ships and aircraft from Singapore, Malaysia, Papua New Guinea, Indonesia, the U. K., and the U.S. have taken part in the past. Designated by year (KANGAROO 92).

KARAT (PO 94) Polish combined forces exercise conducted in May 1994. Air Force units ran a series of attacks against Polish ships in the Baltic.

KARLSBAD (GER 41) The first of a long series of anti-partisan operations conducted by the Germans in an attempt to secure their lines of supply in eastern Europe. This operation began on 12 October 1941 between Minsk and Smolensk, Ukraine.

KE (JPN 42) Evacuation of Japanese forces from Guadalcanal in late January 1942. This escape was conducted with superior skill, and resulted in the U.S. cruiser *Chicago* being sunk on 29 January. See WATCHTOWER and KA-GO.

KEELHAUL (Allied 45) The forcible repatriation of Soviet personnel in the hands of the Western allies at the conclusion of World War II. Many of these people were killed or imprisoned by the Soviet government for becoming prisoners of the Nazis. This repatriation was required by agreements reached at Yalta (ARGONAUT) among the "Big Three." In many instances, force had to be used to return these unfortunates. Some killed themselves rather than fall into the hands of the Soviets.

KE KOA 95 (U.S./CN) A naval exercise in Hawaiian waters based around the American carrier *Carl Vinson* and including the Canadian frigate *Annapolis*. In late August 1995 U.S. Army, Air Force, and Hawaii Air National Guard units conducted training on a number of procedures and techniques.

KEEN EDGE (U.S./JPN 95) Training exercise conducted in mid-1995 by elements of the Colorado National Guard and active Army units working with the Japanese 30th Division at Camp Ojojihara, Japan.

KENNECOTT (Allied 42) A deception operation in support of the invasion of North Africa (TORCH). KENNECOTT falsely depicted the threat of an Allied invasion against southern Italy, Greece, and Crete. See TOWNSMAN.

KERNEL (U.S.) General designator for a program of amphibious exercises conducted by

the U.S. 3rd Fleet throughout the eastern and middle Pacific Ocean region. See VALIANT.

KESTREL (FR 95) See CRECERELLE.

KETSU-GO "OPERATION DECISION" (JPN 45) Plan for the defense of the Japanese home islands against an American-led invasion. Published on 8 April 1945 this plan called for the mobilization of 32,000,000 Japanese civilians into a poorly armed militia to back up almost 3,000,000 soldiers. Suicide planes and boats were to attack the invaders initially and guerrilla bands were to harass the rear areas after the landing. Post-war studies showed that the Japanese accurately predicted the sites of the planned American landings and focused on defense of those areas. See DOWNFALL, SHO-GO, and TO-GO.

KEYHOLE (U.K. 82) British special operation on South Georgia in the South Atlantic. Special Air Services teams were landed covertly to observe Argentine activities. The harsh conditions on the island claimed several of these highly trained commandos. The commandos spotted the Argentine submarine *Santa Fe* in port; it was quickly disabled by British airpower. Part of CORPORATE.

KEYSTONE BLUEJAY
KEYSTONE CARDINAL
KEYSTONE EAGLE
KEYSTONE ROBIN (U.S. 69) The phased withdrawal of American military units from Vietnam. See EAGLE PULL.

KICK OFF

1. (U.N. 51) American shore bombardment of communist defenses at Wonsan, Korea, on 18 July 1951. A phony invasion fleet lured the defenders out of their bunkers, where they were exposed to American air and sea power.

2. (U.S. 52) The modification of F-84 aircraft of the U.S. Air Force's former Strategic Air Command to carry nuclear weapons.

KILLER (U.N. 51) Attack launched in February 1951 by the U.S. 9th Corps to destroy Chinese and North Korean forces east of the Han River, and south of the general line Yangp'yong-Hyonch'on-Haanmiri. This attack was marked by massive American firepower. After reaching the KILLER objectives, the advance continued under the name RIPPER and later COURAGEOUS.

KINDLE LIBERTY (U.S./PN) The annual combined American/Panamanian exercise of plans to defend the Panama Canal. These exercises helped prepare the Panama Defense Forces to accept responsibility for the canal in the year 2000. The Panama Defense Forces were disbanded at the conclusion of the American invasion in December 1992 (JUST CAUSE).

KING I (Allied 44) Planned American landing at Saragani Bay on Mindanao; canceled in November 1944.

KING II (Allied 44) The invasion of Leyte, which culminated in the Battle of Leyte Gulf, the climactic battle of World War II in the Pacific. The first amphibious landings were conducted at Tacloban on Leyte's east coast on 20 October 1944. This landing included Douglas MacArthur's much-photographed wading ashore. The Japanese made a heroic, if suicidal, naval counterattack. A sacrificial task force of carriers, stripped of their air wings, was spotted by the American main force and lured them out of position. The Japanese bait was sunk on 25 October off Cape England. Simultaneously, the remnants of the Japanese battleship fleet approached from the south in 2 task forces. One of these forces was sunk in a night battle in the Surigao Strait that was almost unique as a night battleship gun duel. The second task force (headed by the huge battleship *Musashi*) attacked the American covering force at dawn on the 25th in conjunction with ground-based kamikaze aircraft. The American small carriers still on station protecting the landings (a force dubbed "Taffy 3") were totally outclassed and were decimated by the time the Japanese retired. Despite the stinging blow suffered by Taffy 3, the battle, the greatest in naval history, was a decisive victory for the Americans. This broke the back of Japanese resistance in the archipelago; garrisons on each island could now be attacked one by one. The invasion of the critical island of Luzon (MIKE) followed a month later. The rest of the islands were cleared by the VICTOR series.

KINGFISHER (U.S. 66) The third largest American search and destroy operation conducted in Vietnam as part of an attrition strategy.

KINMEN (P.R.C. 95) Amphibious training exercise conducted by mainland Chinese troops near Nationalist-held islands. This training was conducted the day before the Nationalist's first direct presidential election. This intimidation was aimed at preventing a Taiwanese declaration of independence. Such a declaration, the Chinese announced, would lead to an actual invasion.

KITTENS (U.K. 53) British nuclear safety tests, which studied the components of nuclear weapons but did not involve a nuclear detonation. Conducted between 1953 and 1963 at Emu Field and the Maralinga test areas in Australia. Also called RATS, TIMS, and VIXENS.

KLABAUTERMANN 'HOBGOBLIN" (GER 42) The blockade of Leningrad (St. Petersburg) by German patrol boats on Lake Ladoga in the summer of 1942. The boats were partially dissembled and transported overland to the lake.

KLIPKLOP (R.S.A. 80) July 1980 South African attack on the SWAPO faction in Angola. Followed SCEPTIC, preceded PROTEA.

KLONDIKE I (Allied 42) A deception operation for the raid at Dieppe, France (JUBILEE). The troops scheduled to make the raid were loaded into their boats under the cover of another training exercise KLONDIKE I. In fact the rehearsal was the actual raid.

KLONDIKE KEY (U.S. 88) Plan to conduct Noncombatant Evacuation Operations in Panama. Drawn up in April 1988, this plan called for U.S. troops to set up points throughout Panama City to collect noncombatants and escort them to airports. The Americans feared the Panamanian dictator would seize hostages from the large expatriate American community. Never executed in full scale. Part of the PRAYER BOOK series. See BLADE JEWEL.

KM (Allied convoy) Allied convoys from Britain to North Africa in World War II. Designated by number (e.g., KM 123). Replaced by the OG and OS designations in 1943.

KN (Allied convoy) Allied northbound convoys up the east coast of the U.S. in World War II. Designated by number (e.g., KN 123).

KNIFEDGE (Allied 44) Allied deception operation that falsely depicted preparations for a French ground attack in the Mulhouse-Vesoul area. German agents active in Switzerland were "fed" rumors supporting this phony attack. See JESSICA.

KNIGHT STRIKE (Coalition 91) A large night reconnaissance of the Wadi Al Batin in order to deceive the defending Iraqis that this would be the major attack route

into occupied Kuwait. Conducted on 19 February 1991 by elements of the U.S. 1st Cavalry Division. Moving into the heavily defended area, several American vehicles were struck by concealed Iraqi anti-tank weapons. Followed RED STORM, preceded DEEP STRIKE.

KON (JPN 44) A series of operations to transport Japanese Army reinforcements to the island of Biak (in the Palau Group) after its invasion by the Americans on 27 May 1944. The KON force left Tarakan, Borneo, on 30 May 1944. The fleet was spotted by U.S. aircraft and retired on 4 June. A second attempt was launched on 4 June from Sorong. On 8 June, this force was intercepted by elements of the U.S. fleet. Japanese destroyers towing troops in barges cut loose their tows and fled. One of the 3 barges was sunk, the others proceeded to Biak. A third force including 2 battleships was scheduled to leave Tawitawi on 10 June but was redirected to support A-GO and never left for Biak. The name KON can be loosely translated as "Water Army." KON was a part of the larger A-GO operation.

KONSTANTIN "CONSTANTINE" (GER 43) Reinforcement of German troops in the Balkans and Greece in mid-1943. Increased resistance in the region required a large number of troops to protect supply lines and other facilities.

KOPENHAGEN "COPENHAGEN" (GER 43) Part of the German occupation of Italy (ACHSE). German operation to seize the Mont Cenis Pass, on the Franco-Italian border after the Italian government defected from the Axis cause on 3 September 1943.

KORMORAN "CORMORANT" (GER 43) A month-long anti-partisan sweep in the Minsk Borisov section of the Warsaw-Moscow rail line that began on 22 May 1943.

KORRIDOR "CORRIDOR" (GER 42) The breakout of the German 2nd Corps from their encirclement at Demyansk, Russia, in March 1942.

KOTTBUS (GER 43) See COTTBUS.

KRAAL (R.S.A. 74) Secret South African program that produced 7 primitive nuclear weapons despite a U.N. arms embargo. Ordered by Prime Minister John Vorster in 1974, the first working prototype was completed 3 years later. Working at a secret facility located near the legitimate nuclear research center at Pelindaba, about 150 technicians purified the plentiful supply of "yellow cake" ore into weapons grade uranium 235. The program eventually completed an arsenal of 7 weapons suitable for aircraft delivery. The South Africans felt threatened during this period by Angola and Mozambique. These weapons apparently were meant to be used as a final trump card in the event of an invasion. In late 1990, President F.W. Deklerk directed the weapons be dismantled and all the plans be destroyed. This was completed in July 1991 making South Africa the first nuclear nation to disarm itself. This action by the final white government of that nation precluded the new government from having weapons of mass destruction. A kraal is a native redoubt or fortified village commonly built on hilltops and surrounded by high wooden walls.

KREMEL "KREMLIN" (GER 42) A deception operation, which falsely portrayed that the 1942 German summer offensive would be aimed at Moscow. In fact, the actual offensive (BLAU) was directed at oil fields in southern Russia.

KRUCHEN (Allied 43) British training exercise conducted in April 1943 to develop tactics and techniques to clear German beach defenses.

KRYSTAL BALL (U.S. 88) Plan drawn up in April 1988 to conduct civil-military stability operations in Panama. Succeeded by BLIND LOGIC, then PROMOTE LIBERTY. Part of PRAYER BOOK.

KS (Allied convoy) Allied convoys southbound along the east coast of the U.S. Designated by number (e.g., KS 123). See JW, ON, ONS.

KÜSTE "COAST" (GER 44) An air raid on Warsaw conducted by more than 400 German aircraft dropping over 70 tons of incendiaries on 25 September 1944 in response to the Warsaw ghetto uprising. See ONEG SHABBAT.

KUTUSOV (SU 43) Counterattack launched on 12 July 1943 against the northern shoulder of the Orel salient, part of the Battle of Kursk. This assault did not achieve its geographic objectives but did serve to prevent the Germans from continuing their southward push toward Kursk that began 4 days before. See ZITADELLE.

L

LACE (U. S. Law Enforcement 86) A joint CIA/FBI task force inquiry into the possibility of a Soviet "mole" in the CIA. Suspicions were raised after the fall of the Berlin Wall when East German documents showed every American agent in that country had been detected. This investigation was followed by PLAYACTOR and SKYLIGHT, both of which also failed to detect the traitor. The NIGHTMOVER investigation in 1993 caught the turncoat Aldrich Ames.

LACHSFALLE "SALMON CATCH" (Axis 42) Proposed joint German-Finnish attack on Soviet positions at Kandalaksha and Belomorsk, Russia. Planned for the summer or fall of 1942. The Finns refused to attack beyond their prewar boundaries. Never executed.

LAGOON (AUS/B.I.G. 94) Australian support for the South Pacific Peacekeeping Force (SPPKF) in support of a cease-fire between Bougainville Revolutionary Army (BRA) and the Bougainville Interim Government (BIG). In September 1994, the cease-fire agreement was signed that called for a joint peacekeeping force consisting of troops from Fiji, Tonga, and Vanuatu. These troops in turn were supported by Australian ships (primarily HMAS *Tobruk* and *Success*) and aircraft.

LADBROKE (Allied 43) British glider landing near Syracuse, Sicily, on the night of 9 July 1943 as part of HUSKY.

LAHAV "BLADE" (IS 60) The Israeli effort to undermine the Egyptian armed forces by smuggling drugs from Lebanon through Israel to Egypt. This effort began in the 1960s as an investigation into the drug smugglers operating from Lebanon. The Israelis quickly realized that moving the contraband in military trucks to Egypt would prevent a drug problem in Israel and reduce the efficiency of the Egyptians. The operation continued until the late 1980s, well after peace between the 2 nations. In the late 1960s and early 1970s, up to half the Egyptian military were using hashish. Profits from the operation were fed into secret Israeli accounts used to fund other covert operations.

LAMANTIN "MANATEE" (FR 77) The deployment of French aircraft and troops to Dakar, Senegal, in December 1977. These units conducted raids on Polisario guerrillas who, backed by Mauritania, claimed areas of the former Spanish Sahara. Under the pressure of French and Senegalese attacks, Mauritania gave up its claims to the disputed territory and ended the war. See TACAUD.

LAM SONG (R.V.N. 1960s) Lam Song was a semi-mythical Vietnamese hero who fought the Chinese. The Republic of Vietnam used this name along with a number to designate plans developed by their high command. The plans were designated by number.

LAM SONG 719 (R.V.N. 71) The February 1971 invasion of Laos by the Army of the Republic of Vietnam (ARVN) designed to cut North Vietnamese supply lines running through that country. The operation was a fiasco. Despite intelligence reports that the area was occupied by support troops only, the ARVN force ran into stiff resistance and had to withdraw. Meant to demonstrate the ability of South Vietnam to fight its own war, they in fact showed themselves reliant upon massive American air power to maintain an orderly retreat.

LANCE (CN 93) Canadian participation in the U.N. Observer Mission Uganda-Rwanda (UNOMUR). This mission, established in 1993, observed the frontier between the 2 nations to prevent rebel Rwandans from crossing from bases in Uganda. The Canadians provided an aircraft logistics unit of 45 people (called SCOTCH) at Nairobi, Kenya, from April to September 1994, and a medical unit of 247 personnel (PASSAGE) based at Goma, Zaire, from July to October 1994. Additional units provided security, signal, and other support during this humanitarian effort.

LAND CRAB (U.S. 43) Liberation of the Japanese-occupied Alaskan islands of Attu and Kiska by elements of the U.S. 7th Infantry Division. Attu was invaded on 1 May 1943 and the garrison there was quickly defeated. The invasion of Kiska in mid-August met with no opposition as the Japanese evacuated the garrison on the night of 28 July. See AL.

LARGESSE (Allied 43) Allied amphibious landing near Sfax on the Gulf of Gabes in eastern Tunisia to cut Italian supply lines. Conducted on 5 January 1943.

LARKHILL (Allied 42) Allied deception operation that used "turned" enemy agents, phony radio traffic and other means to exaggerate the size and capability of American forces in the British Isles. Part of COCKADE. See DUNDAS.

LAST (Allied 44) Amphibious training exercise held by Canadian troops in England in April 1944 in preparation for the invasion of northern France (OVERLORD).

LATCH KEY
LATCHKEY (U.S. 66) A series of 27 nuclear test explosions at the Nevada Test Site (with one exception). These tests followed the FLINTLOCK series and were in turn followed by CROSSTIE. The individual explosions were:

SAXON	28 July 66	<20 kilotons, see PLOWSHARE
ROVENA	10 August	<20 kilotons
DERRINGER	9 September	prob. 12 kilotons
DAIQUIRI	23 September	<20 kilotons
NEWARK	26 September	<20 kilotons
SIMMS	5 November	<20 kilotons, see PLOWSHARE
AJAX	11 November	<20 kilotons
CERISE	18 November	<20 kilotons
STERLING	3 December	380 tons, near Hattiesburg, Mississippi
NEW POINT	13 December	prob. 10 kilotons
GREELY	20 December	870 kilotons
NASH	19 January 67	prob. 49 kilotons
BOURBON	20 January	prob. 29 kilotons
WARD	8 February	prob. 10 kilotons
PERSIMMON	23 February	prob. 3 kilotons
AGILE	23 February	prob. 130 kilotons
RIVET III	2 March	<20 kilotons
FAWN	7 April	<20 kilotons
CHOCOLATE	21 April	prob. 7 kilotons
EFFENDI	27 April	<20 kilotons
MICKEY	10 May	prob. 10 kilotons
COMMODORE	20 May	250 kilotons
SCOTCH	23 May	155 kilotons

KNICKER-BROCKER	26 May	76 kilotons
SWITCH	22 June	<20 kilotons, see PLOWSHARE
MIDI MIST	26 June	prob. 9 kilotons
UMBER	29 June	prob. 8 kilotons

LB (Allied 42) The delivery of Spitfire fighters to Malta on 18 May 1942.

LEADER (Allied 43) British and American air attacks on shipping in and around the Norwegian port of Bodo in October 1943. Bodo served as a port for iron ore from neutral Sweden.

LEAP FROG

1. (U.S. 53) A long-range bombing exercise conducted in early August 1953 by 2 B-47 wings of the former Strategic Air Command. The bombers flew from Hunter Air Force Base in Georgia and attacked simulated targets before landing at bases in North Africa. Concurrent with LONGSTRIDE.

2. (CN 52) The movement of Royal Canadian Air Force Sabre fighter jets from Canada to Europe begun May 1952. Followed by RANDOM.

LEAPING LENA (U.S./R.V.N. 64) A series of airborne infiltrations into areas of Laos and Vietnam by 8-man South Vietnamese teams conducted in 1964 as part of OPLAN 34-A. These patrols took heavy casualties as each was detected by the enemy; additional missions were canceled.

LEDO STRIPTEASE (Allied 43) Subordinate plan of ALBACORE III. This involved the movement of 1 regiment of the American trained and equipped Chinese 22nd Division from Ledo to Fort Hertz to protect the left flank of the Chinese 38th Division's thrust south toward Indaw, Burma.

LEFT HOOK (U.S. 56) A fighter competition sponsored by the former Strategic Air Command for its Strategic Fighter Wings at Offut Air Force Base, Nebraska, from 25 October to 14 November 1956. Five wings sent 36 F-84 Thunderjets each. The competition was won by the 506th Strategic Fighter Wing. This competition was held only once; the newly-fielded B-52 bombers did not require fighter escorts, and the Strategic Fighter Wings were disbanded.

LEHRGANG "TRAINING COURSE" (GER 43) Evacuation of German troops from Sicily to the Italian mainland. Executed 11-17 August 1943. See HUSKY.

LEMMING (Allied 45) A combined American/Canadian evaluation of over-snow tracked vehicles conducted near Churchill, Manitoba, in early spring 1945.

LENA (GER 40) Insertion of German spies by submarine into England on 3 September 1940. The 4 misfit secret agents were captured within hours. Three were hanged, but another convinced a British jury he was really a Dutch patriot who simply posed as a spy to escape Nazi-occupied Europe.

LEOPARD

1. (GER 43) German invasion of the Greek island of Leros on 12 November 1943.

2. (Allied 42) A British attempt to land 10 tons of weapons and other supplies for use by the Algerian resistance on the night of 5 November 1942. The Royal Navy failed to make contact with the partisans on the shore, and had to abandon the effort.

LEVER (Allied 45) British attack to clear the area between the Reno River and Lake Comacchio, in northern Italy, conducted in April 1945.

LICHTMEER "SEA OF LIGHT" (GER 40) German air attack on British bomber bases during the Battle of Britain (ADLER).

LIEGE (GER 44) See LÜTTICH.

LIFEBELT (Allied 43) Plan for an amphibious operation against the Azores. These islands were needed as Allied air bases in the Battle of the Atlantic. Never executed. Basing rights were obtained by negotiation in October 1943. The British established an air base at Terceria in the Azores in January 1944.

LIFELINE (U.N. 92) A mostly-British operation to protect truck routes from besieged Muslim communities in the former Yugoslavia (including Sarajevo) to seaports. Conducted in the late summer of 1992, the U.N. troops worked to open roadblocks, disarm bandits, and speed the flow of relief supplies inland.

LIFETIME (U.S.) A reserved first word for the programs and projects of the U.S. Army Security Agency.

LIGHTFOOT (Allied 42) British attack that launched the 3rd Battle of El Alamein on the night of 23 October 1942. British forces were fighting an outnumbered, outclassed Axis force at this point. Allied air activity based on Malta had restricted most resupply by the Italians and Germans. In addition, the TORCH invasion of the Western Desert was scheduled for 8 November, to place the Axis in a powerful pincer. When LIGHTFOOT stalled in the thick German minefields in the northern sector, Field Marshal Montgomery redirected his attack to the south (SUPERCHARGE I). When this attack also bogged down, he returned to his original axis of advance on 2 November and achieved a breakthrough the next day against the much-reduced German force. Despite a 20 to 1 advantage in tanks, the British were unable to cut off their retreating enemy who used bad weather to cover their escape into Tripolotania. See BERTRAM and TREATMENT.

LIGHTNING STRIKE (U.S. Law Enforcement 93) A probe of corruption at the National Air and Space Administration's (NASA) Johnson Space Flight Center in Houston, Texas. Made public in December 1993. FBI investigators posed as representatives of "Southern Technologies Diversified" and offered bribes to contractors and NASA personnel to obtain government funding for a project. At least one astronaut was offered an illegal payment but reported the incident immediately to his superiors. Indictments were returned by a grand jury in February 1994 against 2 federal employees. Martin Marietta and General Electric agreed to pay over $1,000,000 in costs, but did not admit guilt.

LILA "LILAC" (GER 42) German occupation of Toulon, France, executed on 27 November 1942. The major objective of this assault was to capture the 58 French warships in port. The French fleet, under orders of its commander, Admiral Jean de Laborde, scuttled itself to prevent its capture by the Germans. See CATAPULT.

LILAC

1. (Allied 41) Plan to move American forces to the Belem-Natal-Recife region of Brazil in 1941 to defend the region against possible Axis attack. Brazil was an Ally during the war and provided troops who fought in Italy. It was an important way point for aircraft on their way to the Middle East and China. Called POT OF GOLD during planning. See VELLUM.

2. (GER 42) See LILA.

LINEAR (U.S.) A reserved first word for the submarine and anti-submarine warfare programs of the U.S. Navy. See LINEAR CHANCE.

LINEAR CHANCE (U.S.) A program to investigate the use of trained porpoises to mark enemy submarines and naval mines.

LINEBACKER
LINEBACKER II (U.S. 72) American air

attacks on North Vietnamese transportation, power, and supply facilities. LINEBACKER I began in May 1972. By fall, 70 percent of the electrical distribution system was knocked out. These attacks ended on 23 October 1972. LINEBACKER II was ordered by President Nixon on 18 December 1972 to force the North Vietnamese back to peace negotiations in Paris. This attack was a massive 11-day campaign beginning on 18 December 1972 and included over 3,000 sorties that dropped 20,000 tons of bombs. Due to bad weather, the crews could attack targets visually for only 12 hours during the campaign; for the first time, electronics were used for pinpoint bombing. Laser-guided bombs were used to destroy heavily bunkered targets such as Radio Hanoi. Targeting was tightly controlled and the North Vietnamese claimed only 1,623 civilians were killed. The Americans lost 22 aircraft, with 43 crewmen killed, and another 41 captured. Although B-52 Stratofortress bombers flying from Guam and Thailand took center stage in this operation, carrier-based naval aircraft dropped a quarter of the total tonnage. Among some Air Force circles, the success of this operation showed that air power would be decisive in future wars. Politically, LINEBACKER II was denounced by the *New York Times* as a "return to barbarism" and was widely referred to as the "Christmas bombing" campaign. As these attacks occurred after U.S. Secretary of State Henry Kissinger had announced "peace is at hand," the renewal of air attacks against North Vietnam may have been designed to reassure the South Vietnamese that they would not be abandoned by their allies.

LINK (Allied 43) Exercise conducted by the British 61st Infantry Division and the Polish First Armored Division conducted in England in September 1943.

LINNET I

LINNET II (Allied 44) Airborne assaults planned to assist in the breakout from northern France (GOODWOOD, COBRA). Canceled due to bad weather.

LITTERBUG (U.S. 70) The dropping of propaganda leaflets over North Vietnam by American drone aircraft.

LITTLE FELLER (U.S. 62) A series of 4 nuclear tests conducted between 7 and 17 July 1962 at the Nevada Test Site. At one of these blasts, dubbed LITTLE FELLER I, a small tactical warhead was fired by a "Davy Crockett" system. Ground troops then "attacked" into the contaminated area in vehicles for 50 minutes. This exercise was observed by a number of high-ranking Army officials. See DESERT ROCK. Followed NOUGAT; preceded NIBLICK.

LITTLE SWITCH (U.N. 53) The first exchange of prisoners in the Korean War. A total of 6,670 sick or wounded held by the U.N. (5,194 North Korean, 1,030 Chinese, and 446 civilians) were exchanged for 684 U.N. soldiers. The exchange began on 20 April 1953 and ran until 3 May at Panmunjom. See BIG SWITCH and SCATTER.

LITTLE VITTLES (U.S./U.K. 48) Informal program begun by American fliers during the Berlin Airlift (VITTLES) and later adopted officially. U.S. Air Force Lieutenant Gail Halvorsen began to throw candy attached to parachutes made of handkerchiefs from his cockpit while flying over the city. This captured the imagination of the besieged Berliners. It was expanded to include special LITTLE VITTLES flights that visited Berlin without landing, dropping treats to the children in both the Soviet and Allied sectors of the city. Halvorsen became a well-known hero to the city and was included in commemorations ceremonies of the Airlift for many years.

LOCK (U.S.) A reserved first word for the programs and projects of the U.S. Air Force's Communication Service.

LOCUSTA "LOCUST" (IT 90) The Italian contribution of 3 fighter squadrons to the Coalition that liberated Kuwait (DESERT STORM). The units, equipped with Tornado aircraft, were based at Al Dhafra, Abu Dhabi. They used their advanced bombing equipment to destroy critical elements of the Iraqi air defense system.

LOFTY THUNDER (U.S. 91) American effort to develop a nuclear powered rocket engine for use in the "Star Wars" missile defense program. The existence of this program (then called TIMBER WIND) was revealed in 1991 by the Federation of American Scientists. Due to public ridicule, the project was renamed LOFTY THUNDER, and on being exposed again was allegedly canceled. See PLUTO and NERVA.

LOG HORN (U.S.) See TREE TOP.

LOG TREE (U.S.) See TREE TOP.

LOINCLOTH (Allied 43) The first Chindit expedition in Burma. A deep infiltration attack launched by the 77th Indian Brigade (the "Chindits") on 14 February 1943 into Japanese-held territory. The Brigade penetrated 500 miles and destroyed 3 major bridges and numerous Japanese garrisons. Roughly coordinated with CANNIBAL. Followed by THURSDAY.

LOMBARD (Allied 44) Part of the SKYE deception operation that projected the false threat of an Allied invasion of southern Norway. In June 1944, British aircraft flying from the carriers *Victorious* and *Furious* flew reconnaissance and bombing missions (BLUES) over the phony target area.

LONG (U.S.) A reserved first word for the programs and projects of the U.S. Air Force.

LONG ARM (U.S. Law Enforcement 92) An operation by the American Justice Department aimed at electronic bulletin boards featuring child pornography. Begun in 1992, 31 search warrants were executed in March 1993 in 15 states. The operation was made public in August with the indictment of 8 suspects. One of the bulletin boards that attracted the attention of the investigators was based in Aalborg, Denmark.

LONG LIFE (U.S. 65) The only launch of an American intercontinental ballistic missile (ICBM) from an operational silo, conducted on 1 March 1965. A Minuteman I missile of the 44th Strategic Missile Wing was launched from Ellsworth Air Force Base, South Dakota. To prevent the missile from becoming a hazard, it was destroyed 7 seconds after launch. See GIANT PATRIOT.

LONG RIFLE (U.S. 95) A flight by a B-52H Stratofortress on 25 August 1995 from Edwards Air Force Base to a bombing range in Alaska. The flight set a world record speed of 556 mile per hour over 10,000 kilometers in the aircraft category between 200 and 250 tons.

LONG SHOT (U.S.) Periodic U.S. Air Force exercise in which units are deployed at short notice to Nellis Air Force Base in Nevada for tactical training.

LONGSTRIDE (U.S. 53) The self-deployment of 26 F-84G Thunderjet fighters from the U.S. to French Morocco and England executed in late August 1953. These ferrying flights were unique in that they were nonstop; the fighter aircraft used air-to-air refueling to extend their range. The flight from Georgia to North Africa took about 11½ hours. See FOX PETER 1 and FOX PETER 2. Concurrent with LEAP FROG.

LONGSTRIKE (NATO) Annual NATO exercise of long-range surveillance units. Military police teams attempt to capture the scouts as they infiltrate. Designated by year-number (e.g., LONGSTRIKE 92).

LONG THRUST II (NATO 62) An exercise conducted in January 1962 to test the ability of the U.S. to reinforce Europe in an emergency. See BIG LIFT.

LONGTOM (U.S. 45) A plan for an American invasion along the Chinese coast in the final stages of World War II. Never executed.

LOOK (U.S.) A reserved first word used to designate the programs and projects of the U.S. Air Force.

LORRAINE (U.S./R.V.N 52) A mostly-South Vietnamese operation conducted from October 1952 to April 1953 in the Mekong Delta, which captured a Viet Minh supply center at Phu Doan.

LOST TRUST (U.S. Law Enforcement 91) Federal investigation of corruption in the South Carolina legislature conducted in 1991. The investigation began when a former legislator, Ron Cobb, was arrested on an unrelated drug charge. In exchange for a reduction of sentence, Cobb became an operative for the FBI. He rented an elaborate office and began to buy the votes of legislators in support of a pari-mutuel betting bill. Seventeen lawmakers, 10 percent of the entire body, were charged and all but one of those convicted of corruption.

LOVE (Allied 45) A series of small landings in the Philippines designed to secure a line of departure for assaults in the central Philippines (MIKE). American engineers quickly built airfields in the liberated areas to provide air cover for the MIKE landings.

LOVE I American landing at Legaspi Bicol Peninsula on southeast Luzon, conducted on 1 April 1945.

LOVE II The establishment of American air bases on the north coast of Luzon at Apparri to provide protection for convoys passing through the Luzon Straits.

LOVE III The U.S. occupation of southwest Mindanao and the establishment of air bases.

LOVE IV An unopposed American landing on Mariduque Island northeast of Mindoro on 3 January 1945.

LOVE V An unopposed American landing at Bongabong on the east coast of Mindoro.

LOW (U.S.) A reserved first word for the programs and projects of the U.S. Air Force's Air Training Command.

LOYAL (U.S.) A reserved first word for the programs and projects of the U.S. Air Force's Air University.

LUC "LUKE" (BG 40) Intelligence and resistance network setup in occupied Belgium by Walthere Dewe in the summer of 1940. See CLARENCE, DAME BLANCHE, ZERO.

LUCKY DRAGON (U.S. 64) Operations by American U-2 aircraft from Bien Hoa, Vietnam, in 1964. LUCKY DRAGON was one of the operations revealed in the "Pentagon Papers."

LUCKY STRIKE (Allied 44) Plan considered in May and June 1944 for an attack by British 21st Army Group east to capture Seine ports as an alternative to attacking west toward the Channel ports of Brittany.

LUCY

LUCY RING (U.S. 40) Designation for the Soviet spy-master Rudolf Rudessler ("Lucy") and the spy ring run by him during World War II from Lucerne, Switzerland. This Soviet organization included Alexander Foote ("Jim"), a British expatriate. The LUCY RING provided intelligence of extreme importance and accuracy, first to the Swiss, and later to the Soviets. The ring was broken up by the Swiss (under German pressure) in late 1942. LUCY intelligence was so accurate, timely, and important (such as the planned date for BARBAROSSA, its objectives and troop list) that speculation as to its source is still raging. LUCY may have had contact with a high-ranking member of the Nazi government, a member of the Czech or Swiss intelligence agencies, or even may have been a front operated by the British as a means of disguising and passing to the Soviets selected information developed through the ULTRA operation. One indicator that this may have been the case is that the Englishman Foote went to Moscow after the war and continued to work in the Soviet Intelligence. In 1947 he re-defected to Britain where he found a quiet, comfortable post in the Ministry of Agriculture.

LUMBERJACK (Allied 45) The attack by the Allied 12th Army Group that took Cologne and the Ludendorff Bridge over the Rhine at Remagen. This was the first intact bridge captured over that river. On 7 March 1945 elements of the U.S. 9th Armored Division were the first to enter Germany's industrial heartland. See UNDERTONE.

LUSTER

LUSTRE (Allied 41) The dispatch of British troops from Egypt to Greece in March and April 1941. Two infantry and 2 armored divisions were in place in Greece before the German invasion. These forces had no effect on the German invasion (MARITA) and they were quickly evacuated (DEMON). Historians now see that this deployment weakened British forces in North Africa to a point where their COMPASS offensive failed. Some of these units were moved to Crete (SCORCHER), where they were overwhelmed by the airborne invasion of that island.

LÜTTICH "LIEGE" (GER 44) Attack launched by German forces on the left flank of the Allied lodgment at Normandy beginning on 7 August 1944. An Allied counterattack (TOTALIZE) cut off the attacking forces, forming the "Falaise Pocket."

LYDIA (GER 44) A German retreat by phase line that ended at the Arno River in northern Italy in the summer of 1944.

M

MÄCHEN (GER 44) Alternate name for LYDIA.

MADISON (Allied 44) Attack by Lieutenant General George Patton's 3rd Army east to Metz, France, early December 1944. By 15 December, American troops had crossed the German frontier east of Saarbrucken. When the Germans launched their surprise Ardennes Offensive (WACHT AM RHEIN), these troops were perfectly positioned to swing north and pinch off the advance.

MAGIC (U.S. 39) Radio interception and decoding operations directed against the Japanese diplomatic "Purple" code by a U.S. Army team led by Colonel William Friedman beginning in early 1939. The code was largely broken by late 1941; the task then became decoding and translating the huge volume of Japanese radio traffic. By extension, "MAGIC" came to mean the products of this effort. Perhaps the most important contribution of MAGIC was information that allowed an outnumbered U.S. Navy to crush the Japanese at Midway (MI).

MAGIC CARPET (U.S. 45) The use of warships as troop-transports to return American troops home after World War II.

MAGIC FLUTE (GER 43) See ZAUBER-FLÖTE.

MAGNET (Allied 42) The movement of the U.S. 5th Corps to northern Ireland for that region's defense, releasing British troops for duty elsewhere. See BOLERO and SHADOW 82.

MAGNETO (Allied 45) See ARGONAUT.

MAILFIST (Allied 45) British plan to recapture Singapore in early 1946. Never executed. See ZIPPER.

MAINBRACE (NATO 52) An early combined naval exercise sponsored by the Supreme Allied Commander, Atlantic in the fall of 1952. Over 150 ships participated. This exercise highlighted the difficulty in coordinating, supplying, and organizing ships from NATO member states.

MAIN ROUGE "RED HAND" (FR 56) A program of assassination and other covert actions by the French intelligence agencies from 1956 to 1960, designed to suppress Algerian agitation for independence.

MAISKOLBEN "CORNCOB" (GER 43) Plan to intern the rural male population of Serbia in September 1943 to deny the local resistance fighters a recruiting and support base.

MAJESTIC

1. (Allied 45) An alternate plan for the invasion of the southernmost Japanese home island of Kyushu. Rejected in favor of OLYMPIC.

2. (U.S. 47) Supposedly, a highly-secret American investigation of Unidentified Flying Objects begun in July 1947. A segment of society claim the U.S. recovered a crashed flying saucer from a remote area near Roswell, New Mexico, as part of this operation. The Air Force then allegedly froze 2 dead space aliens and transferred the spacecraft to Wright-Patterson Air Force Base in Ohio where their craft was the basis for the impressive advances made by the U.S. in various technical areas in the postwar era. See MOBY DICK and MOGUL.

MALABAR TWO (U.S./IN 95) A joint U.S./Indian naval exercise conducted off the Cochin coast in early June 1995. The exercise featured the American carrier *Abraham Lincoln* and several Indian submarines and destroyers.

MALARIA (GER 42) Anti-partisan operation conducted in February 1942 in the Osipovichi area of Belorussia.

MALLARD (Allied 44) A supply train of gliders that reinforced the British 6th Airborne Division 6 June 1944. See TONGA and OVERLORD.

MALLORY (Allied 44) Air operations by the U.S. 12th Air Force using free-roaming fighter-bombers in late 1944 to destroy railroads and bridges in the Po River Valley to isolate German forces in the region.

MANA (U.K. 92) The British humanitarian relief operation conducted in Bangladesh after the end of the Gulf War. MANA may be a misspelling of MANNA. See SEA ANGEL.

MANATEE (FR 77) See LAMANTIN.

MANCHU (U.N. 50) A local attack launched in late August 1950 from the Pusan perimeter by the U.S. 9th Infantry Regiment (called the "Manchus" from their long service in China). This attack was launched by the regimental reserve across the Nakong River. The attacking force was across the river and became isolated by a major North Korean offensive, which struck across the entire front. With their reserve caught out in the open, the Manchus fought a desperate action that stopped the advancing communists, but which also shattered the regiment.

MANDIBLES (Allied 41) Plan for the invasion of the Dodecanese Islands and Rhodes in 1941. Never executed.

MANDREL (U.S. 69) A series of 43 nuclear test explosions. These tests followed BOWLINE and preceded the EMERY series. All of these tests were conducted at the Nevada Test Site except as noted. The individual blasts of this series were:

ILDRIM	16 July 69	prob. 6 kilotons
HUTCH	16 July	prob. 300 kilotons
SPIDER	14 August	<20 kilotons
PLIERS	27 August	<20 kilotons
RULISON	10 September	47 kilotons, near
	Grand Valley, Colorado, see PLOWSHARE	
MINUTE STEAK	12 September	prob. 10 kilotons
JORUM	16 September	prob. 700 kilotons
MILROW	2 October	1 megaton, near Amchitka, Alaska
PIPKIN	8 October	prob. 82 kilotons
CRUET	29 October	11 kilotons
POD	29 October	20-200 kilotons
CALABASH	29 October	110 kilotons
SCUTTLE	13 November	<20 kilotons
PICALILLI	21 November	prob. 17 kilotons
DIESEL TRAIN	5 December	prob. 16 kilotons
GRAPE A	17 December	prob. 61 kilotons
LOVAGE	17 December	<20 kilotons
TERRINE	18 December	prob. 28 kilotons
FOB	23 January 70	<20 kilotons
AJO	30 January	<20 kilotons
GRAPE B	4 February	prob. 120 kilotons
LABIS	5 February	25 kilotons
DIANA MIST	11 February	prob. 9 kilotons
CUMARIN	25 February	prob. 25 kilotons

YANNIGAN	26 February	prob. 100 kilotons
CYATHUS	6 March	8.7 kilotons
ARABIS	6 March	<20 kilotons
JAL	19 March	prob. 6 kilotons
SHAPER	23 March	prob. 93 kilotons
HANDLEY	26 March	prob. 1.9 megatons
SNUBBER	21 April	prob. 6 kilotons
CAN	21 April	prob. 8 kilotons
BEEBALM	1 May	prob. 1 kiloton
HOD	1 May	prob. 6 kilotons
MINT LEAF	5 May	prob. 28 kilotons
DIAMOND DUST	12 May	<20 kilotons
CORNICE	15 May	prob. 39 kilotons
MANZANAS	21 May	prob. 1 kiloton
MORRONES	21 May	prob. 20 kilotons
HUDSON MOON	26 May	prob. 9 kilotons
FLASK	26 May	105 kilotons, see PLOWSHARE
(Unknown)	28 May	(unknown)
ARNICA	26 June	20-200 kilotons

MANHATTAN ENGINEER DISTRICT (Allied 40) The American program to develop the atomic bomb. Established in October 1940, the project enjoyed top priority for manpower and material. The first atomic bomb test (TRINITY) was conducted at 0530 on 16 July 1945 at Alamogordo, New Mexico. The use of this new weapon against Japan (CENTERBOARD) forced an early end to the war and precluded a land invasion of the home islands (DOWNFALL). See ALSOS, COMBINED DEVELOPMENT TRUST, and TUBE ALLOYS.

MANHOLE (Allied 44) The insertion of a Soviet military mission to Tito's partisan headquarters on 23 February 1944. The delegation was delivered by American gliders flying out of bases in Italy.

MANNA

1. (Allied 44) British expedition to Greece during the German collapse in the Balkans.

Executed on 4 October 1944. On 12 October, the Germans began to evacuate; British paratroopers occupied Athens on 15 October and moved north following the retreat. This strengthened anti-Communist forces in Greece and may have prevented a Soviet occupation of that country. See LUSTER.

2. (Allied 45) The air supply of tons of food to German-occupied Dutch cities beginning in April 1945 to reduce the level of starvation in the Netherlands. Local German commanders agreed not to interfere with these deliveries. Despite this effort, over 16,000 civilians starved. See CHOWHOUND and FAUST.

3. (U.K. 92) See MANA.

MANTA (FR 83) French intervention in the Chadian civil war. French aircraft based at N'djamena attacked rebel forces who were supported by the Libyans. As a result of this effort, the rebel faction was defeated and Chad was prevented from falling into a Libyan orbit.

MAPLE (Allied 44) Naval mine sweeping operations in support of the invasion of northern France (OVERLORD). Part of NEPTUNE.

MAPLE FLAG (U.S./CN 76) Annual air combat training exercises conducted at Cold Lake, Alberta, by U.S. and Canadian crews. Modeled on RED FLAG, and supported by RED FLAG adversary units from U.S.A.F.

MARDER "MARTEN" (GER 44) German plan for the defense of the Italian mainland in the event of an Allied amphibious landing. Executed in response to the Allied attack at Anzio (AVALANCHE).

MARGARETHE I (GER 44) Occupation of Hungary by Nazi forces on 12 March 1944. The Hungarian government had been a German ally but surrendered to the Red Army in early 1944. Hitler ordered this move to recapture critical facilities and to redeem his betrayal by the Hungarians. See MICKEY MOUSE.

MARGARETHE II (GER 44) Plan for a Nazi invasion of Rumania if that government were to surrender to the Soviets. Never executed.

MARIE (Allied 40) Plan for an invasion of the Vichy-controlled French colony of Djibouti on the Horn of Africa by Free French forces. Scheduled for November 1940, but never executed.

MARIGOLD (Allied 43) British landing on the coast of Sardinia on 30 May 1943.

MARION (R.S.A. 86) The secret training of assassination teams from among elements of the Inkatha Freedom Party by the white government of the Republic of South Africa. The Freedom Party was a Zulu political rival to the African National Congress. To encourage black-on-black violence, the white security agencies flew selected recruits to "Camp Hippo" in Namibia (then occupied by South African troops) for a course that included house-breaking, bomb-making, and marksmanship. This operation was made public in the mid-1990s when a Truth and Reconciliation Commission began inquiries into South Africa's "dirty war."

MARITA (GER 41) German invasion of Greece and Yugoslavia on 6 April 1941. Planned under the name OP25. The Italians invaded Greece from Albania in October 1940 but quickly got bogged down. The German troops struck from Rumania and Bulgaria, outflanking the Greeks who had pushed the Italians back into their own territory. British units, transferred from North Africa (LUSTRE) arrived too late to be of any real use. The fighting delayed the invasion of Russia (BARBAROSSA) by 5 critical weeks, forcing the Germans to face bitter cold just as

they were reaching their primary objectives. See BESTRAUFUNG and DEMON.

MARITIME GUARD
MARITIME MONITOR (NATO 93) Alternate names for naval operations in the Adriatic Sea to enforce the international arms blockade on the former Yugoslavia. Components, with SHARP FENCE, of SHARP GUARD.

MARKET (Allied 44) The airborne portion of MARKET-GARDEN. The airborne seizure of bridges over the Maas, Waal, and Neder Rijn Rivers at Grave, Nijmegen, and Arnhem respectively to open a path for a quick armored thrust through the low countries (GARDEN). Executed 7 September 1944. After a 5-day battle, the Germans managed to recapture the Arnhem bridge from the British 1st Airborne Division and the Polish Parachute Brigade. Only 2,000 of the original 9,000 paratroopers escaped the encirclement there. The American 82nd and 101st Airborne Division were quickly relieved by the British 30th Corps. The attack failed to shatter the German lines as hoped, and so ended the Allied hopes for a victory in Europe in 1944. Early planning was under the name CARPET. See COMET.

MARKET-GARDEN (Allied 44) See MARKET and GARDEN.

MARKET TIME (U.S./R.V.N. 65) Supply interdiction operations conducted by the U.S. and South Vietnamese navies from the spring of 1965 to the end of 1966. See GAME WARDEN.

MARQUIS
1. (FR 74) A French open-air nuclear test conducted using a AN52 nuclear bomb delivered by a Jaguar fighter-bomber over the Murroa Atoll in French Polynesia.

2. (CN 92) Deployment of Canadian officers as part of the U.N. Transition Authority in Cambodia in 1992/93.

MARS (GER 18) Attack against British force between Cambrai and Lens, in Picardy. This attack was launched in support of the HEILGER MICHAEL attack. After limited success, this attack fizzled out by 5 April 1918. See KAISERSCHLACHT.

MARSTON (Allied 43) Airborne assault conducted by the British 1st Airborne Division's 1st Brigade against Primosole Bridge in Sicily in July 1943. Part of the invasion of Sicily (HUSKY). See FUSTIAN.

MARTIN (GER 44) Plan prepared by Field Marshal Gerd Von Rundstedt as an alternative to HERBSTNEBEL and WACHT AM RHINE. Never executed.

MASCOT (Allied 44) A British attack conducted on 17 July 1944 against the German battle-cruiser *Tirpitz* in harbor at Kaafjord, Norway. This operation was the largest British naval air strike of the war, involving 95 aircraft flying from the carriers *Formidable*, *Indomitable*, and *Furious*. German smoke generators shrouded the area in a thick haze that hid the target. Two British aircraft were lost. See BRAWN, GOODWOOD, and TUNGSTEN.

MASHER (U.S. 66) See WHITE WING.

MASTERDOM (Allied 45) Franco-British operation to overthrow the nationalist government set up by local freedom fighters in Saigon, Vietnam. Shortly after the end of the war, the British used captured Japanese units to supplement their forces in the French colony. The European effort set off a civil war in Vietnam that ended over 30 years later.

MASTIFF (Allied 45) An aerial supply effort to drop medicine and other items to Allied prisoners in remote Japanese prison camps immediately following the end of World War II. See BIRDCAGE.

MATADOR (Allied 40) Pre-war plan by the British to move into Thailand to deny ports

and other facilities to the Japanese. Never executed.

MATCH (CN 92) Deployment of Canadian officers as part of the United Nations Observer Mission in El Salvador (UNOSAL) from 1992 to 1994. See SULTAN.

MATTERHORN

1. (Allied 44) Air attacks on Japanese targets by B-29 Superfortress bombers from bases near Cheng-tu, China, in 1944. Approved in April 1944, the plan called for 750 sorties to be flown against 6 targets. Due to shortages of fuel, bombs, and engines, the attacks did not begin until 5 June. The first target was the rail yards in Bangkok, Thailand. Supplies for these aircraft had to be flown over "The Hump" from bases in Burma. Despite claims that the B-29 was "self-supporting," the number of raids was limited by poor logistical support. Only 2 raids could be mounted a month. The last attack of the series was flown against the steel factory at Anshan on 26 September. The logistical difficulties of MATTERHORN made the capture of Pacific islands for air bases a high priority. See TWILIGHT and BOOMERANG.

2. (U.K. 63) Deployment of British bombers during the Malayan emergency. Part of CHAMFORM.

MAUD Committee (U.K. 40) The first British organization to evaluate the possibility of building an atomic bomb. The report of this committee, produced in late 1941, speculated that a nuclear bomb might be ready as soon as 1943. This top-secret committee was infiltrated by Soviet agents, although their identities remain unknown. A copy of the report was sent to Moscow in September 1941. The name MAUD is meaningless. See TUBE ALLOYS.

MAURICE (Allied 40) One plan to land an Allied amphibious force at Trondheim,

Norway, during the "phony war" in 1940. German action (WESSERBÜNG) rendered this plan obsolete. Included the planned HENRY landing.

MAYFLIGHT (U.K.) British term used to describe their quick-reaction nuclear bombers during the Cold War.

MAYFLOWER (U.S. 65) American diplomatic initiative designed to bring the North Vietnamese to the negotiating table. On 13 May 1965, President Johnson ordered a secret 2-day pause in the American bombing of North Vietnam (FLAMING DART). He then had Ambassador Foy Kohler deliver a diplomatic proposal to the North Vietnamese legation in Moscow. The Vietnamese returned the letter unopened and the bombing resumed.

ME (Allied) Allied convoys from Malta to Alexandria in World War II. Designated by number (e.g., ME 123).

MEBOS (R.S.A. 82) South African attack on SWAPO forces near Cassinga. Followed DAISY, preceded ASKARI.

MENACE (Allied 40) Plan for the unopposed occupation of Vichy-controlled Dakar in French West Africa (now Senegal). The Anglo-French force attempted to land on 23 September 1940, but were repulsed by the local garrison who drove off the attackers with the French battleship *Richelieu*, submarines, and other naval forces. The operation was canceled on 25 September by Winston Churchill. French West Africa and Dakar remained loyal to the Vichy government until the invasion of North Africa by the Americans (see TORCH). Earlier versions of this plan were called SCIPIO, BLACK, BARRISTER, and PICADOR.

MENGELE (SP) Human experiments conducted on vagrants by the Spanish government in the early 1990s. At least one of these unfortunates died while being used to test drugs designed to be used during interrogations of separatist fighters. Part of Spain's "Dirty War." Named after the Nazi Doctor Josef Mengele who performed inhuman acts on prisoners at Auschwitz.

MENU (U.S. 68) The first American bombing campaign in Southeast Asia by the Nixon Administration. This series of attacks began on 17 March 1968 and was designed to attack communist staging areas in Cambodia with a short, intense series of attacks. In fact the attacks dragged on for 14 months. The American government attempted to keep the attacks on the neutral country secret. The *New York Times* reported on the attacks in May 1973. See LINEBACKER.

MERCURY (GER 41) See MERKUR.

MERIDIAN (Allied 45) British air attacks conducted on 24 and 29 January 1945 on Japanese-held oil refineries at Palembang, on Sumatra. The critical aviation fuel output of these plants was reduced 75 percent. Followed by COCKPIT.

MERKUR "MERCURY" (GER 41) The German invasion of Crete on 20 May 1941. Approved by Hitler on 25 April in War Directive Twenty-eight, the plan called for the 11th Fliegercorps to control an attack by the 7th Airborne and the 22nd Air Landing Divisions scheduled for 16 May; it was postponed to 20 May and the 5th Mountain Division replaced the 22nd Division. Despite massive casualties among the attackers, the invasion was a success. The Royal Navy destroyed most of the seaborne follow-on forces on the night of 21-22 May but additional troops were flown in. The Royal Navy was forced out on 24 May due to heavy air attacks; this allowed the Germans to move in additional forces, which carried the day. The British began an evacuation on the night of 28 May; about 16,500 men were rescued at the cost of 9 ships lost. Although the island fell on 2 June, casualties to the German airborne forces precluded any further major airborne attacks for the remainder of the war and may have influenced planning for SEELOWE. See SCORCHER.

MERRIMAC (U.S. 67) Illegal CIA project conducted from February 1967 to November 1971 to monitor dissident groups in the U.S. A major goal of this effort was to identify any people and groups who might pose danger to CIA personnel and installations. See CHAOS.

MG (Allied) Allied convoys from Malta to Gibraltar in World War II. Designated by number (e.g., MG 123).

MHCHAOS (U.S. 67) See CHAOS.

MI (JPN 42) Operation designed to seize the island of Midway as part of Operation MO, the overall Japanese plan for 1942. This was designed to set off a decisive naval battle with the American fleet during the resulting Battle of Midway, 3-4 June 1942 when 3 American carriers ambushed 4 Japanese carriers. As a result, the advance of the Japanese was halted in the central Pacific. See AL.

MIAMI MOON (US 57) The deployment of the U.S. Air Force's 72nd Bomb Squadron from its home base at Mountain Home Air Force Base to Hawaii in the summer of 1957. While at Hickham Air Force Base, the B-52 bombers flew into clouds produced by British and Soviet atomic tests to collect intelligence information. These missions ended in June 1958.

MICHAEL (GER 44) Plan for the evacuation of German troops from the Crimean Peninsula. Canceled by Hitler.

MICKEY MOUSE (GER 44) Commando operation led by the SS officer Otto Skorzeny that captured the Hungarian leader Admiral Horthy and the Budapest Citadel on 15 October 1944 to ensure Hungarian loyalty. The next day, a puppet regime was set up by local fascists. Also called PANZERFAUST. See MARGARETHE I.

MICKY FINN (Allied 44) A company-sized raid by the Black Watch of Canada on 7 December 1944 on Knapheide, south of Groesbeek, the Netherlands.

MIKE (Allied 45) The American landings that liberated the population of the Philippines. After the recapture of Luzon (KING II), MacArthur felt a moral obligation to free the remainder of the archipelago. MIKE consisted of a large number of proposed landings and other operations. Each plan was numbered, but were executed out of sequence. Followed by VICTOR.

MIKE I The major American invasion of Luzon, the principal island of the Philippines. On 9 January 1945 the U.S. 1st and 14th Corps came ashore at Lingayen Gulf, halfway up the west coast of the island. The Japanese decimated their air power in a heroic but futile kamikaze defense but refused to make a stand on the beaches. The Americans encountered no immediate resistance and rapidly moved inland.

MIKE VII Landing of the U.S. 11th Corps at San Antonia on the west coast of Luzon on 29 January 1945. The Americans quickly took the Subic Bay naval base, but encountered heavy resistance further inland at Zig-Zag Pass. With heavy air support from aircraft based on the recently-captured airstrips, the Corps broke through the Japanese defenses on 7 February and moved on Manila.

MIKE VI The invasion of Luzon at Nasugbu Bay on 31 January 1945. Most of the U.S. 11th Airborne Division landed by boat just south of Manila, while the 511th

Parachute Infantry Regiment jumped in behind the beach.

MIKE V Consolidation operations on Luzon. This included the exceptionally brutal battle for Manila, the largest land battle in the Pacific campaign.

MIKE II Plan for an American invasion along the east coast of Luzon in early 1945. Never executed.

MIKE III Plan for American invasion at Batangas, southwest of Luzon. In later versions of the plan, the site was shifted north to Vigan. Never executed.

MIKE IV Planned American invasion on the west coast of Luzon in early 1945. Never executed.

MILEPOST (Allied 44) Project to ship American supplies to Siberia in preparation for the Soviet Union's entry into the war against Japan. Over 1,000 fighter planes, 3,000 tanks, and 41,000 trucks were delivered.

MILLENNIUM (Allied 42) The first "Thousand Plane Raid" of World War II. On the night of 30 May 1942 over 1,400 tons of bombs were dropped by 1,050 bombers of the Royal Air Force on Cologne in an hour and a half. About 45,000 people were made homeless, 469 were killed. The British lost 41 aircraft.

MINARET (U.S. sometime in the 60s) See SHAMROCK.

MINCEMEAT (Allied 43) A deception operation conducted as part of TROJAN HORSE by the British to convince the Germans that the HUSKY invasion would be directed against Sardinia and the Peloponnesus rather than Sicily. The British outfitted the corpse of a man who died of pneumonia as if it were that of a "Major William Martin, Royal Marines," a courier. The body was attached to an attaché full of bogus documents and was released by a submarine so

that it would be washed ashore in Spain in an area known to have an active German agent. On 12 May 1943 the German High Command directed preparations against an invasion of Sardinia and the Peloponnesus were to have priority over other areas. This was the basis of the book and movie *The Man Who Never Was*. See BARCLAY, BRIMSTONE, and TROJAN HORSE.

MINOS (FR 49) The insertion of French intelligence agents by parachute into Eastern Europe from 1949 to 1954.

MIRAGE GOLD (U.S. 94) An exercise of the American Department of Energy's Nuclear Emergency Search Teams (NEST) conducted in New Orleans in October 1994. The exercise assumed a nuclear device was hidden somewhere in the downtown area; working covertly, the NEST teams used sensitive radiation-sensing equipment to detect and neutralize the "terrorist bomb."

MK (Allied) Allied convoys from North Africa to Britain in World War II. Designated by number (e.g., MK 123).

MO (JPN 42) The overall Japanese plan to cut off Australia by invading Port Moresby to force the U.S. Navy to commit itself to a decisive sea battle. MO included attacks on Midway (Operation MI), the Aleutians (Operation AL), Moresby, and Tulagi. The operation began in early May 1942 and resulted in the Battle of the Coral Sea on 7 and 8 May when the invasion force was ambushed by the Americans. This battle was fought entirely by carrier aircraft and resulted in the loss of the American carrier *Lexington* and the Japanese *Shokaku* and *Shoho* as well as most of the air wing from the *Zuikaku*. The name MO seems to be derived from Port MOresby.

MOBEX (U.S.) The general term used by the U.S. military for mobilization exercises. "MOBEX" is a contraction of "Mobilization Exercise."

MOBILE ZEBRA (U.S. 57) A publicity flight by 5 Royal Canadian Air Force Mustang fighters from Uplands, Ottawa, to Winnipeg via Vancouver in May 1957.

MOBY DICK (U.S. 52) American aerial photographic program directed against the Soviet Union beginning in 1952. Over 500 high-altitude balloons were released from points around the Soviet border to be recovered after exiting Soviet airspace. Fewer than 30 film packages were retrieved. In 1956, the Soviets publicly complained, forcing the Americans to halt the program. See MOGUL and MAJESTIC.

MODULER (R.S.A. 87) South Africa attack into Angola in late 1987. Followed EGRET, preceded HOOPER.

MOGUL (U.S. 47) A program of covert aerial reconnaissance of the Soviet Union conducted using high-altitude balloons. These balloons carried sonic and other sensors designed to detect Soviet nuclear tests (FIRST LIGHTNING). In July 1947, one of these devices crashed near Roswell, New Mexico. The Air Force initially reported that an Unidentified Flying Object (UFO) had crashed. Later, the Air Force maintained the object was a weather balloon. Many years later, Project MOGUL was revealed. See MOBY DICK.

MOKED "FOCUS" (IS 67) The preemptive Israeli air attacks that began the 6-Day War. Conducted on the morning of 5 June 1967 these attacks destroyed the Egyptian Air Force on the ground. In order to make maximum use of the initial surprise of the attack, the Israeli Air Force launched 160 of their 182 aircraft against Egyptian targets. The Jordanian and Syrian Air Forces were considered to be lesser threats that could be destroyed later. Only 4 fighters were assigned to defend the skies over Israel. Twenty-eight airfields were attacked, 469 Arab aircraft were destroyed on the ground, 60 in air combat, 15 to accidents, and 3 to ground fire — for a total of 369. The Israelis lost 46 aircraft to all causes. See GAZELLE.

MONDSCHEINSONATE "MOONLIGHT SONATA" (GER 44) A series of massive raids on British cities by night-flying German bombers using radio-navigation devices. Coventry was attacked on the night of 14 November 1944 by 449 aircraft, killing or injuring nearly 5,000 people. The city's ancient cathedral was destroyed by the resulting fire. Birmingham was attacked the next night. At this late stage of the war, these attacks were simply a pale imitation of the Allied air attacks against the German homeland. After the war, evidence surfaced that the British knew these attacks were being planned but did not react in order to conceal that they were reading coded German radio traffic.

MONGOOSE

1. (Allied 44) The insertion of a 3-man American team by parachute near Stresa, Italy, to establish a local partisan network. Executed 26 September 1944.

2. (U.S. 62) The general name for CIA operations and plans designed to destabilize Cuba and/or to assassinate or discredit its leader, Fidel Castro. Over 30 different plans were considered under this project. These included the use of American Green Berets, destruction of the Cuban sugar crop, and even the possible creation of a rumor that Jesus Christ would return to Cuba after the communists were overthrown. MONGOOSE came into being after the Bay of Pigs invasion (PLUTO) failed and was in full swing during the 1962 Cuban Missile Crisis.

MONTCLAIR (Allied 45) A draft plan for the overall Philippine Campaign drawn up by General Douglas MacArthur in February 1945. This concept called for the first American landings to be on Borneo to force the Japanese fleet into a climatic battle. After the Japanese Navy was destroyed, the Allies could take islands in the region at will. The idea of a single decisive battle was first outlined in the ORANGE plans almost 50 years before. In fact the first American landing was on Leyte, which then precipitated the Battle of Leyte Gulf.

MOONBOUNCE (U.S. 62) A National Security Agency project that envisioned the construction of a 600-foot radio telescope at Sugar Grove, West Virginia, to eavesdrop on the accidental reflection of Soviet communications off the lunar surface. Canceled in 1962.

MOONLIGHT SONATA (GER 44) See MONDSCHEINSONATE.

MORNING LIGHT (U.S./CN78) The joint American and Canadian recovery of the residue of the Soviet satellite *Cosmos 954*, which crashed near Great Slave Lake in January 1978. The debris included radioactive portions of the satellite's power plant and other items of interest to Western intelligence agencies.

MORNING STAR (CN 56) Canadian Army exercise conducted at Camp Gagetown, New Brunswick, in July and August 1956.

MOSAIC (U.K. 56) Two British nuclear tests conducted in the Monte Bello Islands, Australia. Followed TOTEM, preceded BUFFALO.

| MOSAIC 1 | 16 May 56 | 15 kilotons |
| MOSAIC 2 | 19 June | 98 kilotons |

MOSES (IS 84) The evacuation of about 8,000 black Jews (derogatorily called *falashas*) from Ethiopia to Israel in 1984. This was the third and final such evacuation. In 1978 a program where the Israelis traded weapons to the Ethiopians for the black Jews ended when the Israelis acci-

dentally revealed the operation. The second covert evacuation halted in late 1983 when the Sudanese forbade further use of their territory by the Israelis. This evacuation began with an overland pilgrimage by the refugees to camps in Sudan. They were then smuggled to Kenya, and from there by air to Israel. When this route was compromised the Israelis, with considerable American assistance, secretly bought property along Sudan's Red Sea coast. The refugees were taken from the camps in small groups to this "vacation resort" and were ferried out to sea where Israeli ships waited. Thousands escaped, but as it became more difficult to covertly operate this route a new scheme, dubbed MOSES, was developed. The Americans provided a $200,000,000 bribe to the Sudanese government to look the other way as the Israelis repaired an airstrip near Shubak. Israeli military aircraft flew out of this field at night while commercial airlines chartered by the Israelis carried thousands more from Khartoum's international airport. Over 10,000 Jews were flown to Israel. Once again the operation was compromised, this time by a right-wing religious newspaper in the West Bank. The Sudanese refused to ignore the Israeli activity, and so (after an additional bribe) the last thousand or so refugees were flown out of Shubak aboard an American C-130 aircraft on 28 March 1985. See SOLOMON.

MOUNTAIN EAGLE II (NATO 95) A major American exercise conducted at the Grafenwohr training area in Germany to prepare units for deployment to Bosnia and Macedonia.

MÜNCHEN "MUNICH"

MÜNCHEN I (GER 42) Anti-partisan operation launched on 19 March 1942 in the Yelnya-Dorogobuzh region of Russia, west of Moscow.

MÜNCHEN II (GER 42) Anti-partisan operation conducted in December 1942 in the Radoshkovichi region of Belorussia.

MUDHEN (U.S. 71) The illegal surveillance of the American journalist Jack Anderson in 1971 and 1972 by the CIA. Officially, this was to determine who was leaking classified information to Anderson. Since many of these secrets were political in nature, the operation was mostly a political activity.

MURRAY HILL AREA (U.S. 42) Early name for the COMBINED DEVELOPMENT TRUST.

MUSKET (Allied 43) Plan to invade the Italian mainland at Taranto. Never executed.

MUSKETEER

1. MUSKETEER I (Allied 45) A 4-phased plan to liberate the Philippine Islands developed by General Douglas MacArthur's staff as part of the larger RENO V plan. The 4 phases were (in sequence): KING, LOVE, MIKE, and VICTOR. This was a very complex plan that would have required a huge number of troops and landing craft. It might be viewed as a "dream plan," not taking into account the reality of troops, ships, and other resources available. Called MONTCLAIR in some documents.

2. MUSKETEER II (Allied 45) A revision of the basic plan, deleting a number of the landings.

3. MUSKETEER III (Allied 45) The final revision of the MUSKETEER plan. Due to limited resources, the number of landings were further reduced to focus on the landings on Leyte, Luzon, and Mindanao. Never executed as such, although the general concept was carried through. The landings on Leyte lured the Japanese air and sea fleets into the climatic battle of Leyte Gulf, the militarily significant island of Luzon taken by the KING and MIKE invasions. The rest of the archipelago was liberated by the VICTOR landings.

4. MUSKETEER (U.K./FR 56) Anglo-French invasion of Egypt to capture the Suez Canal. Conducted in early October 1956 in rough coordination with the Israeli armored thrust into the Sinai (KADESH). The Nasser government was seeking political control over the canal, an effort resisted by the Europeans. Although landing forces quickly established control over major canal facilities, the Egyptians were able to sink obstacles in the canal, rendering it unusable. Worldwide reaction against this move was massive and negative. The U.S. led in condemnations of the action at the U.N. and in other forums; this marked a sharp break in the "special relationship" between the U.S. and Britain. Due to political considerations, the Anglo-French forces were withdrawn in early November.

MUSTANG (Allied 43) Plan for the overland seizure of Naples, Italy, after the initial landings at Calabria. Never executed.

MUSTANG I (U.N. 51) An early plan to rescue General William Dean from a North Korean prison camp. Canceled in June, see MUSTANG II.

MUSTANG II (U.N. 51) A plan to rescue General William Dean who had been captured by communist forces during the Korean War. A North Korean reported to American intelligence that the general was being held at Kang Dong. The agent accepted American money to bribe the camp commander. The plan called for a small commando team to jump into the camp and mark helicopter landing zones to extract the prisoner and the traitorous commandant. The aircraft carrying the team was shot down on 17 September 1951 when it flew into a communist ambush. The initial report of Dean's location was managed by communist intelligence organs in order to mislead the Americans.

MUSTANG III (U.N. 52) The insertion of a 19-man South Korean special operations team into extreme northwest North Korea on the night of 22 January 1952. Their mission was to link up with and train local anti-communist forces. After a few days, all contact with the team was lost.

MUSTANG IV (U.N. 52) The air insertion of a 16-man South Korean special operations team near Sinuiju on 16 March 1952. After less than a week, all contact with the team was lost.

MUSTANG V
MUSTANG VI (U.N. 52) The insertion of South Korean special operations teams into 2 areas of North Korea on 14 May 1952. Their mission was to locate communist prison camps and establish escape routes for downed aviators. No contact was made with either team after landing.

MUSTANG VII
MUSTANG VIII (U.N. 52) Air insertion of South Korean special operations forces in far northern North Korea to locate communist prison camps and to establish escape and evasion routes for downed air crews. The 2 teams (of 5 and 6 men, respectively) dropped into 2 different areas on the night 31 October 1952 and were never heard from again.

MW (Allied) Allied convoys from Alexandria to Malta in World War II. Designated by number (e.g., MW 123).

N

NADOR 96-1 (U.S./TA 96) A joint U.S./Tunisian naval exercise conducted in mid-January 1996.

NAHSHON (IS 48) The second phase of the Israeli War of Independence. This operation, launched on 3 April 1948, was a counterattack by 3 infantry battalions, the largest force fielded by the Israelis to date. The attackers seized portions of the Jerusalem Road for a time, but were driven back.

NATIVE FURY (U.S. 92) A "war game" conducted by the U.S. Central Command from early August to 21 October 1992 in conjunction with INTRINSIC ACTION and EAGER MACE.

NEPTUN "NEPTUNE" (GER 43) Counterattack by German ground forces against Soviet units near the Black Sea at Myschanko-Berg on 6 April 1943.

NEPTUNE

1. (Allied 44) Naval operations in support of OVERLORD. See GAMBIT and MAPLE.

2. (GER) See NEPTUN.

NEROBEFEHL "NERO'S ORDER" (GER 45) Operation ordered by Hitler on 19 March 1945 to conduct a "scorched earth" policy on German soil in the path of advancing enemy forces. This program was only partially implemented due to obstruction by Albert Speer. The name is an obvious reference to the Roman emperor who "fiddled while Rome burned." See WEREWOLF.

NERVA (U.S. 60) The program to build a nuclear-powered rocket engine. The engine was successfully tested, but was never used operationally. See PLUTO, TIMBER WIND, and LOFTY THUNDER.

NEST EGG (Allied 45) Plan for the liberation of the German-held Channel Islands in the event of a sudden German collapse. The liberation of the islands of Guernsey and Jersey was conducted on 11 May 1945. The task force directed at Guernsey was named AGENT; Task Force BOOTY recaptured Jersey. Both landings were unopposed. See ECLIPSE.

NEUTRALIZE (U.S. 67) A massive series of airstrikes and artillery fire missions that broke up communist troop concentrations surrounding U.S. Marine bases at Con Thien, Camp Carroll, and Dong Ha in Vietnam. Over 900 B-52 missions (ARC LIGHT) were flown in support of this effort, which was conducted from September to the end of October 1967. See NIAGARA.

NEW LIFE (U.S. 75) Strategic Air Command (SAC) support to the American evacuation of Southeast Asia conducted from 23 April to 16 August 1975. The 110,000 or so evacuees rescued by SAC aircraft flew to Anderson Air Force Base on Guam. See EAGLE PULL and FREQUENT WIND.

NEW SPIRIT (NATO 95) An American-led training exercise conducted in Greece in early 1995 featuring Greek, Albanian, Bulgarian, and Romanian units. This exercise focused on a disaster-relief scenario, but was conducted during a period when the NATO effort in the Balkans was becoming more critical as the Yugoslav civil wars continued out of control.

NIAGARA (U.S./R.V.N. 67) Massive air bombardment in support of the U.S. Marines besieged at Khe Sanh by the Communist Tet Offensive from 21 January 1967 to 7 April 1968. Over 100,000 tons of ordnance were dropped on the North Vietnamese troops in an assembly-line operation. Every 3 hours 6 B-52 bombers would drop hundreds of 500-pound bombs into the target area surrounding the base. During the lulls, fighter bombers, artillery, and helicopters would attack identified targets. In reality much of this bombing was done blindly, relying on overwhelming firepower to break up North Vietnamese formations. Although an inelegant solution, NIAGARA worked. The Marine garrison at Khe Sanh acted as bait inviting the Vietnamese to attempt a second Dien Bien Phu, exposing themselves to the full force of American firepower. See NEUTRALIZE.

NIBLICK (U.S. 63) The series of 27 underground nuclear explosions conducted at the Nevada Test Site. Followed the NOUGAT/DOMINIC II series, preceded WHETSTONE. The individual test shots were:

PEKAN	12 August 63	
SATSOP	15 August	
KOHOCTON	23 August	
AHTANUM	13 September	
BILBY	13 September	249 kilotons
GRUNION	11 October	
TORNILLO	11 October see PLOWSHARE	
CLEARWATER	16 October	
SHOAL	26 October	12 kilotons, conducted near Fallon, Nevada
ANCHOVY	14 November	
MUSTANG	15 November	
GREYS	22 November	
SARDINE	4 December	
EAGLE	12 December	
FORE	16 January 64	prob. 19 kilotons
OCONTO	23 January	<20 kilotons
KLICKITAT	20 February	prob. 24 kilotons, see PLOWSHARE
PIKE	13 March	<20 kilotons
HOOK	14 April	<20 kilotons
STURGEON	15 April	<20 kilotons
TURF	24 April	prob. 100 kilotons
PIPEFISH	29 April	<20 kilotons
BACKSWING	14 May	<20 kilotons
MINNOW	15 May	<20 kilotons
ACE	11 June	<20 kilotons, see PLOWSHARE
FADE	25 June	<20 kilotons
DUB	30 June	<20 kilotons, see PLOWSHARE

NICKEL GRASS (U.S. 73) Transfer of American equipment to Israel in 1973 to replace losses in the Yom Kippur War.

NICKLING (Allied, Informal 45) The name commonly used by Allied air crews for missions that involved the dropping propaganda leaflets over liberated and energy territory in Europe to instruct refugees. See BIRDCAGE.

NIFTY NUGGET (U.S. 79) Computer-assisted command post exercise conducted in the fall of 1979 in conjunction with the REX 78 civil emergency preparedness exercise. It simulated the logistical implications of a Soviet-led invasion of Western Europe.

The game assumed a U.S. mobilization 7 days before the 20 October invasion. On that date, almost half of U.S. surface-to-air missiles were unfit to fire. New missiles could not be flown to Europe because of the elaborate plans already in place that accounted for every available transport aircraft for the first 30 days of the war. Many items scheduled for movement were not in stockpiles. Simulated draftees electronically reporting for training did not have uniforms or boots. This exercise clearly showed the U.S. forces to be "hollow" and began a decade-long rebuilding effort. Conducted in conjunction with REX 78.

NIFTY PACKAGE (U.S. 89) A special operation conducted in the opening hours of the American invasion of Panama (JUST CAUSE) to capture, kill, or prevent the escape of the Panamanian strongman Manuel Noriega. Based on the GABEL ADDER plan, this operation included a team of elite Navy Seals who destroyed the dictator's private jet on the ground, but suffered 4 dead.

NIGHT LIGHT (U.S. 70) The loan of 2 American RF-4C Phantom jets to Israel from 1970 to 1971, until 6 RF-4E aircraft could be permanently transferred to that nation.

NIGHTMOVER (U.S. Law Enforcement 93) A combined CIA/FBI counterintelligence operation that led to the arrest of Aldrich H. Ames and his wife for spying for the Soviet and Russian governments. The CIA had long suspected that it had been penetrated by the Soviets. A number of previous investigations (PLAYACTOR, LANCE, and SKYLIGHT) failed to detect Ames. Suspicions deepened after the fall of East Germany. The files of the East German *Stasi* showed that every American agent in that country had been turned. This investigation led to evidence that Ames and his wife had been spying for the Soviets (and later the

Russians) since 1985. They were arrested in late February 1994. As many as 10 American agents in the Soviet Union may have been killed as a result of Ames' actions. The agents included Gennadi Varenik ("FITNESS"), who controlled Soviet "illegals" in Germany. Varenik was executed by the Soviets. Valery Martynov ("GENTILE"), and Sergei Motorin ("GAUZE") were recruited while they worked at the Soviet Embassy in Washington. Both were executed when they returned home. GRU Major General Dimitri Polyakov ("TOP HAT") was shot in 1988, following a 20-year career with the CIA. Another Soviet, Adolph Tolkachev ("SPHERE"), was executed in 1986. Ames' betrayal also led to the executions of Vladimir Piguzov ("JOGGER"), Vladimir Vasilyev ("ACCORD"), Sergei Vorontosov ("COWL"), Gennadi Smetanin ("MILLION"), and Leonid Polyshuk ("WEIGH"). Four agents were betrayed by Ames, but survived: Boris Yuzhin ("TWINE"), Oleg Gordievsky ("TICKLE"), and "PROLOGUE" whose actual name has never been revealed, as well as Oleg Agraniants, whose code name is unknown.

NIGHT TRAIN (U.S. 84) See REX 84 ALPHA.

NIMBUS MOON (U.S. 74) The clearance of land mines from portions of the Sinai peninsula conducted by the U.S. as a part of the Camp David peace treaty between Egypt and Israel. See MUSKETEER, NIMBUS STAR, and NIMBUS STEAM.

NIMBUS STAR (U.S. 74) The clearance of naval mines and other debris from the Suez Canal conducted by the U.S. as a part of the Camp David peace treaty between Egypt and Israel. See MUSKETEER, NIMBUS MOON, and NIMBUS STREAM.

NIMBUS STREAM (U.S. 74) The clearance of naval mines off the Egyptian cities of

Port Said and Damietta. See MUSKE-TEER, NIMBUS MOON, and NIMBUS STAR.

NIMROD DANCER (U.S. 89) Buildup of American forces in Panama during the period of tension before the invasion of that country (JUST CAUSE). See BLADE JEWEL.

NINE LIVES (U.S. 80) A series of civil/military exercises dealing with presidential succession and the control of nuclear release codes. NINE LIVES I was conducted from 6 to 8 May 1980. See TREE TOP.

NOAH'S ARK

1. (Allied 44) Attacks by Greek partisans on retreating German troops near Yanina in September 1944. See MANNA.

2. (IS) Covert Israeli purchase of French-built patrol boats despite an international arms embargo.

NOBALL (Allied 44) A series of Allied air attacks aimed at German V-1 launch sites in the Pas de Calais region of France. A subset of the CROSSBOW attacks.

NOBSKA (U.S. 56) An early U.S. Navy effort to identify future technologies that would aid in submarine and anti-submarine warfare. Named after Nobska Point, near the Wood's Hole Observatory, which was heavily involved in this research.

NORDPOL "NORTH POLE" (GER 43) Counterintelligence operations conducted in the Netherlands by German forces. As a result of these efforts, much of the British network in that country was "turned." See BRUNNENKRESSE.

NORD SEE "NORTH SEA" (GER 42) An anti-partisan sweep in the Mogilev region of Kazakhstan, west of Smolensk, Russia, conducted in September 1942.

NORDWIND "NORTH WIND" (GER 44) German subsidiary ground offensive launched 31 December 1944 in the Alsace region of France in support of the Battle of the Bulge (WACHT AM RHEIN). Three German corps attacked south from the Saar toward the Saverne Gap, while one corps drove north from Colmar towards the town of Bitche. Despite some initial gains by the attackers, by 9 February the assault came to a halt producing the "Colmar Pocket."

NORTHERN EDGE (U.S. 94) A 6-week air/ground deployment exercise conducted in Alaska. This exercise deployed Army and Air Force units to Fort Greely to simulate an American-led peacekeeping mission.

NORTHERN EXPOSURE (U.S. Law Enforcement 92) The botched FBI siege and assault on a family suspected of minor gun-law violations in Idaho in the summer of 1992. Randy and Vicki Weaver fled society to the wilds of Boundary County, Idaho, to isolate themselves from the Federal government they feared. Entrapped by paid informers into selling a number of sawed-off shotguns, Randy Weaver was indicted. A typographical error in a court document caused Weaver to miss his trial date. The FBI responded with a prolonged surveillance of the cabin located near Ruby Ridge. Determining the family to be violent, the government sent heavily armed patrols onto the family's land to provoke a response. On 21 August 1992 one of these patrols killed Weaver's 14-year old son, shooting him in the back. A federal agent was also killed. The next day a federal marksman killed Weaver's unarmed wife while she stood in the cabin's doorway holding her infant daughter. As a result of this siege, the FBI agreed to pay over $3,000,000 to the surviving family members. Randy Weaver was found not guilty. The FBI officials who gave the shoot-to-kill orders destroyed documents to hide their involvement. *Northern*

Exposure was a television program set in Alaska that was popular during this period.

NORTHERN VIKING (NATO) Training exercise series conducted in odd-numbered years involving the deployment of U.S. ground and naval reserve units to Iceland. Designated by year (e.g., NORTHERN VIKING 91).

NORTH POLE (GER 40) See NORDPOL.

NORTH SEA (GER 42) See NORD SEE.

NORTH WIND (GER 44) See NORD-WIND.

NOUGAT (U.S. 61) A series of 32 nuclear tests conducted (with one exception) at the Nevada Test Site during the 1962 Fiscal Year. The individual blasts were:

ANTLER	15 September 61	2.6 kilotons
SHREW	16 September	"low"
BOOMER	1 October	"low"
CHENA	10 October	"low"
MINK	29 October	"low"
FISHER	3 December	13.4 kilotons
GNOME	10 December	3 kilotons,
Carlsbad, New Mexico see PLOWSHARE		
MAD	13 December	500 tons
RINGTAIL	17 December	"low"
FEATHER	22 December	"low"
STOAT	9 January 62	5.1 kilotons
AGOUTI	18 January	6.4 kilotons
DORMOUSE	30 January	"low"
STILLWATER	8 February	3.07 kilotons
ARMADILLO	9 February	7.1 kilotons
HARD HAT	15 February	5.7 kilotons
CHINCHILLA	19 February	1.9 kilotons
CODSAW	19 February	"low"
CIMARRON	23 February	11.9 kilotons
PLATYPUS	24 February	"low"
PAMPAS`	1 March	"low"
DANNY BOY	5 March	430 tons
ERMINE	6 March	"low"
BRAZOS	8 March	8.4 kilotons
HOGNOSE	15 March	"low"
HOOSIX	28 March	3.4 kilotons
CHINCHILLA II	31 March	"low"
DORMOUSE II	5 April	10.6 kilotons
PASSAIC	6 April	"low"
HUDSON	12 April	"low"
PLATTE	14 April	1.85 kilotons
DEAD	21 April	"low"

NUCFLASH (U.S.) A flag-word used in American electronic messages, which announce events that may result in a nuclear war. See FRONT BURNER.

NUT CRACKER

1. (U.K. 64) January 1964 British offensive against rebels in the Rafdan Mountains in the former Aden Protectorate.

2. (U.S. 93) A battalion-sized sweep through the main weapons bazaar of Mogadishu, Somalia conducted on 11 January 1993 in order to reduce the number of weapons in the capital as part of RESTORE HOPE.

NYLON (CN 95) The deployment of 3 Canadian staff officers to support the Organization for Cooperation and Security in Europe mission to monitor the frontier between Armenia and Azerbainjan in the disputed Nagorny-Karabakh region.

O

OAK (GER) See EICHE.

OB (Allied) Allied convoys from Liverpool to North America in World War II. Designated by number (e.g., OB 123).

OBOE (Allied 45) A series of 6 small joint Australian/American landings on Japanese-held Borneo and nearby islands. Australian Army units conducted the landings, assisted by the American fleet and air power. These were the last Allied amphibious landings of World War II and represented the highest statement of the tactics developed over the war. American naval firepower was massive and responsive, reducing the number of Australian casualties considerably. Like the VICTOR landings that preceded them to the north, the OBOE landings were conducted out of their numerical sequence.

OBOE I Australian landing on Tarakan on 1 May 1945. The Japanese had built impressive beach fortifications and destroyed the airfield that was the main objective of the attack.

OBOE VI The 10 June 1945 Australian invasion at Brunei Bay with the objective of the massive oil fields at Seria. The attackers encountered little opposition and quickly turned their hands to fighting the massive fires ignited by the Japanese.

OBOE II The invasion of Balikpapan on the Makassar Strait on southeast Borneo.

The Australian 7th Division landed on 1 July 1945 under an exceptionally effective shore bombardment that destroyed all organized Japanese defenses. The area was declared secure on 22 July.

OCEAN (S.U.) See OKEAN.

OCEAN SAFARI (U.S.) Exercise series conducted by U.S. Atlantic Command during odd-numbered years. OCEAN SAFARI focuses on the protection of sea lanes between the U.S. and Europe. Designated by year (e.g., OCEAN SAFARI 77)

OCEAN VENTURE (U.S.) Exercise series conducted by U.S. Atlantic Command in conjunction with SOLID SHIELD during even-numbered years. These exercises extend beyond the NATO area to include the Caribbean and Gulf of Mexico and include air activities and port security functions. Designated by year.

OCEAN WAVE 97 (U.S./U.K./AUS 97) A combined exercise hosted by Australia scheduled for January to August 1997. American, British, and Australian naval, air, and ground units will train at various training areas in and around Australia.

OCTAGON (Allied 44) Conference held by Churchill and Roosevelt in Quebec from 28 November to 1 December 1944. Commonly called "The Second Quebec Conference" to distinguish it from the earlier QUADRANT meeting. OCTA-GON was held by the Western leaders to prepare for the "Big Three" meeting at Yalta (ARGONAUT) to discuss post-war arrangements in Europe.

OFF TACKLE (U.S.) See BROILER.

OG (Allied) Allied convoys from Britain to Gibraltar in World War II. Designated by number (e.g., OG 123).

OKEAN "OCEAN" (S.U.) Soviet naval exercises held periodically during the 1970s that emphasized the coordination of large fleet groups and anti-carrier operations. These exercises were designated by year and sometimes took on a worldwide character. OKEAN 70 was the largest Soviet Navy exercise since World War II. OKEAN 75 is sometimes called VESNA in Soviet sources.

OLDENBURG (GER 41) German plan for the economic exploitation of the Soviet Union after its capture in World War II. The BARBAROSSA invasion envisioned an eastern frontier of German control along a general line from Archangel to the Volga River. OLDENBURG called for the ruthless stripping of agricultural products from this captured territory to support huge German armies. It assumed that this would result in widespread starvation among the occupied peoples. Never executed.

OLDHAM TWO (U.K.) A flag-word used in British electronic messages to designate the most severe category of nuclear weapons accident. A rough equivalent of the American BROKEN ARROW.

OLIVE (Allied 43) Attack on the German Gothic Line defenses that ran west from Pesaro on the Adriatic to La Spezia. The British 8th Army attacked on the east beginning on 25 August 1943 as a diversion for a heavy attack by the British 5th Army in the west. The fight soon settled into a battle of attrition that broke through the German defenses in mid-September. The operation may have been named after the commander of the 8th Army, General Oliver Leese.

OLIVE NOIRES "BLACK OLIVES" (NATO 78) A naval mine-clearance exercise conducted off Toulon in 1978.

OLYMPIC

1. (Allied 45) Planned American invasion of the southern Japanese island of Kyushu, scheduled for 1 November 1945. Part of DOWNFALL, the overall plan for the invasion of Japan. Fifteen divisions were scheduled to take part in this second landing. The naval armada would have been the largest ever seen, including 42 aircraft carriers, 24 battleships, and almost 400 destroyers and destroyer escorts. Using Okinawa as a staging base, OLYMPIC was to seize the southern portion of Kyushu as an advanced base for the follow-on CORONET operation. Never executed. See TEN ICHI and MAJESTIC.

2. (U.S.) A first word used to designate operations by U-2 aircraft.

OLYMPUS (GER 42) Anti-partisan operation conducted in Greece during May 1942.

ON (Allied 39) Fast Allied convoys from Britain to North America. Designated by number (e.g., ON 123). Replaced "OB" in September 1939.

ONEG SHABBAT "SABBATH DELIGHT" (Zionist 42) Project run by Emanuel Ringelblum in the Warsaw Ghetto in 1942 and 1943, which chronicled the activities of the Jewish underground. An archive was buried in 3 milk cans. The first can was recovered in 1946, the second in 1950. The third can has not been found. See KÜSTE.

"ONE, OPERATION" (JPN 44) See ICHI-GO.

ONS (Allied) Slow Allied convoys from England to Canada. Designated by number (e.g., ONS 123).

ON-TOP (U.S. 50) A program to upgrade American B-29, B-36, B-47, and B-50 bombers with standardized bomb racks to accept nuclear weapons.

OP25 (GER 41) Planning name for MARITA.

OPEN ATOLL (FR) See ATOLL OUVERTE.

OPLAN 34-A

OPLAN 34A (U.S. 64) The 1964 American umbrella plan for covert operations against North Vietnam. This plan intended to conceal direct American participation and therefore relied on Filipino, Vietnamese, and Chinese mercenaries. It included air, ground, and sea raids as well as propaganda operations. This plan was drawn up well before the Gulf of Tonkin Incident (DESOTO) provided justification for overt American involvement in the region. The existence of this operation was leaked with the publication of the "Pentagon Papers" in 1971. "OPLAN" is a contraction of "Operations Plan." See BARREL ROLL, BLUE SPRINGS, BOX TOP, DE SOTO, LUCKY DRAGON, SALEUMSAY, SAW BUCK, SONE SAI, STEEL TIGER, and YANKEE TEAM.

ORANGE (U.S. 04) One of the COLOR SERIES first drawn up in 1904 and updated periodically until 1941 in the event of war with Japan. These plans generally called for a defense of the Philippines by its garrison and local troops until the U.S. Navy could destroy the Japanese fleet at sea in a large decisive battle and impose a blockade on the Home Islands. Replaced by RAINBOW-5 in 1941. Never executed. See RED-ORANGE.

ORIENT (GER 41) General plan for German forces to move southeast after the defeat of the Soviet Union to establish Nazi control of Persia (now Iran), Syria and on into India. Prepared in July 1941 for execution that year or in 1942. Never executed.

ORPHAN (Allied 44) See APHRODITE.

ORYX (IT 92) The Italian component of the international effort rescue Somalia from anarchy and famine (RESTORE HOPE). Begun in December 1992, the performance of the Italian troops was widely criticized. Local Italian commanders cut deals with local warlords to ensure that relief supplies were delivered. The Italians were accused of being too slow to rescue American troops who were surrounded by hostile Somalis. Oryx is a genus of straight-horned African antelopes or gazelles.

OS (Allied convoy) Allied convoys from Britain to West Africa. Designated by number (e.g., OS 123). Replaced by "KM" after April 1943.

OSSEX (Allied 44) See SUSSEX.

OTTO

1. (GER 38) The German occupation of Austria on 12 March 1938. Popularly called the anschluss ("annexation"). At least 35,000 people were killed as the Nazis established control of the country against no organized resistance. The unexpected disappearance of Austria placed Czechoslovakia in a militarily untenable situation. See GRUEN.

2. (GER 40) A program of improvements to Polish roads and railroads leading from Germany to the Soviet frontier to support the planned German invasion (BARBAROSSA). Conducted using Polish and Jewish slave labor from 9 August 1940 to May of the next year.

OUTLAW (U.S.) A reserved first word for the projects and programs of the U.S. Air Force.

OVERBOARD (Allied Unofficial 44) A satire of the OVERLORD plan drawn up by British and American staff officers as a diversion. The heading of the real plan read "Top Secret, Equals British Most Secret" was twisted into "Stupid, Equals British Most Stupid." This parody was actually classified due to its close similarities to the real plan.

OVERCAST (U.S. 45) The evacuation of selected German scientists to the U.S. at the end of the war in Europe. Over 350 scientists and their families were moved. See ALSOS, BIG, and PAPERCLIP.

OVERFLIGHT (U.S. 58) Surveillance of the Soviet Union by U-2 spy planes run by the CIA and the U.S. Air Force. The main bases for these flights were: Lakenheath, U.K., Incirlik, Turkey, and Atsugi, Japan. These flights ended in 1958 as Soviet air defenses became more capable. Later flights were conducted out of bases in Norway, Pakistan, and Taiwan and were considered to be high-risk. On 1 May 1960 Francis Gary Powers was shot down by a surface-to-air missile, ending the U-2 flights over the Soviet Union. This attack led the U.S. to secretly develop a new spy aircraft: the SR-71 Blackbird. Powers was freed when he was exchanged in Berlin for the Soviet spy Rudolph Abel.

OVERLORD (Allied 44) The invasion of northern France. Papers with the actual times and locations for the execution of OVERLORD were marked BIGOT. This information was controlled through a special access list (a "Bigot List"). Executed 6 June 1944, this date has become the pre-eminent "D-Day" in history. Deception operations in support of OVERLORD came under the heading BODYGUARD and included COPPERHEAD, FORTITUDE, GRAFFHAM, HAMBONE, IRONSIDE, JAEL, ROYAL FLUSH, SKYE, and ZEPPELIN. Rehearsals for the invasion included BEAVER, DUCK, FABIUS, FOX, HARLEQUIN, and TIGER. BULBASKET was a special operation as part of OVERLORD. Airborne landings included CHICAGO and DETROIT. Other plans to invade northern France included VERT, QUICKSILVER, and ROUNDHAMMER. See BIGOT and TAXABLE.

OVERTHROW (Allied 42) The Allied deception plan for Europe in 1942. It was designed to convince the Germans that the Allies would land near Calais that summer. As a result of the misinformation spread by this operation, some French resistance units rose up to support the expected invasion, only to be crushed by the occupation forces. Included the CAVENDISH feint.

OVERWHELMING (U.N. 51) Plan drawn up in July 1951 by General Van Fleet's staff calling for a drive by the U.S. 8th Army toward the Pyongyang-Wonsan line, the narrow waist of Korea, starting about 1 September 1951. This was (along with WRANGLER) a plan designed to launch an offensive during the long period of truce negotiations to preserve the initiative and maintain pressure on the communists. Never executed.

P

PACER (U.S.) A reserved first word for the programs and projects of the U.S. Air Force Logistics Command.

PACIFIC WIND (U.S. 90) A planned rescue of American embassy staff members who were isolated in their Kuwait City compound by the 1990 Iraqi invasion. This plan called for a raid by American special operations teams in October or November. Never carried out as the diplomats were allowed to leave peacefully.

PACT DOC (Allied 43) The covert establishment of American medical training units in areas of China threatened by Japanese ground forces. A small school for Chinese medics set up in western Hunan graduated its first class in the summer of 1944. Japanese attacks forced the facility to move to Hangchow. This program, along with a system of coast-watchers, river pirates, and intelligence assets, were supported by the Sino-American Cooperation Organization, an operation largely run by the U.S. Navy.

PAKISTAN (U.K./PK/IN 47) "Operation Pakistan" was a population shuffle conducted in early September 1947 after the partition of India. This movement was accompanied by massive communal violence against religious minorities.

PALACE (U.S.) A reserved first word for the programs and project of the U.S. Air Force.

PANCAKE (Allied 44) A series of Allied air attacks on German supply and support facilities near Bologna, Italy, in October 1944.

PANDA (U.S.) A reserved first word for the program and projects of the U.S. Air Force Communication Services.

PANTHER (Allied 44) British 10th Corps attack on the strong German defenses at Monte Cassino, Italy, launched on 17 January 1944. The assault achieved local success but did not break the German line. Followed by DIADEM.

PANZERFAUST "BAZOOKA" (GER 44) See MICKEY MOUSE.

PAPA (U.S.) A reserved first word for the programs and projects of the U.S. Air Force's former Alaska Air Command.

PAPER (U.S.) A reserved first word for the programs and projects of the U.S. Air Force.

PAPERCLIP (U.S. 45) Operation by the American Office of Strategic Services to seize German scientists to prevent their capture by the Soviets. The key prizes of this operation were Wernher von Braun and Arthur Louis Hugo Randolph, both of whom were critical to the post-war U.S. defense and space programs. Randolph was later found to be a war criminal. See BIG and OVERCAST.

PARAQUET "PARAKEET" (U.K. 82) Plan developed by the Royal Navy as an alternative the Army's CORPORATE plan to liberate the Falkland Islands. Nicknamed by cynics "Paraquat" after the industrial poison. Never executed.

PARKPLATZ (GER 43) A proposed German attack on Leningrad (now St. Petersburg) in the spring of 1944. Never executed.

PARDON (U.S.) A reserved first word for the programs and projects of the U.S. Air Force.

PASSAGE (CN 94) See LANCE.

PASTORIUS (GER 42) Infiltration of 8 German intelligence agents in 2 teams into the U.S. by submarine in 1942. The first team of 4 was landed by U-202 on Long Island on the night of 13 June. A second group was landed in Florida on the night of 17 June by U-584. The spies were quickly denounced by their own team leaders. All 8 were tried and sentenced to death. Six were executed on 8 August. President Roosevelt commuted the death sentence of Georg Dasch and Ernst Burger, who betrayed their comrades, to 30 years in prison. They were released in 1948. The operation was named after the first German immigrant to America, Franz Pastorius.

PATCH (U.S.) A reserved first word for the programs and projects of the U.S. Air Force. Generally, this word is used for medical programs.

PAUKENSCHLAG "DRUM BEAT" (GER 42) Initial German submarine operations conducted along the east coast of the U.S. after the Americans entered World War II. Seven submarines sank 23 merchant ships in January 1942 alone. This period was also called "The Happy Time" by German submariners.

PAUL (Allied 40) The mining of the routes used by ships carrying iron ore from Sweden to Germany. Ore mined in Sweden is taken by rail to ports in Norway where it is loaded and moved south through a series of inland waterways protected from the open sea by islands. Proposed by Churchill in May 1940 but never executed.

PAVE (U.S.) A reserved first word used to designate the programs and projects of the U.S. Air Force. These development programs often produce aircraft or other equipment that then inherit the name of the program that produced it. An example is PAVE LOW, a highly modified transport helicopter used to covertly insert special operations forces far behind enemy lines. PAVE HAWK is a similar helicopter optimized to recover downed airmen. PAVE KNIFE was an early laser target-designation device.

PAWAN (IN 87) Attack launched on 12 October 1987 by units of the Indian Peacekeeping Force against the rebel Tamil Tigers in Jaffna, Sri Lanka.

PBSUCCESS (U.S. 54) See SUCCESS.

PEACE (U.S.) A first word used by the U.S. Air Force to name programs dealing with the transfer of equipment and training overseas. For example, PEACE PHARAOH was the training and equipping of the Egyptian Air Force.

PEACEFUL EAGLE (U.S./AL 95) The first joint American/Albanian military exercise. Conducted in late 1995 in the coastal regions of Albania. The goal of the training was to increase the professionalism of the Albanian Army, build links between the two militaries, and acclimatize the Americans to the Balkan region.

PEACEKEEPER (U.S./RU 95) A joint American-Russian peacekeeping exercise conducted at Fort Riley, Kansas. Elements of the U.S. 3rd Infantry Division and the Russian 27th Guards Motorized Rifle

Division worked on interoperability issues and jointly developed peacekeeping doctrine.

PEACE PEEK (NATO) The use of West German maritime patrol aircraft over the Baltic Sea to eavesdrop on Warsaw Pact communications during the Cold War.

PEACE SHIELD (U.S./UKR 95) A combined American/Ukrainian training exercise conducted in mid-1995 near Lvov. The training focused on interoperability issues that became more critical when Ukrainian units were deployed alongside Americans in the Balkans.

PEACH WINGS (U.S./CN 70) The exchange of Canadian F-101 Voodoo interceptors for newer American F-101B aircraft in 1970. See QUEENS ROW.

PEACOCK (Allied 43) The assassination of Japanese Admiral Yamamoto on 17 April 1943. His transport aircraft was intercepted by American long-range fighters that were tipped off to the Admiral's schedule by a radio intercept. See MAGIC and Z.

PEDESTAL (Allied 42) Very large supply convoy to Malta in August 1942. Months of blockade had threatened the island with starvation, requiring prompt action. This massive effort was made possible by the temporary suspension of convoys to the Soviet Union. Fourteen merchant ships protected by 2 battleships, 3 aircraft carriers, 7 cruisers, and 32 destroyers sailed through the Pillars of Hercules on 9 August. Axis air and sea attacks sank 9 of the cargo ships as well as 1 aircraft carrier (HMS *Eagle*) and 2 cruisers. The British claimed 1 Italian submarine and 39 aircraft. The MV *Ohio*, then the world's largest tanker, suffered 7 direct hits and 20 near misses and lost all power, but was finally towed into port on 15 August. By flying fighters from the carriers to Malta, the British reestablished a creditable air garrison on the island. Malta became a clamp

on Axis supplies immediately before the Battle of El Alamian. Followed BELLOWS, preceded BARITONE.

PEERTO PINE (U.S. 60) The U.S. Army portion of BIG SAM.

PEGASUS (U.S./R.V.N. 68) Helicopter movement of elements of the U.S. 1st Cavalry Division to a landing zone near the besieged city of Khe Sahn. There they linked up with a relief column traveling overland to the city on 7 April 1968. See NIAGARA.

PENITENT (Allied 45) Proposed series of landings along the Dalmatian coast to be conducted in the final days of World War II. The object of these assaults would be to ensure that at least some portion of the Balkans would remain under the influence of the Western Allies. Never executed.

PENKNIFE (Allied 45) A deception operation conducted in February and March 1945 in support of the transfer of Canadian units from Italy to Britain (GOLDFLAKE).

PENNSYLVANIA (U.S. Unofficial 67) The first diplomatic foray of Henry Kissinger (then a private citizen, later Secretary of State) into the Vietnam War. In Paris in the summer of 1967, Kissinger was introduced by a friend to Raymond Aubrac, a Frenchman who in turn knew the Vietnamese leader Ho Chi Minh. Kissinger sent Aubrac to Hanoi to propose a simultaneous end to American bombing and a start to peace negotiations. These private talks continued at a low level for some time but did not produce results.

PENTAGON (Allied 42) The actual occupation of French Somaliland by Free French units on 28 December 1942.

PEPPERMINT (Allied 44) Nuclear defense activities associated with the invasion of Normandy (OVERLORD). Allied officers were concerned that the Germans faced with the invasion might resort to radiological weapons. These weapons would disperse radioactive elements in the form of a poisonous gas or dust. The MANHATTAN ENGINEER DISTRICT prepared manuals dealing with this threat and distributed instruments to detect such an attack. In early 1944 there was a rehearsal for PEPPERMINT, which involved airborne detectors overflying British cities, where they detected no radiation. Never executed.

PERFORMANCE (Allied 42) An attempt on 1 April 1942 by 10 Norwegian merchant ships to break out from the Swedish port of Gothenburg. The ships were savaged by German air and naval forces. Only two completed the dangerous voyage to Britain.

PERPETUAL (Allied) An April 1941 convoy to Malta. Followed WHITE, preceded DUNLOP.

PERSECUTION (Allied 44) Amphibious attack to seize Aitape and Hollandia simultaneously to establish air bases. Both places were invaded on 22 April 1944, a Japanese counterattack against the U.S. 32nd Division on Aitape began on 10 July and was only crushed in late August. Over 20 Japanese were killed for every American lost. Included RECKLESS.

PERSIAN RUG (U.S. 62) The flight of a B-52 Stratofortress bomber of the former Strategic Air Command from Okinawa to Torrejon, Spain, conducted on 10-11 January 1962. This flight of 12,532 miles set a new record for an unrefueled flight from point to point.

PETERSBURG (Allied) Plan to evacuate New Guinea if Guadalcanal fell. Never executed.

PHALANX (U.S. 82) A series of 18 underground nuclear tests conducted at the Nevada Test Site. Two blasts during this period have never been publicly described. These tests followed PRAETORIAN and

preceded FUSILEER. The individual shots of this test series were:

SEYVAL	12 November 82	<20 kilotons
MANTECA	10 December	20-150 kilotons
COALORA	11 February 83	<20 kilotons
CHEEDAM	17 February	<20 kilotons
CABRA	26 March	20-150 kilotons
TURQUOISE	14 April	<150 kilotons
ARMADA	22 April	<20 kilotons
CROWDIE	5 May	<20 kilotons
MINI JADE	26 May	<20 kilotons
FAHAD	26 May	<20 kilotons
DANABLU	9 June	<20 kilotons
LABAN	3 August	<20 kilotons
SABADO	11 August	<20 kilotons
(Unknown)	27 August	(unknown)
TOMME/ MIDNIGHT ZEPHYR	21 September	<20 kilotons
(Unknown)	21 September	(unknown)
TECHADO	22 September	<150 kilotons

PHOENIX

1. (U.S./R.V.N. 68) See PHUNG HOANG.

2. (NATO 96) A command post exercise conducted along with ROYAL SORBET 96 to improve international cooperation in submarine rescue and recovery. Both NATO and Partnership for Peace nations took part in this training hosted by Norway in mid-June 1996.

PHUNG HOANG "PHOENIX" (U.S./R.V.N. 68) CIA-led effort to identify and separate loyal and revolutionary South Vietnamese peasants thus destroying the Viet Cong Infrastructure ("VCI"). In late 1968, intelligence reports from all South Vietnamese intelligence organizations were used to draw up arrest lists. CIA-trained teams were sent into the provinces to make the arrests. These teams faced armed resistance, and so had a natural tendency to shoot first and ask questions later. Policy officially required the capture, not the killing of those identified as VCI. Those arrested were questioned by the South Vietnamese in order to identify other Viet Cong sympathizers. In practice, these interrogations often degenerated into torture and even death. In addition, local officials often modified the arrest lists for bribes. This form of venture capitalism resulted in innocent people being arrested or killed and actual VCI members escaping the net. In 1971, the Director of Central Intelligence reported that 28,000 VCI members had been captured, of whom 20,000 had died. PHOENIX is a loose translation of the Vietnamese name for this operation, PHUNG HOANG. In Vietnamese folklore, the Phung Hoang is a bird that can fly anywhere in the world.

PICADOR (Allied) Plan for the liberation of Dakar during World War II. The name PICADOR replaced BLACK, and was in turn replaced by BARRISTER. The operation was actually executed as MENACE.

PICKET (Allied 42) The delivery of Spitfire fighters to Malta in late March 1942. Preceded PINPOINT.

PIERCE ARROW (U.S. 64) Retaliatory carrier air strikes on targets in North Vietnam in response to the "Gulf of Tonkin Incident." Executed on 5 August 1964.

PIGSTICK (Allied 42) Proposed Allied offensive in Burma during the 1942/43 dry season. Never executed. See CANNIBAL.

PILGRIM (Allied 40) Planning name for TONIC.

PINE CONE II (U.S. 60) The U.S. Army portion of BRIGHT STAR.

PINE RIDGE (U.S.) See TREE TOP.

PINPOINT (Allied 42) The delivery of Spitfire fighters to Malta in July 1942. Followed PICKET.

PIRATE (Allied 43) Amphibious training exercise for British and Canadian troops sched-

uled to take part in the invasion of northern France (OVERLORD). Conducted at Studland Bay, England, in mid-October 1943.

PITCH BLACK (AUS/U.S. 87) Royal Australian Air Force exercise that arrayed defending Australian interceptors against an attacking force of American B-52s and F-14s.

PIVOT (CN 94) Canadian participation in the U.N. effort to restore the elected government of Haiti. In addition to military peacekeepers, Canadian police went to the island to establish an effective civil force to replace the corrupt army. See RESTORE DEMOCRACY and FORWARD ACTION.

PLAINFARE (U.K. 48) The British portion of the Berlin Airlift (VITTLES).

PLAYACTOR (U.S. Law Enforcement 91) An unsuccessful FBI inquiry into an alleged "mole" in the American CIA begun in 1991 in parallel with a similar CIA effort called SKYLIGHT. The turncoat was Aldrich Ames who was uncovered in a second investigation called NIGHTMOVER.

PLOUGH "PLOW" (Allied 43 or so) Training of a combined U.S./Canadian force in deep-snow and mountain operations to attack targets in Norway. The attack never took place, but the elite unit (the 1st Special Service Force) did fight in Italy.

PLOWSHARE (U.S. 61) The development of techniques to use nuclear explosives for peaceful construction purposes. Proposed uses included widening the Panama Canal, constructing a new waterway through Nicaragua, or cutting paths through mountainous areas for highways. These 28 shots were conducted in conjunction with other weapons-related test series. The individual tests were:

GNOME	10 December 61	Carlsbad, NM
		3 kilotons, see NOUGAT

SEDAN	6 July 62	Nevada
	104 kilotons, see STORAX	
ANACOSTIA	27 November	Nevada
	"low," see DOMINIC II	
KAWEAH	21 February 63	Nevada
	"low," see DOMINIC II	
TORNILLO	11 October	Nevada
	"low," see NIBLICK	
KLICKITAT	20 February 64	Nevada
	24 kilotons, see NIBLICK	
ACE	11 June	Nevada
	<20 kilotons, see NIBLICK	
DUB	30 June	Nevada
	<20 kilotons, see NIBLICK	
PAR	9 October	Nevada
	38 kilotons, see WHETSTONE	
HANDCAR	5 November	Nevada
	<20 kilotons, see WHETSTONE	
SULKY	18 December	Nevada
	.09 kilotons, see WHETSTONE	
PALANQUIN	14 April 65	Nevada
	4.3 kilotons, see WHETSTONE	
TEMPLAR	24 March 66	Nevada
	<20 kilotons, see FLINTLOCK	
VULCAN	25 June	Nevada
	25 kilotons, see FLINTLOCK	
SAXON	28 July	Nevada
	<20 kilotons, see LATCHKEY	
SIMMS	5 November	Nevada
	<20 kilotons, see LATCHKEY	
SWITCH	22 June 67	Nevada
	<20 kilotons, see LATCHKEY	
MARVEL	21 September	Nevada
	2.2 kilotons, see CROSSTIE	
GASBUGGY	10 December	Farmington, NM
	29 kilotons, see CROSSTIE	
CABRIOLET	26 January 68	Nevada
	2.3 kilotons, see CROSSTIE	
BUGGY	12 March	Nevada
	5.4 kilotons, see CROSSTIE	
STODDARD	17 September	Nevada
	prob. 13 kilotons, see BOWLINE	
SCHOONER	8 December	Nevada
	30 kilotons, see BOWLINE	
RULISON	10 September 69	Grand Valley, CO
	47 kilotons, see MANDREL	

FLASK	26 May 70	Nevada
	105 kilotons, see MANDREL	
MINIATA	8 July 71	Nevada
	83 kilotons, see GROMMET	
RIO BLANCO	17 May 73	Rifle, CO
	3.33 kilotons, see TOGGLE	

PLUM (U.S. 41) A 9-ship convoy sent from the U.S. to reinforce the American garrison of the Philippines. The convoy left San Francisco on 14 November 1941 headed by the heavy cruiser *Pensacola* and carrying almost 5,000 national guardsmen organized into a provisional artillery brigade. Aircraft, fuel, and ammunition were also included in the shipment. Due to the rapid advance of the Japanese and enemy air superiority over Manila, the convoy was ordered to the Australian port of Darwin. There, on 19 February 1942 they were attacked by a massive Japanese air strike and suffered heavy losses. In history, this ill-fated voyage is remembered as the "*Pensacola* Convoy."

PLUMBAT (IS 68) The covert acquisition of 200 tons of uranium oxide for use in the secret Israeli nuclear weapons program. The *Mossad* bought a ship and several dummy corporations who legally purchased the uranium oxide in November 1968 in Antwerp. The ship, the MV *Scheersburg A*, rendezvoused with an Israeli cargo vessel and covertly transferred its cargo at sea.

PLUMBOB (U.S. 57) A series of 24 nuclear tests shots and 5 non-nuclear safety tests conducted at the Nevada Test Site. Ground forces participated in DESERT ROCK VI and VIII in conjunction with these tests. PASCAL-A was the first American underground test, although the explosion breached the surface. RAINIER was the first American test to be contained completely underground. The individual explosions were:

BOLTZMANN	28 May 47	12 kilotons
FRANKLIN	2 June	140 tons
LASSEN	5 June	5 tons

145

WILSON	18 June	10 kilotons
PRISCILLA	24 June	37 kilotons
COULOMB-A1 July		zero (safety test)
HOOD	5 July	74 kilotons, see
		DESERT ROCK VII
DIABLO	15 July	17 kilotons
JOHN	19 July	2 kilotons
KEPLER	24 July	2 kilotons
OWENS	25 July	9.7 kilotons
PASCAL-A	25 July	"slight"
STOKES	7 August	19 kilotons
SATURN	10 August	zero (safety test)
SHASTA	18 August	17 kilotons
DOPPLER	23 August	11 kilotons
PASCAL-B	27 August	30 tons
FRANKLIN PRIME 30 August		4.7 kilotons
SMOKY	31 August	44 kilotons, see
		DESERT ROCK VIII
GALILEO	2 September	11 kilotons, see
		DESERT ROCK VIII
WHEELER	6 September	197 tons
COULOMB-B6 September		300 tons
LAPLACE	8 September	1.25 kiloton
FIZEAU	14 September	11 kilotons
NEWTON	16 September	12 kilotons
RAINIER	19 September	1.7 kilotons
WHITNEY	23 September	19 kilotons
CHARLESTON28 September		12 kilotons
MORGAN	10 October	8 kilotons

PLUNDER (Allied 45) Crossing of the Rhine at Rees and Wesel by the British 25th Army Group. Executed on the night of 23 March 1945. Included the VARSITY parachute jump.

PLUTO

1. (U.S. 61) The U.S.-backed invasion of Cuba at the Bay of Pigs on 17 April 1961. The new Kennedy administration authorized the invasion, but reduced the air and other support the original plan of the Eisenhower administration called for. The invaders became hung up on offshore reefs and were quickly isolated by Cuban forces. Over

11,000 survivors surrendered on 19 April. The Castro government demanded a ransom from the Americans, who raised the money privately in a vain attempt to preserve the fiction that the attack was not connected to the American government. The participation of the U.S. Navy in this operation was called BUMPY ROAD. See MONGOOSE. Called ZAPATA in some sources.

2. (U.S. 50) An American cold-war project to build a very large cruise missile to deliver nuclear weapons to the former Soviet Union. This program, which ran roughly co-incident with the failed effort to build a nuclear-powered bomber, envisioned an aircraft powered by a nuclear-powered rocket. In addition to its warhead, such an aircraft would spread radiation along its route. Followed by NERVA, TIMBER WIND, and LOFTY THUNDER.

POINTBLANK (Allied 43) Allied bombing offensive against Germany from 1943 to 1945. The U.S. Army Air Forces (USAAF) and Royal Air Force approached this program with different doctrines. The Royal Air Force, battered by many years of war, preferred night attacks on cities to avoid enemy fighters. The USAAF used large, tight formations of bombers in daylight to achieve better accuracy and provide mutual covering fire against the fighters. The Allies agreed to let each air force use its own techniques so as to pummel Germany day and night. POINTBLANK identified 6 classes of targets: submarine facilities, aircraft factories, ball bearing factories, oil production and storage, synthetic rubber plants, and the military vehicle factories. Later, railroads and the German power system were added to the target list.

POLAR BEAR

1. (GER 43) See EISBAER.

2. (Allied 44) A joint American/Canadian program to test and develop Arctic warfare

equipment and techniques. A combined force spent the winter of 1944/45 in the mountains of British Columbia moving between various climatic zones.

POLCO (CN 50) The determination of the exact location of the Earth's magnetic north pole in July 1950 by Royal Canadian Air Force aircraft. POLCO seems to be a contraction of "polar coordinates."

POLECHARGE (U.N. 51) The final phase of COMMANDO to secure the last few hills along the Jamestown Line in Korea. The attack began on 15 October 1951 and was conducted by the U.S. 5th and 8th Cavalry Regiments and the Belgian Battalion (including its Luxembourg elements). The final objective was taken on 19 October, thus ending COMMANDO.

POLE TAX (U.S. 87) The deployment of additional security elements to Panama as a response to Panamanian provocations. In late November 1989, an informant reported to the U.S. Embassy that Colombian drug traffickers were targeting American forces in Panama with car bombs. The American commanders tightened security at all American bases and flew in additional bomb-detection dogs. After about a week of this increased activity, the informant was discredited by a polygraph test and most of the additional troops returned to the U.S. This activity occurred at the same time as the BLADE JEWEL evacuation of American families and the ELOQUENT BANQUET reinforcement of U.S. troops in preparation for the JUST CAUSE invasion. POLE TAX is a misspelling of POLL TAX.

POLE VAULT (U.S. 76) Worldwide command post exercise conducted by all branches of the American armed forces from 1 to 12 March 1976. This exercise confronted the disrupted communications, massive casualties, and civil disorder that would follow a nuclear strike on the U.S. Conducted in conjunction with REX 76.

POLL STATION 81 (U.S. 81) Command post exercise conducted from 9 to 21 March 1981 in conjunction with WINTEX/CIMEX 81 by American units worldwide and centered on chemical and nuclear weapons release procedure. Conducted in tandem with WINTEX/CIMEX 81.

POLLUX The name is an astronomical reference to the twins of Gemini, Pollux, and Castor.

1. (GER 18) Alternative plan to the HEILGER MICHAEL series. This plan called for a pincer attack on French forces near Saint Mihiel, France in the spring of 1918. Never executed. See CASTOR and KAISERSCHLACHT.

2. (FR 53) The consolidation of French Union forces into the fortress of Dien Bien Phu. Executed in November 1953.

POLO HAT (U.S. 86) A series of communication exercises conducted by U.S. forces several times a year since at least 1986.

POMEGRANATE (Allied 44) An attack by the British 30th Corps launched on 16 July 1944 to capture jumping-off points for the GOODWOOD attack.

PONY EXPRESS (US 65) A series of covert Special Forces operations in Laos beginning in 1965.

POOMALAI (IN 87) Indian Air Force humanitarian relief flights that dropped supplies to civilians on the Jaffna Peninsula beginning in June 1987. This marked an escalation in India's involvement in Sri Lanka's civil war.

POPEYE (U.S. 69) A program of weather modification designed to cause heavy rain over the "Ho Chi Minh Trail." Aircraft secretly seeded clouds over Laos with silver iodide. Over 2,000 sorties were flown.

Conducted from March 1967 to November 1968 as COMPATRIOT, then called INTERMEDIARY until March 1969 and finally dubbed POPEYE until March 1972.

POPLAR TREE (U.S. 89) American contingency plan to evacuate noncombatants from El Salvador. Never executed.

POPPY

1. (U.S./U.K.) Reconnaissance flights made by U.S. SR-71 aircraft from British bases. These included flights from the British Isles, Cyprus, and other British-controlled facilities.

2. (CN 44) A Canadian study conducted to identify potential uses of Canadian troops in the Pacific theater at the end of World War II.

PORTO II (GER 42) Deception operation that used a "turned" British agent to convince the British the Dieppe, France, area was very lightly defended. The British used this false information to plan a massive raid on Dieppe (JUBILEE), which resulted in heavy losses.

POSEJDON "POSEIDON" (CT 94) A major Croatian exercise conducted in November 1994 by air and ground units earmarked for STORM 95.

POSITIVE LEAP (U.S. 80) The first command post exercise sponsored by U.S. Central Command. Conducted in the spring of 1980 at Fort Bragg to address communications and logistics aspects of the deployment of an American task force to the Mideast.

POSTERN (Allied 43) Airborne and amphibious attack to seize Nazdab and the Markham/Watut river valleys on New Guinea. After the landings, an airfield was quickly built to support the drive on Lae. Executed 5 September 1943. See CARTWHEEL.

POST TIME (U.S. 88) Plan for the defense of the Panama Canal drawn up in 1988 based on the assumption the Panama Defense Forces would be hostile or neutral to the American effort. This reflected a deterioration of relations between the two nations that eventually led to the American invasion (JUST CAUSE).

POT OF GOLD (Allied 41) Early plan to send U.S. forces to Brazil to protect that national from Axis attack. Executed as LILAC.

POWER FLITE (U.S. 57) The first around-the-world, nonstop flight of B-52 Stratofortress bombers of the former Strategic Air Command. Conducted 16 to 18 January 1957 by 3 aircraft of the 93rd Bomb Wing based at Castle Air Force Base, California.

POWER PACK (U.S. 65) American intervention in the Dominican Republic in 1965/66.

POWER PLAY (U.S. 79) Worldwide command post exercise that tested the relocation of critical personnel and headquarters to alternate sites as well as chemical and nuclear weapon release procedures. This exercise was conducted in conjunction with WINTE/CIMEX 79.

POWER SWEEP 87 (U.S. 86) Worldwide command post exercise conducted from 27 October to 7 November 1986 to test mobilization, crisis management, and the use of alternative national command posts in a multi-theater conventional war.

PQ (Allied convoy) Allied convoys to the northern Soviet ports during World War II.

PQ17 (Allied 42) Allied convoy ravaged by the German ROSSELSPRUNG attack in June 1942.

PRAETORIAN (U.S. 81) A series of 22 underground nuclear blasts at the Nevada Test Site. The HURON LANDING and DIAMOND ACE explosions occurred simultaneously in one of the most complex and most extensively monitored nuclear tests to date. These explosions followed TINDER-BOX and preceded PHALANX. The tests of the PRAETORIAN series were:

PALIZA	1 October 81	20-150 kilotons
TILCI	11 November	20-150 kilotons
ROUSANNE	12 November	20-150 kilotons
AKAVI	3 December	20-150 kilotons
CABOC	16 December	<20 kilotons
JORNADA	28 January 82	20-150 kilotons
MOLBO	12 February	20-150 kilotons
HOSTA	12 February	20-150 kilotons
TENAJA	17 April	<20 kilotons
GIBNE	25 April	20-150 kilotons
KRYDDOST	6 May	<20 kilotons
BOUSCHET	5 July	20-150 kilotons
KESTI	16 June	<20 kilotons
NEBBIOLO	24 June	20-150 kilotons
MONTEREY	29 July	20-150 kilotons
ATRISCO	5 August	20-150 kilotons
QUESO	11 August	<20 kilotons
CERRO	2 September	<20 kilotons
HURON LANDING	23 September	<20 kilotons
DIAMOND ACE	23 September	20-150 kilotons
BORREGO	29 September	<150 kilotons

PRAIRIE (U.S.) A reserved first word for the program of the U.S. Navy. See PRAIRIE FIRE.

PRAIRIE FIRE (U.S. 83) U.S. Navy operations off the coast of Libya in March 1983. The Libyans had claimed the Gulf of Sidra as territorial waters, calling the demarcation a "line of death." The American aircraft carriers *America* and *Coral Sea* supported other surface vessels in order to maintain the "right of innocent passage" in the Gulf. This effort included several air-to-air battles and the sinking of a Libyan missile boat on 25 March with a laser-guided bomb. See EL DORADO CANYON.

PRAIRIE PACIFIC (CN 54) A Royal Canadian Air Force publicity tour in the summer of 1954.

PRAYER BOOK (U.S. 88) A series of plans for operations in Panama drawn up beginning in April 1988 as relations between the U.S. and Panama deteriorated. Included ELDER STATESMAN, BLUE SPOON, KRYSTAL BALL, KLONDIKE KEY, and their successors.

PRAYING MANTIS (U.S. 88) A 3-day American naval war waged against Iran in 1988. The Americans had reflagged Kuwaiti oil tankers to protect them from Iranian attacks during the Iran/Iraq War (EARNEST WILL). In April 1988, an American frigate hit a mine. The Americans responded with a naval task force ("Battlegroup Foxtrot") built around the carrier *Enterprise* which attacked Iranian naval and intelligence facilities on inoperable oil platforms in the Persian Gulf and sank most of the small Iranian Navy. See PRIME CHANCE.

PRESENT ARMS 86 (U.S. 86) Worldwide command post exercise that dealt with recovery after a massive nuclear attack on the U.S. This exercise included play by civil defense organizations of the states called REX 86 ALPHA.

PRESSURE COOKER (U.S. 94) A portion of the civil affairs operations conducted by U.S. forces following their conquest of Haiti in mid-1994. The popularly elected president, Aristide, was scheduled to return in October. Concerned with the possibility of violence from both pro- and anti-Aristide forces, the Americans stepped up their pacification operations. Bumper stickers, newly-commissioned songs on the radio, and other techniques were used to ensure the peaceful reception of President Aristide. See UPHOLD DEMOCRACY.

PRESSURE PUMP (U.N. 52) A massive air attack on the North Korean capital of Pyongyang on 11 July 1952.

PRICELESS (Allied 43) The general name for Allied naval operations in the Mediterranean after the invasion of Sicily (HUSKY).

PRICHA (IS 70) See FLORESCENCE.

PRIME BEEF (U.S.) U.S. Air Force term for their Base Engineer Emergency Force units and personnel.

PRIME CHANCE (U.S. 87) The U.S. Army contribution to the mostly-navy EARNEST WILL operation. The Navy, confronted with the task for protecting Kuwaiti oil tankers flying the American flag in the war-torn Persian Gulf, required small, lightweight helicopter gunships. The American Army recently secretly acquired the AH-6 gunship for its special operations forces. These aircraft were based on navy ships and barges in the region where they took part in the destruction of the Iranian Navy (PRAYING MANTIS).

PRIME RIBS (U.S.) U.S. Air Force term for logistics units used to augment bases in an emergency.

PRIME TARGET 77 (U.S. 77) Worldwide command post exercise to test the ability of key headquarters units and personnel to relocate to alternative command posts while controlling chemical and nuclear weapon release. Followed 2 years later by POWER PLAY 79 and then POLL STATION 81.

PRINCIPAL (Allied 43) A British special operations attack on the Italian Navy. On the night of 2 January 1943 British submarines released raiders in two-man submarines near the ports of Palermo, Cagliari, and Meddelina. These miniature submarines, dubbed "chariots," were used to attach explosive charges to the targeted ships.

PRIZE GAUNTLET 80 (U.S. 80) A worldwide command post exercise testing command and control systems and procedures.

PRODUCTIVE EFFORT (U.S. 92) Planning name for SEA ANGEL.

PROFITEER (U.K. 59) Deployment of Royal Air Force Vulcan heavy bombers to Malaya for possible use during the communist insurrection in that country. The aircraft were never used in combat there.

PROMOTE LIBERTY (U.S. 89) Nation assistance efforts in Panama after the invasion of that country. Based on the BLIND LOGIC plan. See PRESSURE COOKER.

PROPER LADY (U.S.) A plan, current in the early 1980s, to use elements of the U.S. Air Force to conduct special operations, shows of force, and deception operations in the Pacific region.

PROTEA (R.S.A. 81) Attacks by South African forces on SWAPO bases at Ongiva and Xangongo, Angola, in August 1981. Followed KLIPKLOP, preceded DAISY. A protea is a local flower.

PROUD (U.S.) General designator for a series of biennial command post exercises in which senior civil and military leaders focus on command and control, command post operations, and mobilization issues. Exercises of this series included:

PROUD DEEP ALPHA (U.S. 71) A 5-day interruption of the general U.S. halt of the bombing of North Vietnam. Following the ROLLING THUNDER offensive that ended on 31 October 1968 until the LINEBACKER strikes, which began on 8 May 1972, the U.S. called off large-scale air attacks north of the Demilitarized Zone. PROUD DEEP ALPHA attacked targets in North Vietnam from 26 to 30 December 1971. See FREEDOM TRAIN.

PROUD SABER 83 (U.S. 83) Tested the crisis management procedures of the Office of the Secretary of Defense and other senior agencies. Conducted in conjunction with REX 82 BRAVO.

PROUD SCOUT 87 (U.S. 87) Tested mobilization of reserve units and the individual ready reserve. Conducted 12 to 20 November 1987.

PROUD SPIRIT (U.S. 80) The follow-on to the disastrous NIFTY NUGGET 78 exercise. Held in conjunction with REX-80 BRAVO.

PROVEN FORCE (Allied 91) Allied air operations based at Incirlik, Turkey, in support of DESERT STORM. These attacks began on the night of 18 January 1991. Most of the aircraft available were American F-111s so most of the attacks launched from Turkey were conducted at night to take advantage of that aircraft's advanced electronics. These aircraft were critical in suppressing the Iraqi "Scud" missiles fired from the western portion of that country.

PROVIDE ASSISTANCE (U.S. 94) Humanitarian operations following an outbreak of genocidal civil war in Rwanda. American military units provided water purification, transport, and other support to refugee camps in Zaire. See SUPPORT HOPE.

PROVIDE COMFORT (U.S. 90) Operations to prevent Kurds from fleeing their homes in northern Iraq in the aftermath of the Persian Gulf War. A "No-Fly Zone" was established by the U.N. north of the 36th parallel. This was enforced by American and British aircraft. Also included in this effort was the delivery of humanitarian relief and military protection of the Kurds by a small American ground force based in Turkey. On 14 April 1994, 2 U.S. Air Force F-15 Eagle fighters on a PROVIDE COMFORT patrol mistakenly downed 2 United Army Blackhawk helicopters carrying 26 Allied personnel, killing all aboard. The

operation ended officially on 31 December 1996 at the request of the Islamic Government of Turkey who wanted to improve relations with Iran and Iraq.

PROVIDE HOPE (U.S. 92) Political program to coordinate economic assistance to the former Soviet Union from donor nations (Japan, Germany, Belgium, France, Italy, Portugal, Norway, Canada, Qatar, U.K., and U.A.E.). Although some coordination of effort was achieved at a conference held in Washington in 1992, the American government was unwilling to commit substantial resources to the effort. Given the lack of U.S. resolve, this political effort faltered.

PROVIDE PROMISE (U.S. 92) American-led U.N. effort to fly humanitarian supplies in to the Bosnian capital of Sarajevo. Began on 2 July 1992, the effort was suspended when hostilities closed the Sarajevo airport. NATO air strikes (DELIBERATE FORCE) reopened that facility in September 1995. See CHESHIRE, COURLIS, and PROVIDE SANTA.

PROVIDE RELIEF (U.S. 92) The airlift of relief supplies to Kenya and Somalia (via Kenyan airfields) that began on 28 August 1992. By December, the situation in Somalia had deteriorated to the point that the U.N. authorized the use of military force to restore law and order. Somali factions attacked the soldiers sent to save them from anarchy, who were then withdrawn by early 1994, leaving Somalia to return to lawlessness. See RESTORE HOPE.

PROVIDE SANTA (U.S. 93) The airlift of donated toys to Bosnian children aboard PROVIDE PROMISE flights in December 1993.

PROVIDENCE (Allied 42) Plan in 1942 for a covert occupation of sites near Buna on the northeast coast of New Guinea to establish a number of airfields. The plan called for a cross-country movement of some troops and an amphibious landing by others who would build the airfields quickly before they were detected by the Japanese. As executed, the movement was conducted far ahead of schedule in response to Japanese moves. The limited number of troops who did land at Gona on 22 July did not establish an airfield, but instead were forced to fight the advancing Japanese.

PUGILIST (Allied 43) British attack on the Mareth Line, near the Wadi Zigzaou in North Africa in late March 1943. Using the New Zealand Corps to turn the enemy's western flank, Montgomery launched a week-long battle that ended in a rout of the Italian defenders. See SUPERCHARGE II.

PUMA (Allied 41) British contingency plan to capture the Spanish Canary Islands if Spain entered World War II.

"PUNISHMENT" (GER 41) See BESTRAU-FUNG.

PURPLE (U.S. 39) The machine used by the Japanese to encode and decode diplomatic traffic. By extension, the code itself. This traffic was interpreted by the MAGIC operation.

PURPLE STAR (NATO 96) A large amphibious exercise conducted by the U.S. and Royal Navies in April 1996. Sponsored by the U.S. Atlantic Command, the training ran from 25 April to 20 May 1996. The highlight of the exercise was an air and sea assault on Camp LeJeune, North Carolina, simulating a second war in the Persian Gulf. This complex action was coordinated by a combined U.S./U.K. staff aboard the USS *Mount Whitney*. Fourteen Americans were killed in a nighttime helicopter collision during this training. The U.S. Air Force portion of this exercise was called BIG DROP III. The U.S. Army portion was called ROYAL DRAGON. Over 53,000

soldiers took part along with over 50 ships and more than 300 aircraft.

PURPLE STORM (U.S. 89) Exercises conducted in Panama to train for the execution of PRAYER BOOK plans including the U.S. invasion of Panama, BLUE SPOON. In the summer and fall of 1989, these exercises provided training on or near unit's real tactical objectives and supported the deception plan of BLUE SPOON by overwhelming the ability of the Panamanians to monitor American preparations. The large number of Americans aggressively asserting American rights under the Canal Treaties provoked a number of violent episodes that eventually led to war. See JUST CAUSE.

PURPLE WARRIOR (U.K. 87) A British exercise conducted in northern Scotland in November 1987. This exercise was designed to test lessons learned during the liberation of Falkland Islands (CORPORATE).

PUSHOVER (U.S. 49) An early test of the feasibility of launching ballistic missiles from warships. A German V-2 rocket was placed on a mock-up deck at White Sands Proving Grounds. It was then fueled, ignited, and pushed over to simulate an accident during launch. The resulting explosion compounded the disastrous effect of the liquid oxygen spilling over the simulated deck. The spectacular effect of this test convinced the Navy that liquid-fueled missiles were impracticable aboard ship. Part of ABUSIVE. See SANDY.

PYRAMIDER (U.S.) A CIA program to develop a satellite-based method of covert communication with agents and sensors around the world. This program was exposed to the Soviets by William Kampiles, a 23-year old junior CIA employee, in 1978. He was sentenced to 40 years in prison. His treason, trial, and escape from prison was the basis of the book, *The Falcon and the Snowman*.

Q

QP (Allied 41) Allied convoys from the northern Soviet ports to England. Designated by number (e.g., QP 123). Replaced the designation RA in September 1941.

QUADRANGLE (GER 42) See VIERECK.

QUADRANT (Allied 43) The first U.S./British conference held at Quebec. Conducted from 14-23 August 1943; this meeting is commonly referred to as "First Quebec Conference" to distinguish it from the OCTAGON meeting. The Western Allies agreed to a combined effort to produce an atomic bomb (MANHATTAN ENGINEER DISTRICT), attack Europe through northern France (OVERLORD), and to conduct a strategic bombing offensive against German (POINTBLANK) in preparation for this invasion.

QUEEN (Allied 44) Operation by the U.S. 7th Corps on the Ruhr plain. Due to poor weather, the massive air attacks scheduled for this attack were canceled. Executed on 16 November 1944.

QUEEN BEE (U.S. 64) A "sensitive intelligence operation" conducted as part of OPLAN 34-A in Southeast Asia in 1964. This name was leaked with the publication of the "Pentagon Papers" in 1971.

QUEENS ROW (NORAD 61) The U.S. transfer of 56 F-101B and 10 2-seat training versions of the F-101 Voodoo interceptor to Canada. The actual hand-over was conducted in April 1961. See PEACH WINGS.

QUICK DRAW (U.S. 94) The evacuation of U.S. forces from Somalia in late March 1994. Part of UNITED SHIELD.

QUICK KICK

1. (U.S. 56) A publicity flight conducted by 8 B-52 bombers of the former Strategic Air Command on 24 and 25 November 1956. The aircraft used air-to-air refueling to fly completely around North America.

2. (U.S. 62) An American all-service amphibious training exercise conducted in May 1962.

QUICK LIFT (U.S. 95) A U.S. sealift operation to move military and other heavy equipment to the former Yugoslavia in support of international peacekeeping operations (JOINT ENDEAVOR) there. Begun in June 1995.

QUICKSILVER

1. (Allied 44) Sub-plan of FORTITUDE, the 1944 deception plan. QUICKSILVER created a fictional "1st U.S. Army Group" commanded by General Patton that supposedly would invade France at the Pas de Calais. American troops used false signals and decoy installations and phony

equipment to deceive German observation aircraft and radio intercept operators. See BODYGUARD.

2. (U.S. 78) A nuclear test series of 18 blasts conducted at the Nevada Test Site in 1978 and 1979. Preceded TINDERBOX, followed CRESCENT. The individual tests were:

EMMENTHAL	2 November 78	<20 kilotons
QUARGEL	18 November	20-150 kilotons
(Unknown)	1 December	(unknown)
FARM	16 December	20-150 kilotons
BACCARAT	24 January 79	<20 kilotons
QUINELLA	8 February	20-150 kilotons
KLOSTER	15 February	20-150 kilotons
MEMORY	14 March	<20 kilotons
(Unknown)	11 May	(unknown)
PEPATO	11 June	20-150 kilotons
CHESS	20 June	<20 kilotons
FAJY	28 June	20-150 kilotons
BURZET	3 August	20-150 kilotons
OFFSHORE	8 August	20-150 kilotons
NESSEL	29 August	20-150 kilotons
HEARTS	6 September	20-150 kilotons
PERA	8 September	<20 kilotons
SHEEPSHEAD	26 September	20-150 kilotons

3. (U.S. 90) Plan to reduce the size of the U.S. Army in the early 1990s as a result of end of the Cold War. A number of incentives such as early retirement were used to reduce the number of soldiers on active duty by a third.

R

R4 (Allied 40) Planned Franco-British landings at the Norwegian ports of Narvik, Stavanger, and Trondheim to interdict German supplies of Scandinavian iron ore and deny the Nazis air and naval bases that would out-flank the Allied blockade. Planned for 5 April 1940, during the "Phony War" period, but canceled after the German invasion of France (GELB).

RA (Allied) Allied convoys from the Soviet northern ports to Britain and Iceland. Designated by number (e.g., RA 123). Replaced by the designation "QP" in September 1941.

RAILROAD (Allied 41) June 1941 convoy to Malta. Followed ROCKET, preceded SUB-SISTENCE.

RAIN BARREL (U.S. 47) The program that detected the first Soviet nuclear test in September 1949 (FIRST LIGHTNING). A monitoring station in the Aleutian Islands detected traces of cesium in clouds that had traveled over the Soviet homeland. Additional trace elements were detected by modified weather planes.

RAINBOW

1. (U.S. 39) Series of American war plans drawn up between 1939 and 1941. These plans considered a coalition of enemies, unlike the earlier "Color Series," which it replaced. The Rainbow plans were in turn replaced by the ABC series.

RAINBOW-1 The most limited plan of the series called for the defense of all U.S. territory north of 10 degrees south latitude, but without reinforcement of the Philippines. This plan assumed the democracies in Europe and Latin America would remain neutral and only U.S. forces would be available to resist an attack in the Pacific.

RAINBOW-2 expanded RAINBOW-1 to include the Western Pacific and the Philippines.

RAINBOW-3 expanded RAINBOW-1 to include the defense of both North and South America.

RAINBOW-4 Called for the defense of the entire Western Hemisphere in the event of a war against the U.S., France, and Britain by Italy and Germany.

RAINBOW-5 Proposed an initial holding action in the Pacific against the Japanese while attacking Italy and Germany.

2. (GER) See REGENBOEN.

3. (Allied 43) A practice amphibious exercise held in Algeria in the spring of 1943 for American troops earmarked for the invasion of Sicily (HUSKY).

RAINCOAT (Allied 43) Attack by the American 5th Army against the German

"Winter Line" in Italy near the Camino hill complex. Launched on 3 December 1943.

RANCH HAND (U.S. 62) General term for American defoliant programs during the Vietnam War. Begun on 13 January 1962 and conducted for over 9 years; by the end of the war over 18,000,000 gallons of chemicals had been sprayed to deny the communist forces cover from American firepower. In 1969, the primary defoliant used (called "Agent Orange" after the colored stripes that marked its barrels) was found to cause birth defects. On 29 October of that year, Agent Orange was replaced by Agent Blue in RANCH HAND operations. These chemicals denuded large areas, opened them to erosion, and had unintended long-range toxic effects on the environment and people. In 1979, the American Environmental Protection Agency (EPA) banned Agent Orange in the U.S. due to evidence it caused stillbirths. Injuries suffered by the American soldiers became a long-running legal battle that was settled 20 years later when the American government admitted that exposure to these chemicals caused cancer, birth defects, and other medical problems. See TRAIL DUST.

RANDOM (CN 54) The deployment of Royal Canadian Air Force fighter jets to Europe beginning in February 1954. Followed LEAP FROG.

RANGER (U.S. 51) A series of 5 nuclear explosions conducted at the Nevada Test Site west of Las Vegas. All of these were open-air explosions of weapons dropped from B-50 bombers. These tests centered on the practicality of developing a second generation of nuclear weapons using smaller amounts of valuable nuclear materials. Planned under the name FAUST. Preceded GREENHOUSE, followed by SAND-STONE. The shots were:

ABLE	27 January 51	1 kiloton
BAKER	28 January	8 kilotons
EASY	1 February	1 kiloton
BAKER-2	2 February	8 kilotons
FOX	6 February	22 kilotons

RANKIN A
RANKIN B
RANKIN C (Allied 44) Plans for the occupation of Europe in the event of a German collapse. Replaced SLEDGEHAMMER and its variants. RANKIN postulated three possible contingencies: Case A: Substantial weakening of German resistance; Case B: German withdrawal from occupied territories; Case C: unconditional German surrender. See ECLIPSE.

RAPID ROADS (U.S. 62) A U.S. Army exercise conducted in central Texas in the summer of 1962. This training featured the 82nd Airborne Division opposed by the 1st Armored Division. Both units hurriedly returned to their bases to support the mobilization for the Cuban Missile Crisis. See THREE PAIRS.

RAPID STEP (CN 56) Deployment of HMCS *Magnificent* to support United Nationals, peacekeeping efforts in the Sinai region following the Suez Crisis (MUSKETEER).

RATKILLER (R.O.K. 51) Anti-guerrilla operations conducted in 1951 in southwestern Korea in 3 phases. Phase I centered on the town of Chiri-san. On 2 December 1951, South Korean Army units began clearing the area and pushing the guerrillas toward blocking positions manned by security forces, youth regiments, and the National Police. By 14 December 1,612 guerrillas were killed and 1,842 wounded. Phase II was a similar operation conducted in Pukto Province, centered on the city of Chonju from 19 December 1951 to 4 January 1952. Phase III returned to the Chiri-san area to complete the sweep. On 15 March 1952 responsibility for anti-guerrilla operations returned to civil authorities.

RATS (U.K. 53) A series of British nuclear safety tests that studied the components of nuclear weapons but did not involve any nuclear detonations. Conducted between 1953 and 1963 at Emu Field and Maralinga test areas in Australia.

RATWEEK (Allied 44) A coordinated series of attacks launched on 1 September 1944 by Yugoslav partisans and the Royal Air Force against German forces retreating from the Soviets.

RAWLINSON (Allied 44) A planned breakout from the Orne River bridgehead in France to be led by the British 3rd Infantry Division's thrust south of the Bois de Bavent in August 1944. Never executed.

RDS-I (S.U. 47) Name given to the first Soviet nuclear bomb. The designation was meaningless, but members of the project quickly decided it stood for Reaktivnyi dvigatel Stalina (Stalin's Rocket Engine). See FIRST LIGHTNING.

READY SWITCH (U.S. 77) See CREEK SWING.

REBUILD (U.S. 50) The emergency repair of worn American military equipment in Japan to meet the crisis in Korea. The U.S. occupation force in Japan suffered from years of low funding and almost exclusively used equipment left over from World War II. To improve levels of readiness, Far East Command collected equipment from abandoned Pacific battlefields (ROLL UP) and contracted with Japanese companies to repair small arms, vehicles, and other equipment (REBUILD).

RECKLESS (Allied 44) Amphibious invasion of Hollandia conducted on 22 April 1944. This attack bypassed the heavily-defended Japanese positions at Hansa Bay and Wewak, and so avoided heavy casualties. Part of PERSECUTION.

RECORD (CN 91) Canadian participation in the U.N. Iraq-Kuwait Observer Mission (UNIKOM). The Canadians contributed a 300-man engineer regiment as part of a 898-man force from 33 nations. This mission monitors the frontier between the 2 nations.

RED (U.S. 04) American war plan prepared in 1904 dealing with the potential of war against the British Empire arising from commercial rivalry. One of the Color Series. Never executed. See RED-ORANGE.

"RED BEAN" (BG 78) See HARICOT ROUGE.

RED BIRD (U.S. 51) Deployment of B-26 Invader bombers equipped with infrared sights for night operations in Korea.

RED COW (U.N. 52) A series of close air support sorties conducted in Korea in October 1952.

RED DRAGON (BG 64) See DRAGON ROUGE.

RED FLAG (U.S. 75) A 5-week training program periodically conducted by the U.S. Air Force for fighter pilots at Nellis Air Force Base, Nevada. All American fighter units are cycled through this capstone exercise every 2 years. RED FLAG began in November 1975 and includes the firing of live missiles at target drones. French and British forces have periodically taken part in this training. See BLUE FLAG, GREEN FLAG, and MAPLE FLAG.

"RED HAND" (FR 56) See MAIN ROUGE.

RED HORSE (U.S.) Air Force term for heavy airfield repair teams. See PRIME RIBS, PRIME BEEF.

RED MAGIC (U. S. 40) The effort that broke the Japanese "Red" naval code before World War II. By extension, the products of that effort. This decoding was aided by the

FBI illegally breaking into various buildings in the U.S. to photograph the code books. See MAGIC and RED.

RED-ORANGE (U.S. 04) Plan prepared by the U.S. that dealt with a war against both Japan and the British Empire simultaneously. Such a war would require a 2-ocean navy, which became a goal for American naval construction from the early 1900s. Part of the Color Series. Superseded by the RAINBOW plans. Never executed.

RED RAMP (CN 50) Royal Canadian Air Force provision of humanitarian relief to victims of flooding along the Red River in May 1950.

RED STORM (Coalition 91) Deception operation conducted by the 1st Cavalry Division with attached aviation and psychological warfare units to falsely portray a Coalition attack into occupied Kuwait via the Wadi Al Batin. Conducted on 15 February 1991, followed BERM BUSTER, preceded KNIGHT STRIKE.

REDWING (U.S. 56) A series of seventeen nuclear tests conducted in 1956 at Eniwetok and Bikini Atolls in the Pacific Test Area. These explosions were designed to test the reliability of American nuclear weapons. The individual shots were:

PAWNEE	canceled	
LACROSSE	4 May 56	40 kilotons
CHEROKEE	20 May	prob. 3.75 megatons
ZUNI	27 May	3.5 megatons
YUMA	27 May	<.25 kilotons
ERIE	30 May	several kilotons
SEMINOLE	6 June	13.7 kilotons
FLATHEAD	11 June	unknown
BLACKFOOT	11 June	unknown
KICKAPOO	13 June	unknown
OSAGE	16 June	prob. 70 kilotons
INCA	21 June	prob. 15 kilotons
DAKOTA	25 June	unknown
MOHAWK	2 July	several kilotons
APACHE	8 July	prob. 3.4 megatons
NAVAJO	10 July	prob. 4.5 megatons
TEWA	20 July	5 megatons
HURON	21 July	several hundred kilotons

REEFEX (U. S. 94) The general American term for the disposal of obsolete tanks, ships, and other equipment at sea. The material is decontaminated and dumped at sea in such a way as to provide habitat for marine life. Generally this training is conducted by amphibious landing craft units of the National Guard. "REEFEX" is a contraction of "Reef Exercise."

REFLEX (U.S. 53) The general name for the overseas rotation of Strategic Air Command B-47 Stratojet bombers as an alert force. The Stratojet did not have the range to strike at the Soviet Union from the U.S. REFLEX deployments moved bomber wings to foreign bases for short periods, complicating the planning for Soviet staffs. These routine rotations were given individual names (such as REFLEX ACTION) and were conducted continuously from 1953 to 1958. The foreign bases used for these deployments included Nouasseur, Benguerir, and Sidi Slimane in French Morocco, Moron, Torrejon, and Zaragoza in Spain, and the British bases of Brize Norton, Fairford, Greenham Common, and Upper Heyford. In addition, REFLEX aircraft also deployed to Anderson Air Force Base on Guam and Elmendorf Air Force Base in Alaska. As the medium-ranged B-47 was phased out of service, the need for these rotations was reduced. By 1963, operations at the Moroccan bases ceased. The next year operations out of Fairford, Greenham Common, Anderson, and Zaragoza ended. In 1965, REFLEX aircraft left Moron and Torrejon. In late July 1956, during one of these deployments, an aircraft crashed into a nuclear weapons storage bunker at Lakenheath Air Base in England.

REFLEX ACTION (U.S. 57) The deployment of 20 B-47 Stratojet bombers from the U.S. to Sidi Slimane Air Base in French Morocco where they remained on alert for 90 days. Begun in September 1957.

REFORGER (U.S. 67) Annual exercise conducted by the U.S. Army to practice a major reinforcement of Europe. Under the terms of a 1967 agreement with NATO, the U.S. promised to be ready to send 35,000 soldiers and airmen to Europe in the event of a crisis. These exercises ensure that the Americans could meet this commitment. The name REFORGER is a contraction of "REturn of FORces to GERmany." The equivalent Air Force exercise is called CRESTED CAP.

REGATE "REGATTA" (FR 54) The final relief column that linked up with French Union forces in Bien Dien Phu.

REGATTA

1. (GER 42) Anti-partisan operation centered near Gorky, Byelorussia, begun 1 October 1942.

2. (FR 54) See REGATE.

REGENBORGEN "RAINBOW"

1. (GER 43) An ill-fated German naval attack on Allied convoys to the Soviet Union. The German force, built around the battle cruiser Scharnhorst, planned to interdict the convoy route between the North Cape and Bear Island. They left port in late December 1943. The Royal Navy, alerted to the raid by signal intercepts, was able to attack the force, sinking the Scharnhorst and killing all but 36 of her crew.

2. (GER 45) The scuttling of German submarines by their crews in the last days of the war to prevent their capture. Ordered in early May 1945, 231 of the boats were destroyed. See DEADLIGHT.

REGENSCHIRM "UMBRELLA" (GER 40) The German air attack on Birmingham, England, in November 1940.

REINDEER (R.S.A. 78) South African attacks on SWAPO bases near Cossinga and Chetquera, Angola, in early May 1978. Followed SAVANNAH, preceded REKSTOK.

REKSTOK (R.S.A. 79) South African raids into southern Angola in March 1979. Conducted concurrently with SAFRAAN. Preceded SCEPTIC.

RENEGADE (Allied Law Enforcement 96) A 6-year operation conducted by various agencies in America, Australia, South America, and Africa that uncovered a wide-ranging illegal trade in tropical birds. These animals are protected by the Convention on International Trade in Endangered Species. Tony Silva, a well-known member of the legitimate bird industry, who had publicly decried the trade in endangered birds, was found to be the kingpin of the international network.

RENO
RENO II
RENO III
RENO IV

RENO V (Allied 44) Plans for the recapture of the Philippines from the Japanese prepared by General MacArthur's staff. These plans varied in the number of units required and their possible routes. Generally, they were not practical, given the worldwide demand for landing forces and the Allied "Germany First" policy. See MONTCLAIR.

RESCUE EAGLE 2-95 (U.S./AL 95) A combined American/Albanian rescue exercise conducted from 2 to 14 October 1995 in Albanian waters. American forces centered on the assault carrier USS *Wasp*.

RESISTANCE (U.S. 73) A part of CHAOS. This project involved illegal CIA surveillance of dissident groups inside the U.S. and continued until June 1973.

RESTORE DEMOCRACY (U.N. 94) The American invasion and occupation of Haiti. A series of Haitian coups, public pronouncements, and mass emigrations by sea presented the Clinton administration with a long-running diplomatic crisis. On 31 July 1994, the U.N. Security Council authorized member states to use all means necessary to remove the military government of General Raoul Cedras. The invasion force was en route to the island on 18 September when the Haitians surrendered to a delegation led by former President Jimmy Carter. This resulted in an American-led international occupation (UPHOLD DEMOCRACY) and the restoration of the duly elected president, Aristide. On 31 March, the U.N. took command of the remaining forces and began an international effort to improve conditions on the island.

RESTORE HOPE (U.S. 92) The American portion of the U.N.-authorized use of military force to support humanitarian relief efforts in Somalia. This action was approved by the U.N.s Security Council on 3 December 1992. The next day President Bush announced that elements of the 1st Marine Expeditionary Force and the 10th Mountain Division would be used to end lawlessness and establish a multinational peacekeeping force in the nation. See ORYX.

RESUPPLY (CN 52) Annual flights by Royal Canadian Air Force transports to remote Arctic research and weather stations, begun in March 1952.

RETAINER (U.S. 51–54) Follow-on to FANDANGO, modifying F-84 fighter bombers for nuclear weapon carriage.

RETRIBUTION (Allied 43) Air and naval attack designed to prevent the German evacuation of North Africa through Tunis. The *Africa Korps* was surrounded and facing a final Allied attack (STRIKE). Admiral Cunningham, Royal Navy, began this operation on 7 May 1943 with the colorful signal to "Sink, burn, and destroy. Let nothing pass." The Germans were unable to mount a significant rescue effort. The Royal Navy captured 897 men. Only 653 Germans are thought to have escaped to Italy. An unknown number drowned. See FLAX.

RETROSPECT (Allied 44) The Allied occupation of the village of Mandang on the northeast coast of New Guinea on 24 April 1944.

REUNION (Allied 44) Air evacuation of over 1,100 Allied prisoners from Rumania to Italy.

REVIVAL (Allied 45) Flights that returned displaced persons from German and Austria to their homelands after World War II.

REX (U.S.) General term used to designate annual readiness exercises conducted by the Federal Emergency Management Agency (FEMA), the American civil defense headquarters. These exercises are designated by year. Exercises designated ALPHA deal with the continuity of government. Those designated BRAVO address mobilization of military reserves and industrial facilities. REX is a contraction of "Readiness Exercise." Exercises in this series included:

REX 76 (U.S. 76) Conducted in conjunction with POLE VAULT 76, this exercise dealt with recovery from a nuclear attack.

REX 78 (U.S. 78) Conducted in conjunction with NIFTY NUGGET from 10 to 30 October 1978.

REX 80 BRAVO (U.S. 80) Conducted in conjunction with PROUD SPIRIT 80.

REX 82 ALPHA (U.S. 82) Conducted in conjunction with IVY LEAGUE.

REX 82 BRAVO (U. S. 82) Conducted in conjunction with PROUD SABER 83 from 25 October to 4 November 1982.

REX 84 ALPHA (U.S. 84) Conducted in conjunction with NIGHT TRAIN 84 from 5 to 13 April 1984.

REX 86 ALPHA (U. S. 86) Conducted in conjunction with PRESENT ARMS 86.

RHENNUEBUNG "RHINE EXERCISE" (GER 41) The sortie by the *Bismark* and *Prinz Eugen* leaving from Gdynia, Poland, on 12 May 1941. Alerted by agents in the Swedish government, the British mounted an exceptional effort to sink the German flotilla. The ships took a brief refuge in Norwegian waters on 18 May, making a break for the Atlantic shipping lanes on the 22nd. The obsolescent British battlecruiser *Hood* and new battleship *Prince of Wales* made contact with the Germans early on the morning of 24 May. The *Hood* exploded, killing her entire crew of 1,417 when a German shell detonated her magazines. The *Prince of Wales* continued to dog the Germans, reporting their position. Leaking fuel and damaged, the *Bismark* made course for the French port of Ste. Nazaire (CHARIOTEER) while the undamaged *Prinz Eugen* began to raid the convoy lanes. She reached Brest on 1 June. British forces converged on the *Bismark* hitting her with naval airpower that damaged her rudder. She was sunk on 27 May by British shells and torpedoes.

RHINE EXERCISE (GER 41) See RHENNUEBUNG.

RHUMBA (Allied 44) Plan to transship allied combat forces through England to the liberated potions of northern France. In fact, reinforcements from the U.S. arrived so quickly in England that shipping was not available to move them to France, leading to a backlog.

RICE BOWL (U.S. 79) Planning name for EAGLE CLAW.

RIMAU (Allied 44) Raid by British commandos on Singapore harbor in 1944.

RIM PAC (U.S.) A series of naval exercise hosted by the U.S. Pacific Command in even-numbered years. Over the years, ships from the U.S., Canada, Japan, Korea, and Chile have taken part. The name seems to be derived from "Pacific Rim."

RIPPER (U. N. 52) The U.N. attack that recaptured Seoul. The assault began on 7 March 1952 with a massive artillery preparation and was followed by multiple river crossings across the peninsula. The U.N. forces advanced on line to prevent gaps that would allow North Korean infiltration. Day by day, huge amounts of artillery and air support hammered the communist forces and cleared the way for the U.N. advance. Seoul was abandoned by the North Koreans on 15 March. Included HAWK, followed KILLER.

RIVET (U.S.) A reserved first word for the programs and projects of the U.S. Air Force. See RIVET CAP and RIVET MILE.

RIVET CAP (U.S. 87) The deactivation of American Titan II intercontinental ballistic missiles. The Titan II was in the American arsenal from 1963 to the late 1980s.

RIVET MILE (U.S. 85) A program to improve the reliability and extend the life of American Minuteman II intercontinental ballistic missiles. MILE is an acronym for Minuteman Integrated Life Extension. Begun in April 1985.

RO (JPN 43) The Japanese reinforcement of Rabaul with about 200 aircraft from their carriers at the beginning of October 1943. The idea was to destroy the next major Allied operation, wherever it might occur. On 11 November, these aircraft were savaged by U.S. land-based fighters preparing the way for the invasion of New Georgia (TOENAILS). On 12 November, the 120 surviving aircraft were ordered to return to Truk.

ROAD'S END (Allied 46) The postwar destruction of captured Japanese warships in February 1946.

"ROARING BULL" (U.S.) Flag-word used in electronic messages to identify communications concerning the actual mobilization of reserve units and personnel. "Grazing Herd" is used for practice messages and exercises.

ROARING LION (U.K. 93) Training exercise conducted in Britain from 4 to 12 August 1993 by British (and some American) units centered on the 5th Airborne Brigade. This exercise included the largest British airborne drop in 20 years. It marked the revitalization of 5th Airborne Brigade, which had been under-manned and under-funded for a number of years.

ROAST (Allied 45) British attack to clear the area from Lake Comacchio, Italy, to the sea. Conducted in April 1945.

ROBIN QUART (U.S. 90) See JUST CAUSE.

ROCKET (Allied) Allied convoy to Malta in June 1941. Followed DUNLOP, preceded RAILROAD.

ROLAND (GER 18) Alternative plan to the HEILGER MICHAEL series. This plan called for an attack on French forces near Rheims, France. Scheduled for the spring of 1918. Never executed.

ROLLING STONE (U.S./R.V.N. 66) Operation in Bihn Dong Province, Vietnam, that included bridge- and road-building operations along Routes 13 and 16 south of Phuoc Vihn in February 1966.

ROLLING THUNDER (U.S./R.V.N. 65) The general name for the bomber offensive against North Vietnam conducted from 2 March 1965 to November 1973. During this period, there were many pauses in the bombing and changes in targeting. These were used in an attempt to "communicate messages" to the North Vietnamese. In general, these attacks were indecisive and poorly coordinated. Destroyed economic resources were more than made up for by increased support to the North Vietnamese from other communist countries. The steady buildup in the attacks gave the North Vietnamese time to adapt. The tonnage of bombs dropped was impressive. By 1973 the U.S. had dropped more bombs on North Vietnam than had been dropped by all Allied air forces worldwide in World War II; but the campaign was spread over several years and targets were limited by political considerations. Unlike the air campaigns in World War II, enemy cities were not destroyed by bombing; instead entire classes of targets (such as cultural landmarks) were off-limits. At no time did the effect of these attacks overwhelm the North Vietnamese ability to cope with them. See LINEBACKER.

ROLL UP (U.S. 48) A self-help program by U.S. 8th Army in Japan to overcome serious equipment shortfalls. By 1949, the American occupation force in Japan was suffering from years of under-funding. Much of its equipment, left over from the War, was broken, missing, or simply worn out. Teams were sent to abandoned World War II supply depots on Pacific atolls. Equipment, including vehicles, ammunition, and small arms, was shipped to Japan where it was rebuilt by local industry. Much of this material was later used to halt the invasion of South Korea in June 1950.

ROOSTER (Allied 45) The air transport of the U.S. trained and equipped Chinese

22nd Division in April and May 1945 to Chiihchiang, China, to defend American air bases in the region.

ROSIE (Allied 44) A subsidiary landing to the invasion of southern France (DRAGOON). A Free French unit attempted to land near Cannes on 15 August 1944 but was driven off by defenders.

ROSSELSPRUNG "KNIGHT JUMP" This name refers to the Knight in chess.

1. (GER 42) Naval operation conducted by German forces against the British convoy PQ17 on 5 and 6 July 1942. The battleship *Tirpitz*, recently reinforced by *Scharnhorst* and *Gneisenau* (ZERBERUS), operating out of the bases in northern Norway sortied against the ill-fated PQ-17 convoy. This attack was so effective that the convoy was scattered and turned back from its destination of Archangelsk, Russia.

2. (GER 44) German attempt, led by Otto Skorzeny, to capture the Yugoslavian leader Tito at his headquarters at Drvar, Bosnia. The Germans jumped onto the target on 25 May 1944 and continued to chase the partisans until 4 June. Tito escaped, although the Germans did manage to capture his dress uniform.

ROT "RED" (GER 40) The second phase of the conquest of France by the German Army, begun on 5 June 1940. See GELB.

ROUNDHAMMER (Allied 43) Proposed modification of the SUPER ROUNDUP plan discussed at the May 1943 Washington Conference (TRIDENT). This plan called for an emergency invasion of northern France in the event of a sudden German or Soviet collapse. Never adopted.

ROUNDUP

1. (Allied 42) Plan for an invasion of northern France in the spring of 1943. This plan, drawn up by then-Brigadier General Eisenhower in 1942 reflected American enthusiasm for an early entry into Europe. Given the shortage of landing craft and other resources, this plan was unrealistic. Briefings concerning this plan brought Eisenhower's organizational and diplomatic skills to the attention of senior civil and military leaders in the U.S. and Europe, launching his meteoric rise to Supreme Allied Commander, Europe. Although ROUNDUP was never executed, parts of it were incorporated into OVERLORD. ROUNDUP included SLEDGEHAMMER. See ROUNDHAMMER.

2. (U.N. 51) Attack launched by U.S. 10th Corps toward Hongch'on and P'yonch'ang on 5 February 1951.

ROVING SANDS (NATO 95) The world's largest, most elaborate air-defense exercise to date. American trucks were modified to simulate enemy missile launchers. These provided mobile targets that moved through the American desert. Air defense units from the three countries defended the launchers from air attack. German and Dutch air defense units train in the American Southwest to take advantage of the wide-open spaces.

ROYAL DRAGON (NATO 96) See PURPLE STAR.

ROYAL FLUSH (Allied 44) Deception plan in support of the invasion of Normandy (OVERLORD). This operation projected a false threat of an Allied invasion of Turkey or the Balkans in 1944. A series of diplomatic notes were sent to the government in Ankara in June 1944, which implied imminent Allied action in the region. This added to German confusion in the days before D-Day.

ROYAL MARINE (Allied 40) British plan to place naval mines by air in the Rhine river during the "Phony War." Scheduled for 4 April 1940 but never executed.

ROYAL PHOENIX (U.S./R.V.N. 62) A local provincial effort to establish "strategic hamlets" in South Vietnam. See SUNRISE.

ROYAL SORBET 96 (NATO 96) A submarine rescue and recover exercise hosted by Norway in June 1996. The training included major participation from the U.S., U.K., Germany, and Sweden. Several other nations also took part. A sister exercise PHOENIX was conducted at about the same time but did not include the deployment of actual ships.

RUGGED (U.N. 50) Attack by U.N. forces across the 38th parallel to the Imjin River. Executed in April 1950. To be followed by Operation DAUNTLESS.

RUMPELKAMMER "LUMBER ROOM" (GER 44) The first attacks on England by V-1 flying bombs, launched on 12 June 1944.

RUPERT (Allied 40) Planning name for MAURICE.

RURALIST (U.S. 47) See GEM.

RUSTY PROJECT (Allied 42) American aerial mapping operation to support the TORCH invasion of North Africa. Conducted in early 1942.

RUTTER (Allied 42) The original plan for the raid on Dieppe, France. This plan called for the raid to be launched on 2 July 1942 and to last for several days. Bad weather and German air attacks on the assembled troops and ships forced its cancellation. When the Soviet Union continued pressure on the British for a second front against the Germans, Churchill ordered RUTTER reborn in a reduced scale as JUBILEE. See PORTO II.

RYAN (S.U. 80) Soviet intelligence operation conducted in London, Washington, and perhaps other Western capitals in the mid-1980s. Soviet operatives were directed to be alert to a possible Western preemptive nuclear strike against the Soviet Union. This included monitoring of the price of human blood at local blood banks noting which lights were on late at night in key buildings. RYAN is a Russian acronym for "Surprise Nuclear Missile Attack."

S

"SABBATH DELIGHT" (Zionist 42) See ONEG SHABBAT.

SABER (U.S.) A reserved first word for the programs and projects of the U.S. Air Force.

SADDLETREE (U.S. 47) A program of modifications conducted from 1947 to 1952 to retrofit the American bomber fleet (B-29, B-36, and B-50s) to accept nuclear weapons.

SAFARI (GER 43) The German imposition of full martial law in Denmark in August 1943 as a response to a restive population.

SAFE BORDER (U.S./ARG/BZ/CH 94) The U.S. contribution to the international observer mission on the frontier between Ecuador and Peru to support a general reduction in tensions. The U.S., Argentine, Brazil, and Chile are guarantors of the 1919 peace treaty between the 2 nations.

SAFEGUARD (U.S. Law Enforcement 95) Adoption of the border-control techniques developed during BLOCKADE to the area near Tucson, Arizona.

SAFE HAVEN (U.S. 92) Exercise conducted in mid-1992 by the U.S. 6th Fleet in the Mediterranean Sea to practice procedures to evacuate noncombatants. An innovation of this operation was the basing of Marine Corps helicopters and troops aboard the aircraft carrier *Forrestal*. This allowed 1 ship to accommodate both helicopters and fixed-wing aircraft. As this exercise took places as Yugoslavia was breaking apart, it seems likely that it was a rehearsal of an American contingency plan.

SAFE PASSAGE

1. (U.S.) An American Special Forces training effort that instructed Afghan refugees in Pakistan in removing and disarming Soviet mines after the Russian withdrawal from that country.

2. (U.S. 94) The return of Haitian refugees from camps in Panama to camps in Cuba as space there became available in February 1995. See ABLE VIGIL.

SAFE REMOVAL (U.S. 93) The removal of World War I-era chemical munitions from a residential area in Washington, DC, conducted in 1993 and 1994. Over 100 shells, some of which contained mustard gas and Lewisite, were recovered and flown to Pine Bluff, Arkansas, for disposal. The weapons were buried on the campus of American University, which was a training center during the war. They were uncovered during construction activity in the residential neighborhood that had later been built on the site.

SAFRAAN "SAFFRON" (R.S.A. 79) South African raids into the Caprivi Strip area in

Angola. Conducted in March 1979 concurrently with REKSTOK, preceded REINDEER, followed SCEPTIC.

SAGE BRUSH (U.S.) See TREE TOP.

SAGE SCARAB (U.S.) A contingency plan, current in the early 1980s, for the use of Air Force units to conduct special operations, shows of force, and deception operations in the Pacific region.

SAIF SAREEA "SWIFT SWORD" (Oman/U.K. 85) A joint British/Omani air exercise conducted in the Gulf region in November 1985.

SAILMAKER (Allied 44) Plan to capture the Dutch island of Schoven for use as a radar site to support Allied air operations. Never executed.

SAINT GEORGE (GER 18) See HEILIGER GEORG.

SAINT MICHAEL (GER 18) See HEILIGER MICHAEL.

SALEUMSAY "ANNIVERSARY VICTORY No. 2" (U.S./Laos 64) A ground operation conducted by the Royal Laotian Army and local Meo fighters to clear Route 4 north of Tha Thom. This operation included air support flown by the Royal Lao Air Force using American-supplied T-28 aircraft. Conducted in 1964, this operation was mentioned in the leaked "Pentagon Papers." Part of OPLAN 34-A.

"SALMON CATCH" (GER 42) See STORFANG.

SALTY

1. See CHECKED FLAG.

2. (U.S.) A reserved first word for the programs and projects of the U.S. Air Force's Military Airlift Command.

SAN ANTONIO I (Allied 44) This first raid on Japan by B-29 Superfortress bombers flying from the Marianas. Executed on 24 November 1944.

SAN ANTONIO II (Allied 44) A B-29 raid on Tokyo from Saipan, in the Marianas, on 27 November 1944.

SAND FLEA (U.S. 89) A series of training exercises for the JUST CAUSE invasion of Panama. These troop movements and practice assaults were disguised as training to defend the Panama Canal (PURPLE STORM). Conducted in the summer of 1989, these seemingly endless movements overwhelmed the ability of the Panamanians to observe, analyze, and understand the activity. In this way, this program desensitized the Panama Defense Forces to the coming invasion.

SANDSTONE (U.S. 48) A series of 3 nuclear test explosions conducted at Eniwetok Atoll. Preceded RANGER, followed CROSSROADS. The individual shots were:

X-RAY	14 April 48	37 kilotons
YOKE	30 April	49 kilotons
ZEBRA	15 May	18 kilotons

SANDWEDGE (U.S. Political 71) A tentative plan to conduct "offensive intelligence and defensive security" for the 1972 Nixon reelection campaign. White House staffer John Caulfield proposed he leave government service to establish a private firm that would contract with the Committee to Reelect the President to provide these services. SANDWEDGE was rejected, but many of the ideas outlined in it were revived in GEMSTONE.

SANDWICK (Allied 41) British plan to occupy Thailand to preempt a Japanese invasion. Never executed.

SANDY

1. (U.S. 47) The test-firing of a V-2 missile from the flight deck of the USS Midway on 6 September 1947 as part of ABUSIVE.

These tests showed that liquid-fueled rockets were too dangerous to be used aboard ships.

2. (U.S.) A reserved first word for the programs and projects of the U.S. Air Force's Air University. See LOYAL.

SANDY COAST (NATO 95) A small NATO naval exercise conducted in the North Sea in September 1955 with Polish participation under the Partnership for Peace program.

SANGUINE (U.S. 68) A 1968 proposal by the U.S. Navy to build an Extremely Low Frequency (ELF) communication complex in Wisconsin. This plan called for 6,000 miles of cable to be buried 5 feet under 41 percent of the state. Never executed, downsized to SEAFARER.

SAPPHIRE (U.S. 94) The transfer of uranium from Ust-Kamenogorsk, Kazakhstan, to the U.S., conducted secretly in October 1994. The nuclear material was left in central Asia by the collapse of the Soviet Union. Instability in the region threatened the stockpile. After secret negotiations with the Soviet Union, the U.S. agreed to take control of the material. In exchange, Kazakhstan received a massive infusion of American economic aid.

SATELLITE (U.S. 65) See STARLITE.

SATURN

1. (Allied) Plan for the secret establishment of British troops in Turkey during World War II. SATURN was part of the elaborate diplomatic effort mounted by the British to prevent the Turks from supporting the Germans in the World War II. Never executed. See HARDIHOOD.

2. (S.U. 42) The attack of the South-West Front toward Rostov scheduled for November 1942. Due to the Battle of Stalingrad, this attack was delayed until 16 December.

SATURATE (U.N. 52) Bombing of North Korean railroad targets in March 1952. These strikes were designed to place an overwhelming tonnage of bombs on short portions of the enemy rail-net, leaving other sections untouched. This tactic did not increase repair time and was soon abandoned.

SAUCY (Allied 43) Proposed limited offensive by the Chinese from the east and the British from the west to reopen a land route from China to India. A more modest form of the ANAKIM plan, without the amphibious invasion to close the port of Rangoon. Never executed. See CANNIBAL.

SAVANNAH

1. (Allied 41) The first insertion of a British special warfare team into German-occupied France; conducted on the night of 15 March 1941 near Vannes. The 5 commandos failed in their mission to ambush a bus carrying German pilots, but they were extracted successfully by light plane without being detected. This mission demonstrated the practicality of using airdrops and covert landings by aircraft to insert, supply, and recover small units behind German lines.

2. (R.S.A. 76) The first South African operation of the Bush War in Angola and Southwest Africa. Begun on 23 August 1976, the white minority government of South Africa supported the FNLA and UNITA against the Soviet- and Cuban-backed MPLA. SAVANNAH failed to crush the MPLA who then created the Southwest Africa People's Organization as a communist front to continue the fighting in South African controlled territories. Preceded REINDEER.

SAVILLE (U.S.) A reserved first word for the programs and projects of the U.S. Defense Communications Agency.

SAW BUCK (U.S. 62) A series of deployments of American F-100 Super Saber aircraft to

Takhli Royal Thai Air Force base. These aircraft interdicted Pathet Lao supply lines. Followed by BARREL ROLL. The individual rotations of this series were:

SAW BUCK I	18 May - 3 September 62
	428th Tactical Fighter Wing
SAW BUCK II	3 September - 13 December
	430th Tactical Fighter Wing
SAW BUCK III	13 December - 1 June 63
	522nd Tactical Fighter Wing

SC (Allied) Allied convoys from North America to Britain. Designated by number (e.g., SC 123)

SCANATE (U.S.) The initial name for the CIA project that used a team of psychics to gather intelligence. This program of "remote imaging" began in the early 1980s and was initially based at Fort Meade, Maryland. This group, and the intelligence it produced, was later called GRILL FLAME, CENTER LANE, SUNSTREAK, and STARGATE.

SCARLET (U.S.) A reserved first word for the programs and projects of the U.S. Air Force's former Air Defense Command.

SCATTER (U.N. 52) Screening of North Korean and Chinese prisoners to determine which would accept and which would resist repatriation. The interviews began on 3 April 1952. Of about 170,000 prisoners interviewed, only about 70,000 said they would accept return to their nations. This caused a great loss of face for the Chinese and North Korean governments and complicated truce negotiations. See BIG SWITCH.

SCAVENGER (Allied 44) Air attack on Japanese units and facilities on the Bonin Islands and Iwo Jima as part of the overall fighting in the Marianas in August 1944.

SCEPTIC (R.S.A. 80) The largest South African operation of the Bush War. This sweep against SWAPO forces followed

SAFRAAN and REKSTOK but preceded KLIPKLOP.

SCHEUNE "HARVEST HOUSE" (GER 43)

SCHEUNE I Anti-partisan operation launched on 18 January 1943 west of Osipovichi, Belorussia.

SCHEUNE II Anti-partisan operation launched on 28 January 1943 in the vicinity of the Minsk-Slutsk road, over 200 miles behind the front.

SCHNEPFE "SNIPE" (GER 43) Anti-partisan operation launched on 1 November 1943 to protect supply lines north of Vitebsk. See WILDENTE.

SCHWARZ "BLACK" (GER 43)

1. Offensive operation against Partisan forces in Yugoslavia conducted by 100,000 German and satellite forces in February 1943. The Axis units were able to drive Tito's forces out of Montenegro. See TYPICAL and WEISS.

2. One alternative plan to reestablish German control over Italy after the overthrow of Mussolini in 1943. Never executed.

SCIMITAR (CN 90) The Canadian ground and air contribution to the liberation of Kuwait (DESERT STORM). A squadron of CF-18 fighters deployed to the region and a number of Canadian exchange officers served with American and British units. The Canadian naval contribution was called FRICTION.

SCIPIO

1. (Allied 40) Planning name for MENACE.

2. (Allied 43) British attack by 8th Army on German positions at the Akarit Wadi in southern Tunisia. Launched on 6 April 1943.

SCOOP (CN Law Enforcement 93) A long-running investigation of child-pornography and abuse rings centered in London, Ontario. After the accidental discovery of a cache of pornographic videotapes near the local river, police uncovered several interlocking pedophile groups covering large parts of the province and extending into the U.S.

SCOPE (U.S.) A reserved first word for the communication programs and projects of the U.S. Air Force.

SCORCHER (Allied 41) The movement of British troops to Crete in May 1941. These units were originally scheduled to support the COMPASS attack in North Africa but were diverted in time for the German airborne invasion 20 May (MERKUR). Other British units were sent to the Greek mainland (LUSTRE).

SCORPION WIND (U.S. 95) Annual aviation training exercise hosted by the U.S. Marine Corps at the Yuma, Arizona Marine Corps Air Station and the Fallon, Nevada Naval Air Station. These operations feature close air support delivered by Royal Air Force and other Allied units who are limited in their ability to drop live bombs in their own countries.

SCOTCH (CN 94) See LANCE.

SEA ANGEL (U.S. 92) Relief operations conducted by U.S. Marines returning from Operation DESERT STORM for the victims of flooding in Bangladesh. Planned as PRODUCTIVE EFFORT. The British contribution to this effort was called MANA.

SEA DRAGON

1. (U.N. 53) A covert reconnaissance of the Yalu river estuary and its islands by a U.S./South Korean team operating from fishing boats in April 1953.

2. (U.S./R.V.N. 67) Naval operations beginning in 1967 to interdict sea lines of communications between North and South Vietnam and to destroy land targets with naval gunfire.

SEAFARER (U.S. 76) A U.S. Navy proposal in 1976 to build an Extremely Low Frequency (ELF) communication facility in Wisconsin. This proposal was a much-reduced version of the 1968 SANGUINE plan. SEAFARER was in turn replaced by ELF in 1981. Never executed.

SEAHORSE (U.S. 46) The transport of examples of captured German aircraft to the United States. See SURGEON.

SEA SIGNAL (U.S. 94) American interception of Haitian refugees beginning in mid-1994. Initially these "boat people" were held on the hospital ship USNS *Comfort*. When that ship became overcrowded, the Haitians were transferred to a series of large camps set up at Guantanamo Bay, Cuba. When even these facilities were insufficient, some of the refugees were moved to Panama (SAFE HAVEN). By mid-September 1994 the total number of people being held peaked at over 46,000. In September, an international effort, RESTORE DEMOCRACY, established civilian rule in Haiti. Eventually all the refugees were returned to Haiti or allowed to enter the U.S. under a number of programs. The last Haitian left U.S. protection on 1 November 1995.

SEA SWALLOW (U.S./R.V.N. 62) One of several provincial efforts to build "strategic hamlets" in South Vietnam. See SUNRISE and ROYAL PHOENIX.

SECRET SQUIRREL (U.S. 91) A series of extremely long-range missile attacks on Iraq conducted by American B-52 bombers during the liberation of Kuwait (DESERT STORM). These missions were formally called SENIOR SURPRISE, but were quickly dubbed SECRET SQUIRREL by the air crews. The new name stuck. Long runways in the region suitable for the large bombers were being used by short-range tactical aircraft. The Stratofortresses flew to their targets from Barksdale Air Force Base in Louisiana. The total length of these flights were equal to an around-the-world mission. Replaced the BLACK BUCK series as the longest combat mission of all time.

SEDAN CHAIR (U.S. Political 71) A Republican plan to plant spies in the political campaign of Edmund Muskie, who was then contending for the Democratic Party's nomination. This operation had already inserted an operative into the Muskie camp when SEDAN CHAIR came under the overall "dirty tricks" plan, GEMSTONE.

SEED (U.S.) A reserved first word for the programs and projects of the U.S. Air Force.

SEEK (U.S.) A reserved first word for the programs and projects of the U.S. Air Force.

SEELOWE "SEA LION" (GER 40) Plan for a German invasion of England in 1940. After the fall of France, 25 divisions were assembled in the channel ports to await the German Air Force's victory in the Battle of Britain (ADLER). The invasion was postponed on 12 October 1940 and finally canceled on 10 January 1941. The projected invasion beaches were along England's south coast, between Folkestone and Selsey Bill (just east of Portsmouth). Never executed. See ADLER, HERBSTREISE, and JULIUS CAESAR.

SEEWOLF "SEA WOLF" (GER 45) The last major German submarine operation of World War II. Six large U-Boats were sent to the east coast of the U.S. to disrupt convoys. The Americans thought these boats might carry rockets to attack the mainland, and so hunted the group very aggressively. All 6 boats were sunk by the American operation TEARDROP.

SENIOR (U.S.) A reserved first word for the programs and projects of the U.S. Air Force.

SENIOR TREND was the program that developed the F-117 Nighthawk aircraft.

SENIOR SURPRISE (US 91) The official name for the extremely long-range bombing missions aimed at Iraq using B-52 bombers based in the U.S. The air crews preferred the more colorful name SECRET SQUIRREL.

SENTINEL (U.S.) A reserved first word for the programs and projects of the U.S. Air Force.

SENTRY (U.S.) A reserved first word for the programs and projects of the U.S. Air Force.

SENTRY WOLVERINE (U.S./IT 87) A training exercise in which 6 Italian Tornado fighter-bombers were deployed to the Air National Guard facility at Selfridge, Michigan, in June 1987.

SERIOUS (U.S.) A reserved first word for the programs and projects of the U.S. Air Force's Systems Command.

SERVICE (U.S.) A reserved first word for the munitions programs and projects of the U.S. Air Force.

SETTING SUN (Allied 44) A proposal to bomb Japan with B-29s based in China. Never executed. See DRAKE.

SEVEN (U.S.) A reserved first word for the programs and projects of the U.S. Air Force.

SEVER "NORTH" (S.U. 68) Naval exercise conducted in the Norwegian, Baltic, and Barents Seas in July 1968 by the Soviet Navy.

SEXTANT (Allied 43) Conference between Churchill, Roosevelt, and the Chinese leader Chiang Kai-shek in Cairo in late November and early December 1943. The Western leaders were on their way to the Teheran conference (EUREKA), a meeting from which the Chinese strongman was banned by Stalin. Discussion focused on proposed actions in the Far East.

SHADOW 82 (Allied 42) Movement of U.S. air units to northern Ireland during World War II as part of MAGNET. See BOLERO and SICKLE.

SHAKEDOWN (U.S.) Early plan prepared by the Strategic Air Command for a nuclear war with the Soviet Union. Never executed. Replaced by the SIOP series. See DROPSHOT.

SHAMROCK (U.S. 60s) Effort by the National Security Agency and Army Intelligence in the 1960s to intercept international diplomatic communications using commercial cables from Washington and New York City. The government asked for and received the assistance of RCA and Western Union in this effort. Once the intercept system was in place, the FBI established a watch list of American citizens involved in the protest movement against the Vietnam War. The communications of these people were then illegally intercepted. This FBI operation (MINARET) ended when the CIA withdrew its support.

SHARP EDGE (U.S. 90) The 5-21 August rescue of American civilians from Liberian civil war by Marine Corps helicopters flying from the assault ship *Wasp*. Followed by ASSURED RESPONSE.

SHARP FENCE (W.E.U. 93) Naval operation to isolate the warring parties in Yugoslavia. This early operation was conducted under the authority of the Western European Union. When U.S. units joined in, the name was changed to SHARP GUARD. Conducted in conjunction with MARITIME MONITOR and MARITIME GUARD.

SHARP GUARD (U.S. 92) U.S.-led international naval blockade of the former Yugoslavia to prevent weapons from entering

that nation during its civil war. Begun on 22 November 1992, following SHARP FENCE. The naval units boarded and inspected thousands of ships transmitting the area.

SHED LIGHT (U.S. 66) A U.S. Air Force program that sought to build an illumination version of the C-130 cargo aircraft. Such a "Light Ship" would be equipped with flares and a bank of large searchlights. The C-130 would circle a target area allowing other aircraft to conduct strikes in periods of limited visibility. Abandoned when it became apparent such an aircraft drew large amounts of ground fire.

SHINGLE (Allied 44) The American invasion at Anzio, Italy, south of Rome. The operation met with initial success on 22 January 1944, but failed to turn the flank of the German "Gustav" defensive line. As a result the American commander, Lieutenant General John P. Lucas, was relieved of his command and the lodgment was described as "the world's biggest self-supporting POW camp" by German propaganda. The Allied force finally broke out of the encirclement with the BUFFALO attack in May. See DIADEM, WEBFOOT.

SHINING BRASS (U.S. 65) A program of combined American-Montagnard 12-man patrols into Laos to reconnoiter North Vietnamese supply routes. These teams would call in airstrikes on targets they discovered. Over 2,000 patrols were conducted from 1965 to 1972.

SHOESTRING (Allied Unofficial 42) Nickname coined for Operation WATCH-TOWER, the invasion of Guadalcanal, due to the limited resources and planning time available.

SHO-GO "OPERATION VICTORY" (JPN 44) A series of plans for the defense of Japanese territory. The plan was adopted on 24 June 1944 and had several variants:

SHO-1 Included the defense of the Philippine Islands and resulted in the Battle of Leyte Gulf in October 1944. As called for SHO-GO, this battle was decisive; the Japanese Navy lost 3 battleships, 4 aircraft carriers, 13 destroyers, and 5 submarines. See MUSKETEER, WA.

SHO-2 Focused on the defense of Formosa and the Ryukyu Islands.

SHO-3 The defense of the Japanese Archipelago. See KETSU-GO and DOWNFALL.

SHO-4 The final battle for the main Japanese home island of Honshu. See CORONET.

SHOWDOWN (U.N. 52) Limited objective attack during the Korean War by the U.S. 9th Corps to straighten lines and regain the initiative. The attack began with a 2-day artillery preparation on 12 October 1952. The planned battle was to last 5 days and cost about 200 lives. In the event, fighting went on for over 6 months and resulted in about 9,000 casualties.

SHRAPNEL (Allied) Plan for an Allied occupation of the Cape Verde Islands in World War II. Never executed. These islands were a Portuguese possession until 1975. See LIFEBELT and PILGRIM.

SICILIAN (GER 43) See SIZILIEN.

SICKLE

1. (Allied 40) The amphibious landings and subsequent evacuation of an Anglo-French force at the Norwegian ports of Aandalsnes and Molde on Romsdal Fjord in April and May 1940. The troops were landed to aid in the defense of Norway, but were withdrawn when France collapsed, reducing Scandinavia to sideshow status.

2. (Allied 42) Buildup of American bombers in Britain for the POINTBLANK offensive. See SHADOW 82.

SIEGFRIED

1. (GER 41) An early 1941 staff study of the possibility of the capture of the Kola Peninsula and the port of Kandalaksha by German and Finnish troops. See SILBER-FUCHS.

2. (GER 43) Part of ACHSE, this portion of the plan called for the German occupation of the southern coast of France to replace the Italian 4th Army upon the defection of the Italian government. Executed on 25 July 1943.

SIESTA (Allied 44) Planning name for DESTROYER.

SILBERFUCHS "SILVER FOX" (GER 41) Failed German ground attack on the Soviet port of Murmansk begun on 1 July 1941. The German units were based in Finland, but the Finns refused to attack outside their national boundaries.

SILVER (U.K. 49) A British intelligence operation, which ran from 1949 to 1955, that covertly tapped into the landline communications of the Soviet Army headquarters in Vienna. The operation was never discovered and ended only when Austria regained full sovereignty. The British monitoring station was disguised as a shop that sold tweed clothing. In 1951, when the American CIA planned a similar operation in Berlin, the British revealed SILVER to the Americans and the two countries then ran jointly GOLD.

SILVER BAYONET (U.S./R.V.N. 66) The first major battle involving American troops in the Vietnam War. The American 101st Airborne Division crushed 3 North Vietnamese regiments near Pleiku in the Ia Drang valley in November 1965. The Americans shifted their units by helicopter into the valley when they detected the enemy. They then used massive air support (including B-52 bombers) to grind down the communists. The Americans lost 300 dead but claimed 2,000 enemy dead. This battle prevented the North Vietnamese from moving large units from the central highlands to the heavily populated coastline.

SILVER BULLET (U.S. 90) See NIFTY PACKAGE.

SILVER EAGLE (U.S./Botswana 92) Joint training exercise conducted in January 1992. About 200 U.S. paratroopers joined with the Botswana Defense Forces in mock battles near the capital city of Gaborone.

SILVER FOX (GER 41) See SILBERFUCHS.

SILVERPLATE (Allied 45) The training and preparation of U.S. Army Air Force units to drop the atomic bombs over Japan (CENTERBOARD). Units began training at Wendover, Utah, and continued after moving to Tinian. The term SILVERPLATE was used on orders and supply requisitions to indicate their high priority. After the war, the Strategic Air Command called their modified, nuclear-capable B-29 Stratofortresses "Silverplates." See BRONX SHIPMENT.

SILVER SHOVEL (U.S. Law Enforcement 95) A 3-year federal investigation of corruption in the Chicago city government that resulted in a number of indictments. Using an undercover "mole," John Christopher, the FBI recorded a number of alderman, labor leaders, and city workers soliciting and accepting bribes to grant city contracts and licenses, and to allow a variety of illegal activities including drug crimes and illegal dumping.

SIMMER (Allied 42) Amphibious training exercise conducted in the summer of 1942 for the JUBILEE raiders.

SIOP (U.S. 63) A contraction for "Single Integrated Operation Plan"; the SIOP is the American plan for nuclear war. After World War II, the U.S. Air Force held a nuclear monopoly and made a series of rough contingency plans (BROILER) with a minimal consultations with the other services. As the world became more complex and the other services gained nuclear weapons, these single-service plans became unworkable. In the early 1960s the first SIOP (CHARIOTEER) came into effect, which integrated all strategic nuclear weapons into a single effort. The SIOP is updated by a joint staff at Omaha, Nebraska, every 6 months. SIOPs are no longer named; as major changes take place, the SIOP receives a new numerical designation (e.g., SIOP 6). Minor changes are designated by letter (e.g., SIOP 6F, the 6th change to SIOP 6). SIOP 4 was in effect in the mid 1960s. SIOP 5 took effect on 1 January 1976. SIOP 6 took effect on 1 October 1983. SIOP 6F was in effect in late 1989.

SIXTEEN TONS (U.S. 56) A major airlift conducted in late 1956 in support of the U.S. Coast Guard. The Coast Guard requested aircraft to move supplies to Puerto Rico and the Bahamas to upgrade navigation aids. The Air Force assigned the task to the Air Force Reserve, the first time it had been entrusted with a real-world peacetime mission. Over 400 tons of cargo were moved in C-46 and C-119 aircraft flying 164 sorties. "Sixteen Tons" was a popular American country music song at the time.

SIZILIEN "SICILIAN" (GER 43) Raid by German naval forces, including the battleships *Tirpitz*, *Scharnhorst*, and 9 destroyers against Spitzberger, Norway, conducted from 7 to 9 September 1943.

SKI JUMP

1. (U.S. 49) American research operations in the Arctic conducted in 1949.

2. See TREE TOP.

SKOSHI TIGER (U.S. 65) A combat test of the F-5A Tiger I Vietnam that began in July 1965. The aircraft flew out of both Bien Hoa and Da Nang air bases. By the time of the test in February 1966, the F-5 had a good reputation but had not encountered any energy aircraft. The name is a corruption of Sukoshi Tiger, Japanese for "Little Tiger."

SKYBURNER (U.S. 61) A speed-record flight by a YF4H-1 Phantom fighter conducted on 22 December 1961 achieving a speed of 1,606.347 miles per hour.

SKYE (Allied 44) A major subplan of FORTITUDE NORTH that created a fictional "British 4th Army" that threatened an invasion of Norway. The British media cooperated with this effort by broadcasting fake football scores and even wedding announcements for the nonexistent troops. Seventeen German divisions were tied down by this effort. Included LOMBARD.

SKYLIGHT (U.S. Law Enforcement 91) A CIA internal inquest conducted in conjunction with an FBI investigation (PLAYACTOR) into a possible Soviet "mole" in the CIA. SKYLIGHT/PLAYACTOR failed to detect Aldrich Ames, who was caught by a 1993 investigation (NIGHTMOVER).

SKY MONITOR (NATO 92) The electronic monitoring of the airspace over Bosnia that began on 16 October 1992. NATO E-3 Sentry aircraft monitored compliance with a U.N. Security Council resolution passed on 9 October. Initially, these aircraft orbited over the Adriatic, but in late October a second orbit was established over Hungary. By flanking Bosnia, the aircraft were able to monitor all air activity in the region. The aircraft reported widespread violations of the U.N. no-fly order and prompted the world community to begin enforcement actions (DENY FLIGHT) on 12 April 1993.

SKY SHIELD (NORAD/U.K. 61) A joint American/Canadian air defense exercise conducted in October 1961. A force of British Avro Vulcan bombers served as the attacking force. One of these was able to fly from a base in northern Canada and land at Plattsburgh Air Force Base in New York undetected.

SKY SHIELD II (NORAD/U.K. 61) An air-defense exercise conducted in 1961, remarkable in that it grounded all civil air traffic in the U.S. for 12 hours.

SKY TRY (U.S. 53) The first major Air Force exercise using the newly-delivered B-47 Stratojet bomber conducted from 22 January to 20 February 1953. The 306th Bomb Wing was the first unit equipped with this new bomber.

SKYWATCH (NORAD 52) Program designed to protect North America from Soviet air attack prior to the completion of a radar network. SKYWATCH formed a Ground Observer Group Corps of over 10,000 regulars, augmented by 170,000 reservists manning 10,000 observation posts throughout the U.S. This program began on 14 July 1952. By 1953, high-altitude radar coverage across the Arctic was possible; SKYWATCH continued as a means of spotting low-flying aircraft until the Distant Early Warning (DEW) line was completed in 1957.

SL (Allied) Allied convoys from Sierra Leone to Britain in World War II. Designed by number (i.e., SL 123).

SLAPSTICK (Allied 43) Allied invasion near the Italian naval base of Taranto on 9 September 1943. This attack met with no resistance and was the most successful of the 3 nearly-simultaneous invasions of Italy (see AVALANCHE, BAYTOWN). Unfortunately, the invasion force consisted of only the British 1st Airborne Division, an insufficient force to fully exploit the tactical opportunity of the situation.

SLEDGEHAMMER (Allied 42) Contingency plan for a limited-objective invasion of Europe in response to a German or Soviet collapse in 1942. Never executed. Replaced by RANKIN.

SLICK CHICK (U.S. 55) The early deployment of three F-100A Super Saber fighters to the U.S. Air Force Europe to train maintenance and other personnel.

SLIPPERY (Allied 45) Planned deception operation to support the recapture of Singapore scheduled for 1946. The intent of the deception was to project phony preparations for a invasion of Indochina. Never executed.

SMACK (U.N. 52) A company-sized raid conducted by elements of the U.S. 7th Infantry Division to capture prisoners on 25 January 1952. The raid was conducted in conjunction with a series of air strikes on a complex of bunkers. Due to confusion, poor marksmanship by the pilots, and inadequate communications, the raid was a disaster. Over 75 Americans were injured; no prisoners were taken.

SNIPE (GER 43) See SCHNEPFE.

SNOW BIRD

1. (U.S. 80) Proposal for a second attempt to rescue American hostages held in Iran. Planning for SNOW BIRD began 26 April 1980, 2 days after the failure of EAGLE CLAW. Eventually SNOW BIRD was rejected in favor of HONEY BADGER.

2. (N.Z. 85) Royal New Zealand Air Force helicopter operations in support of the Scott Base Antarctic research facility.

SNOW DROP (U.S. 47) An American training exercise that featured a major parachute drop in the snow at Pine Camp, New York.

SNOW FALCON (NATO 88) A practice deployment of British Harrier aircraft to Bardufoss, Norway.

SNOW FALL

1. (U.S. 52) A large-scale winter training exercise conducted at Camp Drum, New York.

2. (U.S.) See TREE TOP.

SNOW FLURRY (U.S. 58) A minor training exercise conducted by B-47 bombers and other aircraft of the American Strategic Air Command, notable for the loss of an unarmed nuclear weapon near Florence, South Carolina, on 3 November 1958. Despite an exhaustive search and a large excavation effort, the bomb was never recovered.

SNOW GOOSE (CN 64) Deployment of HMCS *Bonventure* to support U.N. peacekeeping efforts on Cyprus.

SNOW STORM (U.S.) See TREE TOP.

SOAPSUDS (Allied 43) Planning name for TIDAL WAVE, the attack on the oil fields at Ploesti, Rumania. See STATESMAN.

SOLID SHIELD (U.S. 63) U.S. Atlantic Command exercise conducted in odd-numbered years beginning in 1963 in the Atlantic, Gulf of Mexico, and Caribbean. Denominated by year (e.g., SOLID SHIELD 65). Alternates with the OCEAN VENTURE series.

SOLO I

SOLO II (Allied 42) Deception operations in support of the Allied invasion of North Africa (TORCH). SOLO I depicted a false threat of an invasion of Norway by troops in Britain. SOLO II gave the impression that troops in the U.S. earmarked for TORCH would in fact invade at Dakar. See DRYSHOD.

SOLOMON (IS 91) The evacuation of 14,000 black Jews from Ethiopia in 1991. On one remarkable SOLOMON flight, a Boeing 747 in cargo configuration carried 1,087 passengers to Israel. See MOSES.

SONE SAI "VICTORIOUS ARROW" (U.S./Laos 64) A Laotian ground attack conducted in 1964 to clear communist forces from southern Laos. Part of the overall OPLAN 34-A. See YANKEE TEAM.

SONNENBLUME "SUNFLOWER" (GER 41) Deployment of German troops (the "Afrika Corps") to North Africa in February 1941. These troops reinforced the Italians who were close to collapse from the COMPASS attack.

SONNIE (Allied/Sweden 44) The repatriation of Allied airmen who had been interned in Sweden. This was conducted in unmarked Allied aircraft under cover of night and bad weather between March and December 1944. This operation violated Swedish neutrality but was conducted with the assistance of the Swedish government, which by this point realized the Germans were doomed.

SOURCE (Allied 43) An attack on the German battleship *Tirpitz* in the harbor at Altafjord, Norway, on 20 September 1943 by British midget submarines. Explosive charges laid on the bottom of the fjord severely damaged the German ship, putting it out of action for 6 months. See TUNGSTEN.

SOUTHERN BREEZE (BG 90) Logistic flights conducted in support of the Belgian units taking part in DESERT SHIELD and DESERT STORM. See GULF STREAM.

SOUTHERN PINE (U.S.) See TREE TOP.

SOUTHERN WATCH (Allied 92) Operations by American, British, and French aircraft beginning on 27 August 1992 to enforce a prohibition on Iraqi aircraft flying south of the 32nd parallel. This was an effort to protect religious minorities ("marsh Arabs") in the southern portion of Iraq. On 4 September 1995 the American government extended the restricted area north to the 33rd parallel as part of the DESERT STRIKE action. See ALYSSE, PROVIDE PROMISE, and WARDEN.

SPAN (Allied 44) A deception operation in support of the invasion of southern France (DRAGOON). This operation consisted of fake amphibious landings on Corsica and along the Italian coast immediately following the actual invasion. This tied down German troops and prevented this deployment against the beachhead.

SPARTAN (Allied 43) Major training exercise conducted in England for troops earmarked for the OVERLORD invasion of northern France. This corps-level event focused on breaking out of beachheads.

SPARK (S.U. 43) See ISKRA.

SPECIAL DELIVERY (U.S. Law Enforcement 94) A 2-year investigation of the child pornography industry. The operation began when the U.S. Postal Inspectors came into possession of the mailing list of a supplier of child pornography. Setting up a front company, the Postal Service in cooperation with other agencies solicited customers for their new company with suggestive advertisements. This led to a nationwide series of arrests and a better understanding of pedophile rings.

SPESSART 95 (NATO 95) A small peacekeeping exercise hosted by Germany for NATO and Partnership for Peace countries in December 1995. A international battalion of Polish, German, and Danish troops was formed to improve cooperation.

SPHERICAL (U.K. 65) A deployment of Royal Air Force heavy bombers to support operations during the Malaya Emergency.

SPITFIRE (U.N. 51) The attempted insertion of a joint U.S., British, and South Korean special operations unit behind North Korea lines on 26 June 1951. The drop zone was marked by an underground resistance unit designated BIG BOY. The BIG BOY operation was secretly controlled by the North Koreans, and so most of the team was killed or captured upon landing.

SPLITRAIL (U.S. Law Enforcement 95) The Federal investigation of the derailment of passenger train 50 miles south of Phoenix, Arizona, on 9 October 1995. A train crewman was killed and over 100 passengers were injured when a rail was intentionally damaged, which forced the train into a river bed. A note nearby was signed by "Sons of Gestapo" (sic), prompting fears of internal terrorism. The FBI responded with over 90 agents who combed the area for other clues.

SPOTTER (Allied 42) Delivery of Spitfire fighters to Malta on 7 March 1942. Followed JAGUAR, preceded PICKET.

SPRING

1. (GER 44) See FRÜHLING.

2. (Allied 44) Canadian attack launched on 25 July 1944 in rough coordination with the American COBRA breakout from Normandy. The attack captured local objective around Caen, but also prevented movement of German defenders against the American thrust.

SPRING THAW (U.N. 53) A surge of air attacks against communist supply lines and dumps beginning on 21 March 1953 to prevent a communist spring offensive.

STALEMATE (Allied 44) The American amphibious invasion of Peleliu in the western Carolines. The first Marine Division landed on 15 September 1944 and faced an especially well-prepared force of 6,000 Japanese defenders. Deep tunnels in Umurbrogol Ridge (dubbed "Bloody Nose Ridge") sheltered heavy Japanese guns that pinned down the attackers for over a month. This was the bloodiest amphibious

landing in American history, with 9,171 Marines killed. The Japanese lost over 13,000 soldiers. Part of GRANITE.

STAMINA (Allied 44) Air supply operations in support of surrounded British forces in Kohima, India, that began on 18 April 1944. In the 12-week operation, wounded soldiers of the 4th Battalion, Royal West Kent Regiment, were flown out of the area, while much-needed supplies and reinforcements were brought in. The siege was lifted by relief column arriving in early May. See U-GO.

STARGATE (U.S.) One of a series of names for a CIA program that used psychics to develop intelligence through "remote viewing." See GRILL FLAME, CENTER LANE, and SUNSTREAK.

STARKEY (Allied 43) The general 1943 Allied deception plan in Europe. This operation used radio, news stories, and bombing raids to project the false idea of an Allied invasion of northern France on 9 September 1943. This culminated in the HARLEQUIN convoy. In 1944, the FORTITUDE SOUTH deception reprised STARKEY with another false invasion threat of the same region.

STARLITE (U.S. 65) The first engagement of a major regiment-sized communist unit by the Americans during the Vietnam War. The 7th Marine Regiment of the Marine Expeditionary Brigade attacked the 1st Viet Cong Regiment killing 614 of the enemy at a cost of 45 Marines killed. Originally called SATELLITE the attack was authorized on 18 August 1965 by General Westmoreland. A clerk misspelled the name STARLITE and his error entered history.

STARVATION (Allied 45) The American effort to tighten the blockade of Japan with mines laid by submarines and aircraft, which began in March 1945 and continued until the Japanese surrender.

STAR WATCH (U.S. Law Enforcement 88) A surveillance operation mounted by the FBI against drug trafficker in Colombia. The FBI established an aircraft brokerage in Memphis, Tennessee. This front company sold $45,000,000 worth of long-range aircraft to the smugglers. Each aircraft could carry up to 500 kilograms of illicit cargo and had a covert homing device hidden aboard. The FBI determined these aircraft did not bring drugs directly into the U.S., but instead flew into Canada, Mexico, and other countries. The drugs were then taken overland into the U.S. The operation was closed down in 1991 after other federal agencies were unwilling to use the intelligence generated by the FBI.

STATESMAN (Allied 43) Early name for TIDAL WAVE, the air attacks on the Ploesti oil refineries. See SOAPSUDS.

STEEL BOX (U.S. 90) The removal of U.S. chemical weapons from Europe conducted in 1990. The stockpile was moved from 26 June to 22 September to the remote Johnston Atoll in the Pacific where it is scheduled to be destroyed.

STEEL TIGER (U.S. 65) Interdiction operations conducted by the 1st Marine Air Wing against communist supply lines in Laos from 6 to 31 December 1965. See BARREL ROLL.

STEINBOCK "IBEX" (GER 44) German air operations against Great Britain from January to May 1944, commonly called the "Baby Blitz." These attacks were centered on London, but due to effective defenses, poor navigation, and other factors, only 32 (of 500) tons of bombs actually hit the city. Over 329 German aircraft were lost in this campaign. An Ibex is a type of mountain goat.

STEP (Allied 44) Canadian exercise in England conducted in April 1944 by troops slated for the OVERLORD invasion.

STONE AGE (Allied 42) The merchant convoy that reached Malta from Egypt on 20 November 1942 breaking the siege of that island. Followed TRAIN.

STORAX (U.S. 63) Those blasts of the DOMINIC I and II series that took place in Fiscal 1963, but excluding the SEDAN test, which was part of the PLOWSHARE program.

STORFANG "STURGEON CATCH" (GER 42) Siege operations by the German 11th Army against the Soviet defenses at Sevastopol, Russia, beginning on 7 June 1942. An amphibious assault north of the city outflanked the Soviet defenses and the city fell on 30 June 1942.

STORM 95 (CT 95) The Croatian attack into the self-styled "Krajina Republic" in mid-1995. The Croatian military quickly established control over this area, part of Croatia whose people had ethnic identification with the bordering Serbian state. The operation ended the Serbian-Croatian alliance against Bosnia and placed Serbia in a more difficult position to support the rebellion by Serb ethnics against the Bosnian government. This operation ended in early August 1995.

STORM FURY (U.S. 61) Peacetime effort to reduce the destructiveness of hurricanes while they were at sea, conducted by the U.S. Navy and Air Force in support of civil authorities. Military aircraft "salted" 8 hurricanes with silver iodide crystals to weaken the wall of the storm's eye. These operations, conducted from 1961 to 1983, had questionable results and were halted due to environmental concerns.

STORM TRAIL (U.K. 89) Term used for the occasional deployment of Royal Air Force units and aircraft to take part in MAPLE FLAG.

STRANGLE

1. (Allied 44) Air operations by the U.S. 15th and 21st Air Forces to interdict German supply routes in Italy north of Rome from spring 1943 to spring 1944. See DIADEM.

2. (U.N. 51) The general name for air interdiction strikes and naval gunfire against North Korean targets launched during the latter stages of the war. Although these operations failed to starve the communist forces into submission, it did increase the number of troops devoted to logistics functions and limited the enemy's ability to stockpile supplies for renewed offensives. Included CUTTER.

STRIKE

1. (Allied 43) A planned final offensive on Axis forces in North Africa. Portions of the attack were conducted, but the plan was never completed due to the rapid advance of the ground forces. See FLAX and RETRIBUTION.

2. (Allied 44) One of a series of fighter-bomber sweeps over northern France conducted in June 1944. These strikes were designed to attack German units moving to counterattack the Normandy beachhead (OVERLORD).

3. (U.N. 52) See BLAST.

STUD (Allied 44) See ROYAL FLUSH and FULL HOUSE.

STYLE (Allied 42) The delivery of Spitfire fighters to Malta on 3 June 1942.

STYMIE (Allied 43) Canadian amphibious exercise scheduled for June 1943 at Ayrshire, Scotland. Canceled by bad weather.

SUBSISTENCE (Allied 41) British convoy from Malta to Gibraltar in July 1941. See STYLE.

SUCCESS (U.S. 54) The CIA plot that overthrew the popularly elected government of Guatemala in mid-1954. The Eisenhower Administration, concerned by the election of Jacobo Arbenz Guzman as President, authorized a covert effort to topple his regime. A small force of revolutionaries was created in Nicaragua. Backed by an air force flown by CIA mercenaries and aided by covert propaganda broadcasts, they quickly overran the capital and plunged their country into chaos that led to a long-lived right-wing dictatorship and civil war.

SUDDEN IMPACT (U.S. Law Enforcement 93) Nationwide crackdown on automobile insurance fraud coordinated by the FBI beginning in 1993. This investigation was publicly announced in late May 1995 with a massive roundup over 100 suspects in 32 states.

SUITCASE (Allied 44) A corps-level covering attack for VITALITY launched on 20 October 1944.

SULTAN (CN 90) Deployment of Canadian observers to Central America in 1990 to 1992 and peacekeeping observers. See MATCH.

SUMMIT (U.N. 51) An early use of helicopters to move American Marines in September 1951 near the "Punchbowl" in Korea.

SUMPF-FIEBER "MARSH FEVER" (GER 42) Anti-partisan operation launched on 4 March 1942. The local commander reported "389 partisans killed, 1,274 persons shot on suspicion, 8,350 Jews liquidated."

SUMPHBLUME "SWAMP FLOWER" (GER 42) An anti-partisan sweep conducted in early July 1942 in the Dorogobuzh region of Russia.

SUNBEAM (U.S. 63) Investigation of radiation leakage from the DOMINIC II series of test explosions.

SUNBURN (U.K. 45) British air patrols off the coast of Palestine to prevent Zionist immigration.

SUNDIAL (U.N. 51) Plan for a limited-objective attack launched by the U.S. forces to reach the "Duluth" line during the Korean War. This plan included many features of WRANGLER, but without the amphibious operation. Never executed.

SUNFLOWER (GER 41) See SON-NEBLUME.

SUNRISE

1. (Allied 41) A British air attack on German ships in the French ports of Brest and La Pallice on 24 July 1941. The attack failed and cost the Royal Air Force 17 aircraft.

2. (U.S. 45) Alternative American term for CROSSWORD.

3. (U.S./R.V.N. 62) The first major forced relocation of Vietnamese peasants into "strategic hamlets," begun in April 1962. Strategic hamlets were designated villages that could be defended by government forces. By moving peasants into these hamlets, the government could protect them from Viet Cong terrorism and provide them other government services. By December 1963, over 11,000 hamlets were designated as "strategic." People outside the hamlets were assumed to be supporters of the Viet Cong. Often the relocation effort was seen by the peasants as severance of their ancient ties with the land and forcing them to live under government surveillance. The strategic hamlet program was aimed at denying the guerrillas the support of the people and was the philosophical descendant of a similar tactic developed by the British during the Boer War. The British called their centralized locations "concentration camps." See EXPLOSION.

SUN RUN (U.S. 57) A series of record-breaking flights conducted by 6 RF-101

Voodoo aircraft on 27 November 1957. The flights were conducted from the east to west coast of the U.S. and established new records for both the round trip (6.46.36) and both legs (3.36.32 and 3.7.43).

SUNSET (U.S. 45) The return of American B-29s and other serviceable aircraft to the U.S. at the end of World War II.

SUNSHINE (U.S. 53) A secret research program conducted by the American Atomic Energy Commission to investigate the effect of radiation on the human body. Beginning in 1953, government agents began to collect cadavers from across North America. Without the knowledge or permission of next of kin, the bodies were studied as to the amount of radiation stored in the body from nuclear tests. This program continued until at least 1957 and was declassified in 1995.

SUNSTREAK (U.S.) The name given in the early 1990s to a team of psychics maintained by the CIA to "remotely view" areas of interest to the U.S. This term replaced the earlier terms CENTER LANE, GRILL FLAME, and SCANATE.

SUNTAN (U.S.) A program conducted in the 1950s to build a hydrogen-fueled high-altitude reconnaissance aircraft to replace the U-2. Never completed.

SUN VALLEY (U.S.) American surveillance flights that flew along the Korean Demilitarized Zone using a very large camera to peer into North Korea. Originally conducted using RB-50 aircraft, but changed to modified C-130s in 1961.

SUPERCHARGE I (Allied 42) Attack by the British 8th Army (led by Australian, New Zealand, and Indian troops) west through Axis defenses near El Rahman. The attack began on 1 November 1942 to open a new route into the enemy positions once LIGHT-FOOT failed to achieve a breakthrough.

SUPERCHARGE I also quickly stalled. The next day, the British returned to their original northern thrust and burst the German defenses. See TORCH.

SUPER CHARGE II (Allied 43) Attack by the British 8th Army on the German Mareth Line defenses in southern Tunisia. Conducted in March 1943. See PUGILIST.

SUPER GYMNAST (Allied 42) Planning name for TORCH.

SUPERMAN (U.S. 47) See GEM.

SUPER ROUNDUP (Allied 43) A larger version of ROUNDUP that eventually became ROUNDHAMMER. Never executed.

SUPPORT DEMOCRACY (U.S. 94) The embargo of Haiti by a mostly-American international force that began in May 1994. The goal of the blockade was to keep Haitian from fleeting their country (see ABLE MANNER) and to punish the military regime that had deposed the government of Jean-Bertrand Aristide, the elected president. Followed by the American-led occupation of Haiti, RESTORE DEMOCRACY.

SUPPORT HOPE (U.S. 94) The American relief effort to provide humanitarian aid to refugees fleeing from the genocidal civil war in Rwanda to nearby Zaire. Water purification, medical, and transportation units established a string of refugee camps that were turned over to U.N. control on 24 August 1994.

SURF BOARD (U.S.) See TREE TOP.

SURGEON (U.K. 45) A post-war plan to acquire German aviation equipment, prototypes, and designers to ensure the health of the British aviation industry. See SEASHORE.

SUSSEX (Allied 44) The insertion of intelligence teams into occupied France to support OVERLORD. American teams were designated OSSEX; British teams were called BRISSEX.

SU ZU (JPN 44) Japanese plan to defend Mindanao and the Visayan Islands in the Philippines. Developed by General Sosaku Suzyki, commander of the 35th Army.

SW (Allied) Allied convoys from Suez to South Africa in World War II. Designated by number (e.g., SW 123).

SWALLOW (Allied 43) The insertion by parachute near Vermorsk, Norway, of a 4-man advanced party of resistance fighters. This team conducted reconnaissance and prepared a landing zone on a frozen lake for 6 additional parachutists (GUNNERSIDE). Together the 2 groups succeeded in their mission to blow up a heavy water plant vital to the German nuclear bomb program. See GROUSE.

SWAMP FOX (U.S. 61) Exercise conducted in the old Panama Canal Zone by American troops to test new tropical warfare equipment.

SWARMER (U.S. 50) Exercise by the American 18th Airborne Corps at Fort Bragg and Camp McKall, North Carolina. The scenario was a large airborne raid resupplied entirely by air drops.

SWEET BRIAR (U.S./CN 50) The first large post-war U.S./Canadian exercise, conducted in late February 1950 in Alaska and the Yukon Territory.

"SWIFT SWORD" (Oman/U.K. 85) See SAIF SAREEA.

SWITCHBACK

1. (Allied 44) Attack by the Canadian 3rd Division into the Breskers Pocket south of the West Scheldt estuary in the Netherlands. Began in early November 1944.

2. (Allied 63) The transfer of control of Vietnamese Civilian Indigenous Defense Groups (CIDGs) from the American CIA to the Special Forces of the U.S. Army. Conducted from December to July 1963.

SWORDFISH (U.S. Law Enforcement 81) A very successful "string" operation conducted by the American Drug Enforcement Administration against the financial affairs of drug cartels based in Colombia. An informant, Robert Darius, set up a phony investment company in Miami in 1981 and induced the *narcotrafficantes* to invest money in it to launder the funds. As a result of this operation, several people were convicted in a series of trials ending in 1987.

SWORDHILT (Allied 44) American ground attacks that resulted in the capture of Brest, France, in September 1944. The harbor, a major German submarine base earlier in the war, was demolished by the defenders before they surrendered.

SYMBOL (Allied 43) Allied conference at Casablanca, 14-23 January 1943. Stalin did not attend the conference, due to the Battle of Stalingrad. Churchill and Roosevelt approved the invasion of Sicily (HUSKY) as a means of opening a second front in Europe. Roosevelt also called for the "unconditional surrender" of the Axis countries. In addition, the Western Allies agreed to a combined strategic bombing campaign (POINTBLANK) against Germany and an intensification of the Battle of the Atlantic.

T

T.4 (GER 41) Nazi euthanasia program directed against the deformed, incurable, insane, and the otherwise "defective." In the case of children with serious defects, the goal was to murder the children as soon as possible after birth to prevent the mothers from developing close bonds with their offspring. Over 10,000 people, mostly Germans, were killed under this program. As the activity spread, the use of lethal injections and other "medical" means of death became impractical; centralized facilities with gas chambers were developed. The most infamous of these was located at Gorden. The Health Ministry, which administered the killings, insisted all the murders be supervised by a licensed physician. Hitler, in a unique move prompted by public outrage led by the German clergy, canceled the program on 24 August 1941. The murders continued secretly throughout the Nazi regime. The operation name was derived from the address of a Health Ministry office, at Number 4 Tiergartenstrasse, Berlin.

TA (Allied convoy) Allied convoys of large liners such as the *Queen Mary*. Designated by number (e.g., TA 123).

TABLE LEG (U.S. mid-50s) A joint committee established by the U.S. Air Force and Nuclear Regulatory Commission to investigate the possibility of constructing small, "tactical" nuclear weapons.

TABLE TENNIS (Allied 44) Allied attack on the island of Noemfoor, Dutch East Indies, off the north coast of New Guinea in July and August 1944.

TACAUD (FR 78) The April 1978 deployment of French forces from Dakar, Senegal, to attack Libyan-backed guerrillas in Chad. A tacaued is a type of fish. See LAMANTIN.

TACK (U.N. 51) The use of American cargo aircraft to drop roofing nails to interdict communist supply lines in Korea. Conducted on 9 February 1951.

TAIFUN "TYPHOON" (GER 41) Final German attack toward Moscow. Launched on 2 October 1941; Hitler predicted it would be "the last great decisive battle of the war." Two thousand German tanks started the advance cutting off pockets of defending Soviets at Bryansk and Vyazma and pushing as far as Mozhaisk, just 40 miles from the Communist capital. The attack was exhausted by 6 December as the weakening Germans encountered fresh Soviet reinforcements from Siberia and temperatures as low as minus 40 degrees Fahrenheit.

TAILBOARD (U.N. 50) A plan for an amphibious landing at Wonsan, on North Korea's east coast. Never executed due to the rapid advance of the U.N. ground forces. See CHROMITE.

TALLULAH (Allied 44) Planning name for TRACTABLE.

TALON (Allied 45) British amphibious landing at Akyab in western Burma on 3 January 1945. Conducted without opposition.

TANDEM THRUST (U.S. 94) An amphibious exercise centered on the island of Tinian conducted in December 1994. U.S. Army and National Guard units defended the island from an assault by Marine Corps troops spearheaded by Air Force B-52 aircraft.

TANNENBAUM "FIR TREE" (GER 40) A contingency plan for a German invasion of Switzerland. The concept of the operation called for German troops to invade from occupied France, taking advantage of flatter geography. The Germans planned to occupy all major Swiss cities in 2 or 3 days to preclude organized Swiss units from retreating to the mountains to form the nucleus for a campaign of guerrilla warfare.

TAPER (Allied 45) Allied deception operation conducted in March 1945, which falsely depicted preparations for an Allied airborne attack near Cologne.

TARZAN (Allied 42) Proposed Allied offensive in the China-Burma-India theater during the 1942/43 dry season. Never executed.

TAXABLE (Allied 44) Tactical deception executed as part of the invasion of Normandy (OVERLORD) on 6 June 1944. To increase German confusion as to the location and size of the Allied airdrops behind the invasion beaches, radar-reflecting metallic strips and rubber parachutists were dropped near Boulogne, France, far from the actual landing zones. The entire effect was designed to portray an attack on the Pas de Calais region. See TITANIC.

TB (Allied convoy) Allied convoys from North America to Australia in World War II. Designated by number (TB 123).

TEAL (U.S.) A first word used by several American reconnaissance programs.

TEAM SPIRIT

1. (U.S./R.O.K. 76) Annual ground forces exercise in Korea designated by year (e.g., TEAM SPIRIT 82). This program began in June 1976 and stressed the reinforcement of Korea from the U.S. and U.S./Korean interoperability. The series was suspended in 1992 to encourage North Korea to cooperate with international inspections of its nuclear installations, but resumed in 1993 when that cooperation ended.

2. (JPN 44) See WA.

TEAMWORK 92 (NATO 92) First major NATO exercise after the collapse of the Soviet Union. The exercise involved 11 NATO countries and featured an amphibious invasion of Norway by the U.S. Marines. Conducted 6-25 March 1992.

TEAPOT (U.S. 55) Series of 13 nuclear test explosions conducted at the Nevada Test Site. Immediately after the ESS shot on 23 March 1955, ground forces took part in DESERT ROCK VI, which included an armored task force "Razor" moving within 900 meters of ground zero, under the still-forming mushroom cloud. This series preceded WIGWAM and followed CASTLE. The shots of this series were:

WASP	18 February 55	1 kiloton
MOTH	22 February	2 kilotons
TESLA	1 March	7 kilotons
TURK	7 March	43 kilotons
HORNET	12 March	4 kilotons
BEE	22 March	8 kilotons
ESS	23 March	1 kiloton
WASP PRIME	29 March	3 kilotons
HA	6 April	3 kilotons
POST	9 April	2 kilotons
MET	14 April	22 kilotons
APPLE	25 May	29 kilotons
ZUCCHINI	15 May	28 kilotons

TEARDROP (Allied 45) The American defense against the SEEWOLF submarine wolf pack off the east coast of the U.S. in March 1945. The Americans thought the 6 large U-boats might be armed with missiles to attack the U.S., and therefore used every effort to destroy the flotilla. By May all 6 boats were sunk by aircraft and surface ships.

TEMPEST (CN 93) The deployment of Canadian observers and HMCS *Halifax* to the Middle East to support the peace process in the region.

TEN ICHI (JPN 45) The massive Japanese air and naval attacks on the American fleet off Okinawa in April 1945. These attacks hit about a quarter of the American fleet, sinking 34 ships and killing about 5,000 sailors. In addition to hundreds of suicide aircraft, the Japanese also sent their last battleship, *Yamato*, on a one-way mission. *Yamato* was quickly destroyed by American air power. See ICEBERG.

TERMINAL

1. (Allied 42) A special landing party assigned to the Eastern Task Force in TORCH. Their mission was to land directly on the port of Algiers to prevent sabotage.

2. (Allied 45) Conference held at Potsdam, Germany, from 17 July to 2 August 1945 between Stalin, Churchill, and Truman. During the summit, Churchill was replaced by the new Labor Prime Minister Clement Attlee. Although the war in the Pacific was still in progress, this meeting focused on post-war arrangements in Europe. These decisions eventually led to the division of Germany and the unique position of Berlin in the Cold War era.

TEXAN

1. (U.S. 52) An exercise designed to train observation crews for the IVY nuclear weapons tests. This training was centered on a ship anchored in the Gulf of Mexico and at Bergstrom Air Force Base in Texas.

2. (U.S./R.V.N. 66) The relief of the South Vietnamese garrison at An Hoa. The Vietnamese called their part of the operation LEIN KET 28. Conducted on 28 March 1966.

THAESUS "THESEUS" (GER 42) Offensive in North Africa launched 26 May 1942. This attack split the British 8th Army in half and captured Tobruk on 21 June. The Italian infantry attack that pinned down many defenders was called VENEZIA. The name refers to a mythical hero, the son of Poseidon.

THESIS (Allied 43) Massive British air attacks on German units on Crete on 23 July 1943.

THREE PAIRS (U.S. 62) An Army exercise conducted in central Texas in the summer of 1962. This training featured the 82nd Airborne Division, opposed by the 1st Armored Division. Both units hurriedly returned to their bases to support the mobilization for the Cuban Missile Crisis. See RAPID ROADS.

THROAT (Allied 42) The British capture of Mayotte Island, one of the Comoro Islands off the coast of Madagascar on 2 July 1942. See IRONCLAD.

THUNDERBOLT

1. (Allied 44) Plan for the seizure of Metz, France by the U.S. 12th Army Group. The plan called for a massive air preparation beginning on 21 September 1944. Due to poor weather, the bombardment was repeatedly canceled and reduced. On 27 September, the ground assault was launched in a much-modified form. The city fell after heavy fighting on 22 November 1944.

2. (U.N. 51) Reconnaissance carried out by elements of the U.S. 1st and 9th Corps

in the area bounded by the Suwon-Ich'on-Yojo road and the Han River. Naval forces conducted 2 amphibious feints, one on the east and one on the west coast, to support this operation. Executed 25 January 1951.

3. (U.S. 61) American armored exercise at Fort Hood, Texas, in 1961.

4. (U.S. Law Enforcement 81) A joint operation by aircraft the American Navy, Coast Guard, and various law enforcement agencies which seized 45 drug-laden aircraft.

THUNDERCLAP

1. (GER 42) See DONNERSCHLAG.

2. (Allied 45) The American and British bombing raids on the German cities of Berlin, Chemnitz, Dresden, and Leipzig conducted from 13 to 15 February 1945, less than 3 months before the German surrender. These strikes were designed to assist the advancing Red Army by preventing the movement of German troops through these cities. The raids on Dresden have become especially infamous since the war: over 2,690 tons of bombs hit the ornate Saxon city, which burned for 7 days. Between 30,000 and 60,000 civilians died. The commander of British Bomber Command, Air Chief Marshal (later Sir) Arthur "Bomber" Harris opposed the raids on the grounds that Dresden was at the extreme limit of his aircraft's range. Churchill and Eisenhower insisted on its execution.

THUNDERSTORM (GER 44) Sweep by the German secret police after the 20 July 1944 bomb plot attack on Hitler.

THURSDAY (Allied 44) The second Chindit Expedition in Burma. Five Chindit brigades established airfield strongholds along Japanese lines of supply between Rangoon and northern Burma. They then interdicted the Japanese, forcing them into frontal attacks against their defenses. See END RUN and DRACULA.

TIDAL WAVE (Allied 43) A series of bombing attacks on oil refineries near Ploesti, Rumania, which began on 1 August 1943 when 177 USAAF bombers flying from bases in Benghazi temporarily destroyed 40 percent of total refining capacity. Five Medals of Honor were awarded for this initial attack, the largest ever awarded for a single air mission. Despite the high loss rates, raids continued against this heavily-defended target. Nineteen additional attacks over the next year essentially eliminated all production at the complex. Earlier plans to attack this vital target were SOAPSUDS and STATESMAN.

TIERRA DEL FUEGO (GER 43) See FEUERLAND.

TIGER

1. (Allied 41) British convoy carrying tank reinforcements sent to Egypt in March 1941. Considering the threat of a German invasion of England and the perils of a voyage across the Mediterranean at the time, this was a very risky decision. One ship loaded with tanks was lost to a mine.

2. (Allied 42) A joint British/Canadian training exercise in which the English counties of Kent and Sussex were deemed separate countries to allow a variety of tactical maneuvers in late May 1942.

3. (Allied 44) Exercise by U.S. 5th Corps conducted at Slapton Sands, England, as a rehearsal for the invasion of northern France (OVERLORD). Early on the morning of 28 April 1944 the convoy was attacked by German naval patrol boats, resulting in 736 U.S. dead.

TIGER I (U.S./BZ 94) A deployment of Brazilian Air Force units to Puerto Rice in 1994 to conduct training with their American counterparts.

TIGER II (U.S./BZ 95) The deployment of U.S. Air Force units to Natal, Brazil, for combined training and a static display for the public at the local airport. Conducted in October 1995.

TIGER MEET (NATO 61) A series of exchange visits between NATO squadrons that share a tiger on their shoulder patches. These meetings began in 1961 in Britain and have rotated between various European air bases more-or-less annually since. Since the units involved use a wide eclectic mix of aircraft, little or no tactical training takes place. Instead these occasions serve as a means of improving informal interpersonal relationships between the NATO air forces.

TIMBER LINE (U.S.) See TREE TOP.

TIMBER WIND (U.S. 91) American effort to develop a nuclear-powered rocket engine for use in the "Star Wars" missile defense program. The existence of this program was leaked in 1991 by the Federation of American Scientists. Due to public ridicule, the project was renamed LOFTY THUNDER, and on being exposed again was allegedly canceled. Followed NERVA and PLUTO.

TIMBERWOLF (Allied 43) The movement of Canadian troops from Italy to Britain in November 1943 to prepare for the invasion of northern France.

TIMS (U.K. 53) A British nuclear safety test, which studied the components of nuclear weapons and which did not involve a nuclear ion. Conducted between 1953 and 1963 at Emu Field and Maralinga test areas in Australia. Also called KITTENS.

TINDALL (Allied 43) A deception operation that falsely portrayed an invasion threat against Norway in the summer of 1943. Part of the overall deception plan COCKADE. See FORTITUDE NORTH.

TINDERBOX (U.S. 79) A series of 15 nuclear tests conducted at the Nevada Test Site. These tests followed the QUICKSILVER series and preceded GUARDIAN. The individual blasts were:

BACK-GAMMON	29 November 79	<20 kilotons
AZUL	14 December	<20 kilotons
TARKO	28 February 80	<20 kilotons
NORBO	8 March	<20 kilotons
LIPTAUER	3 April	20-150 kilotons
PYRAMID	16 April	20-150 kilotons
COLWICK	26 April	20-150 kilotons
CANFIELD	2 May	<20 kilotons
FLORA	22 May	<20 kilotons
KASH	12 June	20-150 kilotons
HURON KING	24 June	<20 kilotons
TAFI	25 July	20-150 kilotons
VERDELLO	31 July	<20 kilotons
BONARDA	25 September	20-150 kilotons
RIOLA	25 September	<20 kilotons

TITANIC (Allied 44) The use of metallic, radar-reflecting strips and rubber toy paratroopers to depict an airborne attack on Marigny, France, during the early morning hours of 6 June 1944, at the same time as the actual invasion of Normandy (OVERLORD). See TAXABLE.

TOENAILS (Allied 44) Invasion of New Georgia on 30 June 1944 by Allied forces. Planned under the name OPERATION A. Part of CARTWHEEL.

TOGGLE (U.S. 72) A series of 15 nuclear tests conducted in 1972 and 1973. With the exception of the RIO BLANCO test, these blasts took place at the Nevada Test Site. Followed GROMMET, preceded ARBOR. The individual shots of this series were:

DIAMOND SCULLS	20 July 71	probably 21 kilotons
(Unknown)	25 July	(unknown)
OSCURO	21 September	prob. 130 kilotons
DELPHINIUM	26 September	15 kilotons
(Unknown)	9 November	(unknown)

FLAX	21 December	prob. 27 kilotons
MIERA	8 March 73	prob. 67 kilotons
ANGUS	25 April	prob. 21 kilotons
STARWORT	26 April	90 kilotons
RIO BLANCO	17 May	three 33 kiloton fired

simultaneously near Rifle, CO. See PLOWSHARE.

(Unknown)	24 May	(unknown)
DIDO QUEEN	5 June	prob. 26 kilotons
ALMENDRO	6 June	prob. 570 kilotons
(Unknown)	21 June	(unknown)
PORTULACA	28 June	prob. 60 kilotons

TO-GO

1. (JPN 44) Japanese plan to intercept an American invasion fleet off the Home Islands with suicide aircraft and small boats. Part of KETSU-GO; see TEN ICHI and DOWNFALL.

2. (JPN 44) Plan to overrun American airfields at Sui-Chnan and Nan-Hsiung, China, and to reopen the Canton-Hangchow railroad. Planned for late May 1944.

TOMAHAWK (U.N. 51) Airborne assault conducted by the U.S. 187th Airborne Combat Team on 23 March 1951 near Munsan. Events forced the cancellation of a previously scheduled combat jump, HAWK. Rather than waste the preparations, the objective was rapidly changed and the operation renamed TOMAHAWK. This jump had a northern and a southern drop zone. The regimental commander was forced to return to base after his aircraft developed engine trouble. Navigational error led to all the troops landing on the northern drop zone only. Later, the regimental commander returned and jumped on the empty southern drop zone. Fortunately, communist resistance was minimal and armored units quickly linked up with the paratroopers.

TONGA (Allied 44) British airborne landings in support of the invasion of northern France (OVERLORD). See CHICAGO and DETROIT.

TONIC (Allied 40) British contingency plan to capture the Spanish Canary Islands for use as air bases in the Battle of the Atlantic. Canceled in December 1942. Planned as PILGRIM.

TONNAGE (Allied 44) Logistic training exercise in preparation for OVERLORD.

TOPHAT (Allied 43) Plan for an invasion of Italy in the Naples area. Abandoned in favor of AVALANCHE.

TOP SAIL (U.S. 58) A record-breaking flight by 2 KC-135 Stratotanker aircraft of the Strategic Air Command conducted on 27 and 29 June 1958. The lead aircraft's times were (New York to London) 5:29:14.64 and (London to New York) 5:53:12.77. A third aircraft crashed on takeoff from Westover Air Force Base, killing Brigadier General Donald Saunders, commander of the 57th Air Division.

TORCH (Allied 42) The invasion of North Africa on 8 November 1942. Political considerations were critical to this invasion, with much effort being expended to ensure Vichy French assistance or neutrality. These entreaties were only partially effective. The invasion was roughly coordinated with the British SUPERCHARGE attack launched from Egypt into the eastern flank of the Axis forces. The invasion beaches were designated Apple, Beer, and Charlie, and were anchored on the port cities of Algiers on the east and Casablanca on the west. Planned as GYMNAST and SUPER GYMNAST. Deception operations in support of this attack included KENNECOTT, OVERTHROW, and SOLO. See RUSTY PROJECT, TERMINAL, and BACKBONE.

TOREADOR (Allied 42) Proposed Allied attack in Burma in the 1942/43 dry season. Never executed. See ANAKIM.

TORRID SHADOW 90 (U.S. 90) Exercise designed to test U.S. intelligence and command systems.

TORTUE "TORTOISE" (Allied 44) French resistance attacks on German communications and supply routes to support the invasion of northern France (OVERLORD).

TOTALITY (Allied 45) A war plan drawn up in 1945 by the Supreme Allied Commander, Europe (still General Eisenhower) for a possible ground war with the U.S., Britain, and France aligned against the Soviet Union and her allies. Due to the rapid demobilization of the U.S. and British armies, the Western Allies would have been hard-pressed to contain a Soviet attack without resorting to nuclear warfare. Never executed.

TOTALIZE (Allied 44) A ground attack on 7 August 1944 by Canadian and Polish forces to break out from the Normandy beachhead along the Caen-Falaise road. Although the attack failed in its objective, it did serve as a spoiling attack, disrupting German forces massing for the LÜTTICH attack. Preceded TRACTABLE.

TOTEM (U.K. 53) Two nuclear tests conducted on 14 and 26 October 1953 at Emu Field, South Australia. Due to poor weather conditions, radioactive materials drifted onto nearby aboriginal encampments. Followed HURRICANE, preceded MOSAIC. See HOT BOX.

TOTEM 1	14 October 53	10 kilotons
TOTEM 2	26 October	8 kilotons

TOUCHDOWN (U.N. 51) An attack by the U.S. 2nd Infantry Division (including attached French, Dutch, and Thai battalions) launched on 5 October to capture "Heartbreak Ridge." The terrain feature acquired its nickname after a poorly-planned attack in September. The ridge, located northeast of Hwachon Reservoir in east-central Korea, dominated several local roads needed by U.N. forces. The North Korean 6th and 12th Division defended the area. Using massive artillery and anti-aircraft machine guns, the U.N. forces moved their lines 10 miles north, capturing Kim Il Sung Bridge on 13 October, ending the attack.

TOURGUIDE (GER 42) See BAEDEKER.

TOWNSMAN (Allied 42) Allied naval deception operation in support of the invasion of North Africa (TORCH). The massive number of ships passing through Gibraltar could not be concealed, so a cover story was invented that depicted the movements as part of the relief of Malta.

TOXIC SWEEP (U.S. 92) The use of U.S. Navy ships with advanced sensors to detect toxic waste barrels off the New Jersey coast.

TRACTABLE (Allied 44) A combined Polish/Canadian attack into the Falaise Pocket and onward east toward Paris. This attack, launched on 14 August 1944, was dogged by bad luck. The preliminary air bombardment landed on the attacker's positions, and the defending Germans had managed to capture a copy of the attack plan. Despite these hardships, the attack reached the Seine River in 4 days. Planned as TALLULAH. Followed TOTALIZE.

TRADEWINDS (U.S./U.K. 86) A long-running series of joint naval exercises conducted by American, British, and Caribbean forces annually since 1986. These operations have aimed at improving cooperation in security and disaster relief operations.

TRAIL DUST (U.S.) Escort missions for C-123 spray aircraft conducting RANCH HAND missions.

TRAIN (Allied 42) The delivery of Spitfire fighters to Malta on 24 October 1942. Followed BARITONE, preceded STONE AGE.

TRANQUILLITY (CN 95) The deployment of HMCS *Calgary* to the Persian Gulf to enforce post-war U.N. sanctions against Iraq.

TRANSIT (Allied 45) The transshipment of men and supplies after the defeat of Germany to the Pacific Theater through the Panama Canal.

TRAPPENJAGD "DUCK HUNT" (GER 42) Offensive launched by the German 11th Army on the Kerch Peninsula during the period 8 to 18 May 1942. A total success, the Germans captured over 169,000 Soviet prisoners.

TREACLE (Allied 41) The relief of the 18th Australian Brigade in Tobruk by the Polish Carpathian Brigade, which was transported into the besieged city by the Royal Navy in August 1941. "Treacle" is a sweet cloying liquid. See BREVITY and THAESUS.

TREATMENT (Allied 42) The strategic deception plan in support of the British LIGHTFOOT attack. The large number of units ready for this attack could not be totally concealed, so their presence was falsely depicted as a large-scale training exercise under combat conditions. See BERTRAM.

TREBOR (U.K. 91) The recapture of the British embassy in Kuwait City on 28 February 1991 by a team from the Special Boat Service.

TREE TOP (U.S.) One of a series of plans and exercises to support the succession to the American presidency. Formally titled the "Presidential Succession Emergency Support Plan," it is tested at least once a year. It designates a small staff for each successor to the presidency for use during an emergency and provides the documents needed to assume office. This plan and its exercises are controlled by the Federal Emergency Management Administration, the American civil defense organization.

Exercises that tested this plan included FLASH BURN, JACK POT, LOG TREE, LOG HORN, PINE RIDGE, SAGE BRUSH, SKI JUMP, SNOW FALL, SNOW STORM, SOUTHERN PINE, SURF BOARD, TIMBER LINE, and NINE LIVES. See FEDERAL EMERGENCY PLAN D.

TRIANGLE (GER 42) See DREIECK.

TRICKLE (Allied 42) The movement of single cargo ships without escort from Iceland to the Soviet northern ports. Such movements avoided major German attacks by taking a much longer route.

TRIDENT (Allied 43) U.S.-British conference held in Washington in mid-May 1943. This meeting set the target date for the invasion of northern France (OVERLORD) as 1 May 1944 and approved American plans for an offensive in the Central Pacific.

TRIDENT EXPRESS 95-01 (NATO 95) A naval exercise in the Central Mediterranean conducted in May 1995.

TRINITY (Allied 45) The first explosion of an atomic bomb. Detonated on 17 July 1945 at a remote site in New Mexico. See ALBERTA, CENTERBOARD, and MANHATTAN ENGINEER DISTRICT.

TRIO (Axis 42) A combined German-Italian-Croatian anti-partisan operation conducted in early May 1942 centered near Pljevlja and Cajnice, Yugoslavia. Hostages were murdered in both villages.

TRISUL (IN 88) Operations by Indian peacekeepers in northern Sri Lanka in April and June 1988. Followed PAWAN, preceded CHECKMATE.

TRIUMPHANT (Allied 44) The overall plan to liberate Burma in World War II.

TROJAN (U.S. 43) (Same as BARKLEY) An early plan prepared by the U.S. Air Force for waging a nuclear war with the Soviet Union. This plan was later used as a basis for CHARIOTEER. Never executed. See DROPSHOT and FLEETWOOD.

TROJAN HORSE (Allied 43) Part of the BARCLAY deception plan for the invasion of Italy (HUSKY). The major component of TROJAN HORSE was MINCEMEAT.

TROUSERS (Allied 44) Canadian amphibious training at Slapton Sands, England, on 12 April 1944 in preparation for the invasion of northern France (OVERLORD).

TRUE (U.S. 85) American program of helicopter training conducted in cities at night. Army and Marine Corps pilots practice urban navigation, landings, and other techniques in these unannounced exercises. The cities of Honolulu, Phoenix, San Diego, San Francisco, and Oxnard, California, have hosted these flights.

TRY OUT (U.S. 56) The first exercise conducted by the former Strategic Air Command to develop procedures to keep a third of its aircraft on runway alert at all times. Conducted by the 38th Air Division from November 1956 to March 1957. This was followed by WATCHTOWER and FRESH APPROACH, which further refined the techniques and organizations.

TUBE ALLOYS (U.K. 40 or so) The British term for their early research into nuclear weapons. By extension applied to enriched radioactive products from that efforts. Both British research and materials were turned over to the U.S. in 1940 and were integrated into the MANHATTAN ENGINEER DISTRICT.

TULSA (Allied 42) Series of plans centering on the capture of Rabaul. The TULSA I plan was completed on 27 June 1942 and underwent numerous revisions. These plans evolved into the ELKTON series, which in turn was executed as CARTWHEEL, which suppressed Rabaul with airpower and bypassed it.

TUMBLER-SNAPPER (U.S. 52) A series of 8 atmospheric nuclear tests detonations conducted in 1952 at the Nevada Test Site. Army forces took part in the DESERT ROCK IV exercise in conjunction with one of these explosions. The TUMBLER series focused on collecting data on blast overpressures. The SNAPPER blasts were directed to verifying the design of warheads. These exercises also "sent a message" to the communist forces in the Korean War. Followed BUSTER-JANGLE and preceded IVY. The individual shots were:

TUMBLER

ABLE	1 April 52	1 kiloton
BAKER	15 April	1 kiloton

SNAPPER

CHARLIE	22 April	31 kilotons
DOG	1 May	19 kilotons
EASY	7 May	12 kilotons
FOX	25 May	11 kilotons
GEORGE	1 June	15 kilotons
HOW	5 June	14 kilotons

TUNGSTEN (Allied 44) Attack on the German battleship *Tirpitz* at anchor at Kaafjord, Norway, by aircraft flying from the British carriers *Victorious* and *Furious* and the escort carriers *Searcher, Emperor, Pursuer,* and *Fencer* on 3 April 1944. The attackers scored 14 hits on the target, killing 122 and wounding 316. Although the ship did not sink, she was so crippled she never again moved under her own power. Followed GOODWOOD.

TUNNEL (Allied 43) A raid by a British naval task force of 6 destroyers and the light cruiser HMS *Charybdis* who left England on 23 October 1943 to destroy German merchant shipping in the vicinity of Brest, France. They encountered several

German warships that sunk both the *Charybdis* and the destroyer HMS *Limbourne*, killing over 500 sailors.

TURPITUDE (Allied 44) Allied deception operation of the portrayed fake preparations for an Allied invasion of Salonica. Phony radio traffic, troop maneuvers, and false rumor planted with double agents were used to tie down German troops in Greece and the Balkans.

TURKEY BUZZARD (Allied 42) The transport of gliders by air from Britain to North Africa on 3 June 1942. These gliders were then used in the invasion of Sicily (HUSKY).

TURQUOISE (FR 94) The French intervention in Rwanda designed to end the genocidal slaughter of ethnic Tutsis by the embattled Huti-dominated government. The French action was approved by the Security Council as there were no trained African troops available. About 600 troops, mostly from the Foreign Legion, were deployed in Zaire and made short trips into Rwanda to provide protection and humanitarian relief.

TWILIGHT (Allied 42 or so) Plan to base 10 to 20 groups of B-29 Superfortress bombers in the China-Burma-India Theater, possibly near Changsha, China. Japanese ground attacks in China called into question the security of this arrangement and made the capture of islands to serve as B-29 bases critical. See DRAKE and MATTERHORN.

TYPHOON (GER 41) See TAIFUN.

TYPICAL (Allied 43) The insertion by parachute on 22 May 1943 of a 4-man British delegation into Yugoslavia to coordinate operations with Tito's partisans. The team jumped into the area then under attack by the Germans in their Operation SCHWARZ.

U

UCHI FOCUS LENS (U.S./R.O.K. 76) Command post exercise conducted annually since 1976 by Combined Forces Command in Korea.

U-GO "Plan U" (JPN 44) Abortive Japanese invasion of India launched in early 1944. This was meant to disrupt the "Burma Road" supply route. Japanese forces advanced on 3 February toward Imphal and encircled the British 4th Battalion, Royal West Kent Regiment in Kohima (in Manipur province). The city had to be supplied by air (STAMINA), but the tiny garrison held off the entire Japanese 31st Division until the Japanese forces were battered to pieces by British artillery and the harsh jungle conditions. Further Japanese thrusts toward Ukrul and Kohima (HA-GO) failed to reach their goals. The invaders withdrew in early July due to overextended supply lines and the onset of the monsoon. Kohima marked the furthest Japanese advance into India and was the greatest defeat suffered by their army on the Asian mainland.

ULTRA (Allied 38) Decoding effort directed against German radio communications during World War II. By extension, the products of this effort. A British team based at Bletchley, England, used information provided by the Polish Intelligence Service and a primitive computer (called "The Bombe") to construct a functional duplicate of the German Enigma encoding machine. This effort was amazingly difficult in the age before computers. The first intercepts became available in mid-April 1940 as the "phony war" came to an end. As the British gained experience, the speed with which German messages could be read was increased. Eventually, Allied commanders could read German radio traffic as quickly as the Germans themselves. Exceptional efforts were made to ensure the Germans did not realize that their codes were broken. ULTRA remained highly classified for many years after the war. See MAGIC and Y.

UNDERGO (Allied 4) The Canadian capture of Calais, France, on 10 October 1944.

UNDERTONE (Allied 45) Attack by the U.S. 3rd and 7th Armies through the "West Wall" to establish a bridgehead across the Rhine in the Worms area. Executed in March 1945. This was roughly coordinated with the more famous LUMBERJACK attack north of the Moselle. See FLASH-POINT and PLUNDER.

UNIFIED ENDEAVOR 96-1 (U.S. 96) A major computer-assisted command post exercise sponsored by U.S. Atlantic Command in mid-November 1995.

UNITAS "UNITED" (U.S. 59) An annual series of naval exercises conducted by the U.S. Atlantic Command. In this program,

U.S. Navy ships cruise the Gulf of Mexico through the Panama Canal and around South America, training with local navies en route. These deployments began in 1960 and each lasts 4 or 5 months. Denominated both by fiscal year and iteration (as in UNITAS 95-36).

UNITED EFFORT (U.S.) An early effort to defeat the North Vietnamese SA-2 Guideline missile. Unmanned reconnaissance drones would fly over antiaircraft positions, causing the operators to activate their search radars. A manned intelligence aircraft, flying at a safe distance, would detect and record the emissions of the radar for analysis.

UNITED SHIELD (U.N. 94) A 7-nation evacuation of humanitarian relief forces from Somalia conducted in early 1994. A combined American and Italian force covered the withdrawal as local bandits began looting the air and sea ports. The American portion was called QUICK DRAW. See PROVIDE RELIEF.

UNITED SPIRIT 96 (NATO 96) A major joint naval and air exercise conducted off the east coast of North America in March 1996.

UPHOLD DEMOCRACY (U.S. 94) The American occupation of Haiti that began on 19 September 1994. The elected government of Haiti had been overthrown by the local military in 1991. The country then began a slow drift into anarchy. This resulted in a huge number of refugees fleeing into the U.S. The Americans planned an invasion to be launched after a last-minute diplomatic effort. This diplomatic mission, headed by former President Jimmy Carter, convinced the Junta to step down after the Haitians received separate confirmation that the invasion aircraft had in fact left Fort Bragg, North Carolina. U.S. forces landed on the island without opposition. The Americans at first cooperated

with and then disarmed the Haitian military. See PRESSURE COOKER.

UPSHOT-KNOTHOLE (U.S. 53) A series of 11 nuclear test shots conducted in 1953 at the Nevada Test Site. Over 21,000 soldiers took part in the ground exercise DESERT ROCK V in conjunction with the GRABLE shot. GRABLE was a 280-millimeter shell fired from the "Atomic Cannon" and was viewed by a number of high-ranking military officials. Followed IVY, preceded CASTLE. The individual shots were:

ANNIE	17 March 53	16 kilotons
NANCY	24 March	24 kilotons
RUTH	31 March	.2 kiloton (partial misfire)
DIXIE	6 April	11 kilotons
RAY	11 April	.2 kiloton (partial misfire)
BADGER	18 April	23 kilotons
SIMON	25 April	43 kilotons
ENCORE	8 May	27 kilotons
HARRY	19 May	32 kilotons
GRABLE	25 May	15 kilotons
CLIMAX	4 June	61 kilotons

URGENT FURY (U.S. 83) The American invasion of Grenada on 25 October 1983. The local government had fallen into the hands of a violent anti-democratic element that had began executing its opponents. The Americans responded with overwhelming force that quickly subdued the small local militia and some Cuban engineer units. The victory came quickly, but revealed serious shortcomings in American inter-service coordination and planning. Reforms instituted as a result of these problems paid dividends with the invasion of Panama (JUST CAUSE).

URSULA (GER 43) A 4-day anti-partisan sweep centered on the Rogachev region launched on 12 February 1943.

UTOPIA (Allied 43) Planning name for BUCCANEER.

V

VALEDICTORIAN (Allied 45) Planning name for VENERABLE.

VALIANT (U.S.) General designation (i.e., VALIANT USHER) for amphibious exercises conducted by the U.S. 7th Fleet in the Indian Ocean and Western Pacific regions. See KERNEL.

VALKRIE (GER) See WALKFÜRE.

VANGUARD (Allied 45) Planning name for DRACULA.

VARSITY (Allied 45) Airborne assault launched on the night of 23 March 1945, near Wesel, Germany, in support of the PLUNDER river crossing. Over 1,348 gliders and 14,000 paratroops of the U.S. 17th and British 6th Airborne Divisions took part in the largest combat drop ever conducted.

VELLUM (Allied 42) Movement of U.S. Coast Artillery units (the 56th Coast Artillery Regiment) to Puerto de la Cruz, Venezuela, to build defense batteries and train Venezuelan units. The troops arrived on 13 March 1942 and were withdrawn in March 1943.

VELVETA (IS) The delivery of fighter planes to Israel in the late 1940s. These deliveries involved indirect routes to a secret Israeli facility established in Czechoslovakia near Zatec. This was designed to disguise the true source and destination of the aircraft. More than 89 fighter planes (20 Spitfires and 69 Messerschmitts) and 3 ex-U.S. B-17 Flying Fortress bombers found their way to the new Israeli Air Force.

VELVET GLOVE (CN 50) The failed Canadian effort, begun in 1950, to develop an indigenous air-to-air missile.

VENDETTA (Allied 44) A portion of FORTITUDE, which falsely portrayed the threat of an Allied invasion of the Pas de Calais rather than Normandy. See OVERLORD.

VENERABLE (Allied 45) Ground attack to capture the French port of Bordeaux launched on 14 April 1945.

VENEZIA "VENICE" (IT 42) A wide-ranging Axis attack designed to capture the British stronghold of Tobruk, executed on 26 to 29 May 1942. The German armored units, led personally by Rommel, swung far to the south outflanking the Indian and South African defenders. Turning north, the attack surrounded the defenders at Rotonda Ualeb and struck at the airfield at El Adem. An Italian attack through the main defenses was unable to rupture the South African lines to link up with the main force, which now found itself without a source of supply. Eventually, Rommel withdrew west toward Sidi Muftah, settling for local gains from a massive flanking movement. The German portion of the effort was called THAESUS.

VERITABLE (Allied 45) Attack by the British 30th Corps and Canadian 1st Army from Mijmegen to the region between the Maas and Rhine Rivers. Scheduled for January 1945, but delayed until 8 February 1945. Roughly coordinated with the GRENADE attack.

VERONA (U.S. 43) A massive worldwide effort to break Soviet codes. This program had its origins in World War II, when operational considerations caused the Soviets to reuse some "one-use" cipher pads. A copy of one of these pads was found in a sunken Soviet ship. With this single pad and sufficient intercepts, messages using the same encryption could be found and broken one by one. The VERONA program read critical Soviet communications, but took years to do so. Many of the intercepts were released to the public in late 1995, providing fascinating insights into the Cold War. VERONA revealed the deep Soviet penetration of the MANHATTAN ENGINEER PROJECT and other U.S. secret programs. The intercepts conclusively show that Ethel and Julius Rosenberg, among others, were Soviet spies, but these documents were not used in court in order to protect the VERONA program. See BRIDE.

VERT "GREEN" (Allied 44) Attacks by French resistance fighters on railroad targets in support of the invasion of northern France (OVERLORD). The British Broadcasting Service initiated these attacks by broadcasting the code message "It is hot in Suez." See VIOLET and TORTUE.

VESNA (S.U.) See OKEAN.

VESUVIUS (Allied 43) The liberation of the island of Corsica on 11 September 1943.

Although the Free French invaders expected resistance, the German garrison had already evacuated the island.

VICTOR (Allied 45) Series of amphibious landings conducted to liberate the southern portion of the Philippines. These minor islands had little military value, but were freed to redeem MacArthur's promise that "I shall return." Extremely active guerrilla units on these islands sometimes outnumbered the Japanese garrisons and provided support for the landings. Many of these landings were originally planned as part of the MUSKETEER plan. Additional small landings in the region were called OBOE. Like the MIKE landings that preceded them, the VICTOR landings were conducted out of their numerical sequence:

VICTOR III The landing at Puerto Prinesa on the eastern coast of the island of Palawan by the U.S. 186th Regimental Combat Team on 28 February 1945. As the invasion force approached, the Japanese defenders massacred over 150 Americans taken prisoner in 1942 by burning them in 2 underground bunkers. The island was declared secure on 22 April.

VICTOR IV The landing at Zamboanga, on the extreme tip of Mindanao's Zamboanga Peninsula, by the U.S. 41st Infantry Division on 10 March 1945. The Americans met no initial resistance, the defenders having pulled back to the foothills 3 miles inland. After the area was secured on 24 March, several landings were made to recapture the nearby small islands of Sanga Sanga and Jolo.

VICTOR I The liberation of Panay and the northern portion of Negros. The initial landing on Panay was conducted by elements of the U.S. 40th Infantry Division on 18 March 1945. Resistance fighters met the invasion force on the beach in full uniform and accompanied by a brass band. The few Japanese defenders on Panay were quickly destroyed. Fighting on the northern portion of Negros continued until 4 June.

VICTOR II Landings by the American Division that liberated Cebu, Bohol, and the southern portion of Negros. On 26 March 1945 the landing force encountered extensive minefields on the beaches, but little initial resistance. Moving inland, they met with organized resistance at Cebu City and beyond. Cebu was secured on 18 April; Bohol 2 days later. Fighting continued on Negros until 12 June.

VICTOR V The liberation of Mindanao. By the time the landing force arrived, on 17 April, local guerrillas had mauled the local garrison and sent them into the hills. Japanese units continued to harass the Americans until 15 August.

"VICTORY OPERATION" (JPN 44) See SHO-GO.

VIERECK "QUADRANGLE" (GER 42) Anti-partisan operation conducted in the Bryansk region of western Russia in September 1942. Conducted simultaneously with DREIECK.

VIGILANT WARRIOR (U.S. 94) The emergency deployment of American troops to Kuwait in response to an Iraqi provocation in mid-October 1994. The Iraqis moved 2 Republican Guard divisions near the Kuwaiti frontier to pressure the Security Council to lift economic sanctions. The Americans flew in elements of the 18th Airborne Corps and other units who linked up with equipment stored in Kuwait. The Iraqi pressure backfired; a Franco-Russian effort to lift sanctions was abandoned in the face of the aggression.

VIGOUROUS (Allied 42) See HARPOON.

VIGOUR (U.K. 92) The British contribution to the international humanitarian effort in Somalia, RESTORE HOPE.

"VINE" (GER 42) See WEINSTOCK.

VIOLET (Allied 44) Operations by the French resistance to disrupt German communications in the hours before the Normandy landings (OVERLORD). See VERTE.

VITALITY (Allied 44) Attacks by the Canadian 2nd Division and British 52nd Highland Division to clear South Beveland, the Netherlands, of German defenders. Conducted in October 1944. See SUITCASE.

VITTLES (U.S./U.K. 48) The Berlin Airlift. In order to extend Soviet dominion over the American, British, and French sectors of Berlin, the Soviet occupation authorities closed road, rail, and barge access to the Allied sectors on 24 June 1949. The Allies responded with an airlift of supplies designed to extend the reserves already in those sectors to give diplomats time to solve the crisis. Two additional airfields were built, and the existing Tempelhof field was expanded during the intense operation. Eventually, over 267,000 flights delivered almost 8,000,000 tons of food and fuel to the Allied sectors of the city. During the peak period of the operation, 1,398 flights landed on one of the 3 airfields in a single day. The blockade ended on 12 May 1949, but the airlift continued until the end of September to build up emergency reserves. As a result of the blockade, the Berlin city government maintained emergency supplies of food. This reserve was donated to the city of Moscow at the end of the Cold War. See LITTLE VITTLES.

VIXENS (U.K. 63) A dispersion test of nuclear materials conducted at Maralinga, Australia, in 1963. This test contaminated a wide area while studying the effects of accidental fires or non-nuclear explosions on nuclear weapons. See BRUMBY.

VOGELGEZWITSCHER   "BIRDSONG" (GER 42) Anti-partisan sweep centered near the Roslavvll-Bryansk highway,

Russia, in June 1942. Although 1,193 Soviets died, the fact that fewer than 60 Germans were killed suggests most of those killed were unarmed. In any event, there was no long-term reduction of partisan activities in the area. See VIERECK.

VOLANT (U.S.) A first word used to designate the programs and projects of the U.S. Air Force's C-130 Hercules fleet. VOLANT FOREST is the modification of these aircraft to fight forest fires. VOLANT SOLO is the psychological warfare variant of the C-130.

VOLANT OAK (U.S.) General term for the deployment of Air National Guard C-130 units to Panama to provide local airlift.

VULCAN (Allied 43) Ground attack against German forces in Tunis, Cap Bon, and Bizerte, the last Axis toeholds in North Africa. Executed on 6 May 1943. In June, a major Allied air effort (FLAX) had cut off German supplies to North Africa. The U.S. Army forces surrounded the last defenders at Enfidaville, ending the Axis effort. Followed by RETRIBUTION.

VULTURE (FR/U.S. 54) A plan for the use of heavy American bombers to support French operations in Vietnam in April 1954. The Chairman of the Joint Chiefs of Staff, Admiral Arthur Radford, approved this plan which called for 60 B-29 Stratofortress bombers along with naval aircraft to pound communist positions surrounding the fortress at Dien Bein Phu. This planned attack may have included nuclear weapons. The French government formally requested this assistance, but President Eisenhower was unwilling to go to their aid without British assistance, which would lend a multilateral flavor to the operation. Eventually, the idea was condemned as politically impossible.

WA "TEAM SPIRIT" (JPN 44) A series of Japanese commando raids on American airfields at Leyte, San Pablo, Buri, and Bayug by Japanese ground and airborne forces. The first attack came on the night of 27 November 1944 when 1 Japanese transport plane crashed trying to land on the field at Buri, killing all the raiders. Three other aircraft crashed at sea or on beaches far from their target. On 4 December, a second airborne attack occurred, this one at San Pablo and Buri. Buri had already been overrun by Japanese ground forces. At San Pablo, the 300 paratroops had the bad luck of landing on an American airborne unit based there. The attack was a confused formless battle of small units and individuals. The airfields were recaptured by 10 December. This was the first Japanese airborne assault since February 1942. The term "Wa" may be a play on the name of the plan's author, Lieutenant General Takaji Wacahi, Chief of Staff of 35th Army, or may be translated as meaning "heart" or "team spirit."

WACHT AM RHEIN "WATCH ON THE RHINE" (GER 44) The operation that launched the Battle of the Bulge. Designed to rupture the Allied defenses in the Ardennes and to break through to the sea, the attack was launched on 16 December 1944. After a massive air attack on Allied air bases (HERMANN), 11 panzer and 14 infantry divisions hit 6 American divisions along a 60-mile front from Monchau, France, to Echternach, Luxembourg. The U.S. 106th Infantry Division, newly arrived in Europe, shattered under this unexpected assault. Heroic local resistance by small American units reduced the initial gains of the attackers. The weather cleared on 23 December, allowing massive Allied airpower to attack German units clustered around Bastogne, Saint Vith, and other bottlenecks. Armored forces from Patton's 3rd Army struck from the south to cut off the penetration (MADISON). As supplies ran out, the Germans were unable to continue their drive and the battle ended by early January 1945. This was the last major German attack in the West and cost them 100,000 soldiers and 1,000 aircraft. See GREIF, NORDWIND, and WAHRUNG.

WADHAM (Allied 43) The U.S. Army portion of the overall 1943 deception plan, COCKADE. Deception operations conducted by U.S. 5th Corps were intended to cause the Germans to deploy troops to the Brest Peninsula in France.

WAHRUNG "CURRENCY" (GER 44) Special operation conducted as part of the WACHT AM RHEIN. A small number of German agents infiltrated Allied lines in American uniforms. These agents then used an existing Nazi intelligence network to attempt to bribe rail and port workers to disrupt Allied supply operations. This operation failed miserably. See GREIF.

WALKÜRE "VALKRIE"

1. (GER 18) Planned attack on British forces near Lens, France, in the spring of 1918. Never executed.

2. (GER 43) Plan dated 31 July 1943 to control civil disturbances in Germany. The plan was never executed, although the members of the 20 July 1944 bomb plot intended to use it to capture the reins of the Nazi government. In the confusion following the bomb attack on Hitler, units in Berlin would be ordered to seize key government buildings, communication centers, and vital headquarters. These units would be unaware they were serving the plotters, since their actions would be directed by an established contingency plan. See THUNDERSTORM.

WALLACE (Allied 44) A wide-ranging ground sweep by a 60-man patrol of the British Special Air Service that left Rennes, France, in 20 jeeps on 20 August 1944. At various locations they assisted local partisans, traveling over 200 miles to just south of Sens in 2 weeks.

WANTAGE (Allied 44) The general deception plan that inflated the number and capability of Allied units in Britain. This false "Order of Battle" was created through false radio traffic and the use of double agents. These notional units were later used for a variety of phony invasions and feints to distract the Germans from true Allied intentions.

WARDEN (UK 90) British participation in PROVIDE COMFORT.

WAREHOUSE (Allied 42) Deception plan that portrayed a false threat of a British invasion of Crete by forces based in Egypt. Later renamed WITHSTAND.

WARM WIND (U.S. 52) Airborne training conducted in Alaska by the American 503d Regimental Combat Team.

WARRIOR FOCUS (U.S. 95) An "Advanced Warfighting Exercise" conducted in late 1995 at Fort Polk, Louisiana, to explore the impact of new technologies on military tactics, techniques, and procedures.

WARTBURG (GER 41) Martin Luther translated the Bible in Wartburg Castle. The name is often anglicized as "Warzburg."

1. The mining of the strait between Denmark and Sweden to prevent the escape of the Soviet fleet to England. Begun on 10 June 1941 and completed just before the German invasion of the Soviet Union on 22 June. See WILFRED.

2. The code word sent to German units on 17 June 1941 to indicate the invasion of the Soviet Union (BARBAROSSA) would proceed on schedule.

WARZBURG (GER 41) See WARTBURG.

WATCHTOWER

1. (Allied 42) The invasion of Guadalcanal, in the Solomon Islands, by 16,000 U. S. troops on 7 August 1942. This marked the first American ground offensive in the Pacific. Additional amphibious attacks were launched simultaneously on Florida, Tulagi, Gavutu, and Tanambogo islands. Initially, Guadalcanal itself was occupied only by unarmed Japanese construction and support personnel, allowing the Americans to come ashore almost unhindered. Japanese reinforcements were transported to the island from Rabaul to destroy the Americans (KA GO). These convoys and the resulting land battle on Guadalcanal were

magnets for naval activity on both sides. This resulted in 7 naval battles (Savo Island on 9 August, Eastern Solomons on 24 August, Cape Esperance on 11 and 12 October, Santa Cruz Islands on 26 and 27 October, First Battle of Guadalcanal on 11 and 12 November, Second Battle of Guadalcanal on 14 and 15 November, and finally the Battle of Tassafaronga on 30 November). The naval battles were a draw, but the Japanese were unable to replace their losses. The ground fighting was characterized by extreme desperation; only 3 of the defenders surrendered. Guadalcanal was declared secure on 9 February 1943 after more than 6 months of combat. See KE and SHOESTRING.

2. (U.S. 57) The second of 3 exercises conducted by the former Strategic Air Command to develop and refine organizations, procedures, and techniques needed to keep one-third of its aircraft on alert at all times. Conducted by the 825th Air Division from April to November 1957. Followed TRY OUT and preceded FRESH APPROACH.

WATERFALL (Allied 43) A deception operation designed to support the invasion of Sicily (HUSKY). British units in Egypt used a large number of dummy tanks, landing craft, and aircraft to portray a false threat of an Allied invasion of Crete. Part of BARCLAY. Complimented by MINCEMEAT.

WATERLOO (Allied 41) A major anti-invasion exercise conducted by the Canadian 1st Corps and the British 8th Armored Division to train in techniques to fight German paratroops. Conducted in Sussex, England, in June 1941.

WATERPUMP (U.S. 64) The training of Lao and Thai forces by American Special Forces units during America's involvement in the Vietnam War.

WEARY WILLIE (Allied 44) See APHRODITE. The name "Weary Willie" was a play on the "WW" tail marking placed on aircraft no longer fit for combat.

WEBFOOT (Allied 44) Final training exercise for the invasion at Anzio, Italy (SHINGLE). Conducted 17-19 January 1944.

WEDLOCK (Allied 44) Deception plan designed to falsely project the impression of a potential American invasion of the Kurile Islands in 1944. The Kuriles are the northernmost islands of the Japanese archipelago and were eventually captured by the Soviets in the closing days of the war.

WEHRWOLF "WEREWOLF"

1. (GER 45) An air battle that took place over the German coast near Steinhude between units of the U.S. 8th Air Force and over 150 defending German fighters on 7 April 1945. See NEROBEFEHL.

2. (GER 45) Plan to conduct guerrilla operations against Allied forces in occupied Germany. Never formally executed although some activities did occur.

WEINSTOCK "VINE" (GER 42) A second thrust designed to further widen the neck of the Demyansk Pocket. This attack, in the northern sector, was designed to compliment the August WINKELREID attack. "VINE" was canceled due to a lack of resources.

WEISS "WHITE"

1. (GER 39) The invasion of Poland. This attack opened the overt phase of the European front of World War II. After staging a number of false provocations (HIMMLER), the Germans invaded on 1 September 1939. The Poles were outflanked by the German occupation of Czechoslovakia (GRUEN) and by the basing of military units in the enclave of East Prussia. Their air force was destroyed in less than a day as the

German Army began a series of deep envelopments. Britain and France declared war on Germany on 3 September, but were unable to offer any real assistant to their ally. Warsaw was surrounded on 17 September and bombed until its garrison surrendered 10 days later. Formal resistance ended on 6 October, although the Poles continued to be an extremely restive population under Nazi rule.

2. (Axis 42) A combined Axis counter-partisan operation launched in late January 1942 throughout Croatia. Nine Axis divisions (6 German, 3 Italian) along with 2 Croat divisions and a number of Chetnik and Ustashi formations killed about 8,000 Partisans, capturing another 2,000. Despite these losses, the Partisan formations were able to break out from the encirclement and continue operations. WEISS II followed in February; WEISS III was launched in March. The next major operation in Yugoslavia was SCHWARZ.

WELL HIT (Allied 44) Attack by the Canadian 3rd Division to liberate Boulogne, France, launched on 17 September 1944.

WEREWOLF (GER 45) See WEHRWOLF.

WESERÜBUNG "WESER EXERCISE" (GER 40) The 9 April 1940 German invasion of Denmark and Norway. This plan was drawn up in March 1939 to secure the northernmost ice-free iron ore port, Narvik, and to give the Germans bases from which to hit Britain. The invasion force consisted of 6 divisions and were transported on warships to their targets. Denmark, unprepared for war, fell without resistance. After a stiff fight in northern Norway, the deteriorating situation in France (GELB) forced the Allies to withdraw their troops from Scandinavia (ALPHABET). The Germans then completed their conquest of Norway by mid-May. The Weser is a German river. See HARTMUT, JUNO, and WILFRED.

WESTERN REWARD (AUS) Deployments and operations by the Royal Australian Air Force from their western "bare bases." These facilities, located in isolated areas of the Australian West, provided emergency wartime facilities for the air defense of the region.

WESTERN WAY (CN 59) The transfer of 22 fighter planes from the Royal Canadian Air Force to Turkey in August and September 1959.

WESTERN WEAR (CN 59) The transfer of over 30 fighter planes from Royal Canadian Air Force to France and Greece in September and October 1959.

WESTGOTEN BEWEGUNG "WEST GOTHS' MOVEMENT" (GER 45) Plan to close all German military training units and move their personnel to the nearest front for service.

WHETSTONE (U.S. 64) A series of 36 nuclear tests conducted in 1964 and 1965. These followed the NIBLICK series and were in turn followed by FLINTLOCK. All but one of these blasts were conducted beneath the Nevada Test Site. The individual blasts were:

BYE	16 July 64	20-200 kilotons
CORMORANT	17 July	<20 kilotons
ALVA	19 August	<20 kilotons
CANVASBACK	22 August	<20 kilotons
HADDOCK	28 August	<20 kilotons
GUANAY	4 September	<20 kilotons
AUK	2 October	<20 kilotons
PAR	9 October	38 kilotons, see PLOWSHARE
BARBEL	16 October	<20 kilotons
SALMON	22 October	5.3 kilotons, near Hattiesburg, Mississippi
FOREST	31 October	<20 kilotons

HANDCAR	5 November	12 kilotons, see PLOWSHARE
CREPE	5 December	prob. .1 kiloton
DRILL	5 December	3.4 kilotons
PARROT	16 December	1.3 kilotons
MUDPACK	16 December	2.7 kilotons
SULKY	18 December	92 tons, see PLOWSHARE
WOOD	14 January 65	<20 kilotons
CASHMERE	4 February	<20 kilotons
ALPACA	12 February	<20 kilotons
MERLIN	16 February	10.1 kilotons
WISHBONE	18 February	<20 kilotons
WAGTAIL	3 March	20-200 kilotons
CUP	26 March	prob. .65 kilotons
KESTREL	5 April	prob. 35 kilotons
PALANQUIN	14 April	4.3 kilotons, see PLOWSHARE
GUM DROP	21 April	prob. 4 kilotons
(Unknown)	23 April	(unknown)
TEE	7 May	<20 kilotons
BUTEO	12 May	<20 kilotons
SCAUP	14 May	<20 kilotons
CAMBRIO	14 May	750 tons
TWEED	21 May	<20 kilotons
PETREL	11 June	1.3 kilotons
DILUTED WATERS	16 June	<20 kilotons
TINY TOT	17 June	<20 kilotons

WHIPCORD (Allied 41) A proposed Allied invasion of Sicily in 1941. Never executed. See HUSKY.

WHITE

1. (Allied 40) An attempt to reinforce the air garrison of Malta with aircraft from the British aircraft carrier Argus on 15 November 1940. Due to poor weather, only 5 of the 14 planes landed on the besieged island. Followed by JAGUAR.

2. (GER 39 & 42) See WEISS.

WHITE DRAGON (BG 64) See DRAGON BLANC.

WHITE STAR (U.S. 59) The secret establishment of American Special Forces detachments in Laos in the summer of 1959. Their mission was to train Royal Lao and tribal forces to harass communist supply lines in their country. Despite the military character of this effort, it was controlled by the CIA. See WATERPUMP.

WHITE WING (U.S./R.V.N. 66) Operation by the American 1st Cavalry Division against a communist stronghold area on the Bong Song Plain, Vietnam, beginning at the end of January 1966. The communists had prepared extensive bunkers and other fortifications in villages and hamlets. Despite the presence of civilians, the Americans unleashed their overwhelming firepower. The wounded flooded local hospitals, which were unprepared and overwhelmed. When the communists retreated after 4 days of heavy bombardment, the American and South Vietnamese troops also pulled out, failing to reestablish civil control over the area. Originally called MASHER, this operation was renamed WHITE WING at the direction of President Johnson.

WIGWAM (U.S. 55) A single underwater nuclear test of a nuclear depth charge on 14 May 1955. The blast took place 2,000 feet below the surface about 400 miles southwest of San Diego, California. The device yielded 30 kilotons. Followed TEAPOT. Preceded DIXIE.

WILDENTE "WILD DUCK" (GER 43) Anti-partisan operation launched on 1 November 1943 to protect supply lines north of Vitebsk. See SCHNEPFE.

WILDHORN III (Allied 44) The recovery of parts from a V-2 rocket that were salvaged by the Polish Home Army. An experimental V-2 crashed into a river bend where it was camouflaged by the local Polish resistance. A British C-47 was flown in on the night of 25 July 1944 to recover portions of missile's guidance system. It took off under fire from a German patrol.

WILFRED (Allied) British plan to lay naval mines in Norwegian territorial waters in 1939. On 5 April, the operation was authorized to begin despite misgivings that it might spur the Nazis to invade Norway. The Germans did in fact invade on 9 April (WESERBUNG), but the operation had long been planned and was not a result of the mining effort. The operation was named after a mild and unassuming cartoon character by Winston Churchill.

WILHELM "WILLIAM" (GER 43) A cleanup operation to destroy Soviet forces near Volchansk after the Battle of Kursk. Executed 10 June 1943. Part of FREDERICUS II.

WILLIAM TELL (U.S.) Competition/training exercise designed to identify and reward the best air-to-air pilot and ground crew in the Air Force. Conducted every other year at Tyndall Air Force Base, the competition uses live ammunition fired at drones over the Gulf of Mexico. See GUNSMOKE.

WILLOH 87 (AUS/N.Z. 87) A joint training exercise conducted in March and April 1987 by the Royal Australian and New Zealand Air Force.

WINDMILL (U.S. 47) Antarctic exploration mission conducted by the U.S. Navy during the Antarctic summer of 1947/48. This was a follow-on mission to HIGH JUMP and included ground surveying that produced the first reliable maps of Queen May Coast and Wilkes Land, on the coast of the Indian Ocean, south of Australia.

WINDMILL I (U.S. 51) The first major logistics mission flown by U.S. Marine Corps helicopters. On 13 September 1951 Marine Transportation Helicopter Squadron 161 flew 9 tons of supplies to 2nd Battalion, 1st Marine Regiment, and evacuated 74 casualties using piston-powered Sikorsky.

WINDSOR (Allied 44) Attack by the Canadian 3rd Division to take Carpiquet, France, near Caen. Launched on the night of 7 June, the assault quickly stalled. See EPSOM.

WINKELREID (GER 42) A ground attack that widened the narrow neck of the Demyansk Pocket. Launched in October 1942, the attack broadened access to the troops from 2 to 10 miles. Winkelreid was a character in Norse mythology.

WINTERGEWITTER "WINTER THUNDERSTORM" (GER 42) Attempt to relieve the garrison in Stalingrad (now Volgograd). Executed by 4th Panzer Army on 12 December 1942, but called off 2 days later, far short of its objective. Hitler had ordered the garrison to stand fast, rather than attacking toward the relief column.

WINTERZAUBER "WINTER MAGIC" (GER 43) Anti-partisan operation launched by the Germans in Lithuania in early 1943.

WINTEX/CIMEX (NATO) Multinational exercise conducted in odd-numbered years. These operations address refugee control, port security, and the mechanisms for political consultations with the American exercise POWER PLAY 79. Similarly, WINTEX/CIMEX 81 was run in tandem with POLL STATION 81; and WINTEX/CIMEX 85 was linked with the IVY LEAGUE 85. The name is a contraction for "Winter Exercise/Civil-Military Exercise."

WIRBELSTRUM "HURRICANE"

1. (GER 42) A planned ground attack designed to close off the Sukhinichi Salient from the north as a compliment to the WIRBELSTRUM attack launched from

the south. Scheduled for mid-August 1942 but never executed.

2. WIRBELSTRUM I (GER 44) A very large German anti-partisan operation against an estimated 3,000 Polish guerrillas launched in June 1944. On 10 June, 40 civilians in the Polish village of Pikule were massacred.

3. WIRBELSTRUM II (GER 44) A 6-day anti-partisan operation begun on 18 June 1944. Seven hundred partisans were killed in the Osuchy region of Poland, near Lublin.

WIRBELWIND "WHIRLWIND" (GER 42) An attack launched in August 1942 to pinch off the Sukhinishi Pocket from the south. The drive advanced about 20 miles, less than a third of the distance required, in the face of stiff Soviet resistance. See WIRBELSTRUM.

WITHSTAND (Allied 43) Follow-up to the WAREHOUSE deception. WITHSTAND continued the fake threat of an invasion of Crete with the use of phony radio traffic and reports to enemy intelligence through double agents.

WOP (Allied 43) Eastward attack by the American 2nd Army from the TORCH beachhead on German positions at Gafsa. This was conducted on 17 March 1943 in rough coordination with the British PUGILIST attack from the west.

WOWSER (Allied 45) A series of air strikes in April 1945 by the American 15th Air Force in support of the final U.S. ground attacks of the war in Europe. With no strategic targets left to attack, heavy bombers were free to support front-line units with exceptionally heavy air attacks. See ARC LIGHT.

WRANGLER (U.N. 51) Planned attack along Korea's east coast featuring amphibious landing and a complimentary ground thrust by the R.O.K. 1st and U.S. 10th Corps. Scheduled for October 1951, but never executed. Along with OVERWHELMING, these plans were designed to return U.N. forces to the offensive in the event of the failure of the long truce negotiations.

WS (Allied) Allied convoys from South Africa to Suez in World War II. Designed by number (e.g., WS 123).

X (JPN 43) Phase I of I GO.

X, Project (Allied 42) Delivery flights of tactical aircraft from the east coast of the U.S. to India and on to China. The route went from Florida to Brazil to Africa to India.

XD (Allied 40) The demolition of port facilities in Belgium and the Netherlands by British Army engineers to prevent their capture by the Germans. This operation was authorized on 16 May 1940 and was carried out soon thereafter.

XENOPHON (FR 54) A plan for a sortie to the south by the French Union garrison in Dien Bein Phu. Never executed.

Y

Y

1. (JPN 43) Phase II of I GO.

2. (Allied) Intelligence garnered from German radio traffic that was unencrypted or encrypted using low-grade or manual ciphers. This intelligence was generally of local, tactical value as opposed to strategic intelligence developed by ULTRA breaking of high-grade codes.

3. (Allied 44) Planning name for CAPITAL.

YANKEE TEAM (U.S. 64) The covert use of U.S. Air Force aircraft to provide reconnaissance and fighter protection for the Royal Lao Air Force as it interdicted communist forces in Laos in 1964. These flights began as covert operations in the period before the Gulf of Tonkin Incident. This operation was "leaked" with the publication of the Pentagon Papers" in 1971. Part of OPLAN 34-A. See SALEUMSAY and SONE SAI.

YELLOW (GER 40) See GELB.

YELLOW BIRD (U.S. 89) Assistance to dissident Chinese students and activists (including forged identity and other papers) given by the CIA in the aftermath of the massacre of protesters on Tiananmen Square on 4 June 1989. The dissidents, with this limited U.S. support, set up an escape and evasion network that led many of the students to the Portuguese colony of Macao via high-powered motorboats.

YELLOW FRUIT (U.S. 80) The expansion of the size, training, and capabilities of the American special operations community conducted as a result of national embarrassment of the Iranian hostage incident (EAGLE CLAW). Conducted from 1980 to 1983. See HONEY BADGER.

YUKON I

YUKON II (Allied 42) Two training exercises conducted in June 1942 for the troops preparing for the raid on Dieppe, France (JUBILEE). Conducted near Bridport, Dorset, England.

YULGOK (R.O.K.) The defense procurement program of the Republic of Korea. Begun after the Korean War, this program sometimes totaled more than one-third of total governmental expenditures. In 1993, after the election of Kim Young Sam, a civilian, as President, audits of this program were investigated. Widespread corruption, mismanagement, and poor planning were revealed by these audits. Yulgok was a figure from 16th century Korea who (unsuccessfully) advocated rearmament against the Japanese.

Z

Z

1. (GER 33) A 10-year plan for a buildup of the German Navy to a point where it could challenge the Royal Navy on the high seas. Launched in 1933, "Plan Z" called for a massive surface fleet supported by a large force of submarines. The Nazi leadership lacked the patience to delay their wars of conquest. Only 39 of the projected 300 modern submarines were available at the start of the war in Europe. In addition, the British, alarmed by the German buildup, accelerated activity in their own shipyards, quickly outstripping the German effort.

2. (JPN 41) The aerial attack on the U. S. Fleet at Pearl Harbor executed on 7 December 1941. The Japanese attack force included 6 aircraft carriers, 2 heavy and 1 light cruisers, 9 destroyers, and 3 submarines. In a series of air attacks, the Japanese destroyed 4 American battleships and almost 200 ground-based aircraft. The American carriers were at sea during the attack, escaping damage.

3. (JPN 43) A plan for Japanese naval operations in the Philippine Sea in 1944 that was being carried by Admiral Fukudome when he was killed by American fighter planes (PEACOCK). The plans were recovered from the crash site by Filipino guerrillas who sent them to MacArthur's headquarters. Never executed.

4. (Allied 45) Planning name for DRACULA.

ZAPATA (U.S. 61) Alternate name for the Bay of Pigs invasion of Cuba (PLUTO).

ZAUBERFLÖTE "MAGIC FLUTE" (GER 43) Anti-partisan sweep conducted near Minski, Byelorussia, from 17 to 24 April 1943. The name is from an opera by Mozart.

ZEBRA (Allied 44) The first Allied drops of supplies to French resistance units after the invasion of northern France (OVERLORD). Aid to these groups was curtailed by a shortage of aircraft during the invasion.

ZEPPELIN (Allied 44) A 1944 deception plan designed to depict a potential amphibious landing on Crete, western Greece, or the Romanian Black Sea coast. A compliment to BODYGUARD, the deception plan for OVERLORD (the invasion of Normandy). Followed CASCADE.

ZERBERUS "CERBERUS" (GER 42) The escape of the German ships *Prinz Eugen, Scharnhorst, Gneisenau,* and a number of smaller ships from Brest to ports in Germany and Denmark. Hitler, convinced of an impending British invasion of Norway, ordered the escape. On 11 February 1942 the ships left port at night and escaped British detection for more than 12 hours. Despite massive British air attacks, which cost the RAF 10 planes, by

13 February all the ships had completed their transit. The action has entered history as the "Channel Dash." Cerberus is the 3-headed dog who guards the gate to Hades. See CHANNEL STOP and FULLER.

ZERO (BG 40) Intelligence and resistance network established in occupied Belgium by Walthere Dewe in the summer of 1940. See CLARENCE, DAME BLANCHE, and LUC.

ZIGEUNERBARON "GYPSY BARON" (GER 43) Anti-partisan operation launched on 16 May 1943 in the Bryansk region of western Russia. Five infantry and a tank division were arrayed against an estimated 6,000 guerrillas. Although the Germans claimed to have killed over 1,500 partisans, and captured an equal number, along with 3 tanks and 21 artillery pieces, this action failed to halt Soviet harassment of German rear-area activities.

ZIPPER (Allied 45) British plan to capture either Port Sweettenham or Port Dickson, Burma, as staging areas for the recapture of Singapore. Never executed. The planned deception for this attack was called SLIPPERY.

ZIPPER II (Allied 45) Planned British attack south to the Johore Straits to follow ZIPPER. Never executed.

ZITADELLE "CITADEL" (GER 43) German attack on the Kursk Salient on 5 July 1943 producing the Battle of Kursk, the largest tank battle of the war. The Soviets, alerted to the oncoming attack, heavily reinforced the Salient with infantry operating from elaborate field fortifications. A large mobile force of armor was prepared to counterattack (KUTUSOV). The Soviets deployed about 2,000,000 men and 6,000 tanks in this operation. The northern arm of the German's planned encirclement made little headway. In the south, near Prokhorovka, the Germans met with greater success, and so attracted the attention of General Zhukov's tanks. The Germans lost more than the 300 tanks in a wild, wide-ranging battle fought at close range in darkness and thick dust. The Germans were never again able to reclaim the initiative on the Eastern Front.

ZORRO II (U.S. Law Enforcement 96) An American investigation into Mexican cocaine smuggling rings. These groups gained prominence in the early 1990s, providing transportation of the drugs produced in other countries. This operation was capped by a string of nationwide arrests in May 1996. "Zorro" was a popular character in the works of O. Henry and is Spanish for "fox."

Glossary

AL: Albania

Allied: The alliance of nations that defeated Nazi Germany and Japan. Also used for operations conducted by a number of nations outside of a formal alliance such as NATO.

ARG: Argentina

ARVN: Army of the (former) Republic of Vietnam

AUS: Australia

Axis: The coalition of nations, led by Nazi Germany that began World War II.

BG: Belgium

BZ: Brazil

CH: Chile

CIA: The American Central Intelligence Agency, responsible for overseas intelligence activities and covert operations.

CN: Canada

Coalition: The American-led alliance of over 20 nations that liberated Kuwait (DESERT STORM).

CT: Croatia

DN: Denmark

FBI: The American Federal Bureau of Investigation, responsible for major criminal investigations and internal security.

FEMA: The American Federal Emergency Management Agency, responsible for civil defense planning and disaster relief.

Flagword: A word used in electronic communications to assign a priority or routing to a message (GRAZING HERD, BROKEN ARROW).

FR: France

GER: Germany

G.R.U.: The Military Intelligence Service of the former Soviet Union.

HMAS: His (Her) Majesty's Australian Ship

HMCS: His (Her) Majesty's Canadian Ship

HMS: His (Her) Majesty's Ship

HU: Hungary

IN: India

IS: Israel

IT: Italy

JOR: Jordan

JPN: Japan

Kiloton: A force equal to 100 tons of high explosive.

Megaton: A force equal to 1,000 tons of high explosives.

MV: Merchant Vessel

MY: Malaya

NASA: The American National Aeronautical and Space Administration.

NATO: The North Atlantic Treaty Organization, the American-led alliance that protected Western Europe during the Cold War.

NORAD: The North American Air Defense Command. A joint U.S./Canadian military command that protected North America from air attack during the Cold War.

NZ: New Zealand

Partnership for Peace: A NATO program to increase the professionalism and capabilities of Eastern European militaries as a first step toward joining the alliance. (See COOPERATIVE.)

PK: Pakistan

PN: Panama

PO: Poland

POW: Prisoner of War

PRC: People's Republic of China

RAAF: Royal Australian Air Force

RAF: The (British) Royal Air Force

ROK: Republic of (South) Korea

RSA: Republic of South Africa

RVN: The former Republic of (South) Vietnam

SP: Spain

SS: Steam Ship

SU: The (former) Union of Soviet Socialist Republics

SWAPO: The South West African People's Organization, the communist-inspired rebel group that fought South African forces in Angola and Namibia.

UAE: The United Arab Emirates

UK: The United Kingdom, Great Britain

UKR: Ukraine

UN: United Nations

USAAF: United States Army Air Force(s)

USAF: United States Air Force

USNS: United States Naval Ship, an auxiliary ship owned by the U.S. Navy but manned by civilian crews.

WEU: The Western European Union.

Index

Evacuation of black Jews: MOSES, SOLOMON

Euthanasia, German: T.4

Evacuations
British from France: DYNAMO, ARIEL
Westerners from Africa: FLAG POLE, DRAGON BLANC, ASSURED RESPONSE, SHARP EDGE
Jews from Africa: MOSES, SOLOMON

FFF

F-4 Phantom II
Speed record: SKYBURNER
Transfer to Israel: NIGHT LIGHT

F-5 Tiger
Combat test of: SKOSHI TIGER

F-84 Thunderjet
Deployment of: FOX ABLE 3, FOX PETER 1, FOX PETER 2

F-86 Sabre
Combat test: GUN VAL
Conversion to reconnaissance role: ASHTRAY

F-101 Voodoo
Speed record: SUN RUN
Transfer to Canada: QUEENS ROW, PEACH WINGS

F-111 Raven
Deployment to Southeast Asia: COMBAT TRIDENT, COMBAT REAPER, CREEK SWING, HARVEST REAPER, CONSTANT GUARD V

Falaise Pocket
Formation of: LÜTTICH
Canadian/Polish attack: TOTALIZE, TRACTABLE

Falcon and the Snowman, The (Book title): PYRAMIDER

Falkland Islands
Liberation of: CORPORATE
Alternate plan: PARAQUET
British bomber attacks: BLACK BUCK
Special operations: KEYHOLE

Federal Bureau of Investigation
Investigation of anti-war movement: CHAOS
Investigation of corruption at

Dept. of Defense: ILL WIND
Investigation of South Carolina legislature: LOST TRUST
Investigation of corrupt police: BROKEN FAITH
At Ruby Ridge, Idaho: NORTHERN EXPOSURE
Auto insurance fraud: SUDDEN IMPACT
Corruption at NASA: LIGHTNING STRIKE
Child pornography: INNOCENT IMAGES

Federal Emergency Management Administration (FEMA) Annual exercises: REX

Finland
Proposed attack on Soviet units: LACHSFANG

Formosa
Plan to invade: BLUEBIRD, CRASHER, CAUSEWAY

France
German invasion: GELB
British evacuation: ARIEL, DYNAMO
Invasion of southern: DRAGOON, DOVE
Invasion of northern: OVERLORD (see Normandy)
French Navy in W.W.II: CATAPULT, LILA
German anti-partisan sweep: FRÜHLING
Espionage in eastern Europe: MINOS
Intervention in Lebanon: CHEVESNE

GGG

German Navy (see also Submarine Operations)
Construction program: Z
Surface sorties: JUNO, RHENNUEBUNG, DONNERSCHLAG, FULLER, ROSSELSPRING, ZERBERUS, SIZILIEN, REGENBOGEN

Germany
Scorched earth policy: NEROBEFEHL
Allied plan to occupy: ECLIPSE, JUBILANT

Gibraltar

British plan to defend: GOLDEN EYE
Axis plan to capture: FELIX

"Great Marianas Turkey Shoot": FORAGER

Greece
Planned Axis attack: ALPENVEILCHEN
German invasion: MARITA
British reinforcement: LUSTRE
British evacuation: DEMON
German anti-partisan sweep: OLYMPUS
Planned Allied invasion: ACCOLADE
German invasion of Leros: LEOPARD
Partisan operations: NOAH'S ARK
British entry into: MANNA
Exercise with Turkey: CHECKMATE II
NATO exercise: NEW SPIRIT

Greenland
Mapping of: EARDRUM

Grenada, U.S. invasion: URGENT FURY

Guadalcanal,
U.S. rehearsal: DOVETAIL
U.S. invasion: WATCHTOWER
Japanese counterattack: KA GO
Japanese evacuation: KE
Japanese air attacks on: I GO
As supply base: DRYGOODS

Guatemala
U.S. overthrow of elected government: SUCCESS

Guerrilla Warfare
Plan for German: WEHRWOLF

Gulf of Tonkin incident: DESOTO

HHH

Haiti:
International embargo: SUPPORT DEMOCRACY
Planned U.S. invasion: RESTORE DEMOCRACY
American occupation of: UPHOLD DEMOCRACY, PRESSURE COOKER
International blockade of: ABLE MANNER

Hamburg, Germany